# MEMORY
## in context:

## context in
# MEMORY

# MEMORY
## in context:

## context in
# MEMORY

**Edited by**

Graham M. Davies
*North East London Polytechnic*
and

Donald M. Thomson
*Monash University, Australia*

## JOHN WILEY & SONS

Chichester · New York · Brisbane · Toronto · Singapore

*Library of Congress Catologing in Publication Data:*

Memory in context : context in memory / edited by Graham M. Davies and
    Donald M. Thomson.
        p.  cm.
    ISBN 0 471 91901 2
    1. Memory.   2. Context effects (Psychology)   I. Davies, Graham.
II. Thomson. Donald M.
BF378.C72M45   1988
153.1′2—dc19
87–36004
CIP

*British Library Cataloguing in Publication Data:*

Davies, Graham M. (Graham Michael), 1943–
    1. Man. Memory
    I. Title     II. Thomson, Donald M.
    153.1′2
    ISBN 0  471  91901  2

Typeset by Woodfield Graphics, Fontwell, Arundel, West Sussex.
Printed and bound in Great Britain by Anchor Brendon Ltd., Colchester, Essex.

# Contents

# List of Contributors

John Bain: *University of Queensland, Australia*

Debra Bekerian: *MRC Applied Psychology Unit, Cambridge, UK*

Isabel Birnbaum: *University of California, Irvine, USA*

Martin Conway: *MRC Applied Psychology Unit, Cambridge, UK*

Brian L. Cutler: *University of Wisconsin, Madison, USA*

Graham Davies: *North East London Polytechnic, London, UK*

Eric Eich: *University of British Columbia, Canada*

Edward Geiselman: *University of California, Los Angeles, USA*

Kim Guenther: *Hamline University, Minnesota, USA*

Michael Howe: *University of Exeter, Exeter, UK*

Michael Humphries: *University of Queensland, Australia*

Robert Lockhart: *University of Toronto, Canada*

Elizabeth Loftus: *University of Washington, Seattle, USA*

Andrew Mayes: *University of Manchester, Manchester, UK*

Merrill McSpadden: *University of Washington, Seattle, USA*

Steven Penrod: *University of Wisconsin, Madison, USA*

Jonathan Schooler: *University of Washington, Seattle, USA*

Steven Smith: *Texas A and M University, College Station, Texas, USA*

Donald Thomson: *Monash University, Australia*

Guy Tiberghien: *University of Grenoble, Grenoble, France*

**'Perhaps *This* Will Refresh Your Memory'**

# Preface

This book attempts to bring together the many and disparate threads of applied and theoretical research subsumed under the label of 'context effects'. It arose from discussions between the two editors when Graham Davies visited Don Thomson in Australia in 1984. We were fortunate in knowing most of our collaborators informally and virtually all of those initially approached agreed to take part. We are grateful to them for their promptness in meeting deadlines and the courtesy with which they have dealt with our queries and suggestions. A book co-edited from the opposite side of the world has its own special difficulties and we are indebted to the secretarial staff of the Departments of Psychology at Monash University, Aberdeen University and North East London Polytechnic for their help and support. The indexing has been very effectively performed by John Henderson. We are also grateful to the editorial staff of John Wiley, and in particular Michael Coombs and Wendy Hudlass for their patience and encouragement. Finally, writing and editing books puts an inevitable strain on even the best adjusted families. We are grateful to them and especially our wives, Noelle and Barbara, for their support and it must be to the latter that this book is affectionately dedicated.

GRAHAM DAVIES

DONALD THOMSON

Memory in Context : Context in Memory
Edited by G.M. Davies and D.M. Thomson
© 1988 John Wiley & Sons Ltd.

# CHAPTER 1

# Introduction

D.M. THOMSON

*Monash University*

and

G.M. DAVIES

*North East London Polytechnic*

## ABSTRACT

The focus of the volume is memory but other areas—thinking, perception, problem-solving—are inevitably interlinked. Major issues in the contextual literature include: definitions of context and their classification; the importance of adequate design and the development of context-based theories. The volume focuses on both semantic and episodic contexts, internal and external contexts, theory and applications.

A survey of the psychological literature reveals the increasing importance attributed to context in a wide variety of areas: sensory processes, perception, language, concept-learning, recall and recognition. Perhaps the main reason for context assuming a central role in these various areas is the acknowledgement, explicit or implicit, that organisms, objects and events are integral parts of their environment and cannot be understood in isolation of that environment (see Barker, 1969; Brunswik, 1952; Coe and Sarbin, 1977; Lewin, 1935; Sarbin and Coe, 1972).

As the title of this book, *Memory in Context: Context in Memory*, suggests its focus is on context effects in memory and not context effects in sensory processes, perception, language, concept-learning, or problem-solving. However, to state that the focus is on memory, rather than other cognitive tasks, is not to assert that the effects of context in sensory processes, perception, language, concept-learning and problem-solving are unrelated to context effects in memory. To the extent that memory representations

1

derive from perceptual representations, to the extent that the memory representation is shaped by language and the rememberer's conceptual framework, to the extent that retrieving mnenomic information constitutes a problem-solving task, the effects of context in sensory processes, perception, language, concept-learning and problem-solving are part and parcel of context effects in memory.

A survey of the literature on context effects in memory reveals, not surprisingly, that different investigators have given different emphasis to the role of perception, language, concept-learning and problem-solving in context effects in memory. This differential emphasis is reflected in the chapters of the book. Perhaps a more accurate description of the contents of this book would be context effects in memory tasks. Such a description does not exclude perceptual processes, language processes, concept-learning, problem-solving processes in the encoding, storing and retrieving of memory information.

Context as a concept is also fraught with difficulties. One source of difficulty appears to be a failure to distinguish between the different meanings or senses of context. For some, context refers to the setting in which a target is found. In this sense context is passive and relatively neutral. For others, for example, Koffka (1935), context is assigned an active role, it is the context which determines the figure or the target. Baddeley (1982), for example, distinguishes between interactive and independent context.

Another difficulty can be traced to the conflation of the effects of context occurring at different levels of analysis, context effects emanating from sensory receptors (see Dowling and Boycott, 1966; Hubel and Wiesel, 1959; Kolb and Jones, 1985; Kuffler, 1953) are not distinguished from context effects emanating at a cognitive level (see Boring, 1930; Forster, 1981; Light and Carter-Sobell, 1970; Thomson, 1972, 1986).

The final source of difficulty to be noted here concerns the inappropriate use of context as an explanatory concept. In the absence of any theory of context effects, context as a concept lacks explanatory power. Nevertheless, context is frequently invoked, albeit inappropriately, as an explanation for a particular phenomenon.

Although it is only recently that context has captured the attention of a large number of researchers in diverse areas (see Davies, 1986, for a review) its significance in memory has been acknowledged by various writers for many years. In 1932, in an influential paper in *Psychological Review*, McGeoch underscored the importance of context for remembering. He noted that over time 'contexts alter and it is at least highly probable that such alteration may remove the necessary eliciting stimulus' (p. 365).

Findings from early studies supported McGeoch's contention. Feingold (1914, 1915) manipulated the context of pictures of objects and found that changing contexts impaired the recognition of target pictures; Pan (1926) reported a decrement in recall when the context of stimulus items was changed in a paired-associate learning task.

More recently the gamut of research into context has expanded dramatically. This expansion is reflected in many different ways: the proliferation of contexts manipulated and the increasing array of targets, tasks and response measures. Contexts which have been manipulated include discrete words (Becker, 1979; Bradshaw, 1974; McClelland and Mozer, 1986; Meyer and Schvaneveldt, 1971; Thomson, 1972; Winograd, Karchmer and Russell, 1971), sentences (Conrad, 1974; Fischler and Bloom, 1979; Forster, 1981; Holmes, 1979; Light and Carter-Sobell, 1970), settings (Abernethy, 1940; Davies and Milne, 1982; Feingold, 1914, 1915; Mandler and Parker, 1976; Sanders, 1984; Strand, 1970; Thomson, Robertson and Vogt, 1982) and instructions (Geiselman, Fisher, MacKinnon and Holland, 1985; Malpass and Devine, 1981; Whitten and Leonard, 1981). Context has been used as a vehicle to control the meaning attributed to the target (Bradshaw, 1974; Light and Carter-Sobell, 1970; Schvaneveldt, Meyer and Becker, 1976; Seidenberg, Tandenhaus, Leiman and Bienkowski, 1982; Simpson, 1981; Swiney, 1979; Thomson, 1972; Thomson and Tulving, 1970; Tulving and Thomson, 1971, 1973), the visual and acoustic image or configuration (Beales and Parkin, 1984; Boring, 1930; Bugelski and Alampay, 1961; Dallenbach, 1951; Diamond and Carey, 1977; Mandler and Parker, 1976; Thomson, Robertson and Vogt, 1982), the physiological and emotional states of the observer (Bartlett and Santrock, 1979; Bower, Gilligan and Monteiro, 1981; Eich, 1980) and the focus of attention (Anderson and Pichert, 1979; Craik and Lockhart, 1972; Craik and Tulving, 1975; Morris, Bransford and Franks, 1977).

Concomitant with the proliferation of types of context the kinds of material employed as targets in context experiments have also increased sharply. They range from words (Becker, 1979; Bradshaw, 1974; McClelland and Mozer, 1986; Meyer and Schvaneveldt, 1971; Thomson, 1972; Winograd, Karchmer and Russell, 1971), sentences (Bransford and Franks, 1972; Cairns and Kamerman, 1975; Cofer, 1973; Conrad, 1974; Flagg, Potts and Reynolds, 1975; Foss and Jenkins, 1975; Hogaboam and Perfetti, 1975), pictures of objects (Feingold, 1915; Mandler and Parker, 1976), photos or slides of person or faces (Beales and Parkin, 1984; Baddeley and Woodhead, 1982; Davies and Milne, 1982; Memon and Bruce, 1983; Patterson and Baddeley, 1977; Thomson, Robertson and Vogt, 1982; Winograd and Rivers-Bulkeley, 1977), people (Hilgendorf and Irving, 1978; Krafka and Penrod, 1985; Sanders, 1984) and incidents (Geiselman, Fisher, MacKinnon and Holland, 1985; Loftus, Manber and Keating, 1983; Yuille and McEwan, 1985).

A multitude of tasks has been used to investigate the effects of context. Such tasks include: naming tasks (Broadbent and Broadbent, 1981; Forster,

1981; Marslen-Wilson and Welsh, 1978), lexical decision tasks (Fischler, 1977; McKoon and Ratcliff, 1979; Meyer and Schvaneveldt, 1971; Neely, 1977; Simpson, 1981), semantic decision tasks (Becker, 1982; Burke, White and Diaz, 1987; Holmes, 1979), reading tasks (Mitchell and Green, 1978; Stanovich and West, 1983), speech perception tasks (Marslen-Wilson and Welsh, 1978), problem-solving tasks (Lockhart, Lamon and Gick, 1985; Perfetti, Bransford and Franks, 1983; Weisberg, Dicamillo and Phillips, 1978), word recognition tasks (Light and Carter-Sobell, 1970; Thomson, 1972; Tulving and Thomson, 1973; Winograd, Karchmer and Russell, 1971), word recall tasks (Craik and Tulving, 1975; Thomson and Tulving, 1970; Tulving and Thomson, 1973) and person recognition tasks (Beales and Parkin, 1984; Davies and Milne, 1982; Memon and Bruce, 1983; Thomson, 1981; Thomson, Robertson and Vogt, 1982).

Depending on the task, four main measures have been used to assess the effects of context. These measures are number or proportion of correct responses, number or proportion of incorrect responses, speed in responding, and eye movements. With few exceptions, for example, Ratcliff and McKoon (1978), researchers investigating context effects have assumed that these measures are alternative methods of measuring the same thing, an assumption which may not be valid.

The picture that emerges from the plethora of studies which have examined the effect of context on memory is a confused and confusing one. Some researchers have reported a negative effect (Loftus, Manber and Keating, 1983; Slamecka, 1968, 1972); some have reported no effect (Bower and Karlin, 1974; Lindsay and Wallbridge, 1983; Sanders, 1984); some have reported a weak positive effect (Klee, Leseaux, Malai and Tiberghien, 1982; Memon and Bruce, 1983; Watkins, Ho and Tulving, 1976); and some have reported a strong effect (Brutsche, Cisse, Deleglise, Finet, Sonnet and Tiberghien, 1981; Thomson, 1981; Thomson, Robertson and Vogt, 1982). That no overall pattern has emerged is hardly surprising given the different meanings of the word context, given the wide range of context manipulations, given the diversity of tasks and the variety of dependent variables used to measure the effects of context.

It is tempting, on the basis of conflicting findings, to dismiss context as a useful concept. However, it is our belief that such a course of action would be premature and that an understanding of the various contextual effects may be the key to an understanding of cognitive processes in general and memory in particular. There are three requirements to be met if an understanding of context effects is to be attained.

The first requirement is that more well-designed research be undertaken. The second requirement is that a classification system of context effects be developed. The final requirement is that theories of context be developed. Note that these three requirements are interrelated: the findings from further research should provide a better basis for a classificatory system and for theorizing, which in turn should guide the direction of future research. The chapters reported in this book meet one or more of these requirements and thus advance our understanding of the various context effects.

The contexts and their manipulation reported by the different contributors cover a wide range. Semantic context is discussed in four of the chapters, by Bain and Humphreys, Tiberghien, Thomson, and Lockhart. Bain and Humphreys examine the effect of context on word recognition and recall. Tiberghien explores the effect of context in sentence comprehension tasks. Thomson investigates the effect of semantic context on false recognition and Lockhart its effect on problem-solving.

Two of the chapters are concerned with internal context. Eich and Birnbaum attempt to manipulate internal states or context of subjects by means of alcohol. They explore whether alcohol is a necessary prerequisite to produce a particular internal context or whether the internal state is achieved independently of alcohol but is attributed to the presence of alcohol by the subjects. Guenther reviews experimental and clinical findings of moods on memory performance with particular focus on the congruity of mood and content of the to-be-remembered material.

Naturalistic or environment context of one sort or another is the focus of many chapters. Most of us have had the embarrassing experience of failing to recognize someone we know when that person is observed outside their accustomed setting. This phenomenon is the one explored by Davies. Bekerian and Conway review, among other things, the research evidence pertaining to two types of everyday context: frequently experienced events or situations and rarely experienced events or situations. Bekerian and Conway contrast everyday context with molecular context situations. Four of the chapters, those of Geiselman, Cutler and Penrod, Smith, and McSpadden, Schooler and Loftus probe the efficacy of context reinstatement when the original context is not physically restored but instead imaged by witnesses. McSpadden *et al.* conclude that mental reinstatement is ineffective, a conclusion at odds with that of the other researchers.

The chapters by Lockhart and Howe share a common theme: the role of context in memory tasks which involve problem-solving. Lockhart discusses the role of context in the light of findings from problem-solving tasks in the laboratory. Howe contrasts children's ability to solve complex problems in everyday life with their inability to bring these skills into the classroom.

All of the chapters have implications for applied settings, some more so than others. Thus, Mayes' chapter investigates the relationship between certain types of memory disorder, their loci, and different types of context. Howe's chapter has great significance for our education system. No less than six of the chapters are concerned with matters of direct relevance to the criminal justice system, matters which range from identification issues through to eyewitnesses' testimony.

One final and important feature of the chapters included in this book should be mentioned. In most of the chapters an attempt is made by the authors to develop some sort of classification system of context (Bain and Humphreys, Bekerian and Conway, Davies, Lockhart, Mayes, Smith, Thomson) or to integrate context effects in memory within some sort of theoretical framework (Bain and Humphreys, Bekerian and Conway, Davies, Eich and Birnbaum, Lockhart, Mayes, Thomson). Context has been a theme, either implicit or explicit, in experimental psychology from its earliest days. To our knowledge this is the first volume directly to consider its role in memory. On the evidence presented here, we do not think it will be the last.

## REFERENCES

Abernethy, E.M. (1940). The effect of changed environmental condition upon the results of college examinations. *Journal of Psychology*, **10**, 293–301.

Anderson, R.C. and Pichert, J.W. (1979). Recall of previously unrecallable information following a shift in perspective. *Journal of Verbal Learning and Verbal Behavior*, **17**, 1–12.

Baddeley, A.D. (1982). Domains of recollection. *Psychological Review*, **89**, 708–729.

Baddeley, A.D. and Woodhead, M. (1982). Depth of processing, contexts and face recognition. *Canadian Journal of Psychology*, **36**, 148–164.

Barker, R.G. (1969). Wanted: an eco-behavioral science. In E.P. Willems and H.L. Rausch (Eds), *Naturalistic Viewpoints in Psychological Research* New York: Holt, Rinehart & Winston, pp. 31–43.

Bartlett, J.C. and Santrock (1979). Affect-dependant memory in young children. *Child Development*, **50**, 513–518.

Beales, S.A. and Parkin, A.J. (1984). Context and facial memory: the influence of different processing strategies. *Human Learning*, **3**, 257–263.

Becker, C.A. (1979). Semantic context and word frequency effects in visual word recognition. *Journal of Experimental Psychology: Human Perception and Performance*, **5**, 252–259.

Becker, C.A. (1982). The development of semantic context effects: two processes or two strategies? *Reading Research Quarterly*, **17**, 482–502.

Bilodeau, I.M. and Schlosberg, H. (1951). Similarity in stimulating conditions as a variable in retroactive inhibition. *Journal of Experimental Psychology*, **41**, 199–204.

Boring, E.G. (1930). A new ambiguous figure. *American Journal of Psychology*, **42**, 444–445.

Bower, G.H., Gilligan, S.G. and Monteiro, K.P. (1981). Selectivity in learning caused by affective states. *Journal of Experimental Psychology: General*, **110**, 451–473.

Bower, G.H. and Karlin, M.B. (1974). Depth of processing, pictures of faces and recognition memory. *Journal of Experimental Psychology*, **103**, 751–757.

Bradshaw, J.L. (1974). Peripherally presented and unreported words may bias the perceived meaning of a centrally fixated homograph. *Journal of Experimental Psychology*, **103**, 1200–1202.

Bransford, J.D. and Franks, J.J. (1972). The abstraction of linguistic ideas: a review. *Cognition: International Journal of Cognitive Psychology*, **1**, 211–249.

Broadbent, D.E. and Broadbent, M.H.P. (1981). Priming and the passive active model of word recognition. In R.S. Nickerson (Ed.), *Attention and Performance VIII*. Hillsdale, New Jersey: Lawrence Erlbaum Associates, pp. 419–434.

Brunswik, E. (1952). *The Conceptual Framework of Psychology*. University of Chicago Press, Chicago.

Brutsche, J., Cisse, A., Deleglise, D., Finet, A., Sonnet, P. and Tiberghien, G. (1981). Effets de contexte dans la reconnaissance de visage non familiers. *Cahiers de Psychologie Cognitive*, **1**, 85–90.

Bugelski, B.R. and Alampay, D.A. (1961). The role of frequency in developing perceptual sets. *Canadian Journal of Psychology*, **15**, 205–211.

Burke, D.M., White, H. and Diaz, D.L. (1987). Semantic priming in young and older adults: evidence for age constancy in automatic and attentional processes. *Journal of Experimental Psychology: Human Perception and Performance*, **13**, 79–88.

Cairns, H.S. and Kamerman, J. (1975). Lexical information processing during sentence comprehension. *Journal of Verbal Learning and Verbal Behavior*, **20**, 137–160.

Coe, W.C. and Sarbin, T.R. (1977). Hypnosis from the standpoint of a contextualist. *Annals of the New York Academy of Sciences*, **296**, 2–13.

Cofer, C.N. (1973). Constructive processes in memory. *American Scientist*, **61**, 537–543.

Conrad, C. (1974). Context effects in sentence comprehension: a study of the subjective lexicon. *Memory and Cognition*, **2**, 130–138.

Craik, F.I.M. and Lockhart, R.S. (1972). Levels of processing: a framework for memory research. *Journal of Verbal Learning and Verbal Behavior*, **11**, 671–684.

Craik, F.I.M. and Tulving, E. (1975). Depth of processing and the retention of words in episodic memory. *Journal of Experimental Psychology: General*, **104**, 268–294.

Dallenbach, K.M. (1951). A picture puzzle with a new principle of concealment. *American Journal of Psychology*, **64**, 431–433.

Davies, G. (1986). Context effects in episodic memory: a review. *Cahiers de Psychologie Cognitive*, **6**, 157–174.

Davies, G.M. and Milne, A. (1982). Recognizing faces in and out of context. *Current Psychological Research*, **2**, 235–246.

Diamond, R. and Carey, S. (1977). Developmental changes in the representation of faces. *Journal of Experimental Child Psychology*, **23**, 1–22.

Dowling, J.E. and Boycott, B.B. (1966). Organization of the primate retina: electron microscopy. *Proceedings of the Royal Society (London)*, **166B**, 80–111.

Dulsky, S.G. (1935). The effect of a change of background on recall and relearning. *Journal of Experimental Psychology*, **18**, 725–740.

Eich, J.E. (1980). The cue dependent nature of state dependent retrieval. *Memory and Cognition*, **8**, 157–173.

Feingold, G.A. (1914). The influence of environment on the identification of persons and things. *Journal of Criminal Law, Criminology and Police Science*, **5**, 39–51.

Feingold, G.A. (1915). Recognition and discrimination. *Psychological Monographs*, **78**, 1-128.

Fischler, I. (1977). Associative facilitation without expectancy in a lexical decision task. *Journal of Experimental Psychology: Human Perception and Performance*, **3**, 18–26.

Fischler, I. and Bloom, P.A. (1979). Automatic and attentional processes in the effects of sentence contexts on word recognition. *Journal of Verbal Learning and Verbal Behavior*, **18**, 1–20.

Flagg, P.W., Potts, G.R. and Reynolds, A.G. (1975). Instructions and response strategies in recognition memory for sentences. *Journal of Experimental Psychology: Human Learning and Memory*, **1**, 592–598.

Forster, K.I. (1981). Priming and the effects of sentence and lexical contexts on naming time: evidence for autonomous lexical processing. *Quarterly Journal of Experimental Psychology*, **33A**, 465–495.

Foss, D.J. and Jenkins, C.M. (1975). Some effects of context on the comprehension of ambiguous sentences. *Journal of Verbal Learning and Verbal Behavior*, **12**, 577–587.

Geiselman, R.E., Fisher, R.P., MacKinnon, D.P. and Holland, H.L. (1985). Eyewitness memory enhancement in the police interview: cognitive retrieval mnemonics versus hypnosis. *Journal of Applied Psychology*, **70**, 401–412.

Hilgendorf, E.L. and Irving, B.L. (1978). False positive identification. *Medicine, Science and the Law*, **18**, 255–262.

Hogaboam, T.W. and Perfetti, C.A. (1975). Lexical ambiguity and sentence comprehension. *Journal of Verbal Learning and Verbal Behavior*, **14**, 265–274.

Holmes, V.M. (1979). Accessing ambiguous words during sentence comprehension. *Quarterly Journal of Experimental Psychology*, **44**, 13–35.

Hubel, D.H. and Wiesel, T.N. (1959). Receptive fields of single neurons in the cat's striate cortex. *Journal of Physiology*, **148**, 574–591.

Klee, M., Leseaux, M., Malai, C. and Tiberghien, G. (1982). Nouveaux effets de contexte dans la reconnaissance de visages familiers. *Revue de Psychologie Appliquée*, **32**, 109–119.

Koffka, K. (1935). *Principles of Gestalt Psychology*. New York: Harcourt.

Kolb, H. and Jones, J. (1985). Electron microscopy of Golgi-impregnated photoreceptors reveals connections between red and green cones in the turtle retina. *Journal of Neurophysiology*, **54**, 304–317.

Krafka, C. and Penrod, S. (1985). Reinstatement of context in a field experiment on eyewitness identification. *Journal of Personality and Social Psychology*, **49**, 58–69.

Kuffler, S. (1953). Discharge patterns and functional organization of mammalian retina. *Journal of Neurophysiology*, **16**, 37–68.

Lewin, K. (1935). *Dynamic Theory of Personality*. New York: McGraw-Hill.

Light, L. and Carter-Sobell, L. (1970). Effects of changed semantic context on recognition memory. *Journal of Verbal Learning and Verbal Behavior*, **9**, 1–12.

Lindsay, R.C.L. and Wallbridge, H. (1983). Do the clothes make the man? An exploration of the effect of line-up attire on eyewitness identification. Unpublished manuscript.

Lockhart, R.S., Lamon, M. and Gick, M.L. (1985). Transfer in an insight problem. Unpublished data.

Loftus, E., Manber, M. and Keating, J.P. (1983). Recollection of naturalistic events: context enhancement vs negative cueing. *Human Learning*, **2**, 83–92.

McClelland, J.L. and Mozer, M.C. (1986). Perceptual interactions in two-word displays: familiarity and similarity effects. *Journal of Experimental Psychology: Human Perception and Performance*, **12**, 18–35.

McGeoch, J.A. (1932). Forgetting and the law of disuse. *Psychological Review*, **39**, 353–370.

McKoon, G. and Ratcliff, R. (1979). Priming in episodic and semantic memory. *Journal of Verbal Learning and Verbal Behavior*, **18**, 463–490.

Malpass, R.S. and Devine, P.G. (1981). Guided Memory in eyewitness identification. *Journal of Applied Psychology*, **66**, 343–350.

Mandler, J.M. and Parker, R.E. (1976). Memory for descriptive and spatial information in complex pictures. *Journal of Experimental Psychology: Human Learning and Memory*, **2**, 38–48.

Marslen-Wilson, W.D. and Welsh, A. (1978). Processing interactions and lexical access during word recognition in continuous speech. *Cognitive Psychology*, **10**, 29–63.

Memon, A. and Bruce, V. (1983). The effects of encoding strategy and context change on face recognition. *Human Learning*, **2**, 313–327.

Meyer, D. and Schvaneveldt, R. (1971). Facilitation in recognizing pairs of words: evidence of a dependence between retrieval operations. *Journal of Experimental Psychology*, **90**, 227–234.

Mitchell, D.C. and Green, D.W. (1978). The effects of context and content on immediate processing in reading. *Quarterly Journal of Experimental Psychology*, **30**, 609–636.

Morris, C.D., Bransford, J.D. and Franks, J.J. (1977). Levels of processing versus transfer-appropriate processing. *Journal of Verbal Learning and Verbal Behavior*, **16**, 519–533.

Neely, J.H. (1977). Semantic priming and retrieval from lexical memory: roles of inhibitionless spreading activation and limited-capacity attention. *Journal of Experimental Psychology: General*, **106**, 226–254.

Pan, S. (1926). The influence of context upon learning and recall. *Journal of Experimental Psychology*, **9**, 468–491.

Patterson, K.E. and Baddeley, A.D. (1977). When face recognition fails. *Journal of Experimental Psychology: Human Learning and Memory*, **3**, 406–417.

Perfetti, C.A., Bransford, J.D. and Franks, J.J. (1983). Constraints on access in a problem solving context. *Memory and Cognition*, **11**, 24–31.

Ratcliff, R. and McKoon, G. (1978). Priming in item recognition: evidence for the propositional structure of sentences. *Journal of Verbal Learning and Verbal Behavior*, **17**, 403–417.

Sanders, G.S. (1984). Effects of context cues on eyewitness identification responses. *Journal of Applied Social Psychology*, **14**, 386–397.

Sarbin, T.R. and Coe, W.C. (1972). *Hypnosis: A Social-psychological Analysis of Influence Communication*. New York: Holt, Rinehart & Winston.

Schvaneveldt, R.W., Meyer, D.E. and Becker, C.A. (1976). Lexical ambiguity, semantic context, and visual word recognition. *Journal of Experimental Psychology: Human Perception and Performance*, **2**, 243–256.

Seidenberg, M.S., Tanenhaus, M.K., Leiman, J.M. and Bienkowski, M. (1982). Automatic access of the meanings of ambiguous words in context: some limitations of knowledge-based processing. *Cognitive Psychology*, **14**, 489–537.

Simpson, G.B. (1981). Meaning dominance and semantic context in the processing of lexical ambiguity. *Journal of Verbal Learning and Verbal Behavior*, **20**, 120–136.

Slamecka, N.J. (1968). An examination of trace storage in free recall. *Journal of Experimental Psychology*, **76**, 504–513.

Slamecka, N.J. (1972). The question of associative growth in the learning of categorized material. *Journal of Verbal Learning and Verbal Behavior*, **11**, 73–82.

Stanovich, K.E. and West, R.F. (1983). On priming by a sentence context. *Journal of Experimental Psychology: General*, **112**, 1–36.

Strand, B.Z. (1970). Change of context and retroactive inhibition. *Journal of Verbal Learning and Verbal Behavior*, **9**, 202–206.

Swiney, D.A. (1979). Lexical access during sentence comprehension: (re)consideration of context effects. *Journal of Verbal Learning and Verbal Behavior*, **18**, 645–659.

Thomson, D.M. (1970). Context effects in recognition memory. Unpublished Ph.D. thesis, University of Toronto.

Thomson, D.M. (1972). Context effects in recognition memory. *Journal of Verbal Learning and Verbal Behavior*, **11** 497–511.

Thomson, D.M. (1981). Person identification: influencing the outcome. *Australian and New Zealand Journal of Criminology*, **14**, 49–54.

Thomson, D.M. (1986). Face recognition: more than feeling of familiarity. In H.D. Ellis, H.A. Jeeves, F. Newcombe and A. Young (Eds) *Aspects of Face Processing*. Dordrecht: Martinus Nijhoff.

Thomson, D.M., Robertson, S.L. and Vogt, R. (1982). Person recognition: the effect of context. *Human Learning*, **1**, 137–154.

Thomson, D.M. and Tulving, E. (1970). Associative encoding and retrieval: weak and strong cues. *Journal of Experimental Psychology*, **86**, 255–262.

Tulving, E. and Thomson, D.M. (1971). Retrieval processes in recognition memory: effect of associative context. *Journal of Experimental Psychology*, **87**, 116–124.

Tulving, E. and Thomson, D.M. (1973). Encoding specificity and retrieval processes in episodic memory. *Psychological Review*, **80**, 353–370.

Watkins, M.J., Ho, E. and Tulving, E. (1976). Context effects in recognition memory for faces. *Journal of Verbal Learning and Verbal Behavior*, **15**, 505–517.

Weisberg, R., Dicamillo, M. and Phillips, D. (1978). Transferring old associations to new problems: a nonautomatic process. *Journal of Verbal Learning and Verbal Behavior*, **17**, 219–228.

Whitten, W.B. and Leonard, J.M. (1981). Directed search through autobiographical memory. *Memory and Cognition*, **9**, 566–579.

Winograd, E., Karchmer, M.A. and Russell, I.S. (1971). Role of encoding unitization in cued recognition memory. *Journal of Verbal Learning and Verbal Behavior*, **10**, 199–206.

Winograd, E. and Rivers-Bulkeley, N.T. (1977). The effects of changing context on remembering faces. *Journal of Experimental Psychology: Human Learning and Memory*, **3**, 397–405.

Yuille, J.C. and McEwan, N.H. (1985). Use of hypnosis as an aid to eyewitness memory. *Journal of Applied Psychology*, **70**, 389–400.

# ENVIRONMENTAL CONTEXT

Memory in Context : Context in Memory
Edited by G.M. Davies and D.M. Thomson
© 1988 John Wiley & Sons Ltd.

## CHAPTER 2

# Environmental Context—Dependent Memory

STEVEN M. SMITH

*Texas A&M University*

## ABSTRACT

The impact on recall of reinstatement or change of the environment existing at the time of learning is reviewed. While strong and stable effects have been observed for recall, effects on recognition rarely occur because the word itself is a powerful cue (the outshining hypothesis). A classification of context effects is presented and the conditions where such effects are likely to be maximized or minimized are specified.

## INTRODUCTION

Having lived most of his life in St Louis, Missouri, except for two years at the University of Texas at Austin and four years in the military service during the Second World War, my father returned to Texas after 42 long years of forgetting. Although previously certain that he could recall only a few disembodied fragments of memories of his college days, he became increasingly amazed, upon his return, at the freshness and detail of his newly remembered experiences. Strolling excitedly along the streets of Austin, my father suddenly stopped and animatedly described the house in which he had lived in a location now occupied by a parking lot. He recalled in vivid detail, for example, how an armadillo had climbed up the drain pipe one night and become his pet, and how the woman who had cooked for the residents of his house had informed them of the attack on Pearl Harbor, abruptly ending his college career. Not until he returned to the setting in which those long past events had occurred had my father thought or spoken of them.

This is an example of environmental context (EC)-dependent memory, a class of phenomena in which cognitive processing is affected in subtle, profound, and sometimes important ways by the coincidental background EC in which experiences are set. This particular case is an example of an environmental reinstatement effect (e.g. Smith, 1979), where reinstatement of a previously experienced EC cues memories of events which occurred in that EC. Although reinstatement effects constitute the most commonly described and researched class of EC-dependent memory phenomena, there are other EC-dependent memory effects which have been reported as well, and which will be mentioned briefly herein.

There is a wealth of research on context and memory, but not all studies have manipulated the same types of context, and it is not at all clear that all forms of context are processed alike. Environmental context (EC), as defined in the present discussion, will refer to incidental external stimuli which are not explicitly or implicitly related to the learning material in any meaningful way. This issue of a definition of context will be discussed later in this chapter.

The present chapter will describe naturalistic evidence, laboratory findings, and theoretical accounts of EC-dependent memory, discuss the relevance of such research to some basic issues in cognition, and identify some important lacunae in our understanding of EC-dependent memory. Some similarities and inconsistencies between naturalistic anecdotal experiences and laboratory evidence will be identified.


## NATURALISTIC EVIDENCE

There is a wealth of anecdotal evidence related to EC-dependent memory. Many of us, for example, know of cases of dramatic long-term reinstatement effects such as the one described earlier, as well as more common everyday examples. It is worthwhile to identify some of these naturalistic phenomena to help guide laboratory investigations of EC-dependent memory.


### Long-term reinstatement effects

One of the most commonly noted examples of such dramatic long-term reinstatement effects is the flood of memories one experiences when returning to a former residence after a long absence. Living in a place for a long period of time leads to a rich integration in memory of experiences with environmental information. Physical separation from a former residence is often correlated with important changes in lifestyle, such as career change, marriage, divorce, emigration, enrollment in college, or retirement. Because such new lifestyles often require people to become engrossed with new concerns, new habits and routines, and new friends and acquaintances, memories of former concerns, habits, and friends weaken from interference and disuse. Returning to the former residence can make one poignantly aware that the 'lost' experiences are still quite available in memory.

Another dramatic long-term reinstatement effect has been highly publicized in the news media, namely, revival of wartime experiences caused by returning to the scene of one's former involvement. The return of former prisoners to Nazi death camps, for example, has helped people reconstruct the tragic events of the Second World War even after 40 years of a new life. Vietnam veterans exposed to 15-year-old television images of battles have experienced such vividly revived memories of the war that mental health centers reported considerable increases in the incidence of those veterans requiring mental health care following TV broadcasts.

These dramatic long-term reinstatement effects suggest that the study of long-term separation from a former residence might help in the understanding of a number of clinical concerns, such as infantile amnesia (which might be enhanced by moving from a childhood home), forgetting by the elderly (which might be worsened by retirement in a new residence), or dissociative disorders. Such effects, if brought into the laboratory, might also lead to new insights about the nature of human memory.

**Short-term effects**

Besides long-term environmental reinstatement effects, there are a number of frequently experienced short-term EC effects related to memory. One of the more common of these is the experience of failing to recognize a familiar person (e.g. from work or from a class) when the person is encountered in a new context (e.g. at the grocery store or at the movies). At times one may have a sense of familiarity associated with the person without knowing quite who they are. When the person is viewed back in the original environment, however, recognition may proceed without difficulty.

Momentary forgetting can sometimes be remedied by returning to an event's input context. For example, while working at my desk, I interrupted my work to go to the departmental office for some file folders. Still thinking about my work, I trudged absent-mindedly to the office. Upon arriving at the office, I realized I had forgotten what I needed there. The file folders could not be remembered until I returned to my office. A dramatic example of this type of experience occurred when Beethoven, while riding in a coach, dreamed of a piece of music which he almost immediately forgot. Riding in the same coach the following day, he suddenly recalled the musical canon and wrote it down (Dreistadt, 1971).

Table 2.1 Physical reinstatement—laboratory studies.

| Study | Manipulation | Learning | Test | + | − |
|---|---|---|---|---|---|
| 1. Burri (1931) | Audience | Word pairs | Cued recall | 1 | 0 |
| 2. Canas and Nelson (1986) | Lab vs home | Words | Recognition | 1 | 0 |
| 3. Dulsky (1935) | Color | CVC pairs | Cued recall | 2 | 0 |
| 4. Eich (1985) | Room | Words | Free recall | 1 | 1 |
| 5. Fernandez and Glenberg (1985) | Room | Words | Free recall | 10 | 12 |
|  |  |  | Cued recall | 0 | 3 |
|  |  |  | Recognition | 0 | 1 |
| 6. Frerk, Holcombe, Johnson and Nelson (1985) | Room | Movie | Cued recall | 1 | 0 |
|  |  |  | Recognition | 0 | 1 |
| 7. Geiselman and Glenny (1977) | Voice | Words | Recognition | 2 | 0 |
| 8. Geiselman and Bjork (1980) | Voice | Words | Recognition | 2 | 0 |
| 9. Godden and Baddeley (1975) | Land vs water | Words | Free recall | 1 | 0 |
| 10. Godden and Baddeley (1980) | Land vs water | Words | Recognition | 0 | 1 |
| 11. Jacoby (1983) | Room | Words | Recognition | 0 | 1 |
|  |  |  | Perceptual ident. | 1 | 0 |
| 12. Jensen, Harris and Anderson (1971) | Room | CVC | Serial recall | 1 | 0 |
| 13. Nixon and Kanak (1981) | Room | Words | Free recall | 1 | 1 |
| 14. Pessin (1932) | Sound | CVC | Relearning | 0 | 1 |
| 15. Rand and Wapner (1967) | Posture | CVC | Relearning | 1 | 0 |
| 16. Reed (1931) | Input mode | Word pairs | Cued recall | 1 | 0 |
|  | Response mode | Word pairs | Cued recall | 0 | 1 |
|  | Posture | Words | Serial recall | 0 | 1 |
| 17. S. Smith and Guthrie (1924) | Odor | CVC | Relearning | 1 | 0 |
|  | In vs outdoors | CVC | Relearning | 1 | 0 |
| 18. Smith (1979) | Room | Words | Free recall | 3 | 0 |

| Study | Manipulation | Learning | Test | + | − |
|---|---|---|---|---|---|
| 19. Smith (1986) | Room | Words | Recognition | 3 | 0 |
| | | | Free recall | 1 | 0 |
| 20. Smith (1985a) | Room | Words | Free recall | 0 | 1 |
| | | | Cued recall | 0 | 1 |
| | | | Recognition | 2 | 0 |
| 21. Smith (1985b) | Tank vs lounge | Words | Free recall | 1 | 0 |
| 22. Smith (1985c) | Sound | Words | Free recall | 2 | 0 |
| 23. Smith, Glenberg and Bjork (1978) | Room | Words | Free recall | 2 | 0 |
| | | | Cued recall | 1 | 0 |
| | | | Recognition | 0 | 2 |
| 24. Smith and Heath (1986) | Room | Homophones | Recognition | 0 | 0 |
| | | | Spelling | 2 | 2 |
| 25. Smith and Vela (1986) | Room | Staged event | Face Recognition | 1 | 0 |
| 26. Steuck (1979) | Room | CVC | Cued recall | 1 | 1 |
| 27. Steuck and Levy (1985) | Room | Words | Cued recall | 1 | 0 |
| | | Text | Cued recall | 0 | 1 |
| 28. Vela (1984) | Room | CVC | Free recall | 3 | 0 |
| 29. Weiss and Margolius (1954) | Color | CVC | Cued recall | 1 | 0 |

*Notes*: Numbers in the '+' column indicate numbers of findings of EC-dependent memory effects, numbers in the '−' column indicate failures to find EC-dependent memory. The 'findings' are not equivalent, differing, for example, in numbers of subjects, numbers of conditions finding EC-dependent memory, size of effects. Therefore, attempts to 'total the evidence' would be misleading.

Although in many studies listed the findings and failures to find EC-dependent memory are clear cut, some of the investigations, such as 4, 11, and 12 are difficult to assign exact numbers. In number 11, although EC-dependent memory was found across six age groups, only one finding is listed, because the study is listed as a single experiment. In number 12 there was an EC effect, but only in the primacy and recency portions of the list. The '+s' in number 4 reflect not significant effect, but trends in which subjects in the reinstated conditions scored more than 5% better than those tested under changed context conditions.

'Manipulation' refers to the aspect of the EC which was manipulated to study EC-dependent memory. Learning material and types of tests given are also listed for each study.

**Other effects**

Environmental context-dependent memory phenomena of different sorts
are sometimes experienced in relation to vacations. For example, one of
the basic functions served by a vacation trip is to place the vacationer in
an unfamiliar environment so that the memories and cares of the work
setting can be better forgotten. This example can be labeled either changed
context forgetting or proactive interference reduction. The creative worker
(e.g. author, artist) who becomes 'stale' on the job (e.g. 'writer's block')
may be stimulated by a host of new ideas when away on a sabbatical or
vacation in a new setting. Freed from the hackneyed ideas which one cannot escape in the old work setting, a writer or artist in a new environment
may be more sensitive to new ideas when a changed EC aids forgetting of
the old ideas.

Finally we might note that in a mundane, but very real sense, our everyday memories, situations, and even personal roles are cued constantly by
our environments. Different personal roles are called upon, for example,
when one is at one's work place, one's home, a restaurant, a theater, a
workout gym, a bank, a party, a doctor's office, a campground, or a place
of religious worship. In this way our lives can become compartmentalized
and cued by our environmental surroundings.

## EXPERIMENTAL STUDIES

A number of experimental studies concerned with context-dependent
memory in humans will be briefly reviewed in this section. The investigations deal with physical reinstatement effects in the laboratory and
the classroom, imagined reinstatement of EC, transfer and interference
EC effects, and multiple input context effects. Notably absent from this
review is the growing collection of animal studies of context-dependent
learning and memory. Those interested in EC effects in animal studies
may be referred to Riccio, Richardson, and Ebner (1984), which contains
a review of that literature.

The laboratory studies of physical reinstatement effects (Table 2.1)
demonstrate that although EC reinstatement has been found to aid
memory in a variety of studies by numerous investigators, reported failures
to find EC effects are also numerous. Considering the likelihood that many
failures to find an EC effect have not been reported, the unpredictability
of the effect appears to be one of the most important considerations of
EC-dependent memory.

Five tables summarizing the literature for various EC-dependent memory
phenomena are presented in this section. The numbers of findings and
failures to find EC-dependent memory effects are listed for each study.

Several issues will be considered which help clarify some of the unpredictability of EC-dependent memory phenomena. These issues are effects of EC on recall vs recognition, encoding of EC information, internal manipulation of EC imagery, classroom studies, EC as an organizational cue, and individual differences in EC-dependent memory.

## Recall and recognition

Why is EC-dependent memory generally found with recall, but not with recognition testing (e.g. Smith *et al.*, 1978; Godden and Baddeley, 1980; Jacoby, 1983; Frerk *et al.*, 1985; Eich, 1985)? These studies contradict memory models which identify the recognition process as the locus of context-dependent memory (e.g. Kintsch, 1974; Anderson and Bower, 1974). Kintsch, for example, stated that on a recognition test the following occurs: (a) concepts are retrieved from semantic memory to represent test items; (b) implicitly retrieved concepts are combined with selected elements of the test context to form a memory probe; and (c) the memory probe is matched with encoded event memories. This matching process is enhanced the more overlap there is between the learning context (a component of event memories) and the test context (a component of the memory probe). The lack of EC-dependent recognition in most studies appears to disconfirm such a theory.

One explanation of this pattern of results is the Outshining hypothesis. Outshining is an application of the idea that a heavenly body which is visible on a moonless night is more difficult to see when there is a full moon, and is completely outshone in the daytime by the sun. Similarly, an incidentally encoded EC can cue memory when better cue sources are absent (i.e. they were not encoded or they are missing from the test information), but EC cues can be completely outshone when better cues are present. This Outshining principle has been described by different authors in similar ways (e.g. Smith *et al.*, 1978; Spear, 1978; Eich, 1980; Geiselman and Bjork, 1980; Nixon and Kanak, 1985), both for context- and state-dependent memory. Outshining emphasizes the relativity of EC cuing; a cue's effectiveness depends upon the presence of better cues.

What makes one cue better than another? The potential cuing derived from a piece of information can be increased by a number of factors. For example, the less overloaded a cue (i.e. the fewer items associated with a cue), the better the cue (Watkins and Watkins, 1975). Cues should also be better the more deeply processed they are, the more repetitions they have received, and the better integrated they are with their targets. There may well be other factors related to a cue's usefulness, but this brief description should help convey what is meant by a 'better' cue.

An example of a cue which is better than an incidentally encoded EC cue is a copy of a target word presented on typical recognition test. Copy cues generally outshine EC cues, thus nullifying EC reinstatement effects when recognition tests are given (e.g. Smith *et al.*, 1978; Godden and Baddeley, 1980; Jacoby, 1983; Eich, 1985; Frerk *et al.*, 1985). Demonstrations of state-dependent memory for word lists also typically fail when recognition tests have been used (e.g. Eich, 1980; Bartlett and Santrock, 1979).

Five experiments in two of my own reported studies (Smith, 1985a) have found EC-dependent recognition. In those investigations, however, attempts were made to decrease the use of good memory cues so that the relatively weaker effects of EC cues could be detected. In one set of experiments (Smith, 1986) EC-dependent recognition was found following a shallow, incidental learning task, but the effect disappeared when subjects were asked to use deeper processing during learning. The relatively poorer coding of shallowly processed words increased the cuing effects of the test EC. In another set of experiments (Smith, 1985a) it was hypothesized that when the first few items from a list of learned words are tested, the test words help reinstate the original list context, again nullifying EC cuing effects. To help prevent test words from reinstating a particular list context, test words from several different studied lists were randomly mixed on the recognition test. Without the cuing benefits of interassociated words on the recognition test, the effects of EC cues were relatively greater. It is not the recognition test itself which nullifies context-dependent memory effects; rather, it is the copy cues and interassociated information present on a recognition which cue memory more than the incidentally encoded EC cues.

We may find some confirmation of this description of EC-dependent recognition in naturalistic observation. For example, failure to recognize a familiar person viewed in a new EC may be decreased if that person appears in the presence of good memory cues. If the person is wearing the clothes or associating with friends which are typically seen with the target person, successful recognition may proceed (see the contributions of Davies and Thomson, this volume).

Another example of the Outshining principle is the trend which indicates that better learning (or improved storage of memory cues) appears to reduce EC-dependent memory effects. EC-dependent memory was found to be greater when words were presented as paired associates rather than embedded in meaningful text (Steuck and Levy, 1985). More meaningful CVCs used as targets showed weaker EC-dependent memory effects than low meaningful CVCs (Vela, 1984). Use of an imagery learning strategy may have eliminated the effect of incidental background EC cues in a study by Eich (1985). These studies suggest hints about the relationship between learning and EC-dependent memory, but a more systematic investigation of this relationship is called for.

The Integration hypothesis (Baddeley, 1982) states that context-dependent recognition will not occur unless the context and learning materials are integrated in memory. In Geiselman and Bjork's (1980) terms, only intrinsic situational context cues (i.e. material integrated with the learning material) can be used to induce context-dependent recognition. Extrinsic situational context, which refers to incidentally presented contextual material, should not cause context-dependent recognition. Smith's (1985a; 1986) studies, however, found effects of incidental background ECs on recognition memory. Eich's (1985) study used a condition in which environmental loci were imaged integratively with images of list items, yet no EC-dependent recognition was found. These findings appear to disconfirm the Integration hypothesis.

The SAM hypothesis derives from Gillund and Shiffrin's (1984) treatment of context-dependent memory. Their hypothesis states that increasing the amount of information learned between input and testing (referred to as 'junk') both decreases recognition and increases EC-dependent recognition. The typical list-learning experiment may not provide enough 'junk' for EC-dependent recognition to appear; added junk might reveal hidden effects of the test EC upon recognition. At this time, the SAM hypothesis has not been adequately tested in the laboratory. On the other hand, the naturalistic phenomenon of contextually reviving old memories upon one's return to a former residence may depend upon the large amount of 'junk' occurring since leaving the former residence.

The Sensitivity hypothesis states that recognition accuracy for list words tested in a constant or changed environment is not sensitive enough to detect EC-dependent recognition. Such an experimental situation might result in excessive variability, and it may give subjects opportunities to employ strategic retrieval processes which could nullify EC effects. This paradigm does not take into account recognition latency, a measure which might be more sensitive than accuracy to EC effects on recognition. For example, the common experience of failing to recognize a familiar acquaintance viewed in an unusual context may sometimes be only a brief period of forgetting. After a short time, the acquaintance may be successfully recognized. Thus, EC-dependent recognition may be seen in latency measures even when accuracy is not affected.

Finally, another hypothesis states that studies have not successfully induced changes in subjects' *situational context*, because even though a room change occurs in an experiment, it remains the same experiment. To induce greater situational change in their test of EC-dependent recognition, Canas and Nelson (1986) contrasted subjects' recognition performance tested in the input room vs tested at the subjects' own homes on the telephone. Home environments were assumed to cue a very different situational context than the experimental context. Canas and Nelson (1986) found a robust EC-dependent recognition effect.

Table 2.2 Imagined reinstatement.

| Study | Learning | Test | + | − |
|---|---|---|---|---|
| 1. Fisher, Geiselman, Mackinnon, and Holland (1984) | Dramatic events | Cued recall | 1 | 0 |
| 2. Frerk, Holcombe, Johnson, and Nelson (1985) | Movie | Cued recall | 1 | 0 |
| 3. Krafka and Penrod (1985)* | Staged event | Recognition | 1 | 0 |
| 4. Malpass and Devine (1981)* | Staged event | Recognition | 1 | 0 |
| 5. Smith (1979) | Words | Free recall | 2 | 0 |
| 6. Smith (1984) | Words | Free recall | 2 | 0 |

*Notes*: Numbers in the '+' column indicate findings that imagining one's learning context improved memory. Numbers in the '−' column indicate failures to find such imagined EC reinstatement effects. Learning materials and types of test are also listed for each study.

* These studies used a test procedure in which subjects were asked mentally to reinstate the situation in question, but in both, additional important information was provided to subjects, so it is not clear whether the provided cues or the reinstatement instructions benefited recognition of the target confederate.

## Encoding environmental context

Another issue raised by the reviewed studies concerns whether or not EC cues are encoded during learning. Experimental situations designed to make contextual information very likely to be noticed have usually resulted in context-dependent memory effects. For example, context was integrated with target stimuli in studies of speaker's voice (Geiselman and Glenny, 1977; Geiselman and Bjork, 1980) or background color of CVCs (Dulsky, 1935; Weiss and Margolius, 1954), and such studies produced reliable context effects. Eich (1985) manipulated integration of targets with EC via learning instructions, and found EC-dependent recall only when EC information was integrated with target words. In fact, Eich (1985) and Baddeley (1982) have independently proposed that EC-dependent memory may occur only when contextual and target information are integrated in memory. Consistent with this idea are the findings of Nixon and Kanak (1981), who found that simply asking subjects to encode the learning EC without instructing subjects to integrate list materials with their context, did not lead to EC-dependent recall.

## Internal manipulation of EC imagery

Even if EC information is encoded and not outshone by better memory cues, internal manipulation of EC information can prevent the observation of EC reinstatement effects. That is, subjects can image a previously experienced EC and use the internally generated image as a memory cue even if that EC is not physically present. Table 2.2 lists a number of experimental studies which found cuing effects from imagined EC cues. In those studies instructions to recall the learning context improved subjects' ability to remember words (Smith, 1979; 1984), or more meaningful events (Malpass and Devine, 1981; Krafka and Penrod, 1985; Fisher, Geiselman, Holland, and Mackinnon, 1984; Frerk *et al.*, 1985).

The technique of internally generating one's own contextual memory cues appears to be a promising method for enhancing eyewitness memory, both for recalling events and for identifying photographs of confederates. Malpass and Devine (1981), Krafka and Penrod (1985), and Fisher *et al.* (1984) have found enhanced eyewitness memory using techniques which included, but were not limited to, instructing witnesses to generate contextual cues from memory. Unfortunately, it is not clear whether the self-generated context cues or the experimenter-provided cues were responsible for the noted memory enhancement. Still, the self-generated cuing technique may have great applied value for enhancing eyewitness memory.

This ability to manipulate contextual information internally confirms observations in natural settings which indicate that physical reinstatement of an EC is not always necessary to revive memories associated with that EC. For example, imaging a previously attended school often helps cue memories for people and events associated with that school. Internal manipulation of EC information may also explain some of the frequent failures to find physical reinstatement effects; subjects tested in a new EC might sometimes generate their own EC cues internally. Such an explanation seems especially reasonable in the case where subjects are intentionally directed to notice their learning context during learning (e.g. Nixon and Kanak, 1981). Having been directed to attend to their learning EC during learning, subjects may be quite likely to use internally generated EC cues when tested in a new environmental context.

Table 2.3   Physical reinstatement—classroom studies.

| Study | + | − |
|-------|---|---|
| 1. Abernethy (1940) | 0 | 1 |
| 2. Farnsworth (1934) | 0 | 3 |
| 3. Mellgren (1984) | 1 | 0 |
| 4. Metzger, Boschee, Haugen, and Schnobrich (1979) | 1 | 0 |
| 5. Saufley, Otaka, and Bavaresco (1986) | 0 | 21 |

*Notes*: Numbers in the '+' column indicate findings of EC-dependent memory. Numbers in the '−' column indicate failures to find EC-dependent memory.

### Classroom studies

Table 2.3 presents an interesting, if not surprising, summary of classroom studies concerned with EC reinstatement effects. The preponderance of evidence indicates that students do not score lower on exams as a result of being tested outside their regular lecture room, contrary to a popular belief. Although Abernethy's (1940) study is commonly cited in support of the popular belief, her study stated that no statistically significant effects were found. A likely reason that classroom EC effects have not been found is that students study outside their regular classroom (Chen, 1984); hence, any classroom EC is different from students' predominant learning EC. An exception to the pattern is a study by Mellgren (1984), who did find a classroom EC effect. Mellgren, however, controlled students' study place, having some students spend study time in the regular classroom and others spend study time in another classroom. The only other finding of a classroom EC effect was Metzger *et al.* (1979), who found that when

Table 2.4  Transfer and interference effects.

| Study | Effect | Test | + | – |
|---|---|---|---|---|
| 1. Bilodeau and Schlosberg (1951) | RI reduction | Relearning | 2 | 0 |
| 2. Coggins and Kanak (1985) | RI reduction | Recall | 1 | 0 |
|  | Transfer | Recall | 1 | 0 |
| 3. Dallett and Wilcox (1968) | RI reduction | Serial recall | 1 | 0 |
| 4. Eckert, Kanak and Stevens (1984) | RI reduction | Memory of frequency | 1 | 0 |
| 5. Greenspoon and Ranyard (1957) | RI reduction | Serial recall | 1 | 0 |
| 6. Kanak and Stevens (1985) | RI reduction | Recall | 1 | 0 |
| 7. Strand (1970)* | RI reduction | Recall | 1 | 0 |

Notes: Numbers in the '+' column indicate findings of EC-dependent memory. Numbers in the '–' column indicate failures to find EC-dependent memory. Type of effect and type of test are also shown.
* Strand (1970) found that retroactive interference was reduced if interpolated learning and original learning occurred in different ECs, but she also found that merely disrupting subjects and returning them to their original EC for interpolated learning and final testing reduced interference to a similar degree. This disruption factor has been controlled in studies since Strand's.

one of five exams was given in a new EC, exam performance suffered. A reasonable explanation for their finding, however, is not that reinstatement of the learning EC enhances memory, but that students associated specific exam-taking skills with their regular classroom during the first three or four exams. The classroom EC studies, then, neither support nor refute the ecological relevance of EC reinstatement effects, although they point out a danger of oversimplifying predictions as a result of these experimental findings.

Table 2.5   Multiple input room effects.

| Study | Learning | Test | + | − |
|-------|----------|------|---|---|
| 1. Chen (1984) | Coursework | Exam | 1 | 1 |
| 2. Glenberg (1979) | Words | Free recall | 1 | 0 |
| 3. Smith (1982) | Words | Free recall | 2 | 0 |
| 4. Smith (1984) | Words | Free recall | 1 | 1 |
| 5. Smith (1985d) | Words | Free recall | 1 | 2 |
| 6. Smith, Glenberg, and Bjork (1978) | Words | Free recall | 1 | 0 |
| 7. Smith and Rothkopf (1984) | Lectures | Free recall | 1 | 1 |

*Notes*: Numbers in the '+' column indicate findings of EC-dependent memory. Numbers in the '−' column indicate failures to find EC-dependent memory. Learning materials and type of list are also shown.

### Environmental context as an organizational cue

Another commonly found EC-dependent memory effect is the reduction of interference which occurs when different lists of learning materials are presented in different ECs (Table 2.4). The results of such studies are quite consistent, showing reduced proactive interference (Dallett and Wilcox, 1968; Coggins and Kanak, 1985) and retroactive interference (Bilodeau and Schlosberg, 1951; Eckert, Kanak and Stevens, 1984; Greenspoon and Ranyard, 1957; Coggins and Kanak, 1985; Strand, 1970). Such studies indicate that associated EC information can act as an organizational cue, decreasing interference among sets of learned materials with different contextual referents.

Further evidence of the use of EC organizational cues comes from multiple input room studies (Table 2.5). Those studies show that in the absence of a specific EC cue at the time of testing, recall and clustering are greater for material studied in multiple ECs than for material studied in a single EC. The multiple input ECs may provide extra retrieval cues not available for material learned in one consistent EC.

The studies of interference reduction and multiple input room effects have some parallels in naturalistic experiences. For example, as mentioned earlier, a vacation in a new settng can help prevent the intrusion of everyday problems into one's thoughts, and, unfortunately, a return to one's home or work place diminishes the vivid vacation memories, allowing the work routine to resume almost as if it were uninterrupted. Organization of events by their places of occurrence can aid memory if the places are used as self-generated retrieval cues. For example, one course that I teach is held in the same room every semester, and another course is scheduled in a different room on campus every semester. Not only is it easier for me to remember more students from the 'multiple-room course' than the 'one-room course', but I can also more easily determine the semester or year a student took my multiple-room class, as compared with my one-room class. Rothkopf, Fisher, and Billington (1982) refer to this latter type of memory as attributive memory, or memory for the organization in which an item occurs, which may be improved by incidental contextual organization.

## Individual differences

One explanation of the sizeable variability in EC-dependent memory studies is that individuals may be differentially susceptible to such effects. For example, individuals may differ in terms of encoding EC information, retrieving it from memory, and performing other processes which affect EC-dependent memory.

A reasonable candidate for such a personality factor is field dependence/independence (e.g. Goodenough, 1976). Field dependence is considered to be one aspect of a more general personality factor defined by a holistic (field-dependent) vs an analytical (field-independent) orientation to the world. Field-dependent subjects are less able than field-independent ones to avoid contextual influences in making perceptual judgements; that is, they are more affected by perceptual contexts. It may also be the case that field-dependent subjects are more affected by learning and memory contexts than field-independent subjects. There are some data supportive of this hypothesis found by Smith and Rothkopf (1984), Smith (1985a), and Kanak and Stevens (1985), who found that field-dependent subjects had more context-dependent memories than field-independent ones. Smith (1984), however, found that field-independent subjects were better able to use successfully an imagined EC cue to facilitate memory. The overall pattern of results so far suggests that field-dependent subjects are more influenced by the ambient physical EC, whereas field-independent subjects are better able imaginally to manipulate contextual (or other) images. More research will be needed, however, to clarify this picture.

## WHAT WE STILL NEED TO KNOW

### How to get reliable and dramatic EC effects in the laboratory

Given that EC-dependent memory phenomena are common occurrences for many people, the exercise of trying to prove the existence of such phenomena in the laboratory may well be a trivial one. More importantly, what would be useful would be to discover: (a) whether our laboratory phenomena result from experimental artifacts or from EC-dependent memory; (b) how consistently to produce dramatic EC effects like those experienced in natural settings; and (c) how to manipulate (enhance or inhibit) EC-dependent memory effects. The first two problems are highlighted by failures to find EC-dependent memory (e.g. Fernandez and Glenberg, 1985), which leave open the possibility that laboratory findings of EC-dependent memory may be inconsistent and artifactual.

To say, however, that evidence of EC-dependent memory in the laboratory is sparse or lacking would be far from accurate. In fact, of the 29 studies listed in Table 2.1, 27 investigations found at least some evidence of context reinstatement effects. All of the imagined reinstatement studies (Table 2.2), all of the interference reduction studies (Table 2.4), and all of the multiple-room studies (Table 2.5) have also found evidence of EC-dependent memory.

A good deal of the uncertainty surrounding the EC-dependent memory phenomena may be due to our relative ignorance about factors which may influence the size of the effects. Such factors may include variables related to subjects, learning materials, and experimental tasks.

Field dependence/independence has been one possible subject factor identified as relevant to EC-dependent memory, but there may well be other more predictable factors which have not yet been identified. Other possibly relevant subject factors might include, for example, ability to image, spatial memory, and age.

The importance of learning materials to EC-dependent memory has only been touched upon rather than systematically studied. The meaningfulness, imageability, complexity, or amount of materials, for example, may affect EC-dependent memory.

Among the numerous task factors whose effects upon EC-dependent memory are unknown are time (e.g. presentation time, retention interval), level of processing, and sensory modality of presentation. It may be, for example, that the long years intervening between graduation and a return to one's former school are necessary for finding the dramatic EC-dependent effects noted earlier.

## Decontextualization of knowledge

Some knowledge is based upon memories of specific experiences, whereas other knowledge is primarily abstract, a distinction often referred to as episodic vs semantic memory. Although it may be possible to enter abstract information directly into memory via linguistic communication, it is also the case that abstract knowledge can be derived from specific experiences. This growth process in the development of abstract knowledge structures (e.g. learning schemata, frames, semantic networks) might be referred to as 'decontextualization', or changing from contextually (temporal, spatial, situational) referenced memory to semantically referenced knowledge. At another level, this phenomenon might be referred to as 'generalization', the process of extending learning to situations beyond the original learning context.

Because memory of specific experiences appears to depend upon the background EC, the process of decontextualization apparently must overcome this obstacle of EC-dependent memory. Two reasonable techniques for overcoming EC-dependent memory are varying learning contexts (e.g. Smith *et al.*, 1978; Smith and Rothkopf, 1984) and internally generating one's own EC cues (e.g. Smith, 1979, 1984). Varying learning ECs, in particular, is an attempt to induce learning which is not dependent upon one set of environmental cues.

## Definitions

Rather than leading off the present chapter with definitions of 'context', I have put off such definitions until the end because, although previous research on context-dependent memory has failed to adhere to a common definition, it is hoped that future research will use clearer and more specific definitions. In our 1978 paper (Smith *et al.*, 1978), for example, we referred to the term 'context' as a concept that 'denotes a great variety of intrinsic or extrinsic characteristics of the presentation or test of an item' (p. 342). Indeed, it seems unreasonable, or at least unenlightening, to label posture, syntax, audience, list words, odors, and gross characteristics of the environment all 'context'.

### Focal vs contextual

One way to define 'context' is to contrast it with 'focus'; contextual information is that information processed outside the focus of attention. An analogy is foveal vs peripheral vision, where focal information is likened to foveal vision, and contextual information is analogous to peripheral vision. Another similar analogy is conscious vs unconscious perception, where focal information processing is conscious, and contextual processing is unconscious. These types of definitions point out qualitative differences between contextual and focal information processing.

Alternatively, it may be that there is not a qualitative difference between contextual and focal information processing, but rather there is a quantitative one. Given that attention is a time-sharing process, we might conceive of context as that information which is given relatively little attentional time. According to this definition, however, there should be little need for theories of contextual information processing since all information would be similarly processed.

Is there a difference between contextual and focal information processing? This question cannot be resolved at this time, but the answer is important if we are to consider EC-dependent memory anything more than a case of some subjects using environmental loci as a mnemonic device. An environmental locus used as a mnemonic address would be focally processed, just like the target information encoded with that locus. The naturalistic phenomena noted earlier, however, suggest that EC-dependent memory may well be operating at an unconscious level. Unless there were a special reason to do so, it seems unlikely that people intentionally or focally try to memorize environmental features in association with events in their school, in a prison camp, or in their everyday working and living environs. This is not to imply that we are never consciously aware of environmental objects and loci, but rather that it is unusual to process such information in ways analogous to studying or memorizing material for a later exam.

Furthermore, the apparent elicitation of memories caused by environmental reminders also appears to be unintended, in many cases. The surprise one usually feels at the parade of unbidden memories, or the subtlety associated with falling back into old patterns of speech, driving, and/or social interactions all suggest that people tend not intentionally to generate memories from contextual cues, but rather that such cuing generally occurs without any focal intention on the part of the rememberer. Future research may do well to distinguish between focal and contextual uses of background cues.

*Meaningful vs incidental context*

Another distinction which may help our understanding of context processing is meaningful vs incidental context. Meaningful context refers to verbal or semantic material, such as accompanying words or text which may directly bias meaning selection processes, or it can refer to other schemata in which learning material has been embedded. One's task or situation, for example, may meaningfully encompass the targeted learning material. Incidental context, on the other hand, is not meaningfully related to the learning material in any explicit or implicit way; incidental stimuli just happen to be present during learning. Most studies of EC effects have manipulated EC incidentally, rather than relating learning materials meaningfully to the context.

## General vs specific context

In his component levels theory, Glenberg (1979) differentiated encoded components according to their specificity. Specific cues are included in few item encodings, whereas general cues are represented in many encodings. For example, many encoding specificity studies (e.g. Thomson, 1972) have introduced different context words for each target item; such would be a manipulation of specific context. Most EC studies, however, have used general context manipulations, maintaining the same EC throughout an entire experimental session, so that the same EC cues could be represented in encodings of all target items. General and specific contextual information may have very different cuing properties.

## Internal vs external context

At first glance, the distinction between internal and external context appears to be a clear cut one. External context can refer to any stimuli which are external to the subject, and internal context arises from within the subject. For example, mood states and drug states are called internal and EC is external. Upon further consideration, however, it is clear that internal context is manipulated via external forces (e.g. hypnosis, mood induction, administration of drugs), and external context must be internally represented to cue memory. Given these considerations, then, the best distinction between internal and external context is at the operational definitional level. It may well be, however, that greater cohesiveness will be found between internal and external context effects than between other types of context, since both are externally manipulated and internally represented.

## AUTHOR NOTES

This work was supported by NIMH grant number 1 RO1 MH39977-01 awarded to Steven M. Smith.

# REFERENCES

Abernethy, E.M. (1940). The effects of changed environmental conditions upon the results of college examinations. *Journal of Psychology*, **10**, 293–301.

Anderson, J.R., and Bower, G.H. (1974). A propositional theory of recognition memory. *Memory and Cognition*, **2**, 406–412.

Baddeley, A.D. (1982). Domains of recollection. *Psychological Review*, **89**, 708–729.

Bartlett, J.C., and Santrock, J.W. (1979). Affect-dependent episodic memory in young children. *Child Development*, **5**, 513–518.

Bilodeau, I.M., and Schlosberg, H. (1951). Similarity in stimulating conditions as a variable in retroactive inhibition. *Journal of Experimental Psychology*, **41**, 199–204.

Burri, C. (1931). The influence of an audience upon recall. *Journal of Educational Psychology*, **22**, 683–690.

Canas, J.J., and Nelson, D.C. (1986). Recognition and environmental context: the effects of testing by phone. *Bulletin of the Psychonomic Society*, **24**, 407–409.

Chen, M. (1984). Effects of number of study environments on exam performance. Master's thesis, Texas A&M University.

Coggins, K.A., and Kanak, N.J. (1985, April). Environmental context effects on the learning of a second list. Paper presented at the Annual Meeting of the Southwestern Psychological Association, Austin, TX.

Dallett, K., and Wilcox, S.G. (1968). Contextual stimuli and proactive inhibition. *Journal of Experimental Psychology*, **78**(3), 475–480.

Dreistadt, R. (1971). An analysis of how dreams are used in creative behavior. *Psychology*, **8**, 24–50.

Dulsky, S.G. (1935). The effect of a change of background on recall and relearning. *Journal of Experimental Psychology*, **18**, 725–740.

Eckert, E., Kanak, N.J. and Stevens, R. (1984). Memory for frequency as a function of environmental context. *Bulletin of the Psychonomic Society*, **22**, 507–510.

Eich, J.E. (1980). The cue-dependent nature of state-dependent retrieval. *Memory and Cognition*, **8**, 157–173.

Eich, J.E. (1985). Context, memory, and integrated item/context imagery. *Journal of Experimental Psychology: Learning, Memory, and Cognition*, **11**(4), 764–770.

Farnsworth, P.R. (1934). Examinations in familiar and unfamiliar surroundings. *Journal of Social Psychology*, **5**, 128–129.

Fernandez, A., and Glenberg, A.M. (1985). Changing environmental context does not reliably affect memory. *Memory and Cognition*, **13**, 333-345.

Fisher, R.P., Geiselman, R.E., Holland, H.L., and MacKinnon, D.P. (1984). Hypnotic and cognitive interviews to enhance the memory of eyewitnesses to crime. *International Journal of Investigative and Forensic Hypnosis*, 7(2), 28–31.

Frerk, N., Holcombe, L., Johnson, S., and Nelson, T. (1985). Context-dependent learning in a classroom situation. Unpublished paper, Gustavus Adolphus College.

Geiselman, R.E., and Bjork, R.A. (1980). Primary versus secondary rehearsal in imagined voices: differential effects on recognition. *Cognitive Psychology*, **12**, 188–205.

Geiselman, R.E., and Glenny, J. (1977). Effects of imagining speakers' voices on the retention of words presented visually. *Memory and Cognition*, **5**, 499–504.

Gillund, G., and Shiffrin, R.M. (1984). A retrieval model for both recognition and recall. *Psychological Review*, **91**, 1–67.

Glenberg, A.M. (1979). Component levels theory of the effects of spacing of repetitions on recall and recognition. *Memory and Cognition*, **2**, 95–112.

Godden, D.R., and Baddeley, A.D. (1975). Context-dependent memory in two natural environments: on land and underwater. *British Journal of Psychology*, **66**, 325–332.

Godden, D.R., and Baddeley, A.D. (1980). When does context influence recognition memory? *British Journal of Psychology*, **71**, 99–104.

Goodenough, D.R. (1976). The role of individual differences in field dependence as a factor in learning and memory. *Psychological Bulletin*, **83**, 675–694.

Greenspoon, J., and Ranyard, R. (1957). Stimulus conditions and retroactive inhibition. *Journal of Experimental Psychology*, **53**, 55–59.

Jacoby, L.L. (1983). Perceptual enhancement: persistent effects of an experience. *Journal of Experimental Psychology: Human Learning, Memory, and Cognition*, **9**, 21–38.

Jensen, L.C., Harris, K., and Anderson, D.C. (1971). Retention following a change in ambient contextual stimuli for six age groups. *Developmental Psychology*, **4**, 394–399.

Kanak, N.J., and Stevens, R. (April, 1985). Field independence-dependence in learning and retention and environmental context. Paper presented at the Southwestern Psychological Association, Austin, TX.

Kintsch, W. (1974). *The Representation of Meaning in Memory*, Hillsdale, NJ: Lawrence Erlbaum.

Krafka, C., and Penrod, S. (1985). Reinstatement of context in a field experiment on eyewitness identification. *Journal of Personality and Social Psychology*, **49**, 58–69.

Malpass, R.S., and Devine, P.G. (1981). Guided memory in eyewitness identification. *Journal of Applied Psychology*, **66**, 343–350.

Mellgren, R.L. (April, 1984). The classroom as context. Paper presented at the Convention of the Southwestern Psychological Association, New Orleans, LA.

Metzger, R.L., Boschee, P.F., Haugen, T., and Schnobrich, B.L. (1979). The classroom as learning context: changing rooms affects performance. *Journal of Educational Psychology*, **71**, 440–442.

Nixon, S., and Kanak, N.J. (1981). The interactive effects of instructional set and environmental context changes on the serial position effect. *Bulletin of the Psychonomic Society*, **18**, 237–240.

Nixon, S.J., and Kanak, N.J. (1985). A theoretical account of the effects of environmental context upon cognitive processes. *Bulletin of the Psychonomic Society*, **23**, 139–142.

Pessin, J. (1932). The effect of similar and dissimilar conditions upon learning and relearning. *Journal of Experimental Psychology*, **15**, 427–435.

Rand, G., and Wapner, S. (1967). Postural status as a factor in memory. *Journal of Verbal Learning and Verbal Behavior*, **6**, 268–271.

Reed, H.J. (1931). The influence of a change of conditions upon the amount recalled. *Journal of Experimental Psychology*, **14**, 632–649.

Riccio, D.C., Richardson, R., and Ebner, D.L. (1984). Memory retrieval deficits based upon altered contextual cues: a paradox. *Psychological Bulletin*, **96**, 152–165.

Rothkopf, E.Z., Fisher, D.G., and Billington, M.J. (1982). Effects of spatial context during acquisition on the recall of attributive information. *Journal of Experimental Psychology: Learning, Memory, and Cognition*, **8**, 126–138.

Saufley, W.H., Jr., Otaka, S.R., and Bavaresco, J. (1986). Context effects: classroom tests and context independence. *Memory and Cognition*, **13**, 522–528.

Smith, S., and Guthrie, E.R. (1921). *General Psychology*, New York: Appleton, p. 270.

Smith, S.M. (1979). Remembering in and out of context. *Journal of Experimental Psychology: Human Learning and Memory*, 5, 460–471.

Smith, S.M. (1982). Enhancement of recall using multiple environmental contexts during learning. *Memory and Cognition*, 10, 405–412.

Smith, S.M. (1984). A comparison of two techniques for reducing context-dependent forgetting. *Memory and Cognition*, 12, 477–482.

Smith, S.M. (1985a). Environmental context and recognition memory reconsidered. *Bulletin of the Psychonomic Society*, 23, 173–176.

Smith, S.M. (1985b, April.). Memory and cognition in a flotation tank. Paper presented to Southwestern Psychological Associaion, Austin, TX.

Smith, S.M. (1985c). Background music and context-dependent memory. *American Journal of Psychology*, 98, 591–603.

Smith, S.M. (1985d). Effects of number of study environments and learning instructions on free recall clustering and accuracy. *Bulletin of the Psychonomic Society*, 23, 440–442.

Smith, S.M. (1986). Environmental context-dependent recognition memory using a short-term memory task for input. *Memory and Cognition*, 14, 347–354.

Smith, S.M., Glenberg, A., and Bjork, R.A. (1978). Environmental context and human memory. *Memory and Cognition*, 6, 342–353.

Smith, S.M., and Rothkopf, E.Z. (1984). Contextual enrichment and distribution of practice in the classroom. *Cognition and Instruction*, 1(3), 341–358.

Smith, S.M., and Heath, F.R. (1986, April). *Conscious and unconscious effects of environmental context-dependent memory*. Fort Worth, TX: Southwestern Psychological Association.

Smith, S.M., and Vela, E. (1986, May). *Context-dependent eyewitness recognition*. Chicago, IL: Midwestern Psychological Association.

Spear, N.E. (1978). *The Processing of Memories: Forgetting and Retention*, Hillsdale, NJ: Lawrence Erlbaum.

Steuck, K.W. (1979). The effects of pictures, imagery, and a change of context on young children's oral prose learning. Wisconsin Research and Development Center for Individualized Schooling, Working paper no. 264.

Steuck, K.W., and Levy, V.M. (1985). The effects of change of environmental context on recall of stories and word-lists. Unpublished paper.

Strand, B.Z. (1970). Change of context and retroactive inhibition. *Journal of Verbal Learning and Verbal Behavior*, 9, 202–206.

Thomson, D.M. (1972). Context effects in recognition memory. *Journal of Verbal Learning and Verbal Behavior*, 11, 497–511.

Vela, E. (1984, April). Memory as a function of environmental context. Paper presented at the 30th Annual Meeting of the Southwestern Psychological Association, New Orleans, LA.

Watkins, O.C., and Watkins, M.J. (1975). Build-up of proactive inhibition as a cue-overload effect. *Journal of Experimental Psychology: Human Learning and Memory*, 1, 442–452.

Weiss, W., and Margolius, G. (1954). The effect of context stimuli on learning and retention. *Journal of Experimental Psychology*, 48(5).

Memory in Context : Context in Memory
Edited by G.M. Davies and D.M. Thomson
© 1988 John Wiley & Sons Ltd.

CHAPTER 3

# Faces and Places: Laboratory Research on Context and Face Recognition

GRAHAM DAVIES

*North East London Polytechnic*

## ABSTRACT

People often report being unable to recognise familiar individuals when they are observed in unfamiliar settings. Such an observation seems at variance with many theories involving context effects which emphasise the lack of effect of contextual reinstatement on recognition as opposed to recall. The results of laboratory simulations of this phenomenon are reviewed and related to current conceptions of recall and recognition processes.

It is sometimes said that psychologists inevitably study skills at which they are spectacularly incompetent. An example of this adage concerns this author's prowess at face recognition. Having been fortunate enough to secure a research grant, he spent a busy afternoon interviewing candidates before adjourning to an end-of-year student party. As the evening wore on he approached one young graduate and enquired politely what she intended to do on leaving university. 'Well actually', she replied 'as a result of my successful interview with you this afternoon, I shall start work as your research assistant next week.'

It is tempting to attribute such an incident to context-dependent misidentification. The individual has been observed in one context but is then not recognised when the environment and circumstance of observation change. Most people will own to having had an experience similar in kind to the one described. Indeed in a survey of memory slips associated with faces, confusions or failure to recognise due to changing contexts emerged as the single most potent source of attributed error in everyday face memory (Young, Hay and A.W. Ellis, 1985).

Persuasive though such examples may be, they do not in themselves provide conclusive evidence for the role of context in face recognition.

In the example above, for instance, failure to identify could have arisen because the face had not been noticed sufficiently at the time of initial observation: an encoding rather than a retrieval problem. Likewise, it could be argued that the absent-minded observer had not been expecting to see the interviewee; there was a bias in expectation rather than any real contextual inhibition.

Finally, one must set such everyday misadventures against the impressive accumulation of results from published studies in context and memory which demonstrate significant effects on recall for altered contexts, but with no corresponding impact upon recognition performance.

This chapter surveys first the theoretical and empirical basis for the recall-recognition disjunction in context effects. It then examines the studies which have explored the impact of context on face recognition. Following this, alternative theoretical structures are considered which might accommodate the face data and the fit they provide to existing findings. Finally, broader issues raised by this research are considered and in particular its ecological relevance, both to forensic and everyday memory settings.

## BACKGROUND TO THE CONTROVERSY

Most influential memory theories now accept that encoding and retrieval are not determined solely by the properties of the stimulus itself but also by its context. But how such contextual influences should be defined and what their impact is upon recall and recognition is a matter of continuing debate.

For network theorists like Anderson and Bower (1972, 1973, 1974) or Kintsch (1974), events are represented by nodes in a semantic network. Encounter with an event leads to the tagging or activation of the particular node corresponding to that event in semantic memory. If an event is encountered which is not already represented in the system then a new node is recruited. Tulving's 'encoding specificity' hypothesis (Tulving and Thomson, 1973), on the other hand rejects a network conception of memory in favour of a system where every encounter with a stimulus creates a unique encoding or episode. Thus, episodic memory is distinct from semantic knowledge rather than being parasitic upon it, as in the Anderson and Bower view.

Both theories include reference to context effects and see a role for them in encoding and retrieval, though the particular role and the variety of contextual information emphasised shows significant variation. Anderson and Bower (1972), in their original conception, emphasised the role of extra-stimulus contextual cues present at the time of learning being used as aids to subsequent search. The list of such cues is characteristically comprehensive, including general mood or attitude of the learner, physical position, conspicuous external cues, physiological state, temporal groupings or other words in the list (p. 101). It is important to emphasise that these cues operate to facilitate the search and not the decision phase of retrieval. Thus, effects for contextual change or reinstatement might be expected for recall but not for recognition.

The demonstration by Tulving and Thomson (1973) of the influence of semantic context on recognition as well as recall called for revisions to network theory. In their revised theory, Anderson and Bower (1974) proposed multiple representations for words which are homographs (JAM, PORT) and even for non-homographic words which have a variety of 'distinct uses' (p. 40). However, the extra-stimulus contextual factors identified by Anderson and Bower (1972) were not expected to produce variations in semantic encoding and hence should not influence recognition. A number of findings or non-findings appear to provide support for Anderson and Bower's position. Smith, Glenberg and Bjork (1978) demonstrated a clear impact of physical context at learning and test on word list recall but found no corresponding impact on word recognition. Likewise, studies of the recall of word lists by divers on land or underwater show strong context reinstatement effects upon recall (Godden and Baddeley, 1980). A similar picture emerged from a review of state-dependent learning by Eich (1980) which showed stable and consistent effects of manipulation of internal pharmacological state at learning and test when recall was the measure employed, but few positive findings when the measure was recognition.

How do such results square with Tulving's encoding specificity viewpoint? Central to Tulving's thinking is the idea that events are uniquely encoded and context provides the determinant of such encodings. Context was originally envisaged in semantic terms, although it is clear in his later writings (Tulving, 1983) that Tulving extends contextual influences on encoding to environmental and physiological factors operating at the time of the encounter (p. 150). It is not always clear to what extent he sees non-semantic contextual factors influencing recognition as well as recall. Tulving's views on the identity and distinctiveness of recall and recognition processes have shown some fluctuations over the years (Tulving, 1976; 1982). As the author understands it, Tulving's current position allows for some variation in the impact of semantic and non-semantic factors, with the latter being capable of influencing recall to the exclusion of recognition (Tulving, 1983, p. 45).

The consistency of both theory and data in pointing to a negligible influence of non-semantic contextual factors on recognition must now be arraigned against the more fragile evidence of anecdote and personal experience. How is it possible to reconcile this conflict between experimental research and autobiographical experience? To begin, there are a number of important differences between the studies discussed to date and memory for faces. The studies have almost exclusively been concerned with words. Faces show some important similarities to words as stimulus materials but also produce effects, as with semantic priming, which are quite distinct (see Bruce, 1983). There is thus the possibility that rather different effects of context may be observed under laboratory conditions for recognition of faces than those operating in relation to words.

However, before considering the evidence, some attempt is necessary to define what constitutes context in face recognition studies. As will be demonstrated, researchers have used a variety of interpretations. Following McGeoch (1932) we may distinguish 'internal' from 'external' contexts. Among the internal cues utilised has been mood state at the time of observation and the verbal labels associated with particular faces. Among external cues have been the faces or persons with which the target has been associated, the background against which the individual is initially observed, postural and clothing cues. Such an operational definition of context inevitably avoids the question of a more formal definition of context, a question which has been debated in one form or another since the inception of experimental psychology and is a central issue in a number of chapters in this book. It will, however, provide a suitable orientation with which to survey the face memory literature.

## FACES IN CONTEXT

### Pairing faces

Early research on context effects was dominated by a methodology inherited from studies of word recognition. Bower and Karlin (1974) presented subjects with pairs of faces, rather as other researchers had shown pairs of words, and asked them later to recognise the faces either singly, in their original pairings or re-paired with another face. Attention to the pairs was secured by asking subjects to make forced-choice judgements on the sex of the targets or their likely compatibility. No significant impact of maintained context was found, though compatibility judgements led to better overall performance than classifying by sex. The author concluded that faces were not subject to the variability of encoding associated with homographic words and attributed any failure to recognise faces or unfamiliar surroundings as due to lowered expectancy.

Bower and Karlin's study provoked a response from Tulving's group who criticised the original study for its low statistical power and weak manipulation of context. Watkins, Ho and Tulving (1976) also presented pairs of faces to subjects but sought to ensure that they were encoded as a pair by leading subjects to believe that they would be tested on their ability to identify original pairings. Under these circumstances, a given target face was recognised with 73 per cent accuracy at test if the pairing was maintained compared to 68 per cent when the pairing was disrupted, a small but statistically significant advantage.

A similar advantage of reinstatement of pairing was also reported by Winograd and Rivers-Bulkeley (1977) who sought to induce unitary encoding at presentation by having the male and female faces rated for marital compatibility. Under these circumstances same pairs were recognised 81 per cent of the time compared to 72 per cent when the target face appeared alone and 70 per cent when paired with an entirely novel face. Both studies concluded that faces were subject to modification in encoding by the context in which they appeared, a finding which they saw as compatible with encoding specificity but not a network tagging approach.

### Faces and descriptions

The size of the effects created by pairing faces were small but significant. Watkins *et al.* (1976) introduced a new procedure which appeared to produce rather larger effects. This involved pairing faces with descriptive phrases ('keeps tropical fish'; 'drives an Italian sportscar' etc.). Using this procedure and maintaining, or exchanging labels at test, produced an 84 to 71 per cent advantage for preserving the original pairing of face and label. A similar positive effect was found when a forced-choice procedure was instituted at recall. Pairs of 'old' and novel faces were better discriminated when the phrase associated with the 'old' face accompanied the pair than when no label was present. The latter result was replicated by Kerr and Winograd (1982) who also demonstrated that the effect was independent of whether one or two phrases accompanied the picture. These findings on forced-choice tests help to answer criticisms of the earliest face pairing studies that any facilitation might be due to response-bias elicited by the mere presence of a familiar element (the label or accompanying face) at test (Ellis, 1981; Baddeley and Woodhead, 1982).

### Faces and emotions

A third line of enquiry concerns the role of emotional context and memory. Bower and others have convincingly demonstrated that where successive word lists are learned under contrasting emotional states, recall of a given list may be facilitated through reinstatement of the appropriate mood. Recognition tasks, however, fail to show similar effects (Bower, 1981, 1983). Gilligan and Bower (1984) describe an unpublished study by Gellerman and Bower which involved the same manipulation with sets of unfamiliar faces replacing lists of words. No mood-dependent effects were observed when target faces had to be recognised under the same or a contrasting emotional state as that at the time of initial observation.

The rather sweeping conclusion that emotion has no effects on face recognition needs to be qualified by the interesting findings of Gage and Safer (1985). Their subjects observed ten pictures of faces drawn from the Ekman series (Ekman and Friesen, 1975) under either a happy or sad induced mood. Subsequently they attempted to identify both the individual concerned and the emotion shown in the pictures under the same or contrasting mood state. However, on this occasion, the pictures were presented via a tachistoscope so as to tap processing in either the left or right hemisphere. No mood-dependent effects were observed for faces presented to the left hemisphere but for the right hemisphere, a strong mood-dependent effect was observed with lowered recognition for faces originally seen in the contrasting emotional state. The authors interpret their findings in terms of the differential sensitivity of the two hemispheres to mood detection. In contrast to the analytic processing performed by the left hemisphere, the right hemisphere stores sensory and motor information concerning the observer's mood and this is encoded along with a wholistic representation of the target face, causing the observed interactions. However, under normal viewing conditions, there is co-operation between the hemispheres and this mood-dependent sensitivity is hidden. It appears that Bower (1981) was correct in dismissing as a fiction the spectre raised in the film *City Lights* of Charlie Chaplin being recognised and treated as a pal by one character when drunk but being unrecognised and ignored when the same character was sober—unless, of course, he had suffered brain damage to the left hemisphere!

### Faces and backgrounds

A second group of studies has sought to manipulate context for faces by taking as their starting point, the idea that face recognition may be moderated by the physical environment in which a given face is observed. The most comprehensive of these is probably that of Thomson, Robertson and Vogt (1982) who report a total of seven studies of person recognition where context was systematically varied between study and test. Context was defined by Thomson *et al.* as a combination of setting, activity and clothing. Subjects observed slides of actors engaged in different activities against a variety of backgrounds before being tested for recognition of the persons with different combinations of the three contextual elements reinstated. Recognition accuracy was impaired by changes in any one element with the three contextual components contributing approximately equally to the effect.

Thomson was aware of the problems of response bias and included in his lures appropriate numbers of novel actors in similar poses, clothing or settings to the actual targets. In all but one of his experiments, the presence of old contextual components increased the rate of false positive responding, but in no instance was this sufficient to explain the facilitatory effect. Adjusting for response bias, either by using a subtraction procedure or by employing signal detection measures (Davies, 1986) still leaves a large and statistically significant impact for contextual reinstatement.

Thomson *et al.* are not alone in finding such effects, similar effects being reported by other laboratories. In France, Brutsche, Cisse, Deleglise, Finet, Sonnet and Tiberghien (1981) manipulated the clothing worn by target persons in slides between study and test and found a large and significant advantage for maintaining clothing cues. A similar contextual facilitation was claimed by Klee, Leseaux, Malai and Tiberghien (1982) when backgrounds were used as contrasts and were either changed or reinstated at test. In Britain, Memon and Bruce (1983) reported a similar improvement in recognition accuracy for target persons when the background against which they had been originally posed (a church, a public house) was reinstated at test.

In all of these studies, combinations of 'old' targets with 'old' contexts yielded highest rates of positive responding and 'new' foils against 'new' contexts the lowest. While in all cases, higher false alarm rates occurred for combinations of 'new' foils against 'old' contexts compared to 'new' foils and 'new' contexts, the mere presence of a familiar cue was insufficient to explain the context effect. With the possible exception of Klee *et al.*, all studies show an improvement in accuracy associated with contextual reinstatement, independent of response bias.

Must the context be precisely the same in order to obtain a facilitating effect? Memon and Bruce (1983) compared the impact on recognition of substituting for the original context, one which was highly associated with it—thus a person who had been shown against one church at presentation would be seen against a different church at test. This combination produced results intermediate in strength between reintroduction of the original context and substitution of an entirely novel one. Klee *et al.* (1982) also included this manipulation in their study and found a functional equivalence for the original and associated contexts. Whatever the reason for the discrepancy between these findings, they do suggest a parallelism between faces and words, in that highly associated contextual cues produce some facilitating effects on recognition for both classes of stimuli (see for instance Light and Carter-Sobell, 1970, for a study on word recognition).

An important critique of the methodology employed in these and associated studies was offered by Baddeley and Woodhead (1982). They argue that it is not sufficient to demonstrate a contrast in recognition accuracy for 'old' and 'new' faces shown against 'old' contexts. In order to eliminate entirely a response bias interpretation it is necessary to show similar effects when 'old' faces are recognised against their original contexts compared to other 'old' faces re-paired with existing contexts. Only if the original combination of target and setting prove superior to the rearranged combinations can a genuine context effect be said to be demonstrated. Baddeley and Woodhead failed to demonstrate such an effect on face recognition when context was induced by pairing target faces with descriptive phrases. However, discrimination performance by their subjects was rather low and any effect could have been obscured by basement effects. Their negative results may be contrasted with the positive findings of Watkins *et al.* (1976) and Kerr and Winograd (1982) who used a very similar procedure. Watkins *et al.* preceded their main study by a preliminary task designed to induce subjects to integrate phrases with faces and it may be that the absence of such training led to an inadequate linkage in the later study.

Further support for this argument comes from two other studies which have employed the more powerful contextual procedure of linking face with backgrounds and have still reported a contextual effect even with the modified design. Beales and Parkin (1984) reported that their subjects recognised 91 per cent of the faces when paired with their original scenic backgrounds compared to only 37 per cent for the rematched targets. A rather different technique was used in an unpublished study by J.A. Smith which came to similar conclusions. She too presented target individuals against scenic backgrounds and then primed recognition of the targets against plain grounds either with the original background or that associated with another and different target face. Shorter response latencies were found for identifying targets when primed with appropriate backgrounds. Thus, even when the more rigorous testing procedures suggested by Baddeley and Woodhead are employed, a strong residual context effect remains. How are such effects to be explained and how may they be reconciled with the traditional concepts of the role of context in recognition and recall?

## EXPLAINING FACE CONTEXT EFFECTS

It is apparent that the context in which faces are observed can influence the subsequent ability of subjects to recognise the same faces. However, context effects are not invariable and when they occur, they are not always of the same strength. This review has shown fluctuations as a function of the familiarity of the face concerned, the type of context employed and the instructions tendered to the subjects. The fact that context effects occur at all with faces seems evidence against a simple network model and in favour of encoding specificity, but even Tulving acknowledges that context effects are not automatic when recognition is the measure employed. What theoretical conceptions can determine when and when not context effects will occur?

## Independent and interactive contexts

Baddeley (1982) has suggested that one way of resolving the issue is to consider the relationship between the contextual cue and the stimulus. Where stimulus and context bear an arbitrary relationship to each other and are perceived as such by the subject, then the addition of the appropriate context or its deletion or substitution by another will have no influence on recognition performance. The example of independent contexts selected by Baddeley is of his study with Woodhead where random combinations of faces and job descriptions did not produce a context reinstatement effect. An interactive context, according to Baddeley, would arise when actors are posed against scenic backgrounds which will tend to induce in the subject speculations concerning the appropriateness of the individual to the environment against which they are placed leading to an integration of figure and ground. Under these circumstances, the presence of the same figure placed against an alien background at test may well be encoded differentially and hence not recognised. Thus, an actor posed outside a church may be identified once more if seen subsequently against this or another church, but rejected if seen dressed casually emerging from a bar.

It is apparent that Baddeley's argument shares many similarities to Bower's original position on the importance of encoding variability in producing context effects. The major change is that new faces as well as words are belatedly seen as being capable of being interpreted differently depending upon circumstances. The problem for either theorist is to specify under what circumstances interactive encoding will take place and when independent encoding is more likely. One approach is to manipulate the instructional set employed by subjects when initially observing the faces. Instructions emphasising integration of person and context might be expected to produce a context effect while those inducing attention to the individual alone might alleviate the effect entirely. Such instructional procedures had been employed in two of the earliest studies, with equivocal results. Bower and Karlin's contrast of sex and compatibility judgements led to differences in overall performance but no interaction with the presence or absence of appropriate context. Winograd and Rivers-Bulkeley required subjects to rate their face pairs either for marital compatibility ('interactive') or individual friendliness ('independent'). Neither instruction influenced performance when the other member of the context pair was reinstated or deleted at test, but performance was significantly lowered for the 'interactive' group when contexts were changed.

It can be legitimately argued that such materials only induce weak context effects and that a rather stronger influence of instructional set might be found in studies where actors are placed against backdrops. The demonstrations by Parkin and his associates that subjects making trait or character judgements on such individuals subsequently recall the backdrops better than those making parallel judgements on facial features is certainly consistent with Baddeley's argument. However, the recognition data are less clearcut. Memon and Bruce (1983) manipulated background context following trait or feature judgements on the actors. A strong context effect on recognition was found for trait judgements but none for features, a result entirely consistent with Baddeley's argument. But this result must be set beside that of Beales and Parkin which, while finding a stronger effect for trait judgements, still found a residual context effect following feature judgements.

Another approach to Baddeley's hypothesis would be to examine context effects for classes of stimuli which by his criterion, appeared likely to lead to independent and interactive encoding. This approach was explored in an as yet unpublished study by Henderson and Davies. Subjects saw a selection of faces or national flags superimposed on scenic backgrounds. It was predicted that the faces should produce significant context effects but that no such effects should be present for the flags. Contrary to prediction, both classes of stimuli produced significant context effects. Of course, it could be argued that the flags had been encoded interactively, but such *post hoc* judgements do little to escape the circularity of the existing distinction. Peris (1985) attempted to vary independent and interactive encoding within the same stimulus. Subjects were shown a series of slides depicting an actor holding a tool or implement (hammer, chisel). In the background was a portion of a poster. In the recognition test, they had to discriminate targets from foils which varied both in the tool being brandished (judged an interactive element) and the fragment of poster shown in the background (seen as an independent element). The overall results appear to provide striking support for the independent/interactive distinction: changing the implement used by the actor significantly reduced recognition accuracy but amending the poster had no significant impact. However, Peris also recorded whether the subject's eye movements during the test phase fixated on the poster, on the tool, or both. Context effects were observed, irrespective of whether poster or tool was changed, provided the subject fixated the item concerned at test. This result suggests that maintenance of the context effect was dependent on whether a given element had been encoded at the initial inspection. Provided such encoding had taken place, then the element influenced the subsequent decision on the identity of the target, irrespective of any preconceptions as to what was independent and what interactive.

Finally, Baddeley's distinction needs to be viewed in the light of more recent work by S.M. Smith (1986) described below, which demonstrates environmental context effects for such non-interactive stimuli as lists of unrelated words. It would, of course, always be possible retrospectively to reclassify such tasks as interactive, a move which would be unlikely to add plausibility to the distinction. Baddeley (1978) wrote of the levels of processing approach that it 'provides a useful rule of thumb' but in the absence of independent measures of specifying levels, it was not likely to be theoretically fruitful (p. 140). Much the same comment seems to apply to the independent/interactive distinction.

## The conditional search model

It is possible to develop network theory in such a way as to account for both positive and negative effects of context on recognition memory. One such approach embodying the idea of conditional search was originally suggested by Juola, Fischer, Wood and Atkinson (1971) and developed independently by Tiberghien (1976) and Mandler (1980). According to this viewpoint, two distinct mechanisms may mediate recognition. The first is a fast, perceptually-based system which is automatic in character and is activated where the stimulus is highly familiar, very recent or both. The second mechanism is slower, more cognitively-based and is brought into action if the initial 'pass' is unsuccessful. This latter system operates by checking network connections and tags, in other words invoking contextual information to reach a formal decision. The cognitive system is likely to be invoked with stimuli which are less distinctive, less frequently encountered and/or when long delays separate encoding and retrieval.

Support for such a dual process approach has emerged in the verbal learning field from the work of Atkinson and associates (Atkinson and Juola, 1974) but for the purposes of this review, the key study is one by Mandler, Pearlstone and Koopmans (1969). Their subjects classified random sets of words into categories based on subjective similarity before being asked to either recall or recognise the words. When tested immediately after presentation, effectiveness of categorisation influenced recall but not recognition. However, as delay increased to two and five weeks, so the significance of category cues increased for recognition until it reached the same level as for recall. According to the conditional search model, initial recognition was based on the faster perceptual system, but with delay became increasingly dependent on the slower cognitive system.

Although the theory was originally proposed for verbal memory, Mandler (1980) has argued for its relevance to faces, a view explicitly developed and extended by Tiberghien (1983, 1986). Among the best evidence for conditional search operating with faces is a study by Peris and Tiberghien (1984). Subjects were shown a series of pictures of girls' faces, each accompanied by a different christian name spoken in a distinctive voice. Later they were asked to recognise the faces accompanied by either the same, or a different name, spoken by the original or a different voice. Both latency and error data were recorded and analysis focussed on the latencies for correct responses to the different varieties of recognition stimuli. Each subject's reaction times were partitioned at the midpoint into a 'fast' and 'slow' group. This produced a contrasting pattern of contextual influence: for 'fast' responses there was no effect of context, whereas for 'slow', context had its usual impact. The authors interpret this result in terms of the conditional search model with fast responding being mediated by the familiarity component and the slower responding reflecting the contextually sensitive cognitive component. As Tiberghien (1986) notes, this finding was, however, only found for correct responses and not for errors, nor is it clear whether reaction times were bimodally distributed as the theory seems to require.

Another potential technique for separating out the proposed components would be to replicate the original Mandler *et al.* (1969) study, this time using faces rather than words. According to the theory, as time passes and familiarity wanes, recognition performance should become increasingly influenced by contextual cues. At least three unpublished studies have examined this issue with no clear support. The most ambitious was conducted by Thomson (1984) using groups of subjects varying in age from 7 to 13 years and five delay intervals stretching from an immediate test to one week. Results were consistent in showing no interaction over time between accuracy and vulnerability to contextual influences. Memon (1985) too failed to find any interaction with undergraduate subjects tested after delays of 15 minutes and two days. Memon also included an instructional condition designed to increase the probability of integrated encoding of face and background, but without any apparent effect on the pattern of results over time. Similar negative findings arose from an unpublished study at Aberdeen by Brown (1986) who did find a significant interaction but only for correct responses; increases in false alarms were no greater for same than altered, context conditions. One possible confounding factor in all of these studies is the relative rate of decay of stimulus and context information. If the latter declines at the same or even a faster rate than the stimulus, then contextual influences may be obscured, a point noted by Riccio, Richardson and Ebner (1984) in their discussion of contextual influences on animal discrimination learning. All three studies used unique links between context and face. Perhaps a better analogy with the original Mandler *et al.* study would be to use a smaller number of contexts shared with a number of stimulus persons.

Quite apart from its empirical base, some of the theoretical constructs of the conditional search model are in need of clarification. Just as in Baddeley's theory, there is a need to proscribe the conditions likely to elicit judgements based on familiarity as opposed to cognitive search. There is also some confusion regarding the contextual relationship between the class of material on which the original theory was based (words) and the class to which it has been extended (faces). The former already exists in the mental lexicon of the subject prior to the experiment; the purpose of the subject in a verbal recognition study is to differentiate relevant known words from the irrelevant. For subjects in face memory studies, however, all stimuli are novel at the inception of the experiment. Thus, recognition may take place later purely on the basis of whether the face has been seen before or not; an absolute not a relative judgement.

On this basis it can be argued that a subset of familiar faces might provide a better test of at least Mandler's version of conditional search. In fact, where contextual manipulations of the kind described have been employed using the faces of celebrities or colleagues known to the subjects, little or no contextual influence on recognition has been reported (Thomson *et al.*, 1982; Davies and Milne, 1982). However, personal experience and the work of Young *et al.* (1985) suggests that known faces do evoke contextually-based errors of recognition. However, all experimental studies to date have used arbitrary conjunctions of persons and backdrops. Perhaps more careful matching—and mismatching—of contexts (Sebastian Coe on the race track as opposed to the Houses of Parliament) might produce more contextually sensitive results. For the moment, however, it must be concluded that, Peris and Tiberghien's interesting result apart, there is little positive basis for extending the conditional search hypothesis from the verbal to the non-verbal domain.

## Depth and elaboration

S.M. Smith (1986) has recently reported a series of experiments on recall of word lists which show apparently stable effects on recognition memory for environmental context. This surprising discrepancy from the previous negative findings in this area is attributed by Smith to the nature of the processing induced in his new studies relative to that in the traditional intentional learning study. In his most recent work, subjects learn and recall lists of five words, ostensibly as part of a test of short-term memory. Later they are unexpectedly asked to recognise all the words previously presented. This new procedure, Smith argues, leads to shallow processing, compared to the deeper, more elaborate processing of the traditional memory test. Under such incidental learning, he states, the influence of contextual cues normally marginalised by the availability of more elaborate processing strategies, comes once more to the fore in recognition as well as recall tests.

Apart from noting the incompatibility of his findings with an interactive interpretation, Smith does not apply his theory beyond the materials for which it was developed. No study in the face literature has so far contrasted an incidental and intentional learning task. However, it seems difficult to reconcile the theory with the repeated finding that traditionally 'shallow' processing tasks like judging facial features lead to much weaker context effects than the deeper processing exemplified by trait or character ratings (e.g. Memon and Bruce). To the extent that everyday slips in face identification are the result of incidental learning of context, the theory has a potential relevance to faces, but clearly there is as yet no direct evidence for its applicability to non-verbal material.

## FACES AND PLACES

From the review of the literature it appears that a wide variety of context effects have been reported with faces. In ascending order of strength these appear to be altered mood states, a companion face, a descriptive phase and postural clothing and environmental cues. It is unclear whether these separate contextual elements are independent of each other or summative in their impact, as the Encoding Specificity approach implies. There is some evidence for additivity of dress, postural and background information (Thomson *et al.*, 1982; Davies and Milne, 1982) and perhaps affective and environmental cues (Davies and Milne, 1985), but much more needs to be uncovered before a true taxonomy of context can be established. Context effects are not inevitable, they depend crucially upon how the subject perceives the situation. Instructions which emphasise the relationship between stimulus and context, figure and ground, increase the likelihood of an effect being observed. Such effects are not restricted to encoding as the work of Thomson (1981) makes clear; the size of any contextual facilitation can be manipulated by instructions which emphasise adopting a strict or lax criterion toward the possibility of error.

As has been argued, none of the existing theories provides an entirely satisfactory or comprehensive account of the observed effects with faces. This probably results from their grounding in verbal learning studies with the only occasional foray into non-verbal materials. There is now a growing literature on face recognition in general and this has brought in its wake theories specifically concerned with recognition of individuals (Davies, Ellis and Shepherd, 1981; Ellis, Jeeves, Newcombe and Young, 1986).

One criticism of face recognition theories to date has been their concern for facial appearance identification without regard for the moderating influence of context (Davies, 1986). Contextual factors tend to be merged into a heterodox group of variables in a box labelled 'other cognitive influences' (e.g. Hay and Young, 1982). However, if the current results are accepted, it appears that for novel faces at least, contextual influences can exert as powerful and moderating influence or recognition as more directly facelike factors such as orientation and expression. There is a need to build contextual variables into the core of such models rather than as a bolt-on after-thought (Tiberghien, 1986). Nonetheless even existing models may be adapted to deal with context in a new and innovative way.

Memon and Bruce (1985) offer one example of such an adaptation, this time of the Bruce and Young (1986) theory of face recognition. This envisages that faces may give rise to a variety of encoded representations in memory. These range from superficial picture codes (representing the surface details of the particular view of the face), through invariant structural codes (concerned with feature information) through to deeper semantic codes (inferences and attributions generated by the subject). Recognition memory involves achieving a match between encoded information and the stimulus at test. Memon and Bruce argue that settings and clothing could well influence the form of attribution made by subjects at encoding (a portrait of a man will be encoded with different semantic elaborations if shown against a school as opposed to a building site). Such a theory copes well with much of the face context literature. It explains the basic context effect and how that effect is enhanced by specific instructions to make inferences and attributions. It also explains the failure of familiar faces to evoke context effects under laboratory conditions by arguing that prior established semantic information will be insufficient to override any rival encodings suggested by the background shown in the slide. What is now required is a series of studies aimed at directly testing specific implications of the model. For instance, if the theory is correct, then subjects should remember less about the context of a familiar face compared to a novel one. Likewise, an environmental context which is semantically rich for the subject should produce different effects than one which is impoverished. Tiberghien (personal communication) has demonstrated that familiar contexts produce a weaker effect compared to ones which are novel to the observer.

While the Memon and Bruce approach looks promising, it is also time to examine the ecological relevance of the paradigms employed to date. How representative are they of failures to recognise under conditions of changed context? Or improved recognition under reinstated context?

Psychologists must continuously be aware of 'the functional autonomy of methods' whereby a paradigm which starts as a means to an end becomes an end in itself.

Turning first to failures to recognise, Young *et al.* in their study of face memory studies reveal that, of the 922 incidents reported, 135 or 15 per cent involved context-based confusions. Moreover, the great majority of these were resolved by the generation of context relevant cues: some 64 per cent by the observers themselves and a further 25 per cent by information contributed by others. However, there is an important discrepancy in that in nearly all cases, the experience was accompanied by a 'feeling of knowing', the problem was one of deciding precisely who was the individual concerned. This emphasis on a problem of *identification* contrasts with laboratory studies which use novel faces and are concerned purely with *recognition*.

However, the existing studies should not be dismissed prematurely. First, Young *et al.* note that context-based errors occurred most frequently for little-known faces rather than for habitual acquaintances, which parallels and bolsters existing laboratory findings. Second, it can be argued that a total failure to recognise is different only in degree rather than kind from 'a feeling of knowing'. We may well not be aware when we pass a distant acquaintance on a foreign beach and it requires a circumstance of the kind outlined in the Introduction to bring the phenomenon to the notice of the observer. However, there is clearly a need for experimental studies which mimic more convincingly the circumstances of real-life contextual errors.

Turning to attempts to improve recognition through reinstating context, the strong and stable effects of this manoeuvre must be contrasted with the more modest and equivocal findings reported in the Applied portion of this book. Why are context reinstatement effects in real-life settings so unreliable? Apart from noting that the effects of laboratory-isolated variables are inevitably weaker in realistic settings (Davies, in press), there is a definite need for laboratory-based studies which make more concessions to forensic realism. An example of a study which exemplifies this 'bridging' role is that of Maas and Brigham (1982) who found significant effects of contextual cues when the initial single target was observed live behind a one-way mirror before being identified in a photospread involving either different or reinstated contextual cues.

Studies should also examine forensic situations where context effects do *not* occur: the so-called 'unconscious transference' phenomenon where a person seen in one setting is subsequently identified as being present at another (Tiberghien, 1986). It is exemplified in the phenomena of an innocent suspect who is seen in a mugshop display and then selected mistakenly at an identification parade as the actual criminal (see Shepherd, Ellis and Davies, 1982, for examples). What circumstances lead to such 'context free' identification? Are they more likely to be made to familiar faces or novel ones? Is it necessary for criminal attributions to be made to the 'innocent' person in order for them to be confused at the subsequent parade? In other words, under what circumstances will context operate to protect a memory and when will it become a free-floating non-contextualised representation? These are issues which deserve to be explored and which any theory of the impact of places on faces must adequately encompass.

## REFERENCES

Anderson, J.R. and Bower, G.H. (1972). Recognition and retrieval processes in free recall. *Psychological Review*, **79**, 97–123.

Anderson, J.R. and Bower, G.H. (1973). *Human Associative Memory*, Washington DC: A. Winston.

Anderson, J.R. and Bower, G.H. (1974). A propositional theory of recognition memory. *Memory and Cognition*, **2**, 406–412.

Atkinson, R.C. and Juola, J.F. (1973). Factors influencing speed and accuracy of word recognition, in S. Kornblum (Ed.), *Attention and Performance*, *IV* New York: Academic Press, pp. 583–612.

Baddeley, A.D. (1978). The trouble with levels: a re-examination of Craik and Lockhart's framework for memory research. *Psychological Review*, **85**, 139–151.

Baddeley, A.D. (1982). Domains of recollection. *Psychological Review*, **89**, 708–729.

Baddeley, A.D. and Woodhead, M. (1982). Depth of processing, context and face recognition. *Canadian Journal of Psychology*, **36**, 148–164.

Beales, S.A. and Parkin, A.J. (1984). Context and facial memory: the influence of different processing strategies. *Human Learning*, **3**, 257–264.

Bower, G.H. (1981). Mood and memory. *American Psychologist*, **36**, 129–148.

Bower, G.H. (1983). Affect and cognition. *Philosophical Transactions of the Royal Society*, **302B**, 387–402.

Bower, G.H. and Karlin, M.B. (1974). Depth of processing pictures of faces and recognition memory. *Journal of Experimental Psychology*, **103**, 751–757.

Brown, P. (1986). Recognition of unfamiliar faces: effects of context and display. Unpublished Honours Thesis, University of Aberdeen.

Bruce, V. (1983). Recognising faces. *Philosophical Transactions of the Royal Society*, **302B**, 432–436.

Bruce, V. and Young, A. (1986). Understanding face recognition. *British Journal of Psychology*, **77**, 305–327.

Brutsche, J., Cisse, A., Deleglise, D., Finet, A., Sonnet, P. and Tiberghien, G. (1981). Effects de contexte dans la reconnaissance de visages non familiers. *Cahiers de Psychologie Cognitive*, **1**, 85–90.

Craik, F.I.M. and Lockhart, R.S. (1972). Levels of processing: a framework for memory research. *Journal of Verbal Learning and Verbal Behavior*, **11**, 671–684.

Davies, G.M. (1986). Context effects in episodic memory: a review. *Cahiers de Psychologie Cognitive*, **6**, 157–174.

Davies, G.M. (in press). On the applicability of applied face research. In A.W. Young and H.D. Ellis (Eds), *A Handbook of Face Processing*, Amsterdam: North Holland.

Davies, G.M., Ellis, H.D. and Shepherd, J.W. (1981). *Perceiving and Remembering Faces*, London: Academic Press.

Davies, G.M. and Milne, A. (1982). Recognising faces in and out of context. *Current Psychological Research*, **2**, 235–246.

Davies, G.M. and Milne, A. (1985). Eyewitness composite production as a function of mental and physical reinstatement of context. *Criminal Justice and Behavior*, **12**, 209–220.

Eich, J.E. (1980). The cue-dependent nature of state-dependent retrieval. *Memory and Cognition*, **8**, 157–173.

Ekman, P. and Friesen, W.V. (1975). *Unmasking the Face*, Englewood Cliffs, NJ: Prentice-Hall.

Ellis, H.D. (1981). Theoretical aspects of face recognition. In G.M. Davies, H.D. Ellis and J.W. Shepherd (Eds), *Perceiving and Remembering Faces*, London: Academic Press, pp. 171–200.

Ellis, H.D., Jeeves, M.A. Newcombe, F. and Young, A. (1986), *Aspects of Face Processing*, Dordrecht, The Netherlands: Nijhoff.

Gage, D.F. and Safer, M.A. (1985). Hemispheric differences in the mood state-dependent effect for recognition of emotional faces. *Journal of Experimental Psychology, Learning, Memory and Cognition*, **11**, 752–763.

Gilligan, S.G. and Bower, G.H. (1984). Cognitive consequences of emotional arousal. In C.E. Izard, J. Kagan and R.B. Zajonc (Eds), *Emotions, Cognition and Behavior*, Cambridge: Cambridge University Press, pp. 547–588.

Godden, D.R. and Baddeley, A.D. (1975). Context dependency in two natural environments on land and underwater. *British Journal of Psychology*, **66**, 325–331.

Godden, D.R. and Baddeley, A.D. (1980). When does context influence recognition memory? *British Journal of Psychology*, **91**, 99–104.

Hay, D.C. and Young, A. (1982). The human face. In A. Ellis (Ed.), *Normality and Pathology in Human Functions*, London: Academic Press.

Juola, J.F., Fischer, I., Wood, C.T. and Atkinson, R.C. (1971). Recognition time for information stored in long-term memory. *Perception and Psychophysics*, **10**, 8–14.

Kerr, N.H. and Winograd, E. (1982). Effects of contextual elaboration on face recognition. *Memory and Cognition*, **10**, 603–609.

Klee, M., Leseaux, M., Malai, C. and Tiberghien, G. (1982). Nouveaux effects de contexte dans la reconnaissance de visages familiers. *Revue de Psychologie Appliquée*, **32**, 109–119.

Kintsch, W. (1974). *The Representation of Meaning in Memory*, New York: Wiley.

Krafka, C. and Penrod, S. (1985). Reinstatement of context in a field experiment on eyewitness identification. *Journal of Personality and Social Psychology*, **49**, 58–69.

Light, L. and Carter-Sobell, L. (1970). Effects of changed semantic context on recognition memory. *Journal of Verbal Learning and Verbal Behavior*, **9**, 1–11.

Maas, A. and Brigham, J.C. (1982). Eyewitness identifications: the role of attention and encoding specificity. *Personality and Social Psychology Bulletin*, **8**, 54–59.

Mandler, G. (1980). Recognising: the judgement of previous occurrence. *Psychological Review*, **87**, 252–271.

Mandler, G., Pearlstone, Z. and Koopmans, H.S. (1969). Effects of organisation and semantic similarity on recall and recognition. *Journal of Verbal Learning and Verbal Behavior*, **8**, 410–423.

McGeoch, J.A. (1932). Forgetting and the law of disuse. *Psychological Review*. **39**, 352–370.

Memon, A. (1985). The role of environmental context in facial memory: some applied studies. Unpublished Ph.D. Thesis, University of Nottingham.

Memon, A. and Bruce, V. (1983). The effects of encoding strategy and context change on face recognition. *Human Learning*, **2**, 313–326.

Memon, A. and Bruce, V. (1985). Context effects in episodic studies of verbal and facial memory: a review. *Current Psychological Research and Reviews* (Winter), 349–369.

Peris, J.L. (1985). Reconnaissance et metaconnaissance. Unpublished Ph.D. Thesis, University of Grenoble II.

Peris, J.L. and Tiberghien, G. (1984). Effet de contexte et recherche conditionelle dans la reconnaissance de visages non familiers. *Cahiers de Psychologie Cognitive*, **4**, 323–334.

Riccio, D.C., Richardson, R. and Ebner, D.L. (1984). Memory Retrieval deficits based upon altered contextual cues: a paradox. *Psychological Bulletin*, **96**, 152–165.

Shepherd, J.W., Ellis, H.D. and Davies, G.M. (1982) *Eyewitness Evidence: A Psychological Evaluation*, Aberdeen: Aberdeen University Press.

Smith, J.A. (1984). The effect of natural context priming on face recognition. Unpublished Honours Thesis, University of Durham.

Smith, S.M. (1979). Remembering in and out of context. *Journal of Experimental Psychology, Human Learning and Memory*, **5**, 460–471.

Smith, S.M. (1986). Environmental context-dependent recognition memory using a short-term memory task for input. *Memory and Cognition*, **14**, 347–354.

Smith, S.M., Glenberg, A.M. and Bjork, R.A. (1978). Environmental context and human memory. *Memory and Cognition*, **6**, 342–353.

Thomson, D.M. (1981). Person identification: influencing the outcome. *Australian and New Zealand Journal of Criminology*, **14**, 49–54.

Thomson, D.M. (1984). Context effects on recognition memory: a developmental study. Paper presented to the Experimental Psychology Conference. Deakin University, Gelong, Australia.

Thomson, D.M., Robertson, S. and Vogt, R. (1982). Person recognition: the effect of context, *Human Learning*, **1**, 137–154.

Tiberghien, G. (1976). Reconnaissance à long terme: pourquoi ne pas chercher? *Bulletin de Psychologie*, Numéro Spécial: *La Mémoire Sémantique*, 188–197.

Tiberghien, G. (1983). La mémorie des visages. *L'Année Psychologique*, **83**, 153–198.

Tiberghien, G. (1986). Context effects in recognition memory of faces: some theoretical problems. In H.D. Ellis, M. Jeeves, F. Newcome and A. Young (Eds), *Aspects of Face Processing*, Dordrecht, The Netherlands: Nijhoff, pp. 88–104.

Tulving, E. (1976). Ecphoric processes in recognition and recall. In J. Brown (Ed.), *Recall and Recognition*, London, Wiley: pp. 37–74.

Tulving, E. (1982). Synergistic ecphory in recall and recognition. *Canadian Journal of Psychology*, **36**, 130–147.

Tulving, E. (1983). *Elements of Episodic Memory*, New York: Oxford University Press.

Tulving, E. and Thomson, D.M. (1973). Encoding specificity and retrieval processes in episodic memory. *Psychological Review*, **80**, 352–379.

Watkins, M.J., Ho, E., and Tulving, E. (1976). Context effects in recognition memory for faces. *Journal of Verbal Learning and Verbal Behavior*, **15**, 505–517.

Winograd, E. and Rivers-Bulkeley, N.T. (1977). Effects of changing context on remembering faces. *Journal of Experimental Psychology, Human Learning and Memory*, **3**, 397–405.

Young, A., Hay, D.C. and Ellis, A.W. (1985). The faces that launched a thousand slips: everyday difficulties in recognising people, *British Journal of Psychology*, **76**, 495–524.

INTERNAL CONTEXT

Memory in Context : Context in Memory
Edited by G.M. Davies and D.M. Thomson
© 1988 John Wiley & Sons Ltd.

CHAPTER 4

# Mood and Memory

R. KIM GUENTHER

*Hamline University*

## ABSTRACT

This chapter examines the role of moods in selective memory. Reviewed
are repression, mood selectivity, mood state dependent retrieval, and
reduced capacity due to depression. Briefly discussed are demand characteristics, interpretation of and inconsistencies in experimental findings and
asymmetrical effects of moods on memory.

## MOOD AND MEMORY

Why do we remember some of our experiences but forget others?
Psychologists have long been intrigued by the possibility that moods like
depression, elation, and anxiety influence memory. Historically much of
the research on the role of moods in memory has focused on the Freudian
notion of repression which claims that memories of experiences associated with anxiety are inhibited from entering conscious awareness. More
recently, experimental psychologists have borrowed concepts from modern
cognitive psychology in order to uncover the mechanisms by which moods
influence what we store and retrieve from our memories.

I will begin this chapter with a brief review of some of the research on
repression, then move to a review of the more recent work influenced by
the modern cognitive perspective on memory and finally conclude with a
discussion of some of the attendant problems associated with mood and
memory research.

## REPRESSION

Repression is a theoretical defence mechanism whereby memories of
disturbing events are stored in the unconscious and unintentionally
inhibited from entering consciousness. The memories are not lost,

however. If the negative affect associated with the event can somehow be removed then the memory may be allowed to return to awareness (Freud, 1915– [1957]). Usually the disturbing quality of an experience thought to give rise to repression is ego-threatening anxiety—for example, the kind of anxiety associated with social or sexual embarrassment.

A variety of experiments have attempted to establish the psychological validity of repression (for an extensive review, see Holmes, 1974). One line of research is typified by Zeller (1950). He required subjects first to learn a list of nonsense words to criterion. Immediately afterwards, the subjects were given a psychomotor task; however, the experiment was rigged so that some of the subjects experienced repeated failure on the task while the rest experienced success. The assumption was that the embarrassment over failure on the psychomotor task would induce anxiety which would generalize to the experience of learning the nonsense syllables. Subjects were then required to recall the nonsense syllables—as predicted by the repression hypothesis, the anxiety-induced subjects recalled less than the neutral control subjects. Later, the anxiety-induced subjects were allowed to experience success on the psychomotor task—they were now able to recall as many nonsense syllables as the neutral control group. Apparently the anxiety had been lifted so that memories of the nonsense syllables which had been repressed could now enter consciousness.

A number of other experiments have replicated Zeller's basic set of findings (e.g. Merrill, 1954; Flavell, 1955; Penn, 1964). Unfortunately, explanations other than repression can account for the results of these sorts of experiments. D'Zurilla (1965) and Holmes (1974), among others, have argued that anxiety associated with a memory creates competing thoughts whenever a portion of that memory is accessed. These thoughts then interfere with the cognitive activity required to accomplish recall of more of the details of the experience.

Consistent with the interference hypothesis, D'Zurilla (1965) found from extensive interviews that the anxiety-induced subjects in his experiment thought a lot more about the experiment than did the neutral controls; possibly the anxiety-induced subjects were concerned about the embarrassment they endured. Yet repression would predict that anxiety-induced subjects ought to think less about the experiment than the control subjects.

More direct evidence for the interference hypothesis is provided by Holmes (1972) who required subjects to learn lists of words; for one group the words were associated with ego-threatening personality feedback, for a second group the words were associated with ego-enhancing personality feedback, while for a third group the words were associated with neutral feedback. Consistent with the interference hypothesis, both the ego-enhanced and ego-threatened subjects recalled fewer words than did the control subjects—presumably thoughts about either positive or negative feedback interfered with the memory processes required to recall the word list. When subjects were told of the deception, both the ego-enhanced and the ego-threatened group's recall then improved to the level of the neutral group's recall. Note that the repression hypothesis cannot explain why the response pattern of ego-threatened subjects would be the same as ego-enhanced subjects (see Holmes, 1974, for a more complete discussion of the interference hypothesis).

Not all research on repression can be explained away by interference, however. Blum and Barbour (1979), for example, report a series of experiments in which subjects were required to solve anagrams for a fixed set of words. In the course of the experiment subjects were asked to associate some of the words with Blacky pictures (Blum, 1950) which are pictures of a young dog engaged in various activities. Some of the associations between the word and the picture connoted pleasure while other associations connoted anxiety. For example, anxiety connotations might be induced by asking subjects mentally to associate the word 'lick' to a picture of Blacky licking himself (herself) by imagining that Blacky is licking his (her) sexual organ and so feels afraid that his (her) parents might disapprove of masturbation. Pleasure associations might be induced by asking subjects instead to imagine that Blacky is licking a spot where a flea was. Each subject learned both the anxiety and pleasure associations, though not to the same words.

The main finding of their experiment was that if a word was associated with anxiety, response times to solve an anagram of that word were slowed down relative to anagrams of neutral words. Response times to anagrams of words associated with pleasure, on the other hand, were generally faster than to anagrams of neutral words. It is difficult to see how interference could account for these results. Presumably interference would generalize to all the words, yet an inhibiting effect was observed only for the anagrams of anxiety-laden words. Furthermore, the interference hypothesis would predict that positive emotional associations ought to distract from anagram problem-solving, yet anagrams for pleasure-laden words were solved more quickly than neutral anagrams. The repression hypothesis, on the other hand, predicts inhibition only for anagrams of words associated with ego-threatening anxiety, as was found. Unfortunately, Blum and Barbour (1979) report that many subjects did not show any inhibition on anxiety-laden words—the effect was absent in 10 out of 25 subjects in one of their experiments.

Another kind of paradigm frequently employed to investigate repression requires subjects to learn and later recall material with either emotionally positive, negative, or neutral connotations to see if subjects recall less of the negative material. Unlike the studies discussed earlier, the research investigating the recall of positive and negative information does not attempt to induce anxiety into one group of subjects or in some sessions of the experiment.

One example of this sort of research is provided by Wilkinson and Cargill (1955) who asked subjects to read and later recall a story which either contained ego-threatening material (a boy dreams he slept with his mother and then climbs to a temple surrounded by foliage) or contained only neutral material (the boy dreams he slept with his brother and then walked towards a lake). Presumably the Oedipal complex implied in the ego-threatening story was threatening only to males. Consistent with the repression hypothesis, male but not female subjects recalled less of the ego-threatening story. Unfortunately, a problem with this experiment and others like it (e.g. Sharp, 1938; Jacobs, 1955; Smock, 1957) is that the anxiety-laden and neutral material may differ on dimensions other than emotional ones. Perhaps the difficulty in recalling the negative material stems from these other differences—for example, negative words or imagery which connote psychosexual themes may be less frequently encountered, more abstract, or suggestive of fewer associations than neutral or positive material. Any one of these differences, independent of anxiety, could account for the poorer recall of the negative material.

Similar research requires subjects to recall personal experiences which are then classified as positive, negative, or neutral. An example is provided by Meltzer (1931) who asked subjects to write down and evaluate their experiences during a Christmas vacation. Six weeks later the subjects attempted to recall those experiences—a greater percentage of the negative experiences were forgotten than of the positive experiences (for an early review of other such experiments, see Gilbert, 1938).

Not all experiments, however, have found that positive material is remembered better than negative material (e.g. Menzies, 1936; Sears, 1944; Thompson, 1985); furthermore, even in the cases where such a trend is observed, we cannot be sure that repression is the explanation. Perhaps people talk more about their positive experiences or connect these experiences more with other events in their lives than they do with negative experiences. Such activities would make the positive event more memorable. It is not even clear that all negative experiences induce ego-threatening anxiety—the death of a loved one, for example, may be laden with negative emotion but not induce a threat to one's personality.

In summary, then, a lot (though not all) of the research employing anxiety induction or comparing positive and negative materials demonstrates that negative or anxiety-laden material is not remembered as well as emotionally neutral or positive material. As discussed above, there are probably a variety of reasons for this tendency—the initial recall of negative feelings may interfere with the processing required to recall in more detail or negative material may be less memorable for reasons unrelated to the material's emotional content. And finally, humans may employ defense mechanisms which operate to repress some ego-threatening experiences thereby making them difficult to remember. The importance of repression in everyday memory, however, remains uncertain.

An implicit assumption made by the repression hypothesis is that the cognitive processes underlying memory for stimuli associated with anxiety are different from the cognitive process underlying memory for other stimuli. It is as if the mechanism of repression remains dormant until a person tries to remember an anxiety-laden event, at which time the mechanism springs into action to inhibit the memory. In contrast to the repression hypothesis, the assumption of much of the current work on mood and memory is that the same cognitive processes which account for remembering and forgetting in other contexts also account for remembering and forgetting in various mood states (Bower, 1981). No special cognitive mechanism is needed to explain the effects of moods on the storage and retrieval of information. Much of the rest of this chapter will develop this theme.

## MOOD, MEMORY, AND INFORMATION PROCESSING

Most current models of memory adopt an information processing perspective which suggests that memory includes a storage phase during which information is connected to representations of information residing in memory and a retrieval phase during which information in the current physical, emotional, and cognitive environment accesses representations of stored information (see Klatzky, 1980; Anderson, 1985). Memory failure may be due to either storage or retrieval operations. For example, information in the environment may be ignored, or the information may be processed but not well integrated into previously existing representations, or the retrieval environment may not provide the cues needed to access the target memory. Most theories of human memory assume that the cognitive system is limited by how much information can be stored or retrieved at any one time (e.g. Kahneman, 1973); if the amount of information or the task requirements overburden the cognitive system, then information will also be lost.

The information processing perspective provides a convenient framework for organizing and understanding much of the current research on the role of moods in selective memory. In this section I will first consider how moods affect the storage of information, then discuss how moods affect retrieval operations, and finally consider how moods might affect the limited capacity of the cognitive system for storing and retrieving information.

**Mood effects during storage**

A variety of mood and memory research has made the general point that people will store more information consistent than inconsistent with their mood—an effect sometimes called mood selectivity or mood congruency. For example, a person who feels elated is more likely to notice and later remember positive information (like being praised for doing good work) than negative information (like forgetting a person's name). Similarly, a depressed person is more likely to notice and later remember negative than positive information.

Often this research uses the strategy of mood induction. Subjects are induced to feel a certain mood through techniques like hypnosis, manipulated success or failure in games-playing, or the Velten (1968) mood-induction procedure in which subjects read lists of either positive statements (e.g. 'I feel so good I almost feel like laughing'), negative statements (e.g. 'Looking back on my life, I wonder if I have ever accomplished anything worthwhile') or neutral statements (e.g. 'Utah is the beehive state'). The idea behind mood induction is to provide the experimenter with control over what mood a subject experiences so that any differences in memory may be attributed to mood and not to any extraneous variables.

A well known mood-induction experiment demonstrating mood selectivity is that of Bower, Gilligan and Monteiro (1981). In one of their experiments subjects were hypotized to feel either sad or happy and then required to read a story about two fictional characters, Jack and Andre. Jack is an unhappy character who has a series of rather depressing experiences such as losing his girlfriend while Andre is a happy character who has positive experiences such as winning at tennis. Twenty-four hours later the subjects recalled in a neutral mood as much of the story as they could remember. Subjects who had been induced to feel sad recalled more about sad Jack than happy Andre while elated subjects recalled more about Andre than Jack. Induced mood did not affect how many facts the subjects were able to remember: the elated and depressed subjects recalled overall about the same number of facts. Bower *et al.*'s (1981) research has been replicated (e.g. Gilligan, 1982, in Bower, 1983) although a failure to replicate has also been reported (e.g. Mecklenbrauker and Hager, 1984).

Mood selectivity has also been found in paradigms in which subjects are asked to read a list of positive and negative adjectives while in an induced mood and later remember the adjectives. Again, the usual finding is that induced elation biases the subjects to recall (or recognize) the positive adjectives while induced depression biases subjects to recall the negative adjectives (Nasby and Yando, 1982; Natale and Hantas, 1982; Bower and Mayer, 1985; Alexander and Guenther, 1986; Brown and Taylor, 1986; for a failure to find this result, see Clark, Teasdale, Broadbent and Martin, 1983).

An example of this paradigm is provided by Nasby and Yando (1982) who induced happy and sad moods in fifth-grade children using guided fantasy. The children then read a list of positive (e.g. 'funny') and negative (e.g. 'mean') adjectives and later tried to recall them. While there was a general tendency for the children to recall more positive than negative traits, the depressed children recalled fewer positive adjectives than did children for whom no mood was induced (neutral controls) while the elated children recalled more positive adjectives than did the neutral controls.

Another line of research compares naturally depressed individuals (who are often hospitalized for depression) to non-depressed controls. These investigations cannot, of course, control for other possible differences between depressed and non-depressed people besides current mood. However, if a person's mood does bias them to store mood-congruent information, then the effect should be observed in naturally occurring moods. In fact, a variety of investigations comparing clinically depressed to non-depressed have found evidence for mood selectivity (Nelson and Craighead, 1977; Davis, 1979; Breslow, Kocsis, and Belkin, 1981; Derry and Kuiper, 1981; Finkel, Glass, and Merluzzi, 1982; Slife, Miura, Thompson, Shapiro, and Gallagher, 1984). For example, Derry and Kuiper (1981) required clinically depressed and non-depressed controls to read a list of adjectives and say whether or not the adjectives described themselves. The clinically depressed but not the controls recalled more negative adjectives. As another example, Breslow *et al.* (1981) compared hospitalized depressed patients to non-depressed controls for their recall of a story containing positive, negative, and neutral elements. The depressed patients recalled fewer of the positive elements than did the controls. In general, then, the research on naturally occurring depression is consistent with the mood-induction research—both sorts of research find evidence for mood selectivity.

Other research on depression has suggested that depressed people do not necessarily remember more negative information in general; rather, they seem to be biased to remember only negative information that is in some sense related to themselves. Bradley and Mathews (1983), for example, asked clinically depressed psychiatric patients and control subjects to study lists of negative and positive adjectives and then to judge, on some trials, if the adjectives applied to themselves, or to judge, on other trials, if the adjectives applied to another person. The depressed patients remembered more negative than positive adjectives, but only for the adjectives applied to themselves.

For adjectives applied to others, the depressed patients recalled more of the positive than negative adjectives. The control subjects, on the other hand, recalled more of the positive than negative adjectives for adjectives applied to themselves or applied to another person. As another example, Brown and Taylor (1986) found that subjects induced to feel depressed recalled more negative traits than did subjects induced to feel elated, but only for traits that subjects agreed described themselves. For traits that subjects judged did not describe themselves, there was no effect for induced mood. Similarly interpreted results are reported by Derry and Kuiper (1981), Kuiper and Derry (1982), Kuiper and McDonald (1983), Ingram, Smith, and Brehm (1983), and Pietromonaco and Marcus (1985).

Not all research comparing naturally depressed to non-depressed controls has found evidence for mood selectivity. One well known failure is that of Hasher, Rose, Zacks, Sanft, and Doren (1985) who required subjects to read and later recall stories which contained both positive and negative events. In three different experiments the recall of subjects who rated themselves depressed did not differ from the recall of non-depressed subjects. There may be several reasons for their failure to obtain mood selectivity, however. For example, the naturally occurring mood variations experienced by otherwise rather normal individuals (the subjects were college students) may not have been strong enough to produce mood selectivity, the paper and pencil tests used to assess temporary mood states may have instead measured enduring personality traits, or the positive and negative elements of the stories may have been too interconnected (Mayer and Bower, 1985).

What might explain mood selectivity? One explanation is based on schema theory, a popular concept in modern cognitive psychology (Minsky, 1975; Schank and Abelson, 1977). Generally, a schema is like an outline of a commonly occurring event or a prototype of a concept. Examples of schema include the knowledge of the events that occur when eating at a fancy restaurant or the typical features of a college student. When a schema is activated in the course of information processing, attention is directed towards information relevant to the schema, ambiguous data are interpreted according to the biases induced by the schema, and information consistent with the schema is more readily elaborated upon and so better connected to other facts in memory.

A nice demonstration of how schemas affect memory is provided by Pichert and Anderson (1977) who asked subjects to read a story about a house from the perspective of either a home buyer or a burglar. Subjects who took the home buyer perspective later recalled more facts relevant to home buying (e.g. the house needed painting) while subjects who took the burglar perspective recalled more facts relevant to burglarizing (e.g. the stereo was in the living room). The suggestion made by a number of theorists (e.g. Beck, 1967; Bower *et al.*, 1981; Johnson and Magaro, 1987) is that moods also function as schemas for selecting, organizing, and elaborating upon information. To put it in another way, a mood is like any other perspective a person might take; information consistent with the mood is more likely to be noticed, is likely to be connected to other facts about that mood, and is likely to promote elaborations which embellish its meaning. Later on, any cue to remember the information will result in more mood-congruent information coming to mind (see Roth and Rehm, 1980 or Davis and Unruh, 1981 for additional evidence for the schema hypothesis).

Another explanation for mood selectivity proposes that events associated with more intense moods (either good or bad) become more memorable presumably because such events are distinctive or inspire semantic elaboration (Bower *et al.*, 1981). Therefore, any time a person processes a story or list whose emotional tone is inconsistent with their prevailing mood, the intensity of their mood will diminish and that material will then become less memorable. A variety of experiments have found that experiences rated as intensely emotional, regardless of the type of emotion, are better recalled (Menzies, 1936; Waters and Leeper, 1936; Holmes, 1970; Dutta and Kanungo, 1975). Gilligan (1982; in Bower, 1983), in a mood-induction experiment, used hypnosis to vary the intensity of elation, anger, and depression and then required subjects to read (while mood-induced) and later recall (in a neutral mood) a list of descriptions of events such as finding money or missing a bus. Besides replicating the mood selectivity effect, he found that the more intense the induced mood, the more likely the associated event was later recalled. But for depression, the effect was just the opposite—events associated with severe depression were poorly recalled. Subjects induced to feel severely depressed acted tired and listless—behaviors which undermined their learning. It is not clear, then, if the intensity hypothesis can explain mood selectivity for people feeling severely depressed.

In summary, research using mood induction or comparing clinically depressed to non-depressed people suggests that people are likely to store information consistent with their mood. One possible explanation suggests that moods function like any other cognitive schema in the manner in which information is assimilated. Another explanation is based on the idea that mood-consistent information helps subjects maintain a more intense mood and so inspires more rehearsal or semantic elaboration of that information. Severe depression, however, may disrupt the storage of new information.

## Mood effects during retrieval

The research in the previous section focused on the effects of moods during the storage phase of memory. Now the focus moves to the effects of mood states on the retrieval of previously learned material.

Some mood-induction research has investigated whether mood induced at the time of recall selectivity influences what is remembered from previously learned material. The results of these studies have been inconsistent. Some experiments investigating mood induced only at recall have found no mood selectivity effect (Bower et al., 1981) while others have found mood selectivity effects (Laird, Wagener, Halal, and Szegda, 1982; Teasdale and Russell, 1983; Forgas, Bower, and Krantz, 1984; Fiedler and Stroehm, 1986). Isen, Shalker, Clark, and Karp (1978) induced positive and negative mood by manipulating whether subjects won or lost while playing a video game. Subjects who won (and presumably felt happy) recalled more positive traits from a list of traits presented previously, but subjects who lost (and presumably felt sad) were no more likely to recall negative than positive words. Similar results were reported by Nasby and Yando (1982). Finally, Clark and Teasdale (1985) found mood selectivity for mood induced at recall, but only for their female subjects.

Several explanations for these inconsistencies are possible. The affective associations to material may sometimes be lost by the time subjects attempt to recall or the material may not inspire much of an emotional reaction if learned or experienced in a neutral mood. In general, it is probably true that the selective effects of a schema are greater when the schema is evoked during learning than when it is evoked only during recall (see, for example, Bransford and Johnson, 1972; Mayer, 1975). So it is not surprising that mood selectivity effects for mood induced at the time are not always observed.

Other research has examined what effect the similarity between the mood experienced during storage and the mood experienced during retrieval has on recall. Some anecdotal evidence suggests that people will remember better if they are in the same mood when they recall an experience as they were in when they originally had the experience, a phenomenon called mood state dependent retrieval. For example, Diamond (1969) reports that Sirhan Sirhan, the man who assassinated Robert Kennedy in 1968, initially claimed he could not remember committing the murder which he in fact committed while in a greatly agitated state. Under hypnosis to help him remember, Sirhan became greatly aroused and was only then able to recall the assassination. Bower (1981) has suggested that

Sirhan's case illustrates the general phenomenon of mood state dependent retrieval. Sirhan could only recall the event when he was placed in the same greatly agitated and angry mood as he was in when he originally carried out the assassination.

A variety of mood-induction experiments have looked for mood state dependent retrieval. For example, Bower, Monteiro, and Gilligan (1978) induced moods using hypnosis and required subjects to learn two lists of random (and emotionally neutral) words, one while experiencing elation and the other while experiencing depression. Later, subjects were put into one mood or the other and asked to recall both lists. Depressed subjects recalled more items from the list learned while depressed while elated subjects recalled more items from the list learned while elated. Compared to subjects who had learned both lists and recalled in the same mood, subjects who learned lists in different moods showed interference when recalling the list which mismatched their mood but facilitation when recalling the list which matched their mood. Important to the demonstration was that the cues to induce mood were different at recall than at storage—otherwise the results could be attributed to the similarity of the cues rather than the similarity of mood states.

Bower *et al.* (1978) found no mood state dependent retrieval effect when subjects were required to learn only one list (in one mood) and recall in either the same or different mood. In the one list paradigm subjects recalled as many words when their moods matched as when they mismatched. Other failures to find a mood state dependent effect in the one list paradigm include Nasby and Yando (1982) and Duncan, Todd, and Perlmutter (1985). The memory trace for a single list is probably so distinctive that it is easy for subjects to recall the list even when in an altered mood (Bower, 1981). Generally no mood state dependent retrieval effect is found when it is easy for subjects to remember the material—as, for example, when the experiment tests memory using recognition rather than recall (Bower, 1983; see also Eich, 1980, for similar results in which states are induced with drugs).

Mood state dependent retrieval using the list learning paradigm has been replicated by Schare, Lisman, and Spear (1984) who used the Velten (1968) technique to induce mood, by Bartlett and Santrock (1982) who found the effect in young children, and by Gage and Safer (1985) who found the effect in a recognition test of previously presented photographs but only for photographs first presented to the right cerebral hemisphere. Surprisingly, Bower and Mayer (1985) report a failure to replicate the mood state dependent effects (as does Wetzler, 1985). Probably mood state dependent retrieval in list learning experiments is a rather weak effect, especially since the to-be-learned material has little if any connection to the induced mood.

Another paradigm which provides more consistent evidence for mood state dependent retrieval requires subjects to feel happy or sad and to recall real life experiences. Such subjects typically recall more positive events when elated and more negative events when depressed. I regard this as a state dependency effect since the recalled events were likely experienced in the same mood as induced during retrieval (Blaney, 1986, however, regards these results as examples of mood selectivity).

This paradigm is typified by the research of Teasdale and his associates (Teasdale and Fogarty, 1979; Teasdale, Taylor, and Fogarty, 1980; Teasdale and Taylor, 1981). In their research, moods were induced by the Velten (1968) mood-induction procedure. Subjects were then given stimulus words (such as 'money') and asked to retrieve a real life experience brought to mind by the stimulus word. In general, happy memories were more likely to be retrieved when subjects were induced to be in an elated mood while unhappy memories were more likely to be retrieved when subjects were induced to be in a depressed mood. In addition, the time it took subjects to retrieve a memory was longer if their induced mood and the affective connotations of the experience mismatched than if the mood and affective connotations of the experience matched. Similar results have been reported by Bower (1981), Natale and Hantas (1982), Snyder and White (1982), and Alexander and Guenther (1986).

Mood state dependent retrieval is also observed in severely depressed people who typically report a high frequency of unpleasant memories (Beck, 1967; Beck, Rush, Shaw, and Emery, 1979). Research which compares clinically depressed to non-depressed controls has generally revealed that non-depressed controls more quickly and readily retrieve positive than negative experiences while clinically depressed patients tend to take longer or are less likely to retrieve positive experiences (Lloyd and Lishman, 1975; Weingartner, Miller, and Murphy, 1977; Clark and Teasdale, 1982; Fogarty and Hemsley, 1983). Other research has shown that people who come to an experiment in a cheerful mood are more likely to recall positive experiences than people who are depressed (see Bousfield, 1950 for a review of some of this work which was done as early as 1917).

What might explain mood state dependent retrieval? Many theories of memory propose that information is stored in memory in a network of connections between concepts (e.g. Collins and Loftus, 1975; Anderson, 1985). In fact, a schema is one kind of network. When a concept is activated either by presentation of its corresponding stimulus or by a prior thought, then activation temporarily spreads to other related concepts. If a collection of concepts receives enough activation, then that collection enters consciousness and is experienced as memory for a fact, an image or an event.

An important implication of this sort of network model of retrieval is that memory for an event or fact depends on the similarity between the environmental and cognitive elements that make up the event or fact and the environmental and cognitive elements present during retrieval. When those elements overlap, memory for the event or fact becomes more probable. The idea that such overlap is essential for successful retrieval is central to several theories of memory (e.g. Guthrie, 1959; Tulving and Thomson, 1973).

Network activation provides then an explanation for mood state dependent retrieval (Bower, 1981; Johnson and Magaro, 1987). A mood can be thought of as a collection of concepts that includes degree of arousal, expressive behaviors, beliefs, and so on. When an event is experienced under a given mood, the elements of that mood will become connected to the elements of the event. If a person later tries to recall the event in the same mood, then the same mood elements will be activated and spread excitation to the elements of the event. That activation may combine with activation from other retrieval cues to raise the total activation of the elements of the target event above the threshold necessary for recall. If a person is in a different mood during retrieval than when the event was experienced, the activation prompted by that mood will spread excitation to the wrong part of the memory network—and so will not combine with activation prompted by the other retrieval cues. Consequently memory should be better when the moods during storage and during retrieval match rather than mismatch.

In summary, research consistently demonstrates mood state dependent retrieval when subjects are asked to recall past experiences while in a particular mood. List learning demonstrations of mood-dependent learning are not as consistently obtained, although that may be because the information in the list is unrelated to the prevailing mood. Network activation models used to explain retrieval in other contexts would also seem to account for the mood state dependency effect.

### Depression and limited capacity

Most current models of human memory emphasize that information processing is limited by how much information can be processed at the same time. The usual interpretation is that the cognitive system has limited resources (Kahneman, 1973; Anderson, 1985). The sense in which human cognition is limited, though, remains a matter of debate (e.g. Neisser, 1976). Whatever the basis of our cognitive limits, many researchers have suggested that moods—in particular depression—can affect the capacity of the cognitive system (Hasher and Zacks, 1979; Weingartner, Cohen, Murphy, Martello, and Gerdt, 1981).

Certainly, a common observation made of the very depressed is that their level of cognitive functioning seems reduced. For example, many depressed people frequently complain of memory failures and often find it difficult to learn new information (Beck, 1967; Sternberg and Jarvik, 1976; see Johnson and Magaro, 1987 for a review). However, not all of the research on depression finds that depression reduces memory (e.g. Davis and Unruh, 1980). Indeed many of the experiments on mood selectivity and mood state dependent retrieval show that overall recall levels or recall latencies are about the same under depression as under elation (for example, Bower *et al.*, 1981; Teasdale and Russell, 1983: Alexander and Guenther, 1986). So there is no consistently observed effect of depression on overall level of recall.

Ellis, Thomas, and Rodriguez (1984) have tried to resolve this inconsistency by arguing that depression may inhibit only the cognitive processes which are effortful—especially the kind of processing required to encode material in a way that makes that material more memorable. Generally, information that is difficult to recall (isolated words or sentences) may be made more memorable if a person embellishes or elaborates upon the information (see Stein and Bransford, 1979). Presumably such elaboration creates more connections between the information and other concepts already stored in memory.

A variety of evidence support Ellis *et al.*'s (1984) claim. For example, Ellis *et al.* (1984) presented subjects with lists of sentences like 'The old man bought the paint' and sentences like 'the old man bought the paint to color his cane'. Some subjects were induced (through the Velten mood-induction procedure) to feel depressed. Later, subjects were given a cued recall test (e.g Who bought the paint?). For the shorter sentences it is harder to recall the subject (e.g. 'old man') because there is no inherent connection between the subject and predicate (Stein and Bransford, 1979). But for the longer sentences, the additional phrase suggests a meaningful connection between the subject and predicate (e.g. the fact that the old man is coloring his cane with paint clarifies the idea that the man is old). But subjects must be willing or able to extract and process that additional information in order to make the sentence more memorable. Ellis *et al.* (1984) found that for the short sentences there was very little difference in recall between depressed and non-depressed subjects. However, the non-depressed subjects recalled many more of the longer sentences than did the depressed subjects. Apparently the depression-induced subjects were unwilling or unable to engage in the effortful processing required to take advantage of the additional phase.

Research comparing clinically depressed to non-depressed controls also supports the notion that depression interferes mainly with the effortful cognitive processing (Weingartner *et al.*, 1981; Silberman, Weingartner, Laraia, Byrnes, and Post, 1983; Jackson and Smith, 1984). For example, Weingartner *et al.* (1981) found that depressed people failed to use processing which might have enabled them to organize input. In their experiment, clinically depressed and normal subjects were allowed to study a list of words taken from several categories like flowers or animals. For some lists the words were blocked by category (all the words from the same category were presented together) while for other lists the words were randomly ordered. The depressed and control subjects recalled about an equal number of words from the blocked lists, but the depressed recalled fewer words from the random lists. Presumably, successful recall of the random lists requires engaging in rather effortful reorganizing processes; the depressed subjects were less willing or able to do so.

For what reason might depression interfere with the elaborative processing required to store information effectively in memory? One possibility is that the low arousal associated with depression reduces the overall cognitive capacity for information processing. If a task requires only a little effort, depression may not interfere since enough capacity is retained in spite of the depression. But if a task requires a lot of capacity, then depression may inhibit memory performance. There is reason, though, to doubt the idea that information processing limitations are due to the quantity of cognitive resources (Neisser, 1976).

Another explanation for the inhibitive effects of depression may be that depressed people simply lack the incentive to work hard in memory experiments (but have plenty of incentive to work hard at other tasks such as reflecting on past mistakes) or may be so preoccupied with themselves and their predicament that they become easily distracted and so are ineffective at processing information unrelated to their predicament. If so, depression will only interfere with effortful tasks which are unrelated to their depression (recall the experiments which show that the depressed readily remember negative information about themselves). Depression may not be so much a state of reduced cognitive capacity as it is a state in which cognitive effort is inner directed or directed towards environmental events that bear directly on the depression.

Finally, there is evidence that clinically depressed people may be as likely to retrieve an item from memory but are less likely to report the item than non-depressed controls (Miller and Lewis, 1977). Perhaps the confusion and sense of failure that typically accompanies depression undermines the confidence depressed people have in their memory (Johnson and Magaro, 1987).

## ATTENDANT PROBLEMS WITH MOOD AND MEMORY RESEARCH

In this section I will briefly review four kinds of attendant problems with research on mood and memory; these include: inconsistencies in the research findings, demand characteristic explanations of the results, asymmetrical effects of moods, and the unresolved issue concerning the role cognitions play in emotions.

## Inconsistencies

One general problem plaguing mood and memory research is the inconsistencies in many of the findings; especially in the experiments in which mood is induced (see Blaney, 1986). As discussed earlier, some experiments have failed to find a mood selectivity effect for moods induced (or measured) at the time of storage (e.g. Mecklenbrauker and Hager, 1984; Hasher *et al.*, 1985), others have failed to find a mood selectivity effect for moods induced only at recall (e.g. Bower *et al.*, 1981), others have failed to find mood state dependent retrieval for list learning experiments (e.g. Wetzler, 1985), and finally others have failed to find an inhibitory effect for depression (e.g. Teasdale and Russell, 1983).

I have suggested in the previous sections some of the reasons for these inconsistencies. Mood selectivity at recall might depend on material in which positive and negative elements are not intertwined, mood-biasing effects in general may be stronger when the material can be meaningfully connected to the prevailing mood, and the inhibitory effects of depression may require material that is inherently difficult to remember unless a person is willing or able to engage in effortful processing. Collectively, though, these inconsistencies suggest that mood-biasing effects on memory depend to a considerable extent on the particulars of the experimental task. Human memory is influenced by a large number of variables (including the nature of the information, motivation to recall, processing strategies, mood, and so on). It may be difficult to predict, then, which of these variables will provide the dominant effect on memory performance in any given situation.

## Demand characteristics

Another concern in mood-induction research is with the possibility that subjects may be performing only to fulfil the expectations of the experimenter—that is, a subject's memory performance may not be due to the induced mood but due instead to the demand characteristics of the experiment. This issue is rather difficult to formulate clearly and may entail several issues such as: do mood-induction procedures induce real moods that are experienced as are naturally occurring moods? Is it meaningful to claim that a person can simulate a mood in all of its behavioral aspects but not really feel the mood? Can a person really feel an induced mood yet retain control over what they chose to remember from memory in a manner independent of that induced mood? For that matter, is it possible that even people who experience natural moods nevertheless respond to demand characteristics when participating in a memory experiment? It may not be possible to answer to answer all of these questions. Many researchers, though, have played down the role of demand characteristics in mood and memory experiments.

Bower (1981) notes that moods induced under hypnosis or by the Velten mood-induction procedure do not appear to be faked—rather, subjects behave as if they really are in the induced mood. Bower notes, too, that in some experiments subjects who are told to respond as quickly as possible (creating a demand to recall everything quickly) still show mood state dependent effects on response latency (e.g. Teasdale and Fogarty, 1979). Furthermore, subjects do not always show a mood selectivity or state dependent effect even when the experimental demands imply the occurrence of the effect. For example, in some experiments subjects show no mood selectivity effect when mood is induced only at the time of recall (e.g. Bower et al., 1981). Finally, many of the mood biasing effects like selectivity or state dependency observed in mood-induction experiments are also observed in studies which compare clinically depressed to non-depressed people.

Still, these observations may not completely dispel the demand characteristic explanation for the results of mood-induction experiments. Several researchers have argued that the cognitive effects of the Velten mood-induction procedure are due mainly to its demand characteristics and not induced mood (Polivy and Doyle, 1980; Buchwald, Strack, and Coyne, 1981). Similar arguments have been made for hypnotically induced moods (e.g. Spanos, 1982). Subjects told to respond quickly in an experiment may nevertheless remain sensitive to the rather obvious demand characteristics implied in mood induction. That sometimes subjects do not show mood selectivity effects when mood is induced at recall may only mean that positive and negative information may be difficult to sort out after they begin to forget the material or that the material is not perceived as emotional if they originally learn it in a neutral mood. Finally, that depressed patients show mood biasing does not prove that experimental subjects are ignoring demand characteristics; rather, subjects induced to feel depressed may simply base their pattern of recall on their knowledge of how depressed people behave.

Recently, Alexander and Guenther (1986) explicitly varied the demand characteristics in one of their experiments and found that a suggestion made to subjects that people remember information inconsistent with their moods eliminated the mood selectivity effect (measured by the recall of traits presented while in an induced mood) usually observed in this sort of paradigm. Their finding suggests that demand characteristics may have a rather potent effect on recall in mood-induction experiments.

Presumably mood-biasing effects on memory observed in seriously depressed people are not due to demand characteristics. Indeed,
depressed people often find it difficult to prevent the occurrence of
depressing thoughts in spite of the very clear and strong demands of
other people (including their therapist) to dwell on more positive thoughts.
If demand does play an important role in mood-induction research then the
mechanisms which account for mood-biasing effects in clinically depressed
people and in experimental subjects undergoing mood induction may be
different. Depressed people usually report that they cannot easily control
their feelings and accompanying negative thoughts (Beck, 1967). Subjects
in mood-induction experiments, on the other hand, are only playing the
role of a depressed or elated person—they presumably remain in control
of their feelings. Perhaps, too, they retain control over what they chose
to store into or retrieve from memory. Hopefully, future research can
help clarify how and under what circumstances demand characteristics
influence behavior in mood and memory experiments.

## Asymmetry of mood effects

Much of the research investigating the effects of elation and depression
on memory has implicitly assumed that these moods are symmetrical in
their effects—depressed subjects store and retrieve negative information
while elated subjects store and retrieve positive information. Isen (1985),
however has challenged this assumption. She notes that in some experiments depressed subjects do not show as great a tendency to recall negative
materials as do elated subjects to recall positive materials. That is, mood
selectivity and state dependent retrieval effects may be less for depression
than for elation (e.g. Isen *et al.*, 1978; Bartlett and Santrock, 1982; Nasby
and Yando, 1982; Brown and Taylor, 1986; see Isen, 1985, or Blaney, 1986,
for a review).

Isen (1985) has suggested several reasons for this asymmetry. One
reason may be that mildly depressed individuals are motivated to try
to repair their moods by deliberately thinking about or noticing positive
events. Elated individuals, on the other hand, would be motivated to
maintain their moods and so deliberately attend to positive events.
Another basis for the asymmetry between depression and elation may
be that the cognitive schema associated with depression may connect to
fewer facts or events than schema associated with elation. Mild depression
is usually about something like loss while elation may be associated with
a wider range of situations. The mood state of elation, then, may activate
more facts, images, and events stored in memory.

The reader should note, however, that a variety of studies have
found symmetrical effect for mood selectivity and mood state dependent

retrieval (e.g. Bower *et al.*, 1981; Teasdale and Russell, 1983; Alexander and Guenther, 1986). Furthermore, processes like mood repair may not characterize the behavior of the clinically depressed. They may have depressive schemas that are quite general or they may be too overwhelmed by their depression to engage successfully in mood repair.

## The role of cognitions in mood

Up to this point, I have only considered how moods might affect what and how much people remember. I will conclude this chapter by considering how thoughts and memories might affect moods. Some researchers have suggested that the thoughts and memories that accompany moods also help to maintain or change them. So, for example, depression may trigger negative thoughts and memories which in turn cause a deepening of the depression (Teasdale and Russell, 1983). However, as Blaney (1986) has pointed out, such an interpretation predicts that people will invariably drift toward an extreme and permanent emotional state. Yet people are generally in a neutral mood despite having positive and negative thoughts. Even the seriously depressed usually recover.

A possibility is that memories and thoughts which accompany moods do not actually cause the mood—rather, such cognitions are only by-products of moods elicited by other variables. This possibility is, of course, related to the longstanding debate on whether cognition precedes emotion or emotion precedes cognition (Plutchik, 1985). Another possibility is that thoughts do influence moods but that people deliberately engage in cognitive activities that help then escape from negative mood states like depression. Isen's mood repair is an example of such an activity.

A third possibility is that cognitions influence moods, but the cognitions that do so are not memories of pleasant experiences and the like but rather are the schemas by which experiences are interpreted and problems are solved. That is, semantic rather than episodic memory may play the more important role in affecting moods (see Tulving, 1972, for a discussion of the difference between semantic and episodic memory). Certainly merely thinking of pleasant thoughts is not likely to reduce depression (Teasdale, 1978) but changing the schema by which one understands oneself and one's relationship to events may help (Beck, 1967). People recover from severe depression because they change the way they interpret events and because they find new ways to obtain gratification. Such changes probably depend more on having positive experiences than on directing thoughts towards pleasant memories. Perhaps future research on mood and memory can help better clarify the role cognitions have in controlling mood states.

## REFERENCES

Alexander, L., and Guenther, R.K. (1986). The effect of mood and demand on memory. *The British Journal of Psychology*, **77**, 343–350.

Anderson, J.R. (1985). *Cognitive Psychology and Its Implications*. New York: Freeman.

Bartlett, J.C., and Santrock, J.W. (1982). Emotional mood and memory in young children. *Journal of Experimental Child Psychology*, **34**, 59–76.

Beck, A.T. (1967). *Depression: Clinical, Experimental, and Theoretical Aspects*. New York: Harper Row.

Beck, A.T., Rush, A.J., Shaw, B.F., and Emery, G. (1979). *Cognitive Therapy of Depression*. New York: Guilford.

Blaney, P.H. (1986). Affect and memory: a review. *Psychological Bulletin*, **99**, 229–246.

Blum, G. (1950). *The Blacky Pictures: A Technique for the Exploration of Personality Dynamics*. New York: Psychological Corporation.

Blum, G.S., and Barbour, J.S. (1979). Selective inattention to anxiety-linked stimuli. *Journal of Experimental Psychology: General*, **108**, 182–224.

Bousfield, W.A. (1950). The relationship between mood and the production of affectively toned associates. *Journal of General Psychology*, **42**, 67–85.

Bower, G.H. (1981). Mood and memory. *American Psychologist*, **36**, 129–148.

Bower, G.H. (1983). Affect and cognition. *Philosophical Research Society of London*, **302**, 387–402.

Bower, G.H., Gilligan, S.G., and Monteiro, K.P. (1981). Selectivity of learning caused by affective states. *Journal of Experimental Psychology: General*, **110**, 451–473.

Bower, G.H., and Mayer, J.D. (1985). Failure to replicate mood-dependent retrieval. *Bulletin of the Psychonomic Society*, **23**, 39–42.

Bower, G.H., Monteiro, K.P., and Gilligan, S.G. (1978). Emotional mood as a context for learning and recall. *Journal of Verbal Learning and Verbal Behavior*, **17**, 573–585.

Bradley, B., and Mathews, A. (1983). Negative self-schemata in clinical depression. *British Journal of Clinical Psychology*, **22**, 173–181.

Bransford, J.D., and Johnson, M.K. (1972). Contextual prerequisites for understanding: some investigations of comprehension and recall. *Journal of Verbal Learning and Verbal Behavior*, **61**, 717–726.

Breslow, R., Kocsis, J., and Belkin, B. (1981). Contribution of the depressive perspective to memory function in depression. *American Journal of Psychiatry*, **138**, 227–230.

Brown, J.D., and Taylor, S.E. (1986). Affect and the processing of personal information: evidence for mood-activated self-schemata. *Journal of Experimental Social Psychology*, **22**, 436–452.

Buchwald, A.M., Strack, S., and Coyne, J.C. (1981). Demand characteristics and the Velten mood induction procedure. *Journal of Consulting and Clinical Psychology*, **49**, 478–479.

Clark, D.M., and Teasdale, J.D. (1982). Diurnal variation in clinical depression and accessibility of memories of positive and negative experiences. *Journal of Abnormal Psychology*, **91**, 87–95.

Clark, D.M., and Teasdale, J.D. (1985). Constaints on the effects of mood on memory. *Journal of Personality and Social Psychology*, **48**, 1595–1608.

Clark, D.M., and Teasdale, J.D., Broadbent, D.E., and Martin, M. (1983). Effect of mood on lexical decisions. *Bulletin of the Psychonomic Society*, **21**, 175–178.

Collins, A.M., and Loftus, E.F. (1975). A spreading-activation theory of semantic memory. *Psychological Review*, **82**, 407–428.

Davis, H. (1979). Self-reference and the encoding of personal information in depression. *Cognitive Therapy and Research*, **3**, 97–110.

Davis, H., and Unruh, W.R. (1980). Word memory in nonpsychotic depression. *Perceptual and Motor Skills*, **51**, 699–805.

Davis, H., and Unruh, W.R. (1981). The development of the self-schema in adult depression. *Journal of Abnormal Psychology*, **90**, 125–133.

Derry, P., and Kuiper, N. (1981). Schematic processing and self-reference in clinical depression. *Journal of Abnormal Psychology*, **90**, 286–297.

Diamond, B. (September, 1969). Interview regarding Sirhan Sirhan. *Psychology Today*, 48–55.

Duncan, S.W., Todd, C.M., and Perlmutter, M. (1985). Affect and memory in young children. *Motivation and Emotion*, **9**, 391–405.

Dutta, F., and Kanungo, R.N. (1975). *Affect and Memory: A Reformulation*. Oxford: Pergamon Press.

D'Zurilla, T. (1965). Recall efficiency and mediating cognitive events in 'experimental repression'. *Journal of Personality and Social Psychology*, **3**, 253–256.

Eich, J.E. (1980). The cue-dependent nature of state-dependent retrieval. *Memory and Cognition*, **18**, 157–173.

Ellis, H.C., Thomas, R.L., and Rodriguez, I.A. (1984). Emotional mood states and memory: elaborative encoding, semantic processing, and cognitive effort. *Journal of Experimental Psychology: Learning, Memory, and Cognition*, **10**, 470–482.

Fiedler, K., and Stroehm, W. (1986). What kind of mood influences what kind of memory: the role of arousal and information structure. *Memory and Cognition*, **14**, 181–188.

Finkel, C.B., Glass, C.R., and Merluzzi, T.V. (1982). Differential discrimination of self-referent statements by depressives and nondepressives. *Cognitive Therapy and Research*, **6**, 173–183.

Flavell, J. (1955). Repression and the 'return of the repressed'. *Journal of Consulting Psychology*, **19**, 441–443.

Fogarty, S.J., and Hemsley, D.R. (1983). Depression and the accessibility of memories. *British Journal of Psychiatry*, **142**, 232–237.

Forgas, J.B., Bower, G.H., and Krantz, S.E. (1984). The influence of mood on perception of social interactions. *Journal of Experimental Social Psychology*, **20**, 497–513.

Freud, S. (1957). Repression, 1915. *The Complete Psychological Works of Sigmund Freud*, vol. 14. London: Hogarth.

Gage, D.F., and Safer, M.A. (1985). Hemisphere differences in the mood state-dependent effect for recognition of emotional faces. *Journal of Experimental Psychology: Learning, Memory, and Cognition*, **11**, 742–763.

Gilbert, G.M. (1938). The new status of experimental studies on the relationship of feeling to memory. *Psychological Bulletin*, **35**, 26–35.

Guthrie, E.R. (1959). Association by contiguity. In S. Koch (Ed.), *Psychology: A Study of a Science*, vol. 2, New York: McGraw-Hill.

Hasher, L., Rose, K.C., Zacks, R.T., Sanft, H., and Doren, B. (1985). Mood, recall, and selectivity in normal college students. *Journal of Experimental Psychology: General*, **114**, 104–108.

Hasher, L., and Zacks, R.T. (1979). Automatic and effortful processes in memory. *Journal of Experimental Psychology: General*, **108**, 356–388.

Holmes, D.S. (1970). Differential change in affective intensity and the forgetting of unpleasant personal experiences. *Journal of Personality and Social Psychology,* 15, 234–239.

Holmes, D.S. (1972). Repression or interference: a further investigation. *Journal of Personality and Social Psychology,* 22, 163–170.

Holmes, D.S. (1974). Investigations of repression: differential recall of material experimentally or naturally associated with ego threat. *Psychological Bulletin,* 81, 632–653.

Ingram, R.E., Smith, T.W., and Brehm, S.S. (1983). Depression in information processing: self-schemata and the encoding of self-referent information. *Journal of Personality and Social Psychology,* 45, 412–420.

Isen, A.M. (1985). Asymmetry of happiness and sadness in effects of memory in normal college students: comment on Hasher, Rose, Zacks, Sanft, and Doren. *Journal of Experimental Psychology: General,* 114, 388–391.

Isen, A.M., Shalker, T.E., Clark, M., and Karp, L. (1978). Affect, accessibility of material in memory, and behavior: a cognitive loop? *Journal of Personality and Social Psychology,* 36, 1–12.

Jackson, R.L., and Smith, L.R. (1984). The effects of uncontrollable failure and depression on memorial processes. *Journal of Research in Personality,* 118, 463–479.

Jacobs, A. (1955). Formulation of new associations to words selected on the basis of reaction-time-GSR combinations. *Journal of Abnormal and Social Psychology,* 51, 371–377.

Johnson, M.H., and Magaro, P.A. (1987). Effects of mood and severity of memory processes in depression and mania. *Psychological Bulletin,* 101, 28–40.

Kahneman, D. (1973). *Attention and Effort,* Englewood Cliffs, NJ: Prentice-Hall.

Klatzky, R.L. (1980). *Human Memory: Structures and Processes,* San Francisco: Freeman.

Kuiper, N.A., and Derry, P.A. (1982). Depressed and nondepressed content self-reference in mild depressives. *Journal of Personality,* 50, 67–79.

Kuiper, N.A., and MacDonald, M.R. (1983). Schematic processing in depression: the self-based consensus bias. *Cognitive Therapy and Research,* 7, 469–484.

Laird, J.D., Wagener, J.J., Halal, M., and Szegda, M. (1982). Remembering what you feel: effects of emotion on memory. *Journal of Personality and Social Psychology,* 42, 646–657.

Lloyd, G.G., and Lishman, W.A. (1975). Effect of depression on the speed of recall of pleasant and unpleasant experiences. *Psychological Medicine,* 5, 173–180.

Mayer, J.D., and Bower, G.H. (1985). Naturally occurring mood and learning: comment on Hasher, Rose, Zacks, Sanft, and Doren. *Journal of Experimental Psychology: General,* 114, 396–403.

Mayer, R.E. (1975). Different problem solving competencies established in learning computer programming with and without meaningful models. *Journal of Educational Psychology,* 67, 725–734.

Mecklenbrauker, S., and Hager, W. (1984). Effects of mood on memory: experimental tests of mood-state dependent retrieval hypothesis and of a mood-congruity hypothesis. *Psychological Research,* 46, 355–376.

Meltzer, H. (1931). Sex differences in forgetting pleasant and unpleasant experiences. *Journal of Abnormal Psychology,* 25, 450–464.

Menzies, R. (1936). The comparative memory value of pleasant, unpleasant, and indifferent experiences. *Journal of Experimental Psychology,* 18, 267–297.

Merrill, R. (1954). The effect of pre-experimental and experimental anxiety on recall efficiency. *Journal of Experimental Psychology*, **48**, 167–172.

Miller, E., and Lewis, P. (1977). Recognition memory in elderly patients with depression and dementia: a signal detection analysis. *Journal of Abnormal Psychology*, **86**, 84–86.

Minsky, M. (1975). A framework for representing knowledge. In P.H. Winston (Ed.), *The Psychology of Computer Vision*, New York: McGraw-Hill.

Nasby, W., and Yando, R. (1982). Selective encoding and retrieval of affectively valent information: two cognitive consequences of children's mood states. *Journal of Personality and Social Psychology*, **43**, 1244–1253.

Natale, M., and Hantas, M. (1982). Effect of temporary mood states on selective memory about the self. *Journal of Personality and Social Psychology*, **42**, 927–934.

Neisser, U. (1976). *Cognition and Reality*, New York: Freeman.

Nelson, R.E., and Craighead, W. E. (1977). Selective recall of positive and negative feedback, self-control behaviors, and depression. *Journal of Abnormal Psychology*, **86**, 379–388.

Penn, N. (1964). Experimental improvements on an analogue of repression paradigm. *Psychological Record*, **14**, 185–196.

Pichert, J.W., and Anderson, R.C. (1977). Taking different perspectives on a story. *Journal of Educational Psychology*, **69**, 309–315.

Pietromonaco, P.R., and Marcus, H. (1985). The nature of negative thoughts in depression. *Journal of Personality and Social Psychology*, **48**, 799-807.

Plutchik, R. (1985). On emotion: the chicken-and-egg problem revisited. *Motivation and Emotion*, **9**, 197–200.

Polivy, J., and Doyle, C. (1980). Laboratory induction of mood states through the reading of self-referent mood statements: affective changes or demand characteristics. *Journal of Abnormal Psychology*, **189**, 286–290.

Roth, D., and Rehm, L.P. (1980). Relationships among self-monitoring processes, memory, and depression. *Cognitive Therapy and Research*, **4**, 149–157.

Schank, R.C., and Abelson, R. (1977). *Scripts, Plans, Goals, and Understanding*, Hillsdale, NJ: Lawrence Erlbaum.

Schare, M.L., Lisman, S.A., and Spear, N.E. (1984). The effects of mood variation on state-dependent retention. *Cognitive Therapy and Research*, **8**, 387–408.

Sears, R. (1944). Experimental analyses of psychoanalytic phenomena. In J. McV. Hunt (Ed.), *Personality Behavior Disorders*, vol. 1, New York: Ronald Press.

Sharp, A. (1938). An experimental test of Freud's doctrine of the relation of hedonic tone to memory revival. *Journal of Experimental Psychology*, **22**, 295–418.

Silberman, E.K., Weingartner, H., Laraia, M., Byrnes, S., and Post, R.M. (1983). Processing of emotional properties of stimuli by depressed and normal subjects. *The Journal of Nervous and Mental Disease*, **171**, 10–14.

Slife, B.D., Miura, S., Thompson, L.W., Shapiro, J.L., and Gallagher, D. (1984). Differential recall as a function of mood disorder in clinically depressed patients: between-and-within-subject differences. *Journal of Abnormal Psychology*, **93**, 391–400.

Smock, C.(1957). Recall of interrupted or non-interrupted tasks as a function of experimentally induced anxiety and motivational relevance of the task stimuli. *Journal of Personality*, **25**, 589–599.

Snyder, M., and White, P. (1982). Moods and memories: elation, depression, and the remembering of the events of one's life. *Journal of Personality*, **50**, 142–167.

Spanos, N.P. (1982). A social psychological approach to hypnotic behavior. In
    G. Weary and H.L. Mirels (Eds), *Integrations of Clinical and Social Psychology,*
    New York: Oxford University Press.
Stein, B.S., and Bransford, J.D. (1979). Constraints on effective elaboration:
    effects of precision and subject generation. *Journal of Verbal Learning and Verbal
    Behavior,* **18,** 769–777.
Sternberg, D.E., and Jarvik, M.E. (1976). Memory functions in depression.
    *Archives of General Psychiatry,* **33,** 219–224.
Teasdale, J.D. (1978). Effects of real and recalled success on learned helplessness
    and depression. *Journal of Abnormal Psychology,* **87,** 155–164.
Teasdale, J.D., and Fogarty, S.J. (1979). Differential effects of induced mood
    on retrieval of pleasant and unpleasant events from episodic memory. *Journal
    of Abnormal Psychology,* **188,** 248–257.
Teasdale, J.D., and Russell, M.L. (1983). Differential effects of induced mood
    on the recall of positive, negative and neutral words. *British Journal of Clinical
    Psychology,* **22,** 163–171.
Teasdale, J.D., and Taylor, R. (1981). Induced mood and accessibility of
    memories: an effect of mood state or of induction procedure? *British Journal
    of Clinical Psychology,* **20,** 39–48.
Teasdale, J.D., Taylor, R., and Fogarty, S.J. (1980). Effects of induced elation
    depression on the accessibility of memories of happy experiences. *Behavior
    Research and Therapy,* **18,** 339–346.
Thompson, C.P. (1985). Memory for unique personal events: effects of pleas-
    antness. *Motivation and Emotion,* **9,** 277–289.
Tulving, E. (1972). Episodic and semantic memory. In E. Tulving and W.
    Donaldson, (Eds), *Organization and Memory,* New York: Academic Press.
Tulving, E., and Thomson, D.M. (1973). Encoding specificity and retrieval
    processes in episodic memory. *Psychological Review,* **80,** 352–373.
Velten, E. (1968). A laboratory task for induction of mood states. *Behavior
    Research and Therapy,* **6,** 473–482.
Waters, R., and Leeper, R. (1936). The relation of affective tone to the retention
    of experiences in everyday life. *Journal of Experimental Psychology,* **19,** 203–215.
Weingartner, H., Cohen, R.M., Murphy, L., Martello, J., and Gerdt, C. (1981).
    Cognitive processes in depression. *Archives of General Psychiatry,* **38,** 42–47.
Weingartner, H., Miller, H., and Murphy, L. (1977). Mood-state dependent
    retrieval of verbal associations. *Journal of Abnormal Psychology,* **86,** 276–284.
Wetzler, S. (1985). Mood state-dependent retrieval: a failure to replicate.
    *Psychological Reports,* **56,** 759–765.
Wilkinson, F., and Cargill, D. (1955). Repression elicited by story of material
    based on the Oedipus complex. *Journal of Social Psychology,* **42,** 209–214.
Zeller, A. (1950). An experimental analogue of repression: 11. The effect of
    individual failure and success on memory measured by relearning. *Journal
    of Experimental Psychology,* **40,** 411–422.

Memory in Context : Context in Memory
Edited by G.M. Davies and D.M. Thomson
© 1988 John Wiley & Sons Ltd.

CHAPTER 5

# On the Relationship Between the Dissociative and Affective Properties of Drugs

ERIC EICH

*University of British Columbia*

and

ISABEL M. BIRNBAUM

*University of California/Irvine*

## ABSTRACT

In studies of state-dependent learning, it is unclear whether drugs exert an influence on memory directly or indirectly via changes in mood. A pilot study is reported which attempted to manipulate mood independent of drug action. Modest effects on recall of subjective mood reinstatement were found independent of actual pharmacological state. The implications of these findings for future research and contextual theory are discussed.

Though it has often been observed that events encoded in a particular pharmacological context or state are most retrievable in that state, the mechanisms responsible for human dissociative or drug-dependent memory remain obscure. In this chapter, we explore a plausible but unproven theory concerning these mechanisms. In essence, the theory represents the novel integration of two familiar facts. First, as a rule, drugs that produce reliable dissociations of human memory also produce reliable, sometimes radical, alterations of affect or mood. Alcohol, for example, has been found to facilitate the retrieval of events that had been encoded in an earlier state of intoxication (e.g. Eich and Birnbaum, 1982) *and* to foster feelings of elation, relaxation, and subjective 'high' (e.g. Persson, Sjoberg, and Svensson, 1980). Several other centrally acting agents, such as amphetamine and marijuana, have also been shown to possess both dissociative and affective properties (e.g. Eich 1980; Johanson and

Uhlenhuth, 1981; Jones, 1971; Swanson and Kinsbourne, 1976). Second, people tend to remember events better if they are able to reinstate, during retrieval, the affect or mood they had experienced during the encoding of the events. This appears to be true regardless of whether the people involved are young children (e.g. Bartlett and Santrock, 1979), college students (e.g. Teasdale and Fogarty, 1979), or manic/depressive patients (e.g. Weingartner, Miller, and Murphy, 1977), and regardless of whether the affects involved are artificially induced or naturally occurring (e.g. hypnotically suggested happiness in contrast to endogenous depression; see Bower, 1981; Bower and Cohen, 1982; Isen, 1984; Leight and Ellis, 1981). Tying these two facts together, the theory proposes that drugs achieve their dissociative effects on human memory by virtue of the effects on mood. Drug-dependent memory is thus seen to represent a special case of mood-dependent memory, with drug-produced alterations of affect providing the internal cues or subjective sensations that underlie drug-produced dissociations of memory (Bower, 1981; Overton, 1978, 1984; Weingartner, 1978).

What evidence is there to defend or deny the theory that drug-dependent memory is a mood-dependent phenomenon? At present, the answer either way is: not much. To the theory's credit, research reviewed by Eich (1980, 1986) indicates that reliable dissociative effects are rarely detected unless the dose of drug administered is high enough to produce overt signs of intoxication, such as ataxia or slurred speech—signs that seem likely to occur in conjunction with covert changes in affect, mood, or associated aspects of subjective experience. Of related interest is a study by Weingartner (1978), in which depressed patients generated verbal associations while under the influence of either *d*- or *l*-amphetamine, and were asked to reproduce these associations four days later, while drug free. On each occasion the patients rated various characteristics of their current subjective state, including their levels of activation and euphoria. Weingartner found that the greater the subjective change in state between the generation and reproduction phases of the study, the greater the number of words forgotten—a finding that would seem to square with the mood-mediation theory of drug-dependent memory. However, Weingartner (1978) also found clear evidence of dissociation in a separate study in which normal subjects were treated with physostigmine, an anticholinesterase agent that appears to have little subjective impact apart from some increase in arousal (Bower, 1981; Mewaldt and Ghoneim, 1979). Moreover, Overton and Batta (1977) found no evidence of a relationship between the discriminability of a drug (as defined by the rate at which rats learn to respond differentially in a T-maze depending on whether they are drugged or undrugged) and the drug's potential for abuse (as defined by the United States Drug Enforcement Agency). A robust relationship might have been expected to emerge were it the case, as Overton (1973, 1978) had conjectured, that discriminability and abuse are caused by the same drug actions, and that abuse is caused by the positive affective consequences of drug self-administration.

Since all of the results reviewed in the preceding paragraph are correlational in nature, none can be regarded as compelling evidence either for or against the mood mediation theory. One way to obtain more telling data might be to set up an experimental situation in which the *objective* similarity between study and test states is held constant, while the *subjective* similarity between these states is systematically varied. To illustrate, suppose that college students study a list of words after they have consumed a moderate amount of alcohol, and that several days later, the subjects are tested for recall of the words after they have consumed a non-alcoholic beverage. Suppose further that some of the subjects know that they are sober during the test of recall, while others have been led to expect that their second drink contains as much alcohol as did their first. Given the situation sketched above, might subjects who are subjectively intoxicated, but objectively sober, during the recall test outperform those who are 'straight' by either standard? In other words, is it possible that memory performance depends not on the objective similarity or dissimilarity between study and test states—that is, on whether or not the subjects have alcohol in their blood and brains during recall—but rather, on the subjective similarity or dissimilarity between study/test states—that is, or whether or not the subjects act, think, and most important, feel as though they have alcohol in their system? This possibility would seem to follow directly from the mediation theory discussed above, and we tried to test it in the 'expectancy experiment' that is described below. As will soon become apparent, our attempts to persuade selected subjects that they were intoxicated during recall, when in fact they were not, met with only partial success, and so we were unable to control the subjective similarity between study/test states as completely as we would have preferred. Nevertheless, the expectancy experiment did reveal some suggestive results, and it also raises a number of interesting issues for future research—issues which we will explore in the concluding section of the chapter.

## THE EXPECTANCY EXPERIMENT

### Methods

Twenty-four male undergraduates at the University of California/Irvine averaging 22 years of age, served as subjects in the experiment. Prospective participants were screened, by means of a questionnaire, for serious physical or psychological problems. This questionnaire also provided data on the nature and frequency of alcohol use, which enabled us to select subjects who drank regularly, in moderation, for recreational purposes. The subjects were instructed to eat a prescribed breakfast 3 hr before each experimental session, and to refrain from taking any psychoactive drug for 24 hr prior to their arrival at the laboratory.

Subjects were treated individually throughout the course of the experiment, which comprised two sessions, termed *study* and *test*, separated by seven days. At the start of the study session, the subject was told that the aim of the research was to examine the effects of alcohol on one's ability to learn and recall a list of conceptually categorized words. Next, the subject's current level of alcohol intoxication was assessed both objectively (via a Breathalizer test) and subjectively (via a subject-supplied rating on a 4-point scale ranging from 'not at all intoxicated' [0] to 'slightly intoxicated' [1] to 'moderately intoxicated' [2] and lastly to 'extremely intoxicated' [3]).

Following the baseline assessment of objective and subjective effects, the subject was administered an 0.55 ml/kg dose of absolute alcohol in the form of two equivalent drinks, each containing a 1:4 mixture of 80-proof vodka and decarbonated tonic water. The research assistant in charge not only told the subject that the drinks contained alcohol, but also asked for his help in preparing them. By implementing these unorthodox procedures, we hoped to gain credibility with the subject, and thereby make him more receptive to the expectancy manipulation that we planned to apply in the next session.

The drinks were served to the subject one at a time, over ice, 15 min. apart. Following a 15 min. absorption period, the subject rated his current level of intoxication, and provided a new Breathalizer sample; the resulting reading, expressed in mg% blood alcohol, was shown to the subject.

The list learning task came next. For this purpose, the subject was presented with a list composed of 12 category names and four exemplars of each category (e.g. *chemical elements*: HELIUM, COPPER, SODIUM, CARBON). The list was presented only once, by means of an audio cassette tape, at a rate of 3 sec. per category name or exemplar. Following presentation of the list, the subject was given 1 min. to work on a distractor task (written alphabetical recall of the American states), and was then given 5 min. to reproduce, in writing, as many of the category exemplars as possible, in any order, without benefit of any explicit reminders or cues.

Following the test of immediate recall, objective and subjective intoxication levels were again assessed. The subject was then engaged for the next 30 min. or so in a variety of non-verbal cognitive tasks. Afterwards, he was offered a light lunch and was driven home once he no longer showed any signs of intoxication. On leaving the laboratory, the subject was instructed to return at the same time, one week later, to carry on with the research. The subject was not informed that, during his return visit, he would again be asked to recall the categorized list he had learned earlier this day.

At the outset of the test session, baseline blood-alcohol and subjective-intoxication levels were measured. Depending on which of the two *expectancy conditions* the subject had been randomly assigned, the research assistant then told the subject that he would receive either (a) two drinks composed entirely of flat tonic water, or (b) two drinks containing the same mixture of vodka and tonic that he had received the week before. In the expect-tonic condition, the subject watched as the assistant filled two glasses with an equal volume (6.90 ml/kg) of tonic water from a newly opened bottle. In the expect-alcohol condition, the subject looked on as the assistant prepared two drinks, each of which appeared to contain one part vodka per four parts tonic. Unbeknown to the subject, the original contents of the vodka bottle had been replaced with tonic water.

Procedures involved in delivering the drinks were the same as those summarized earlier, except that in the expect-alcohol condition, the assistant discretely swabbed each glass with a few milliliters of real vodka, in an effort to disguise its true non-alcoholic contents.

Following the absorption period, the subject rated his current level of subjective intoxication, and then took another Breathalyzer test. In the expect-alcohol condition, the Breathalyzer device had been preset to produce a reading of about 40 mg% blood alcohol—the reading one would expect had the subject actually received the same dose of alcohol that he had taken during the study session—and the subject was shown this false reading. In the expect-tonic condition, the Breathalyzer produced an accurate reading of 0 mg% blood alcohol, and this too was shown to the subject.

To the subject's surprise, he was next asked to write, on a blank piece of paper, all of the category exemplars he remembered studying the week before. This test of delayed recall lasted 5 min., and it was followed by a final assessment of objective and subjective levels of intoxication. Afterwards, the subject was thoroughly debriefed, paid $20, and offered a lift home.

### Results

Uniformly zero ratings of blood-alcohol and subjective-intoxication levels were obtained at the beginning of either experimental session. Since all subjects were treated identically throughout the course of the study session, their performance during this session should, in principle, be independent of whichever expectancy treatment they were due to receive during the test session. This was in fact the case. To be specific, blood-alcohol

levels measured shortly before list presentation, and shortly after immediate recall, averaged 40 mg% among subjects who would later serve in the
expect-alcohol condition, and 39 mg% among prospective expect-tonic participants. Also, as indicated in Table 5.1, the two expectancy conditions
were comparable with respect to: (a) mean study session ratings of subjective intoxication [expect alcohol = 2.0, expect tonic = 2.1; $t(22) < 1$];
(b) mean immediate recall of categories [0.51 vs 0.53; $t(22) < 1$]; and (c)
mean immediate recall of words within recallable categories [0.68 vs 0.71;
$t(22) < 1$]. As in an earlier experiment (Eich and Birnbaum, 1982), we
defined category recall as the proportion of different conceptual categories
from which at least one previously presented exemplar was recalled, and
word-per-category recall as the proportion of recalled exemplars divided
by the proportion of recalled categories.

Table 5.1  Mean ratings of subjective intoxication (Sx) and mean proportions of
categories ($R_c$) and words-per-category ($R_{w/c}$) recalled as a function of experimental
session and test-session expectancy.

| Test-session | Study session | | | Test session | | |
|---|---|---|---|---|---|---|
| Expectancy | Sx | $R_c$ | $R_{w/c}$ | Sx | $R_c$ | $R_{w/c}$ |
| Alcohol | 2.0 | 0.51 | 0.68 | 0.6 | 0.36 | 0.51 |
| ($n = 12$) | (0.7) | (0.11) | (0.15) | (0.6) | (0.11) | (0.13) |
| Tonic | 2.1 | 0.53 | 0.71 | 0.1 | 0.37 | 0.59 |
| ($n = 12$) | (0.7) | (0.14) | (0.17) | (0.3) | (0.14) | (0.09) |

*Note*: Standard deviations are enclosed in parentheses.

Turning now to the data for the test session, it is apparent in Table
5.1 that the expectancy manipulation worked, but just barely. Of the 12
expect-alcohol subjects, 7 registered a non-zero rating of subjective intoxication, suggesting that they had, to some extent, been taken in by the ruse.
In contrast, 11 of the 12 expect-tonic subjects rated themselves as being
completely sober during the test session. (The single exceptional subject
evidently did not believe us when we told him that his test-session drinks
contained only tonic water, for he claimed to be slightly intoxicated after
consuming them.) Note, however, that although the mean test-session rating of subjective intoxication was significantly higher in the expect-alcohol
than in the expect-tonic condition [0.6 vs 0.1; $t(22) = 2.64$, $p < 0.01$
on a one-tailed test], the expect-alcohol subjects were obviously not as
subjectively intoxicated during the test session as they had been during

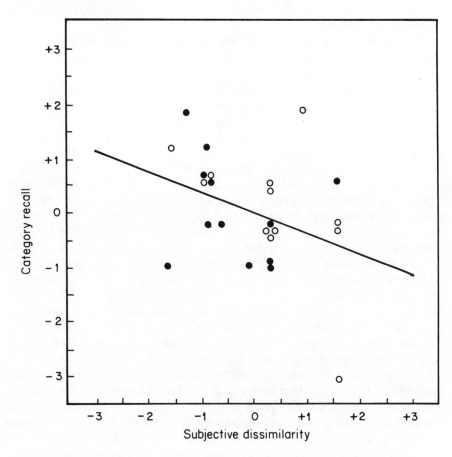

Figure 5.1 Relation between probability of delayed category recall and the difference between study and test session ratings of subjective intoxication (i.e. subjective dissimilarity). The raw data for each variable are expressed as standard (z) scores. Black and white circles correspond to expect-alcohol and expect-tonic conditions, respectively.

the study session [mean difference of 1.4; $t(11) = 6.76$, $p < 0.01$]. Thus, the expect-alcohol treatment did not succeed in returning subjects to their original subjective state; it only made the subjective difference between study and test states somewhat smaller than it would have been had the subjects known for a fact that they were drinking pure tonic. For this reason, it seems unreasonable to suppose that the expect-alcohol subjects should perform significantly better than their expect-tonic counterparts on the test of delayed recall, and indeed they did not. As is shown in the two right-most columns of Table 5.1, the mean proportions of categories and words-per-category recalled in the delayed test were similar in the two expectancy conditions.

The results of the delayed test may not be completely inconsequential, however. If we correlate the probability of delayed category recall with the difference between study and test session ratings of subjective intoxication (i.e. 'subjective dissimilarity'), the coefficient obtained is modest and marginally significant [$r(22) = -0.36$, one-tailed $p < 0.05$]. (The relationship between delayed category recall and subjective dissimilarity is illustrated in Figure 5.1; for convenience, the raw data for each variable have been transformed into standard ($z$) scores.) Further, if we classify subjects according to whether they are above or below the overall mean probability of delayed category recall, and whether they are above or below the overall mean difference between study/test ratings of subjective intoxication, the relationship between category recall and subjective dissimilarity again emerges as modest and marginally significant [$X^2(1) = 2.59$, one-tailed $p < 0.07$]. Interestingly, the relationship between subjective dissimilarity and delayed recall of words within recallable categories does not approach statistical significance on either of the two analyses described above [$r = -0.22$, $X^2 = 0.05$, one-tailed $ps > 0.10$]. This, perhaps, is how it should be. In a number of earlier experiments involving alcohol or other drugs (see Eich, 1986; Eich and Birnbaum, 1982), a change of pharmacological context has been found to impair the nominally non-cued recall of conceptual categories, but to have little impact on the recall of words within these categories. The present results reveal a similar pattern, and more important, they imply that category accessibility depends to some degree on the subjective similarity between study and test states, even under conditions where these states are objectively different. To determine whether this implication is valid, one would need experimentally to control the subjective similarity between study/test states in a more complete and convincing manner than we were able to manage in the current expectancy study. Several strategies and techniques that might be applied to achieve this aim are discussed in the next section.

## PROSPECTS FOR FUTURE RESEARCH

At the outset of this chapter, we used the terms 'plausible' and 'unproven' to describe the theory that the dissociative effects of drugs on human memory are mediated by alterations of affect or mood. This description still seems appropriate in view of the results of the expectancy experiment reported here. If we regard differences between study and test session ratings of subjective intoxication as a rough but reasonable measure of affect change (see Ekman, Frankenhaeuser, Goldberg, Hagdahl and Myrsten 1964), then the correlational data discussed earlier (see Figure 5.1 and related text) would appear to at least be consistent with the mediation theory, and may even enhance its plausibility. However, the present experiment did not produce any results that can be taken as proof of the theory's correctness, or as evidence that drug-dependent effects are due to alterations of affect or related aspects of subjective experience. Nevertheless, our intuition is that the reason we failed to find evidence of a causal relationship between affect change and drug-induced dissociation is not that the relationship does not exist, but rather, that our experiment lacked sufficient sensitivity to detect it. How, then, might a suitably sensitive test of the mediation theory be devised?

One possibility is to try the expectancy experiment again, this time relying on more sophisticated and effective techniques, such as those recently developed by Sher (1985), to bias people's beliefs about the alcoholic content of their drinks, independent of their actual contents. Alternatively, it might be advisable to replace alcohol with a drug whose physical and psychological effects are potentially more malleable vis-a-vis the experimental manipulation of expectancy. In this regard, nitrous oxide ($N_2O$) would appear to be an ideal agent. Being a colorless and faintly scented gas (see Wynne, 1985), $N_2O$ cannot be easily discriminated from pure oxygen, making it suitable for expectancy manipulations. Moreover, $N_2O$, when administered in dilute (subanesthetic) concentrations, produces profound alterations of affect or mood (see Steinberg, 1956), giving it good potential as a dissociative drug. Most important, few if any prospective subjects will have any conscious (i.e. non-surgical) experience with or preconceived notions about the subjective and physiological properties of $N_2O$, which may make them particularly responsive to expectancy manipulations.

While it makes good sense to study the mediation theory in relation to expectancy effects, other strategies also merit careful consideration. As an example, prior research (e.g. Ekman *et al.*, 1964; Persson *et al.*, 1980) indicates that alcohol has a biphasic impact on mood, such that positive affects (euphoria, relaxation) are experienced primarily during the absorption phase, while negative affects (drowsiness, lethargy) predominate during the elimination phase. If the dissociative effects of alcohol on memory are mediated by moods, then it should be possible to show that information transfers more completely between corresponding phases of the absorption/elimination cycle than between complementary phases, even under conditions where the concentration of alcohol in the bloodstream is the same at absorption as it is at elimination. As a second example, Smith (1979) has shown that impairments of memory caused by a change of environmental context can be eliminated by instructing subjects to remember the room in which learning took place. By extension, it is possible that if subjects who have experienced a change of pharmacological context can be induced cognitively to reconstruct their original drug state, a marked improvement in memory performance might result.

Yet another way of gaining purchase on the mediation theory may be to explore the relations among alcohol, mood, and autobiographical memory. According to several studies (see Bower, 1981; Teasdale, 1983), goodness of memory for episodes or events of the personal past depends critically on the match between the mood in which the events were experienced, on the one hand, and the mood in which recollection of the events is attempted, on the other. To cite just one specific study, Teasdale and Fogarty (1979) found that whereas happy subjects retrieve memories of pleasant personal experiences more rapidly than those of unpleasant experiences, sad subjects retrieve sad memories faster than happy ones. Given that alcohol, at least under certain circumstances (see Freed, 1978), leads to an elevation of positive mood, and in view of the mood-dependent nature of memory for personal experiences, it seems reasonable to suppose that alcohol may affect autobiographical memory in much the same manner as mood. More to the point, the idea is that alcohol, by promoting a positive mood, selectively enhances the accessibility of autobiographical memories with positive affective overtones, while it selectively diminishes the accessibility of negative-affect experiences. This hypothesis, if confirmed, is important for three reasons. First, it is clearly compatible with the theory that the dissociative effects of drugs on memory are mediated by modifications of mood. Second, it suggests a simple but psychologically plausible explanation for one of the many reasons people drink socially: simply put, they do so to remember the good times of their lives, and to forget, if only for a while, the bad. Third, the hypothesis challenges the generally accepted conclusion that alcohol has no appreciable influence on the utilization or retrieval of events that had been encoded under conditions of sobriety (see Birnbaum, Parker, Hartley and Noble, 1978; Ryback, 1971). The evidence on which this conclusion is based comes mainly from experiments in which subjects study simple stimulus items (words, pictures, or the like) while sober, and are later tested for recall either while sober or while demonstrably intoxicated. Under these conditions, intoxicated subjects usually fare about as well as their sober counterparts in the number or simple proportion of items recalled, thus implying that information acquired in the absence of alcohol is as accessible for retrieval in the presence of the drug as in its absence. It is important to note, however, that in the prototypical experiment in which no evidence of impaired retrieval under alcohol has been found, the stimulus items used have no particular personal significance to the subjects or any distinct affective quality (positive or negative). The implication of the new hypothesis advanced here is that alcohol may indeed impair the retrieval of information that had been stored in its absence, but that the impairment is specific to experiences that are both personally significant to the rememberer and distinctly negative in affective coloration. In light of this implication, and in consideration of the other points raised earlier, the relations among alcohol, mood, and autobiographical memory would seem to represent a rich subject for future study.

Up to now, the focus of discussion has been on whether memory impairments produced by a change of pharmacological context are caused by a change of affect or mood. Recently, Eich (1985) has conjectured that mood changes may also play a prominent role in memory failures that occur following a change of physical setting or environmental context (see Godden and Baddeley, 1975; Nixon and Kanak, 1981; Smith, 1979, 1982). Briefly, the idea is that how well information transfers from one place to another depends less on how similar or dissimilar the environments *look* than on how similar or dissimilar the subjects *feel* in each environment. In an attempt to test this idea, one of us (EE) is currently collecting normative data on subjects' judgments of both the affective and the perceptual similarity between various pairs of places situated on or around a university campus. From these normative data, four pairs of environments will eventually be selected which will represent the factorial combination of two variables: type of interpair similarity (affective vs perceptual) and degree of interpair similarity (high vs low). One member of each pair will serve as the environment in which subjects encode a series of to-be-remembered or target events, and the other member will serve as the environment in which retrieval of the targets is tested. If it is indeed the case that alterations of affect or mood are responsible not only for drug-dependent memory, but for place-dependent memory as well, then retrieval performance should depend chiefly on the affective, rather than the perceptual, similarity between encoding/retrieval environments. If validated, this hypothesis would help explain some otherwise puzzling failures to demonstrate place-dependent memory that have appeared in the literature (see Eich, 1985 and Smith, this volume). More important, it would give credence to the mediation concept detailed here, and thereby aid the development of a unified theoretical approach to understanding the dissociative effects of drugs, emotions, and environments on human memory.

## ACKNOWLEDGEMENTS

Preparation of this chapter was aided by grants from the (Canadian) Natural Sciences and Engineering Research Council (U0298) and the (American) National Institute on Alcohol Abuse and Alcoholism

(AA03506). Our thanks to Doris Margolis and Karen Schenk for the expert assistance they provided throughout the course of the research reported here.

## REFERENCES

Bartlett, J.C. and Santrock, J.W. (1979). Affect-dependent episodic memory in young children. *Child Development*, **50**, 513–518.

Birnbaum, I.M., Parker, E.S., Hartley, J.T. and Noble, E.P. (1978). Alcohol and memory: retrieval processes. *Journal of Verbal Learning and Verbal Behavior* **17**, 325–335.

Bower, G.H. (1981). Mood and memory. *American Psychologist*, **36**, 129–148.

Bower, G.H. and Cohen, P.R. (1982). Emotional influences in memory and thinking: data and theory. In M.S. Clark and S.T. Fiske (Eds), *Affect and Cognition*, Hillsdale, NJ: Lawrence Erlbaum.

Eich, E. (1980). The cue-dependent nature of state-dependent retrieval. *Memory and Cognition*, **8**, 157–173.

Eich, E. (1985). Context, memory, and integrated item/context imagery. *Journal of Experimental Psychology: Learning, Memory, and Cognition*, **11**, 764–770.

Eich, E. (1986). Epilepsy and state specific memory. *Acta Neurologica Scandinavica*, **74**, 15–21.

Eich, E. and Birnbaum, I.M. (1982). Repetition, cuing, and state-dependent memory. *Memory and Cognition*, **10**, 103–114.

Ekman, G., Frankenhaeuser, M., Goldberg, L., Hagdahl, R. and Myrsten, A. (1964). Subjective and objective effects of alcohol as functions of dosage and time. *Psychopharmacologia*, **6**, 399–409.

Freed, E.X. (1978). Alcohol and mood: an updated review. *International Journal of the Addictions*, **13**, 173–200.

Godden, D.R. and Baddeley, A.D. (1975). Context-dependent memory in two natural environments: on land and underwater. *British Journal of Psychology*, **66**, 325–331.

Isen, A.M. (1984). Toward understanding the role of affect in cognition. In R.S. Wyer and T.K. Srull (Eds), *Handbook of Social Cognition*, Hillsdale, NJ: Lawrence Erlbaum.

Johanson, C.E. and Uhlenhuth, E.H. (1981). Drug preference and mood in humans: repeated assessment of *d*-amphetamine. *Pharmacology Biochemistry and Behavior*, **14**, 159–163.

Jones, R.T. (1971). Marijuana-induced 'High': influence of expectation, setting, and previous drug experience. *Pharmacology Review*, **23**, 359–369.

Leight, K.A. and Ellis, H.C. (1981). Emotional mood states, strategies, and state-dependency in memory. *Journal of Verbal Learning and Verbal Behavior*, **20**, 251–266.

Mewaldt, S.P. and Ghoneim, M.M. (1979). The effects and interactions of scopolamine, physostigmine and methamphetamine on human memory. *Pharmacology Biochemistry and Behavior*, **10**, 205–210.

Nixon, S.J. and Kanak, N.J. (1981). The interactive effects of instructional set and environmental context changes on the serial position effect. *Bulletin of the Psychonomic Society*, **18**, 237–240.

Overton, D.A. (1973). State dependent learning produced by addicting drugs. In S. Fisher and A.M. Freedman (Eds), *Opiate Addiction: Origins and Treatment*, Washington, DC: Winston.

Overton, D.A. (1978). Major theories of state dependent learning. In B.T. Ho, D.W. Richards and D.L. Chute (Eds), *Drug Discrimination and State Dependent Learning*, New York: Academic Press.

Overton, D.A. (1984). State dependent learning and drug discriminations. In L.L. Iverson, S.D. Iverson and S.H. Snyder (Eds), *Handbook of Psychopharmacology*, **18**, New York: Plenum.

Overton, D.A. and Batta, S.K. (1977). Relationship between the abuse liability of drugs and their degree of discriminability in the rat. In T. Thompson and K. Unna (Eds), *Predicting Dependence Liability of Stimulant and Depressant Drugs*, Baltimore: University Park Press.

Persson, L.O., Sjoberg, L. and Svensson, E. (1980). Mood effects of alcohol. *Psychopharmacology*, **68**, 295–299.

Ryback, R.A. (1971). The continuum and specificity of the effects of alcohol on memory. *Quarterly Journal of Studies on Alcohol*, **32**, 995–1016.

Sher, K.J. (1985). Subjective effects of alcohol: the influence of setting and individual differences in alcohol expectancies. *Journal of Studies on Alcohol*, **46**, 137–147.

Smith, S.M. (1979). Remembering in and out of context. *Journal of Experimental Psychology: Human Learning and Memory*, **5**, 460–471.

Smith, S.M. (1982). Enhancement of recall using multiple environmental contexts during learning. *Memory and Cognition*, **10**, 405–412.

Steinberg, H. (1956). 'Abnormal behaviour' induced by nitrous oxide. *British Journal of Psychology*, **47**, 183–194.

Swanson, J.M. and Kinsbourne, M. (1976). Stimulant-related state-dependent learning in hyperactive children. *Science*, **192**, 1354–1357.

Teasdale, J.D. (1983). Negative thinking in depression: cause, effect, or reciprocal relationship? *Advances in Behaviour Research and Therapy*, **5**, 3–25.

Teasdale, J.D. and Fogarty, S.J. (1979). Differential effects of induced mood on retrieval of pleasant and unpleasant events from episodic memory. *Journal of Abnormal Psychology*, **88**, 248–257.

Weingartner, H. (1978). Human state dependent learning. In B.T. Ho, D.W. Richards and D.L. Chute (Eds), *Drug Discrimination and State Dependent Learning*, New York: Academic Press.

Weingartner, H., Miller, H. and Murphy, D.L. (1977). Mood-state-dependent retrieval of verbal associations. *Journal of Abnormal Psychology*, **86**, 276–284.

Wynne, J.M. (1985). Physics, chemistry, and manufacture of nitrous oxide. In E.I. Eger (Ed), *Nitrous Oxide/N₂0*, New York: Elsevier.

# SEMANTIC CONTEXT

Memory in Context : Context in Memory
Edited by G.M. Davies and D.M. Thomson
© 1988 John Wiley & Sons Ltd.

CHAPTER 6

# Relational Context: Independent Cues, Meanings or Configurations?

JOHN D. BAIN and MICHAEL S. HUMPHREYS

*University of Queensland*

ABSTRACT

Interpretation of the episodic/semantic context effect in terms of item and relational information accessed independently through the target and context cues. Alternative interpretations considered are meaning selection during study and test and configural encoding and retrieval. Cue and information analysis advocated as level of explanation in preference to information processing metaphors.

## RELATIONAL CONTEXT: INDEPENDENT CUES, MEANINGS OR CONFIGURATIONS?

It is now a commonplace observation that episodic tasks in the laboratory require subjects to restrict their recalls and their recognition judgments to events that occurred earlier in the experiment. The unresolved problem for memory theorists is how this feat is accomplished. Since the appearance of two seminal papers some 15 years ago (Anderson and Bower, 1972; Tulving, 1972) most researchers have assumed that context is strongly implicated in the recovery of relevant memories. That is, whether one assumes that it is the matching of study and test context tags (Anderson and Bower, 1972, 1974), or the matching of test cues to study traces (both being assumed to include contextual features—Flexser and Tulving, 1978), context is seen to be the major factor that prevents irrelevant memories from intruding, particularly when the target items are familiar. The dilemma that this approach encounters is that most overtly manipulated context variables have relatively weak effects[1].

In one way or another, all context investigations have compared two performances, one with some aspect of the study context reinstated at test, the other with that feature absent or mismatched. Contextual reinstatements such as background environment (Bain, Humphreys, Tehan and Pike, 1986; Fernandez and Glenberg, 1985; Smith, 1985; Smith, Glenberg and Bjork 1978) subject mood (Bower, 1981; Bower and Mayer, 1985), and stimulus presentation features (speaker's voice—Geiselman and Bjork, 1980; type font—Kirsner, 1973) have been found to have weak effects on word recall and recognition relative to the absence/mismatch base rate. This suggests either that much of the experimental context contributes little to episodic performance, or that our methods for investigating it are wide of the mark. We have argued elsewhere (Bain *et al.*, 1986; Humphreys, Bain and Pike, 1986) that the latter may very well be the case, because the primary vehicle for the reinstatement of the study context is not some specific feature of that context but the instructions that link the test and study tasks. That is, when subjects acknowledge that they know to what you are referring when you say 'the words that you rated for pleasantness last month', they have thereby reinstated the operative features of the study context. Specific reinstatements usually add only small increments to this instructional baseline.

Nevertheless, specific contextual reinstatements continue to hold great interest, in part because they have generated their own puzzles, but also because they might provide adequate models for all context effects. By far the most researched and fiercely debated is the context provided for target words by the presence of *other* words at study and test. When a word is tested in its original study pairing, for example, it is a little easier to recognize than when tested either by itself or in the presence of some other word. This effect is obtained with homographs (Light and Carter-Sobell, 1970; Pellegrino and Salzberg, 1975), with weak associates (Humphreys, 1978; Thomson, 1972) and with unrelated word pairs (Humphreys, 1976; Thomson, 1972). Elsewhere we have referred to this as the relational context effect (Humphreys and Bain, 1983), and in what follows we consider three major classes of explanation for it.

The first explanation, which the evidence favours, proposes that when a target word is tested in its study pairing there are two cues from which information about the target can be recovered: the target itself and its study associate. In its simplest form this explanation assumes that two processes can subserve target recognition—target recognition *per se* (elicited by the target word), and recall (from the context word). The two formal models of this proposal (Humphreys, 1978; Mandler, 1980) have in common the assumption that the two cues operate independently. That is, they neither moderate each other's test encodings nor interact to form a configural test stimulus. The alternative explanations assume on the contrary that the target and context words behave interactively at study and test.

The *meaning selection* hypothesis, for example, assumes that the verbal context in which a target is studied will select the meaning of the target that is encoded. Access to this meaning at test (and hence recognition of the target) is assumed to be greater when the recognition and study contexts are the same (Anderson and Bower, 1974; Martin, 1975; Reder, Anderson and Bjork, 1974). We will argue that although this explanation, or aspects of it, may be applicable in special cases, it is not to be preferred as the general model. A related but formally distinct proposal is that the study and test pairs are encoded *configurally*, so that trace access during recognition is more probable if study and test configurations are identical. We assume that this is what Tulving and Thomson (1973, p. 367) intended in their discussion of a Gestalt interpretation of recognition failure. An analogous concept is embodied in recent global matching models which assume a unified or configural representation of study and/or test pairs (Gillund and Shiffrin, 1984; Hintzman, 1984; Humphreys, Pike, Bain and Tehan, 1986; Murdock, 1982; Pike, 1984). We will show that this class of explanation predicts a performance pattern that is not observed in several data sets.

## Recognition using independent cues

Although there are important differences between the two formal models of this hypothesis (Humphreys and Bain, 1983; Mandler, 1980) we shall postpone consideration of those differences until after some general properties of all three explanations have been considered.

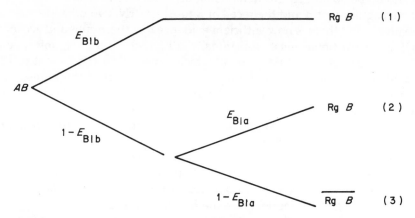

Figure 6.1 The General Independent Cues Model for the recognition of an item (*B*) in an intact pair (*AB*). Evidence for *B* can be recovered from *B* itself (with probability $E_{B|b}$) or from its study pair member, *A* (with probability $E_{B|a}$).

A formal representation of the general independent cues model is presented in Figure 6.1. It is assumed that subjects have studied pairs $AB$, and are attempting to recognize $B$ in the context of $A$. The target, $B$, will be recognized either when evidence for $B$ is recovered using $B$ itself as the cue (with probability $E_{B|b}$, path 1) or when using the context word $A$ as the cue (with probability $E_{B|a}$, the last transition in path 2). Since these events are assumed to be independent, the probability of recognizing $B$ in the context of $A$ is the sum of their disjoint probabilities, as in equation (1) below. When $B$ is tested alone or in the presence of some word other than $A$ ($\overline{A}B$), the only source of evidence for $B$ is from $B$ itself, as in equation (2):

$$\rho(\text{Rg } B|AB) = E_{B|b} + (1 - E_{B|b})E_{B|a} \tag{1}$$

$$\rho(\text{Rg } B|\overline{A}B) = E_{B|b} \tag{2}$$

Research favouring this general model comes from two basic demonstrations. Humphreys (1978) had subjects study pairs ($AB$), recognize individual targets ($B$) from those pairs and then recall those targets given the other member of the study pair as the cue (Rc$A$__). There was a close correspondence between recognition in context and a derived recognition score that was calculated by adding the words that had been recalled but not recognized to those that had been recognized. That is, across several criterion levels, estimated from confidence ratings, the following equation held:

$$\rho(\text{Rg } B|AB) = \rho\text{Rg } B|B) + \rho(\overline{\text{Rg}B} \cap \text{Rc}A\_\_) \tag{3}$$

It should be noted that this demonstration relies on two distinct operations, the recognition of $B$ and the recall of $B$ to $A$. Clearly, two different cues are involved, and there is now sufficient evidence that these cues and accompanying instructions elicit functionally different forms of information (Humphreys and Bain, 1983), about which more will be said later. It suffices for the present to note that Humphreys (1976) proposed the phrase 'relational information' to refer to the recall-based evidence used in item recognition. It is from this phrase that we have coined the label 'relational context effect' to refer to the advantage of intact over other test item arrangements in recognition.

The second demonstration involved a generalization of the independent cues model to the recognition of intact study *pairs* amidst mixed (one old, one new) and new (two new words) distractor pairs (Mandler, 1980). For this situation the general model gives the following probability for recognizing intact pairs assuming that, in the absence of rearranged pairs, subjects will recognize a pair as intact if both words are old, whether or not they know them to come from the same study pair (cf. equation (7) in Mandler, 1980):

$$\rho(\text{Rg}AB) = (E_{A|a})(E_{B|b}) + (1 - E_{A|a})E_{A|b} + (1 - E_{B|b})E_{B|a} \qquad (4)$$

Although Mandler (1980) corroborated this prediction in terms of estimates of his familiarity and retrieval parameters, we have shown elsewhere (Humphreys and Bain, 1983, Appendix A) that in terms of observable variables his model and Humphreys's (1978) are not identifiable, and that both conform to the following:

$$\begin{aligned}
\rho(\text{Rg}AB) = \ &\rho(\text{Rg}A|A)\,\rho(\text{Rg}B|B) \\
&+ [1 - \rho(\text{Rg}A|A)]\rho(\text{Rc}\_B) \\
&+ [1 - \rho(\text{Rg}B|B)]\rho\text{Rc}A\_)
\end{aligned} \qquad (5)$$

The force of Humphreys's and Mandler's demonstrations is that the item recognition and cued recall estimates were obtained separately (i.e. without the opportunity for the other study pair member to influence the test stimulus encoding), and were then combined according to the assumption that the cues operate independently even when they are presented as an intact pair in recognition. There is no room in this formulation for the interactive encoding of study and test pairs.

Although Mandler's (1980) demonstration was concerned with the recognition of intact study pairs, not the individual words in those pairs (and hence its bearing on the relational context effect could be considered problematic) we will show in Experiment 1 that the analogous prediction holds for the relational context effect itself. That is:

$$\rho\text{Rg}B|AB) = \rho\text{Rg}B|B) + [1 - \rho(\text{Rg}B|B)]\rho(\text{Rc}A\_) \qquad (6)$$

Comparison of expressions 3 and 6 will make clear that, although both involve cued recall, they provide different methods for estimating the rightmost component of equation (1), that is for estimating the additional evidence for $B$ that is recovered independently using $A$ as the cue[2]. Collectively, therefore, they provide substantial evidence for the independent cues position.

### Meaning selection

Light and Carter-Sobell (1970) had subjects study noun homographs that were qualified by an adjective and embedded in a sentence context. The nouns were then tested for recognition either in the presence of the study adjective (strawberry jam), with a meaning-preserving adjective (rasberry jam), or with a different meaning adjective (traffic jam). There was a large recognition advantage for targets tested in intact rather than meaning-preserving pairs which in turn produced better performance than the different meaning pairs. Light and Carter-Sobell attributed this pattern of results to the different semantic and phonological features sampled at study and test, an approach that was developed in greater detail by Pellegrino and Salzberg (1975). Other researchers, however, have restricted this proposal to the hypothesis that the meanings selected at study and test determine the relational context effect (Anderson, 1983; Anderson and Bower, 1974; Martin, 1975; Reder *et al.*, 1974). This explanation is said to apply not only to explicit homographs but to all word samples because, it is claimed, no words have context-free meanings (Anderson and Ortony, 1975). Thus meaning selection is said to account for context effects reported with unrelated words (Humphreys, 1976; Thomson, 1972) and pre-experimental associates (Humphreys, 1978; Thomson, 1972; Tulving and Thomson, 1971) as well as with homographs.

There are several lines of evidence against this position. Firstly, the pattern of homographic effects is not consistent. On the one hand, as meaning selection would predict, recognition usually is better with same than with different meaning contexts (Marcel and Steel, 1973; Pellegrino and Salzberg, 1975; Smith *et al.*, 1978). On the other hand, same and neutral contexts produce no reliable differences (Hunt and Ellis, 1974; Underwood and Humphreys, 1979). Moreover, the two conditions that should be equivalent, identical and same meaning contexts, produce large differences (Light, 1972; Light and Carter-Sobell, 1970; Hunt and Ellis, 1974; Marcel and Steele, 1973).

Secondly, because both relational context (Humphreys, 1978) and pair recognition effects (Mandler, 1980) can be estimated from separate measurements of item recognition and cued recall, the meaning selection hypothesis must either provide a mechanism from which such estimations would follow, or treat them as coincidental. The first of these has to cope with the fact that the parameter estimations were based on context-free performances. That is, neither the recognition targets nor the recall cues were jointly presented. Because separate presentation would be expected to lower the probability of selecting the study meanings of both types of test items (with item recognition and cued recall performances suffering correspondingly), it seems unlikely that the relational context advantage could be derived from such performances. Coincidence is an equally unsatisfactory resolution of the issue.

More critical still, however, are some observations made by Humphreys (1976, 1978) as a result of requiring subjects to make recognition judgments about both words of a test pair. Test items were presented in intact (study) pairs, rearranged pairs (two old words from different study pairs), mixed pairs (one old, one new), and new pairs (both new words). The predictions of interest concern the probability of missing both old words in a test pair. According to the meaning selection hypothesis, this probability will be lower for intact than for rearranged pairs, but for the independent cues model no difference is predicted (Humphreys, 1978). Since this difference has been overlooked in recent treatments of the topic (e.g. Anderson, 1983), it will be restated in detail here. The independent cues model for the recognition of items presented in intact pairs is given in Figure 6.2. It will be noted that the relational context effect is represented by paths 2 and 4, and the probability of recognizing neither member of the pair by path 6. This latter probability is given by the product of the probabilities of not recovering evidence for *A* with itself as the cue, and of not recovering evidence for *B* with itself as the cue:

$$[\rho(\overline{RgA}) \cap \rho(\overline{RgB})] | \text{Intact} = (1 - E_{A|a})(1 - E_{B|b}) \tag{7}$$

Clearly, since the test cues operate independently, the probability of missing both old words would not be altered by rearranging items so that *A* and *B* come from different study pairs. However, the relational context effect would be eliminated by such a rearrangement—that is, paths 2 and 4 would reduce to zero.

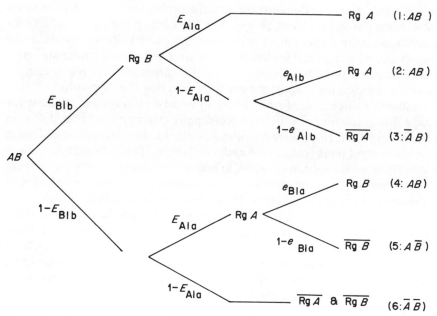

Figure 6.2 The General Independent Cues Model for the recognition of the two items of an intact pair. Evidence probabilities are analogous to those used in Figure 6.1, except that evidence for one word using the other as a cue (e.g. $E_{B|a}$ in the case of *B* being cued by *A*) is conditional on recognition of the cue (with probability $E_{A|a}$ in this example). Thus, $E_{B|a}$ in path 2 of Figure 6.1 corresponds to $(E_{A|a})(E_{B|a})$ in path 4 above, and the analogous relation holds for the recognition of *A* from *B* as the cue (path 2 above).

The meaning selection model for items presented in intact pairs is given in Figure 6.3. According to this model, item *A* (for example) will be recognized if its study meaning is selected and if recognition evidence is recovered for that meaning. The correct meaning of *A* is represented in Figure 6.3 by *A*(b), the probability of its selection by $\alpha$, and the recognition probability for that meaning by $E_{A(b)}$. Note that if an incorrect meaning is selected, $A(\overline{b})$, recognition will fail. The relational context effect is obtained under this model by assuming that the probability of selecting the correct meaning of *A* is greater when it is tested in an intact rather than in a rearranged pair (i.e. $\alpha > a$, where a is the probability of correct meaning selection in a rearranged pair). Given this assumption, the probability of recognizing neither of the old words in a test pair is given in equations (8) and (9):

$$\rho(\overline{RgA}) \cap \rho(\overline{RgB}) | \text{Intact} \quad = \{\alpha(1 - E_{A(b)}) + (1 - \alpha)\}\{\beta(1 - E_{B(a)}) + (1 - \beta)\} \quad (8)$$

$$\rho(\overline{RgA}) \cap \rho(\overline{RgB}) | \text{Rearranged} = \{a(1 - E_{A(b)}) + (1 - a)\}\{b(1 - E_{B(a)}) + (1 - b)\} \quad (9)$$

It is straightforward to demonstrate that the probability of a double miss for intact pairs (equation 8) will be less than the corresponding probability for rearranged pairs (equation 9) whenever the probability of selecting the correct meaning is greater for intact than rearranged pairs (as meaning selection assumes), provided, however, that the probability of recognizing a correctly selected meaning is greater than zero (see the Appendix).

Available evidence confirms the independent cues model, at least for study lists consisting of unrelated word pairs (Humphreys, 1976, 1978). In Humphreys's data there were no differences in the double miss rates of intact and rearranged pairs (columns 3 and 4 of Table 6.1) even though there was a significant relational context effect in both experiments (i.e. the recognition of items presented in intact pairs exceeded item recognition in rearranged pairs—columns 1 and 2 of Table 6.1). It is not known, however, whether this pattern of results would apply without qualification to homographs, fractured words (e.g. amnes-ty, Watkins, 1974), compounds (air-port, Tulving, 1968) and idiomatic phrases (e.g. hot-dog, Horowitz and Manelis, 1972). It also is not known whether different encoding instructions (e.g. interactive imagery) would limit the applicability of the independent cues model, as Begg (1978a, 1983) for example, has implied.

## Configural cue

In the meaning selection model formalized in Figure 6.3 the test words interact to determine their respective encodings, but once encoded they function as separate cues. The configural hypothesis, on the other hand,

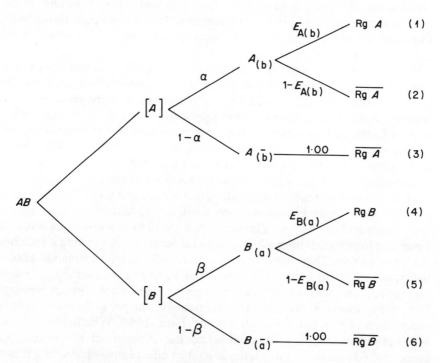

Figure 6.3   The Meaning Selection Model for recognition of the two items of an intact pair. The correct (study) meanings of each word are denoted by $A_{(b)}$ and $B_{(a)}$, and the incorrect meanings by $A_{(\bar{b})}$ and $B_{(\bar{a})}$. The probability of selecting the correct meaning of $A$ is $\alpha$, and of recovering evidence for this meaning is $E_{A(b)}$. The corresponding probabilities for $B$ are $\beta$ and $E_{B(a)}$.

Table 6.1   Summary of recognition data reported by Humphreys (1976, 1978).

| Experiment | p(Hit) | | p(Double miss) | |
|---|---|---|---|---|
| | Intact | Rearranged | Intact | Rearranged |
| Humphreys (1976) Exp 1 ($n$ = 32) | 0.69 | 0.54 | 0.20 | 0.21 |
| Humphreys (1978) Exp 2 ($n$ = 44) | 0.74 | 0.65 | 0.13 | 0.13 |

assumes that the words of a pair interact to form a joint representation. At test, this joint representation becomes the relevant cue. Although this joint cue would suffice in special cases (e.g. in the discrimination of intact from all other test pairs), a more general version of this model would have to assume that the two test words can function separately as well as jointly. That is, when subjects are required to make item judgments they typically do not only recognize both members or neither member of a test pair. Henceforth, therefore, we will assume that both separate and joint cues are part of the configural cue model.

How does such a model fare in relation to available evidence? In general terms it would be able to predict the relational context effect from the fact that an intact joint cue would have a greater probability of accessing a memory trace than would any other joint cue. Also, unlike meaning selection, a configural cue model could accommodate the invariance of the double miss rate described in the previous section with one of two sets of assumptions. It could be assumed, for example, that the greater probability of accessing a joint trace with an intact pair is offset by the greater probability of at least one single match succeeding in a rearranged pair[3]. This of course involves some arbitrary assumptions about the probability of trace access with single and joint cues. Alternatively, it could be assumed that subjects never use joint match information unless at least one of the single matches reaches criterion. This would ensure that the additional information potentially available with intact pairs would not be used if neither single match succeeded. This also is arbitrary, although it is consistent with an assumption of the independent cues model, namely that recall to a cue entails recognition of that cue (Humphreys and Bain, 1983). Whichever of these assumptions is adopted, there remains the problem of accounting for successful estimation of the relational context effect from separate measures of item recognition and cued recall (Humphreys, 1978; Mandler, 1980). It seems that these demonstrations would have to be treated as accidents of the experimental procedures employed, because, as with maning selection, access to a configural trace should occur with an interactively higher probability when all of its components are jointly presented as cues.

It is relatively difficult to evaluate these intuitive ideas about the configural use of cues. However, recent global matching models in which items are combined configurally have clear implications for recognition performance (Humphreys, *et al.*, 1986). One class of these models assumes that memory traces are distributed (aggregated) over elements representing stimulus attributes (Murdock, 1982; Pike, 1984). An association between two items is represented by some multiplicative (configural) combination of corresponding attribute values. When test items are presented in pairs a joint cue may be formed in the same manner as the original associations and then matched to the distributed memory. An alternative class of models (Gillund and Shiffrin, 1984; Hintzman, 1984) assumes that traces are stored independently but are aggregated during the recognition operation. In all these models intact pairs produce the strongest joint match, and thus they are able to predict the relational context effect. However, all global matching models also predict that the joint cue produces a stronger match for rearranged than for mixed test pairs which in turn produce a stronger match than new pairs.[4] Thus these models predict that hit rates will be higher to old words in rearranged than in mixed pairs, and that false alarms will be higher to new words in mixed than in new pairs. The independent cues and meaning selection hypotheses do not predict such hit and false alarm differences[5].

Most studies have not used all of the required test pair types so it is difficult to determine whether the predictions of the global matching models are supported. The one study that did use all pair types (Humphreys, 1976) failed to find the predicted differences. Further evidence is required.

## Summary

The argument so far is best summarized in relation to Experiment 1. In this experiment subjects studied randomly formed word pairs and were then tested for item recognition and cued recall in that order. The study method was varied with instructions. Some subjects rehearsed both words of a pair jointly throughout the presentation interval, whereas others rehearsed the words separately in successive halves of the presentation interval. These methods were known to vary the level of cued recall in favour of the joint condition. The item recognition test consisted of intact, rearranged, mixed and new pairs. It was predicted: (a) that there would be a relational context effect (item recognition greater in intact than in other pairs); (b) that this effect would be greater when the level of cued recall was higher (i.e. in the joint rehearsal condition); (c) that the magnitude of the relational context effect in both instructional conditions would be estimable from item recognition and cued recall, as predicted by the independent cues model (equation 6), but contrary to meaning selection and to intuitive and formal versions of configural cueing; (d) that the double miss rates for intact and rearranged pairs would be equal, consistent with the independent cues model (equation 7), but contrary to meaning selection (equations 8 and 9); and (e) that rearranged and mixed pairs would produce equivalent hit rates, and mixed and new pairs equal false alarm rates, as predicted by the independent cues and meaning selection models, but not by unrestricted versions of distributed models. The remaining predictions for Experiment 1 derived from differences between the two variants of the independent cues model (Humphreys and Bain, 1983; Mandler, 1980), and we turn first to those differences before continuing with Experiment 1.

## Variants of the independent cues model

The Humphreys–Bain (Humphreys, 1978; Bain, 1979) and Mandler (1980) models differ in two key respects. One concerns the nature of the evidence for singly presented items, whereas the other reflects a difference in the relationship between the evidence recovered for an item from itself as the cue and that recovered from its pair member.

Two functionally distinct forms of information are assumed by the Humphreys–Bain model. *Item information* records the occurrence of an item in the study list and thus enables that item to be discriminated from non-list words. This information could consist only of a 'strength' difference between list and non-list items (recency, familiarity), but it may also include contextually descriptive elements. The probability of recovering item information ($I$) can be estimated from the probability of recognizing items presented singly (10a) or in non-intact pairs (10b). That is, in relation to the general form of the model (equation 2):

$$\rho(RgB|B) \quad = I_b = E_{B|b} \tag{10a}$$

$$\rho(RgB|\bar{A}B) = I_b = E_{B|b} \tag{10b}$$

*Relational information* on the other hand records the co-occurence of the two items in a study pair, and this enables intact pairs to be discriminated from rearranged pairs of old words and it also mediates the recall of one pair member given the other as a cue. Provided there are no response production limitations (as there would be in the recall of faces rather than words, for example) the probability of recovering relational information can be estimated from cued recall. An important assumption, however, is that the retrieval of relational information depends on cue recognition but not vice versa (Martin, 1972). Thus the probability of recalling $A$ to $B$, assuming high response availability, is

$$\rho(Rc\underline{\quad}B) = I_bAB_b = E_{A|b} \tag{11}$$

where $I_b$ and $AB_b$ refer respectively to the probabilities of recovering item and relational information to $B$. Since recall occurs on a subset of occasions on which the cue is recognized, recall to that cue does not provide additional evidence for its recognition. However, in conformity with the general model, when $B$ is tested in the presence of its study pair member, additional evidence for the recognition of $B$ may come from the other cue, assuming that that cue can be recognized as a list item. That is, substituting appropriately in equation (1):

$$\rho RgB|AB) = I_b + (1 - I_b) I_aAB_a \tag{12}$$

Different substitutions are required for Mandler's (1980) model. His theoretical constructs are familiarity and retrieval. *Familiarity* is a context-free strength variable that varies directly with presentation frequency and recency. *Retrieval* (in the case of associative learning) refers to the recovery of the holistic *AB* unit, and can be estimated directly from cued recall. Unlike item and relational information in the Humphreys–Bain model, familiarity and retrieval are assumed to be recovered independently. Thus the recognition of an item presented either singly or in a non-intact pair (cf. equation 2 of the general model) is given by:

$$\rho(RgB|\overline{A}B) = F_b + (1 - F_b)R_{ab|b} = E_{B|b} \tag{13}$$

where $F_b$ refers to the probability that *B* is familiar, and $R_{ab|b}$ is the probability of retrieval with *B* as the cue. According to this approach the recognition of an item presented in an intact pair (equation 1) occurs either when the item is familiar or when retrieval of the *AB* unit occurs to either cue. That is,

$$\rho(RgB|AB) = F_b + (1 - F_b)R_{ab} \tag{14}$$

where retrieval to either cue occurs with probability:

$$R_{ab} = R_{ab|a} + R_{ab|b} - (R_{ab|a})(R_{ab|b})$$

Comparison of equations (10) and (13) makes it clear that in contrast to the Humphreys–Bain model, Mandler assumes that recall can assist the recognition of the cue from which recall is elicted. In other words, given two study conditions that produce equal familiarities, recognition should be higher in the condition with the higher probability of recall. Conversely, if the two conditions result in equal recognition performances, then the higher recall condition will be estimated to have lower familiarity, as can be seen by rearranging equation (13) to solve for familiarity:

$$F_b = \frac{\rho(RgB|AB) - R_{ab|b}}{1 - R_{ab|b}} \tag{15}$$

Thus there are empirical circumstances in which familiarity and retrieval will vary inversely, not independently as required by Mandler's model. Of course Mandler's prediction holds at the item level and cannot be evaluated with list averages unless a trade-off in the encoding or the use of familiarity and retrieval can be eliminated. For example, if higher recall is achieved through a study procedure that de-emphasizes item encoding in favour of pair encoding, then it is possible for $F_b$ and $R_{ab|b}$ to be dependent at the list level but independent at the item level.

The remaining objective of Experiment 1 therefore was to examine whether there would be a significant difference in Mandler's $F_b$ across two conditions that differed in recall levels but not in recognition. As noted earlier, encoding (and thereby cued recall) was manipulated with separate and joint rehearsal instructions. These instructions were designed so that the *organization* of rehearsal varied (items versus pairs) rather than the number of rehearsals of each item. The aim was to minimize an encoding trade-off between familiarity and retrieval. The alternative possibility of a different familiarity criterion operating in the two instructional conditions was examined with false alarm rates.

## EXPERIMENT 1

### Method

*Subjects*

The 80 subjects were introductory psychology students fulfilling a course requirement though their participation. They were assigned randomly to conditions in order of arrival, and were tested in groups of 2 to 5.

*Materials*

Four different configurations (sets) of a common word pool were used in this experiment. In each set the recognition list was pivotal: from it five study lists were derived and from each of these study lists two recall lists were generated. In all, there were 20 study lists (4 × 5), four recognition lists, and 40 recall lists (4 × 5 × 2). The word pool comprised 224 nouns having a Thorndike–Lorge frequency of 20 per million or greater and concreteness and imagery ratings of 6 or higher in the Paivio, Yuille and Madigan (1968) or the Friendly, Franklin, Hoffman and Rubin (1982) norms.

Each recognition list consisted of 80 pairs randomly formed from 160 words sampled randomly from the word pool. When considered in relation to its five corresponding study lists, each pair in a recognition test served in all five recognition functions, that is as an intact, rearranged, old-new, new-old, or new-new pair (cf. Humphreys, 1976). This was achieved by randomly partitioning the 80 recognition pairs into 5 sets of 16 and rotating the test functions across the five study lists according to a 5 × 5 latin square.

Each study list also consisted of 80 pairs. Sixteen of these pairs were transferred *intact* from the recognition list. A further 32 study pairs were generated so that the left-hand member of one pair and the right-hand member of another were the corresponding elements of a recognition test pair (which therefore functioned as a *rearranged* pair). Thirty-two additional words were drawn randomly from the pool to enable these study pairs to be formed. The remaining 32 study pairs each drew one item from a recognition pair and one from the pool to result in 16 recognition pairs having an old-new function and 16 with a new-old function (referred to collectively as *mixed* recognition pairs). This exhausted the remaining 32 words in the pool. The left/right position of an item in its recognition pair was retained in its study pairing. Pair presentation order was separately randomized for each list.

For each study list there were two recall lists that differed in the cues used. For one recall list the cues appeared in the recognition list (the 'cue primed' recall list). For the other list the recall targets, not the cues, appeared on the recognition list (the 'target primed' recall list). Each recall list consisted of 48 cues such that intact pairs in the recognition list were not cued in recall. Thus 16 recall cues were drawn from the 32 study pairs corresponding to rear-ranged recognition pairs (with one of the two study pairs being chosen randomly for this purpose), 16 cues were drawn from the 16 study pairs corresponding to the old-new recognition pairs, and the remaining 16 cues were drawn from the 16 study pairs corresponding to the new-old recogni-tion pairs. Again intrapair positions were equated across the cues, and these positions were preserved in the test format—for example recall of the left-hand word of a study pair was always cued as: '____cue word'.

## Design

The between subjects variables were rehearsal instruction (separate vs joint), recall list (cue vs target primed) and materials (four sets). Five subjects (one per study list) were assigned to each of the 16 conditions defined by these between subjects variables. The within subjects variables were the type of pair in the recognition test (analysed as intact, rearranged, mixed and new) and intrapair position (left- or right-hand member).

## Procedure

Each study list was presented as a booklet of four pages on each of which 20 pairs were typed in a well-spaced column. Subjects were instructed to proceed from the top to the bottom of the column keeping place with their finger. A tape recorder presented a low-frequency tone (750 hz) of 0.5 sec. duration at 10 sec. intervals, interspersed every five seconds by a higher (1700 hz) tone also of 0.5 sec. duration. Written instructions were given to all subjects. Subjects in the *separate rehearsal* condition were asked to rehearse the left-hand member of a pair subvocally as often as possible within the first 5 seconds (initiated by a low tone), then to rehearse the right-hand member subvocally as often as possible for the remaining 5 seconds (signalled by the high tone). *Joint rehearsal* subjects were asked to rehearse the two words of a pair subvocally, in left to right order, as often as possible in the 10 seconds allowed. They were instructed to ignore the high tone. An additional 0.5 sec.

was allowed at the completion of each 20 pairs so that subjects could turn the page in readiness for the next rehearsal.

The recognition test immediately followed study. The recognition list was presented in booklet form. There were four pages, 20 pairs to a page arranged in a column. The written instructions were identical for all subjects and gave full information on the different types of pairs in the list. Subjects were instructed that if in their judgment both words of a test pair were old (whether intact or rearranged) they were to circle both words. If instead only one was old they were to circle that word, and if neither was old then neither word should be circled. Nine minutes were allowed for the test, and the experimenter notified each elapsed minute.

Recall immediately followed recognition. The 48 cues and corresponding response blanks were distributed evenly over three pages, each page arranged as a vertical column. All subjects were informed that they had studied the cues given and that they were to recall the missing members of the study pairs. Wild guessing was discouraged. Nine minutes were allowed for the test with elapsed minutes signalled by the experimenter.

**Results**

Two statistical conventions are adopted for this and all subsequent experiments: (a) the alpha level is set at 0.05, two-tailed; (b) error mean squares are reported for an initial $F$ value, and hold for all subsequent $F$ values until explicitly altered.

The mean hit, false alarm, double miss, recall and familiarity ($F_b$) rates are given in Table 6.2 as a function of the main experimental conditions. For the hit and false alarm analyses the full five variable design was used, namely Rehearsal Instruction × Recall Priming × Materials (all between subjects) × Recognition Pair Type × Intrapair Position (both within subjects). Only the first four of these variables were used in the anlysis of double miss rates because intrapair position was not applicable to this pair-based statistic. For the analysis of recall rates and Mandler's familiarity parameter ($F_b$ in equation 15) the data were collapsed over the two within subject variables so that more stable estimates could be obtained. Recall priming (cue versus target occurrence during recognition) was a dummy variable in all recognition analyses. It produced no significant effects either in these analyses or the recall data, and thus will not be considered further.

*Hits*

The pair type main effect for hits was decomposed into two planned comparisons, one examining the relational context effect (intact versus rearranged + mixed pairs), the other examining the difference between the rearranged and mixed pairs. There was a significant relational context effect, $F(1,128) = 39.98$, $MS_e = 0.0221$, and this effect interacted with rehearsal instruction, $F(1,128) = 8.43$. As predicted, the relational context effect was greater for the joint rehearsal condition, although only for three of the four sets of materials, as evidenced by the relevant interaction, $F(3,128) = 3.00$. The difference between rearranged and mixed pairs was not significant, $F(1,128) < 1.0$, nor was this effect qualified either by instructions, $F(1,128) < 1.0$, or by materials, $F(3,128) = 2.05$. The only other significant effect in hit rates was for intrapair position, $F(1,164) = 6.35$, $MS_e = 0.0139$, the left-hand pair members being slightly better recognized (0.65) than right-hand pair members (0.62).

Table 6.2 Mean hit, false alarm, double miss, recall, and familiarity rates in Experiment 1.

| Recognition | Rehearsal instruction | |
|---|---|---|
| Pair type | Separate | Joint |
| *Hits* | | |
| Predicted intact* | 0.67 | 0.72 |
| Intact | 0.66 | 0.73 |
| Rearranged | 0.62 | 0.60 |
| Mixed | 0.61 | 0.60 |
| *False alarms* | | |
| Mixed | 0.12 | 0.10 |
| New | 0.10 | 0.08 |
| *Double misses* | | |
| Intact | 0.21 | 0.18 |
| Rearranged | 0.18 | 0.19 |
| *Cued recall* | | |
| Rearranged + mixed | 0.14 | 0.30 |
| *Familiarity* | | |
| Rearranged + mixed | 0.56 | 0.42 |

* Predicted according to equation 6.

*False alarms*

As inspection of the false alarm data in Table 6.2 suggests, there were no significant main effects for study insructions, $F(1,64) < 1.0$, $MS_e = 0.0463$, or pair type, $F(1,64) = 3.11$, $MS_e = 0.0045$, $p < 0.08$, nor was there a significant interaction between these two variables, $F(1,64) < 1.0$. The only significant effect was the interaction between intrapair position and materials, $F(3,64) = 2.80$, $MS_e = 0.0053$. This reflected the occurrence of more false alarms to the left-hand members of test pairs in one set of materials, and the reverse in another set.

*Double misses*

None of the theoretically critical effects in the double miss rates (Table 6.2) were significant. That is, there were no main effects for rehearsal instructions or pair type (both $F(1,64) < 1.0$, $MS_e = 0.0485$ and $0.0115$ respectively), nor was their interaction significant, $F(1,64) = 1.12$, $MS_e = 0.0115$. In fact only one effect was significant, the three-way interaction between rehearsal instruction, pair type and materials, $F(3,64) = 3.26$. For three of the four sets of materials there either was no difference between intact and rearranged pairs, or a slight tendency for double miss rates to be higher in intact pairs. For the remaining set, however, the intact vs rearranged difference reversed across rehearsal conditions, being 0.24 vs 0.15 for separate rehearsal, but 0.12 vs 0.23 for joint rehearsal. Since this form of interaction did not replicate in later experiments it will not be considered further.

*Cued recall*

As predicted, significantly more words were correctly recalled in the joint rehearsal (0.30) than in the separate rehearsal (0.14) condition, $F(1,64) = 9.87$, $MS_e = 0.0552$. No other effects were significant.

*Familiarity*

There were two significant effects in the familiarity ($F_b$) data. Firstly, as suggested in Table 6.2, mean familiarity was lower in the condition in which recall was higher (joint rehearsal), $F(1,64) = 12.32$, $MS_e = 0.0336$. Secondly, there was a materials main effect, $F(3,64) = 3.39$, reflecting lower values with one of the four sets.

*Predicted intact hits*

Equation (6) was used to estimate the hit rates for intact test pairs according to the general independent cues model. The recognition hit and recall rates for the rearranged and mixed pairs were pooled across materials and intrapair position for this purpose. The resultant estimates, 0.67 for separate rehearsal and 0.72 for joint rehearsal, were very close to the obtained values (0.66 and 0.73 respectively).

**Discussion**

Considered in their entirety the results of this experiment are in most accord with the independent cues model, and favour the Humphreys–Bain over the Mandler version of that model. This can most readily be seen by a process of elimination.

All theories would concur on two basic findings: the occurrence of the relational context effect (hits being greater to intact than to other pairings); and the dependence of this effect on the method of encoding (being better for joint than for separate rehearsal). Thus, although the phenomenon has not always been regarded as robust (e.g. Slamecka, 1975), it is by now well documented and in need of explanation (Humphreys and Bain, 1983).

The explanation that enjoys the greatest favour in the literature, the meaning selection hypothesis, accounts for the relational context effect by assuming that word meanings that are encoded at study are more likely to be re-selected at test when an intact study pair is presented for recognition (Anderson, 1983; Martin, 1975; Reder *et al.*, 1974). A direct prediction of this model is that the double miss rate for intact pairs will be less than for rearranged pairs (equations 8 and 9). This was not observed in the present data, nor was it found in three subsequent experiments (3a, 3b, and 3c). Another result that presents difficulties for meaning selection is the accurate estimation of the intact hit rate from non-intact hits and cued recalls (equation 6). It is difficult to see how meaning selection could account for this result other than by an appeal to coincidence. That is, since meaning selection should not be optimal in either non-intact recognition or in cued recall, the combination of these two conditions in accordance with equation (6) should *under-predict* the relational context effect.

Thus, we infer that the relational context effect cannot be attributed to meaning selection, at least for word pairs randomly formed from relatively concrete nouns. This is not to say that meaning selection is absent in other circumstances. Indeed we show in Experiment 2 that there are conditions in which the independent cues and/or configural cues models have to be supplemented by meaning selection. Nevertheless, in our discussion of that experiment we shall argue that meaning selection is only a minor variant on the fundamental process responsible for the relational context effect.

The results from Experiment 1 also favour independent over configural cueing, although the latter is not ruled out. The general form of the indpendent cues model (equations 1, 4 and 7) not only predicts the occurrence of the relational context effect, but it also accurately estimates its magnitude from item recognition and cued recall. The general model also predicts the constancy of the double miss rate across intact and rearranged pairs, and it predicts that hit and false alarm rates will be uninfluenced by the presence of other words in a test pair, intact pairs excepted. Nevertheless it is possible that the continuous process that is inherent in the configural cue model (the joint match) can mimic the discontinuous process (cued recall) envisaged in the independent cues model. We will discuss this possibility in the introduction to experiments 3a, 3b, and 3c, which provide a more explicit test of the configural cue model.

Assuming for the present that cue independence is the correct interpretation of the present data, there remains the further question of whether the Humphreys–Bain (1983) or the Mandler (1980) version is to be preferred. Essentially the choice hinges on the explanation of the recognition of old items in non-intact pairs. The joint and separate rehearsal conditions were equivalent in their recognition of these items. Is this equivalence attributable to comparable levels of item information generated by the two study conditions (Humphreys–Bain), or is it due to some trade-off between familiarity and retrieval (Mandler)? Again we proceed by a process of elimination.

According to Mandler's model (equation 13), an item in a rearranged or mixed pair is recognized either if it is familiar or if it results in a correct retrieval, these being independent events. If we assume for the moment (as Mandler has done) that the probabilities of these events may be estimated from the relevant list averages, and that the two study conditions produce equivalent levels of familiarity, then recognition accuracy should be higher for the joint rehearsal condition (because of its higher retrieval ability). This was not observed. On the contrary, as already noted there was no difference between the performances of the two conditions, and as a consequence list-based estimates of familiarity and retrieval varied inversely (equation 15). That is, Mandler's familiarity parameter, $F_b$, was significantly lower for the condition in which cued recall was significantly higher. Hence either Mandler's assumption of the independence of familiarity and retrieval at the item level is incorrect, or the retrieval component is inadequately estimated by overt recall, or the dependence of familiarity and retrieval at list level is the result of some list-wide trade-off.

Considering the last of these first, a trade-off could occur during either recognition or study. Humphreys (1976) has suggested, for example, that if there is a high probability of recall subjects may rely heavily on recall as the evidence for their recognition judgments, thereby restricting their use of familiarity to those items that meet a high familiarity criterion. Such a conservative strategy would result in a lower estimated familiarity for the high recall (joint rehearsal) condition despite familiarity and retrieval being independent at the item level. However, our subjects do not appear to have used this strategy. A high familiarity criterion should have resulted in a lowered false alarm rate, yet the joint and separate rehearsal conditions did not differ in their false alarms.

In the absence of any evidence for a criterion shift it appears that either there was a trade-off at the item level between familiarity and retrieval, or that overt recall did not properly estimate the retrieval component of Mandler's (1980) model. Either alternative seriously weakens Mandler's theory. If there was a trade-off at the item level then familiarity must depend on something more than frequency and recency of presentation[6]. This would challenge the link that Mandler has forged between his familiarity construct and performance on item completion tasks (c.f. Graf and Mandler, 1984). If on the other hand overt recall inaccurately estimates retrieval then the successful prediction of the magnitude of the relational context effect (Table 6.2) must be considered a coincidence. Neither of these options seems a compelling or parsimonious way to account for very straightforward effects.

In our view the invariance of item recognition with non-intact pairs is best explained by assuming that item information is comparable for the separate and joint rehearsal conditions[7]. According to the Humphreys–Bain model, if two study conditions are equal in item information then they will be equal in the recognition of items presented singly or in non-intact pairs (equation 10). If recall does occur under these presentation conditions it will be redundant (equation 11), and hence any difference in the probability of recall between the two study conditions will have no effect on item recognition performance, contrary to Mandler's model (equation 13). However, recall can add to the evidence for an item when it is elicited by the *other* study pair member (equation 12). This, of course, is the relational context effect that occurs with the presentation of intact pairs.

We turn next to the boundary conditions for the general independent cues model. Two conditions are examined that, *prima facie*, should increase the influence of meaning selection (Experiment 2) or configural matching (Experiment 3) on item recognition performance.

## EXPERIMENT 2

Our aim in this experiment was to explore a condition in which meaning selection was likely to occur in addition to recall. To this end we substituted interactive and separation imagery instructions for the joint and separate verbal rehearsal instructions used in the first experiment.

The choice of the imagery conditions was prompted partly by the literature and partly by some pilot work following up that literature. Initial studies employing mnemonic imagery (Begg, 1978a; Bower, 1970; Dempster and Rohwer, 1974) reported that there was no difference between interactive and separation imagery in item recognition, whereas interactive imagery produced superior recall. In essence, these were the benchmarks of the joint and separate rehearsal conditions used in Experiment 1, and thus from these initial studies there was little reason to believe that imagery would produce different results from those obtained in Experiment 1 (Humphreys and Bain, 1983). However some more recent experiments suggested otherwise. McGee (1980), for example, reported that although interactive imagery resulted in better pair recognition than separation imagery, the reverse was true for item recognition. Begg (1979) obtained analogous findings. Both researchers interpreted their item recognition data as indicating that access to a joint trace with a single cue (item recognition) is problematic because of variations in the study and test representations of the cue (cf. Begg, 1982, 1983).

In our pilot work we first verified that item recognition was poorer following interactive imagery, then we examined the alternative explanation which assumes that the interactive/separation difference is localized entirely at the *study* stage; that is, that item and relational information trade-off in opposing ways during image formation. This alternative explanation was tested by trying to optimize item encoding in the interactive imagery condition. In our first attempt we modified the interactive instructions so as to stress the importance of forming accurate item images within the combined image. The second attempt involved the use of two study trials. The separation condition formed separate images on both trials, but the interactive condition had one trial (the first or the second) using interactive imagery and the other trial using separation imagery. Again there was emphasis on the formation of accurate item images. Our expectation was that the separation trial in combination with the accuracy emphasis would facilitate item encoding in the interactive group. However, the effects were essentially the same whatever the intervention; interactive imagery produced poorer item recognition but better cued recall. Thus it seemed possible that interactive imagery might violate the assumptions of the independent cues model.

However we were not entirely satisfied with our pilot manipulations, if only because they did not evaluate both joint and separate cues. More convincing demonstrations of cue dependence would show that the double miss rate to intact pairs was lower than to rearranged pairs, contrary to equation (7), and that the relational context effect could not be estimated from the independent cues model (equation 6). Thus Experiment 2 was designed largely as a repetition of Experiment 1 except that imagery instructions were substituted for verbal rehearsal, and pair recognition was assessed as well as cued recall. Given replication of the McGee–Begg findings, and also given that these findings imply cue dependence, the basic predictions were: (a) that interactive imagery would result in poorer item recognition but better cued recall and pair recognition than separation imagery; (b) that there would be a relational context effect that was stronger for the interactive imagery condition; (c) that the double miss rate would be lower to intact than to rearranged pairs; (d) that the relational context effect would not be derivable from the independent cues model; (e) that, assuming meaning selection is the source of cue dependence, the hit rates to items in rearranged and mixed pairs would be equal as would the false alarm rates to items in mixed and new pairs; (f) that, assuming on the contrary that configural cueing is the source of cue dependence, hit rates would be higher to items in rearranged than in mixed pairs and false alarms would be higher to items in mixed than in new pairs (subject to caveats discussed in relation to Experiments, 3a, 3b and 3c).

## Method

### Subjects

There were 80 subjects in the experiment. They were sampled, assigned and tested as in Experiment 1.

### Materials

The item recognition and cued recall (response primed) lists developed for Experiment 1 were used in this experiment, together with a pair recognition test. For each set of materials this test consisted of 32 pairs, 16 being the intact pairs and 16 the rearranged pairs used in the item recognition test. Pairs were assigned randomly to serial position within the list with the constraint that not more than four of a type were permitted to occur consecutively.

### Design

The between subjects variables were rehearsal instruction (separation vs interaction imagery), final test (cued recall vs pair recognition), and materials (one of four sets). Five subjects were assigned to the 16 conditions defined by the cross of these variables. Thus there were 20 subjects in each of the four instruction × final test conditions. Within subjects variables were test pair type and intrapair position.

### Procedure

Study occurred on day 1, and was followed 24 hours later by an item recognition test, which in turn was followed immediately by *either* a cued recall or a pair recognition test. The study procedures were identical to those used in Experiment 1 except that separation and interactive imagery instructions replaced separate and joint rehearsal instructions respectively. Separation instructions required subjects to form two separate images for each study pair. One image (to be formed during the first 5 sec. of study) was to correspond to the left-hand study word, whereas the other image (to be formed during the second 5 sec. period) was to correspond to the right-hand study word. Interactive instructions, on the other hand, stressed the generation of an image in which the interaction of the A and B terms occurred, and the full 10 sec. were to be used for this purpose.

Item recognition and cued recall procedures were identical to those used in Experiment 1, except that 5 rather than 9 minutes were allowed for recall. The pair recognition test consisted of two pages on each of which there were 16 pairs arranged in a column. An instruction sheet informed subjects of the two types of item in the test and requested that they circle just the intact pairs. Five minutes were allowed for the test, with elapsed minutes signalled by the experimenter.

## Results

### Item hits

Item hit rates were analysed within a $2 \times 4 \times 3 \times 2$ ANOVA design representing Rehearsal Instruction × Materials × Pair Type (intact, rearranged, mixed) × Intrapair Position. The main effect for instructions was significant, $F(1,72) = 6.53$, $MS_e = 0.1526$, separation imagery resulting in the higher hit rate (Table 6.3). The pair type main effect was divided into two comparisons, one assessing the relational context effect (intact vs rearranged + mixed pairs, $F(1,144) = 122.13$, $MS_e = 0.0160$), the other examining the difference between rearranged and mixed pairs ($F(1,144) < 1.00$). Pair type interacted with rehearsal instruction. The context effect was greater for the interactive imagery condition, $F(1,144) = 73.89$, but there was no instructional difference in the rearranged/mixed effect, $F(1,144) < 1.00$. The only other significant effect was the interaction of materials with intrapair position, $F(3,72) = 2.79$, $MS_e = 0.0104$. For two lists hits were slightly higher to left-hand pair members whereas for the other two list the reverse applied.

### Item false alarms

A $2 \times 4 \times 2 \times 2$ ANOVA was used to analyse the item false alarm rates. The variables were the same as those in the hits analysis except that test pair type had two levels, mixed and new. The only significant effect was the interaction between materials and intrapair position, $F(3,72) = 3.50$, $MS_e = 0.0057$. In two of the lists there were no left/right-hand differences in false alarms, but in the other two lists there were small but opposing differences.

### Double misses

Double miss rates were analysed with a $2 \times 4 \times 2$ ANOVA (rehearsal instructions × material × pair type). There were significant main effects for rehearsal instructions, $F(1,72) = 6.79$, $MS_e = 0.0459$, and for pair type $F(1,72) = 42.56$, $MS_e = 0.0050$. However these effects interacted, $F(1,72) = 24.81$. The higher double miss rate to rearranged pairs was attributable almost entirely to the interactive imagery condition (Table 6.3). There were no other significant effects.

Table 6.3   Mean hit, false alarm, double miss, recall, familiarity and pair recognition
rates in Experiment 2.

| Recognition | Rehearsal instruction | |
| --- | --- | --- |
| Pair type | Separation | Interaction |
| | Item hits | |
| Intact | 0.71 | 0.76 |
| Rearranged | 0.67 | 0.51 |
| Mixed | 0.68 | 0.52 |
| Observed intact hits* | 0.66 | 0.78 |
| Predicted intact hits** | 0.64 | 0.62 |
| | Item FAs | |
| Mixed | 0.12 | 0.13 |
| New | 0.12 | 0.15 |
| | Double misses | |
| Intact | 0.12 | 0.15 |
| Rearranged | 0.14 | 0.28 |
| | Cued recall | |
| Rearranged + mixed | 0.01 | 0.18 |
| | Familiarity | |
| Rearranged + mixed | 0.63 | 0.44 |
| | Pair recognition | |
| Intact (hits) | 0.38 | 0.73 |
| Rearranged (False alarms) | 0.25 | 0.21 |

  * Data taken from the groups tested for recall.
 ** Predicted from the sum of the last two terms of equation (5)—the first term is omitted because
     of the presence of rearranged pairs.

## Cued recall

The recall data were analysed in terms of two variables, rehearsal instructions and materials (in a 2 × 4 ANOVA). Only the main effect for
instructions was significant, $F(1,32) = 34.39$, $MS_e = 0.0081$. As will be
apparent from Table 6.3, interactive imagery resulted in higher recall than
separation imagery.

## Pair recognition

Pair hits and false alarms were analysed separately with an Instructions × Materials ANOVA. The only significant effect was an instructional
difference in hit rates, $F(1,32) = 28.94$, $MS_e = 0.0423$. Interactive imagery
instructions resulted in a much higher level of pair recognition (0.73) than
separation imagery (0.38).

*Mandler's F*

Mandler's familiarity parameter, $F_b$, was computed for each subject in the recall groups and analysed with a 2 × 4 ANOVA (Instructions × Materials). Rehearsal instruction was the only significant effect, $F(1,32) = 16.18$, $MS_e = 0.0231$, and as Table 6.3 indicates, familiarity was estimated to be higher in the separation imagery condition.

*Predicted intact hits*

Intact hit rates were derived according to equation (6) (the general independent cues model) from the cued recall and item hit rates of recall subjects (hits being pooled across rearranged and mixed pairs). The observed and predicted values for these subjects are given in Table 6.3. It is apparent that equation (6) does not predict the recognition of items in intact pairs if those pairs have been studied with interactive imagery.

**Discussion**

The independent cues model is clearly inadequate for these results. There is a large intact/rearranged difference in the double miss rate, and the separate estimates of item recognition and cued recall underpredict the relational context effect. Our interpretation, however, is not that the independent cues model is wrong but rather that in this instance it has to be supplemented by meaning selection. To sustain this argument we need to consider three issues: (a) why meaning selection would occur with interactive imagery instructions but not with joint rehearsal instructions; (b) why meaning selection is to be preferred over a configural cue interpretation; and (c) why meaning selection is not sufficient to explain the results with interactive imagery. Each of these questions will be considered in turn.

Evidence relevant to the first question is rather sparse and indirect, despite the large literature concerned with the role of imagery in memory processes (e.g. Begg, 1983; Paivio, 1971). Begg (1982) has argued that 'an item could lose identity by being imaged in the context of another item. For example, if *mother* is imaged in interaction with *railroad* the adult female in the image might be so uncharacteristic of mothers that the test item "mother" would fail to contact the appropriate trace, while related test items, such as "woman" might be falsely recognised.' The most direct evidence for this conjecture comes from the recall intrusion data of Anderson and Hidde (1971). They had subjects rate simple sentences either for their image-evoking value or for their pronounceability. Unexpected recall was better following the imagery ratings, but so too was the tendency to make synonym intrusions. Kuiper and Paivio (1977) found with an incidental recognition task that concrete sentences were better recognized than abstract sentences, yet concrete paraphrases were more often misidentified than abstract ones. Humphreys and Yuille (1973) and Yuille (1973) had subjects draw the images that they had used to learn concrete word pairs. Subsequent examination of these drawings (by Humphreys, unpublished) suggested that some of the original items were altered in meaning. Although indirect, all these data are at least consistent with the view that when some form of integrative imagery is involved (either generated by the subject or induced by sentences and phrases), the encoded meanings of target words may be context dependent.

This does not mean, however, that the cue dependence found in Experiment 2 necessarily reflects meaning selection. On the contrary, a configural model could also account for the data. Indeed it could be argued that, although configural cueing is an inappropriate interpretation of joint rehearsal effects, it is paricularly appropriate for the memory traces formed by interactive imagery. We are unable to evaluate this possibility for intuitive configural models (Tulving and Thomson, 1973) because their predictions have not been made explicit. However, the data are contrary to formal configural models. Hit rates for old words in rearranged and mixed pairs did not differ, nor did false alarm rates to new words in mixed and new pairs. The failure to find differences in these rates suggests that the memory traces produced by joint rehearsal and interactive imagery are not accessed in fundamentally different ways. Rather, they would appear to differ in the degree of meaning selection occurring at the time of pair encoding, much as Begg (1982) has speculated. Moreover, since meaning selection would not inevitably result from interactive imagery, this could also account for the absence of meaning selection effects in some imagery studies (Begg, 1982, 1983).

If it is conceded that interactive imagery may induce subjects to select particular meanings of the to-be-learned words, it could also be argued that meaning selection provides a sufficient account of the relational context effect following the use of such imagery. That is, contrary to the independent cues model (equation 1), recall to members of intact pairs need not be posulated if meaning selection will suffice (Figure 6.3). However, this proposal ignores the relational information made available by interactive encoding. Why would subjects abandon recall as an aid to item recognition just because particular meanings of the items have been encoded? Indeed, given that interactive encoding typically produces higher levels of recall than joint rehearsal (e.g. Bower, 1970; Begg, 1983), it seems more rather than less likely that recall would be used. Thus we conclude that meaning selection plays a supplemental not a primary role in the relational context effect, and that its occurrence depends on special circumstances, one of which is the use of interactive imagery encoding. Essentially the same conclusion has been reached by Begg (1983), but with less compelling evidence of cue dependence than that provided by Experiment 2.

## EXPERIMENTS 3A, 3B and 3C

The results from Experiments 1 and 2 pose problems for configural cue models. We doubt that any proponent of these models would have predicted the invariance of the double miss rate across intact and rearranged pairs or the ability to derive recognition in context from separate estimates of single item recognition and cued recall. On the other hand, the model proposed by Murdock (1982) does predict another feature of the data, namely the invariance of the hit and false alarm rates across rearranged, mixed and new pairs. An examination of how Murdock's model predicts this latter invariance also suggests the very particular circumstances in which all global matching models could be modified to predict the entire pattern of findings. We now turn to this reasoning before reporting data that were generated to evaluate it.

Murdock (1982) proposed that the elements comprising the item vectors in his model could be represented as independent identically distributed random variables all having a mean of zero. The result is that the expected joint matching strengths are zero for the configural cues derived from rearranged, mixed and new pairs, and thus the hit and false alarm rates in these pairs are invariant, except perhaps for small effects due to variance and criterion placement differences (Humphreys *et al.*, 1986a). However, there is a major problem with Murdock's assumptions about the elements in his item vectors. These assumptions imply that the average similarity between two words in a list is zero. For this to be true words would be no more similar to each other than they would be to numbers or pictures. We doubt that a viable model could sustain such an assumption.

Using a mathematically tractable model that is very similar to Murdock's, Humphreys *et al.* (1986) have shown that Murdock's assumptions about the vector elements lead to large differences in the variances of the joint matching strengths. That is, the variance of the joint matching strengths for non-intact pairs is considerably less than the variance of the joint matching strengths for intact pairs. Under these conditions the continuously distributed matching process inherent in configural models could mimic the discontinous recall process envisaged in the independent cues model. That is, a subject could set a criterion for the use of a joint match that was well above the expected matching strength for a rearranged pair. In this circumstance the joint match would contribute to the recognition of words in intact pairs, but even if its expectation were non-zero (as most global models predict), it would make only a negligible contribution to the recognition of words in rearranged, mixed and new pairs, producing the invariance in hit and false alarm rates across these pairs.

Such a high joint match criterion would also help to explain the invariance in the double miss rate and the fact that recognition in context can be predicted from separate estimates of single item recognition and cued recall. That is, if the joint match almost never exceeds its criterion unless one of the two separate matches exceeds the separate match criterion, then there is no difference expected in the double miss rates. Similarly, a high criterion for the use of a joint match should mean that there are few occasions on which the joint match exceeds its criterion yet the target is not recallable given the cue. The use of a high criterion for a joint match is thus consistent with the relationships needed to produce the invariance in the double miss rate and the relationship between single item recognition, recall, and recognition in context. Nevertheless, these findings are predictions of the independent cues model but can only be accommodated by global matching models after several arbitrary assumptions are made about the joint and separate match criteria.

In Experiments 3a, 3b, and 3c, we attempted to test a prerequisite to these arbitrary assumptions, namely that if the underlying relational process in recognition uses *continuous* information it should be possible to lower the criterion for the use of that information. In particular, we contrasted item recognition (item bias) instructions with instructions requiring subjects to detect intact pairs as well as items (pair bias). We assumed that the pair bias instructions would induce subjects to use pair information more readily than under an item bias, particularly if they were misled into believing that there were many intact pairs in the recognition list (Experiment 3c).

Assuming that the criterion manipulations would be successful we expected to see higher hit rates in rearranged than in mixed pairs and higher false alarm rates in mixed than in new pairs. We also expected to find a lower double miss rate in intact than in rearranged pairs, but to ensure that this would not be confused with meaning selection, joint rehearsal rather than interactive imagery instructions were used. If none of these predictions were to be confirmed, it would imply that a discrete recall outcome was being used (Jorm and Bain, 1978), thus strengthening the independent cues model of the relational context effect.

## Method

These three experiments were run in close succession, and were identical except for minor changes to the recognition instructions for Experiment 3c. Accordingly this section describes the method adopted in all three experiments, and notes the procedural differences where applicable.

### Subjects

There were 120 subjects in all, 40 in each experiment. They were sampled, assigned and tested as in Experiment 1.

*Materials*

The materials developed for Experiment 1 were used for the three experiments, except the recall tests, which were not used.

*Design*

Within each experiment the between subjects variables were recognition instruction (item vs pair bias) and materials (four sets defined by study list), and five subjects were assigned to each of the 8 conditions defined by the cross of these variables. The within subjects variables were the type of pair in the recognition test (intact, rearranged, mixed and new) and intrapair position (A or B).

*Procedure*

Experiment 1 procedures were used in these experiments except as follows: (a) study was by joint rehearsal only; (b) no recall test was administered; (c) subjects were given one of two biases for their recognition judgments— either to detect old items, or to detect intact pairs as well as old items. In all three experiments, the item bias instructions were identical to the recognition instructions used in Experiment 1. In experiments 3a and 3b, the pair bias instructions required that intact test pairs be circled as *pairs*, in contrast to the old *words* in rearranged and mixed pairs. The same requirement applied in Experiment 3c, but greater emphasis was placed on the detection of intact pairs. This was achieved by misinforming subjects about the proportion of intact pairs in the test (they were told that 'about half' were intact, whereas the true proportion was one-fifth), and by emphasizing the importance of detecting intact pairs.

**Results**

Hit and false alarm rates for items, and the double miss probabilities, are given in Table 6.4, and the pair judgment rates for the pair bias condition are given in Table 6.5. The data were analysed for each experiment separately as well as in a combined analysis in which experiment was a factor. To simplify presentation, the results for the combined analysis are given in detail, and any major departures in the individual experiments noted where applicable.

*Item hits*

Hit rates were analysed within a $3 \times 2 \times 4 \times 3 \times 2$ ANOVA design in which experiment, recognition instructions (item vs pair bias) and materials (one of four sets defined by the study list) were between subjects variables, and test pair type (intact, rearranged, mixed) and intrapair position (A,B) were within subjects variables. As in Experiment 1, the pair type main effect was decomposed into two comparisons, one examining the relational context effect (intact vs rearranged + mixed pairs), the other examining the difference between the rearranged and mixed pairs.

Table 6.4  Mean hit, false alarm and double miss rates in experiments 3a, 3b and 3c.

| Recognition instruction | p(Hit) | | | p(FA) | | p(M&M) | |
|---|---|---|---|---|---|---|---|
| | Intact | Rearr'd | Mixed | Mixed | New | Intact | Rearr'd |
| Experiment 3a | | | | | | | |
| Pair bias | 0.79 | 0.64 | 0.57 | 0.16 | 0.10 | 0.14 | 0.16 |
| Item bias | 0.76 | 0.68 | 0.68 | 0.12 | 0.11 | 0.13 | 0.15 |
| Experiment 3b | | | | | | | |
| Pair bias | 0.81 | 0.66 | 0.63 | 0.12 | 0.10 | 0.14 | 0.14 |
| Item bias | 0.78 | 0.67 | 0.65 | 0.09 | 0.08 | 0.14 | 0.14 |
| Experiment 3c | | | | | | | |
| Pair bias | 0.73 | 0.63 | 0.58 | 0.13 | 0.12 | 0.21 | 0.18 |
| Item bias | 0.77 | 0.62 | 0.61 | 0.11 | 0.10 | 0.14 | 0.17 |
| Pooled data | | | | | | | |
| Pair bias | 0.78 | 0.64 | 0.59 | 0.13 | 0.11 | 0.16 | 0.16 |
| Item bias | 0.77 | 0.66 | 0.65 | 0.11 | 0.10 | 0.14 | 0.15 |

There was a significant relational context effect in the combined analysis, $F(1,192) = 161.45$, $MS_e = 0.0189$, and this effect was slightly larger for the pair bias condition, $F(1,192) = 4.15$. However, only the first of these effects was significant in all experiments; the interaction of relational context with recognition instruction was significant in Experiment 3a only.

The main effect advantage of rearranged over mixed pairs was significant in the combined analysis, $F(1,192) = 5.406$, but not in any of the individual analyses. The rearranged/mixed difference did not interact significantly with recognition instructions in any analysis, including the combined data, $F(1,192) = 1.88$. However, to provide a more lenient test of the global matching predictions, the simple effects also were evaluated. The rearranged advantage was significant for the pair bias condition, $F(1,192) = 6.83$, but not for the item bias condition, $F(1,192) < 1.00$. These effects also occurred in Experiment 3a, but not in the other two studies, although the trends were consistent throughout (cf. Table 6.4).

The only other significant effect in the combined data was a three-way interaction between experiment, recognition instructions and materials,

$F(6,96) = 2.46$, $MS_e = 0.1677$. The pattern was not ordinal—the list effects varied irregularly across instructions and experiments.

## False alarms

False alarms were analysed within a $3 \times 2 \times 4 \times 2 \times 2$ ANOVA design that paralleled the hit rate analysis except for the restriction of pair type to two levels, mixed and new. The pair type main effect was significant in the combined data, $F(1,96) = 6.20$, $MS_e = 0.0074$, reflecting the slightly greater false alarm rate to mixed than to new pairs (Table 6.4). This effect was not significant in any of the separate analyses, however. The interaction of pair type with recognition instructions was not significant in any analysis ($F(1,96) = 1.68$ for the combined data). However, in the combined analysis (though not in the others), the mixed/new simple effect was significant for the pair bias condition, $F(1,96) = 7.16$, but not for the item bias condition, $F(1,96) < 1.00$. No other effects were significant in the false alarm data.

## Double misses

Double miss rates were analysed in a $3 \times 2 \times 4 \times 2$ ANOVA corresponding to Experiment $\times$ Recognition Instruction $\times$ Materials $\times$ Pair Type (intact vs rearranged). The intact/rearranged main effect was not significant in any analysis (in the combined data, $F(1,96) < 1.00$, $MS_e = 0.0086$). Additionally, this effect did not interact with recognition instructions in any analysis ($F(1,96) < 1.00$ in the combined data).

There were two significant effects involving materials in the combined analysis, however. One was the interaction of pair type with materials, $F(3,96) = 4.84$. For two sets of materials there were no intact/rearranged differences at all, but for the other two sets the intact/rearranged differences were antagonistic (0.22 vs 0.18 respectively in one set as against 0.12 vs 0.20 in the other). The other significant effect was a three-way interaction between experiment, recognition instructions and materials, $F(6,96) = 2.32$, $MS_e = 0.0394$. There was no interpretable pattern to this interaction, the materials differences being distributed irregularly across experiments and instructions.

## Pair responses

Subjects in the pair bias conditions were required to circle those pairs that they believed to be intact. These pair responses could be distributed over the four pair types in the recognition test (Table 6.5). This within subjects variable was divided into three comparisons: intact versus rearranged + mixed + new, rearranged vs mixed + new, and mixed versus new. The other two variables, both between subjects, were experiment and materials, resulting in a 3 × 4 × 4 ANOVA.

Table 6.5   Mean pair recognition rates for the pair bias condition in Experiments 3a, 3b and 3c.

|  | Intact | Rearranged | Mixed | New |
|---|---|---|---|---|
| Experiment 3a | 0.67 | 0.08 | 0.03 | 0.01 |
| Experiment 3b | 0.72 | 0.04 | 0.02 | 0.01 |
| Experiment 3c | 0.64 | 0.13 | 0.04 | 0.02 |
| Pooled data | 0.67 | 0.08 | 0.03 | 0.02 |

Two effects were significant in the combined data. The comparison of intact with other pair types confirmed that intact pairs were selected much more frequently than other pairs, $F(1,144) = 1156.27$, $MS_e = 0.0155$. This main effect comparison was significant in all the separate analyses. Rearranged pairs were selected more often than mixed and new pairs in the combined data, $F(1,144) = 9.27$, but this was corroborated only for Experiment 3c in the separate analyses. The mixed versus new difference was not significant in any analysis (for the combined data, $F(1,144) < 1.00$).

## Discussion

The results from Experiments 3a, 3b, and 3c provide some support for configural cue models. There were tendencies: (a) for the relational context effect to be larger with the pair bias instructions; (b) for the hit rate to be larger in rearranged than in mixed pairs; and (c) for the false alarm rate to be larger in mixed than in new pairs. These trends are consistent with global matching models in which the matching strength of the configural cue is greatest for intact pairs, followed by rearranged, mixed and new pairs (Humphreys *et al.*, 1986a). However, there was no evidence that the double miss rate was affected by the pair bias instructions. Had the double miss rate been lower to intact pairs, it would have been convincing evidence that the invariance in Experiment 1 was a coincidence, not a fundamental aspect of the relational context effect. As they stand, the trends are marginal for a configural model because they are weak and incomplete.

The weakness of the trends is of some importance given the power of the analysis and the nature of the pair bias instructions. Bias differences in item hit and false alarm rates only clearly emerged in the combined analysis in which there were 140 subjects. This implies that the role of global matching in item judgments is marginal. This conclusion is reinforced by the nature of the pair bias instructions. In Experiment 3c, in particular, those instructions should have induced subjects to adopt a very lenient criterion for the use of joint match information, because they were led to believe that 50 per cent of the pairs were intact. However, the increase in the number of rearranged pairs circled as intact in that experiment was very small. Clearly there were very few pairs that were of intermediate matching strength.

One explanation for this pattern of results is that decisions about the intactness of pairs are based *primarily* on the output of a discrete recall process (Wolford, 1971), a process that also can assist the recognition of individual words presented in intact pairs (equations 3 and 6). It is possible that, under the extreme conditions created by pair bias instructions, subjects will occasionally use a configural match instread of, or in addition to, recall. An alternative explanation assumes that global matching is the primary basis both of pair judgments and of the relational context effect, but that the continous nature of global matching is masked by a large difference in matching strength variances for intact and non-intact pairs (Humphreys *et al.*, 1986b). Of these two possibilities, the first appears more satisfactory because it explains the data without appeal to arbitrary assumptions about the joint and separate match criteria.

In any event, whether recall or global matching is taken to be the underlying mechanism, each can be subsumed under the concept of relational information (Humphreys, 1976). That is, each mechanism implies that information about the *joint* occurrence of two items can be used to supplement decisions about single items. This general concept is different from the idea that *item* encoding (meaning selection) is context sensitive.

## EXTENSIONS AND FUTURE RESEARCH

In brief, our claim is that with the materials and procedures typically employed to examine the word pair context effect, an explanation cast in terms of relational information is to be preferred over one expressed in terms of meaning selection, and that an independent cues model is to be preferred over a configural cue model. However, the ecological validity of this claim does not extend automatically to materials other than word pairs (generally weak associates or unrelated pairs) nor to learning procedures other than those involving relatively brief study opportunites. Nevertheless our results do permit some generalizations, and our methodology should contribute to an understanding of contextual effects with other materials and procedures.

For example, it may well be the case that meaning selection normally accompanies the storage of relational information. Begg (1982, 1983) argues otherwise, but we no longer have to speculate about this question given the methodology developed for the present research. Thus, we could provide subjects with (Baker and Santa, 1977), or instruct subjects to generate (Begg, 1979, 1983), a phrase or sentence linking the two words in a pair and check to see: (a) whether the relational context effect can be predicted from separate estimates of item recognition and cued recall; (b) whether the double miss rate is equivalent for intact and rearranged pairs; and (c) whether hit and false alarm rates are invariant in the absence of relational context. None of these steps was taken by Begg (1979, 1983) or by Baker and Santa (1977), so it is not known whether their observation that item recognition was hurt following verbally mediated encoding is another instance of meaning selection (as they assume) or an example of configural retrieval.

Even if meaning selection turns out to be more prevalent than previous learning materials and procedures suggest, there nevertheless are important theoretical consequences of the 'standard' relational context effect. Linguistic intuition suggests that the meaning of all words is context sensitive (Anderson and Ortony, 1975) and this intuition has been directly reflected in the basic structural assumptions of some models of human memory (Anderson and Bower, 1974; Anderson 1983). However, when it is ultimately acknowledged that there are associative learning situations in which meanings do not change, these models will have to be altered, perhaps radically.

Although the independent cues model is to be preferred over configural retrieval in the situations that we have considered, we have no doubt that the reverse may occur when a broad range of tasks is considered. A likely candidate for configural retrieval is the recognition of persons in their 'perceptual' context (Beales and Parkin, 1984; Davies, this volume; Thomson, Robertson and Vogt, 1982). Unlike all other context manipulations, perceptual context has large effects, suggesting that it is tapping a different phenomenon. We anticipate that it will not be possible to estimate the magnitude of the perceptual context effect from separate estimates of cued recall and recognition. Of course, one reason for this failure could be the inability to measure covert recall (of persons and faces) with overt recall techniques, in which case the independent cues model need not be incorrect. It is imperative therefore that the double miss rates for intact and rearranged person-context pairs be obtained in such studies, together with the hit and false alarm rates in non-intact pairs.

Lastly, we need to discuss our level of theoretical discourse—that is, our emphasis on the cues employed and the information made available by those cues. We have argued at length elsewhere (Humphreys and Bain, 1983) that both cues and information are necessary to understand the basic memory phenomena, and our view is largely supported by Begg (1982, 1983) and by Hunt (e.g. Hunt and Seta, 1984). It has been our experience, however, that when we present these ideas at seminars and conferences, one of two reactions occurs. Either the item/relational distinction is thought to be so obvious that it hardly needs mentioning, or the distinction is regarded as not constituting a proper theory. We address each of these in turn.

To us the item/relational distinction *is* obvious, but it is not salient to all. For example, the Estes and Da Polito (1967) study of the effects of incidental and intentional learning on recognition and recall has been cited by Kintsch (1970), Mandler (1980) and others as supporting their *item* recognition theories. However, it was a *pair* recognition study and thus essentially irrelevant to those theories. Analogously, most studies of the relational context effect have ignored the possibility that the reinstatement of context may add information to the normal process, concentrating instead on the hypothesis that the removal of context subtracts information from the normal process. One consequence is that neutral conditions in which context is neither added nor deleted have frequently been omitted (Underwood and Humphreys, 1979). Another consequence is that relational information is often ignored in theoretical accounts of the relational context effect. We have demonstrated that this is a substantial oversight.

Is a cue and information theory a 'proper' theory? When our critics answer 'no' to this question they typically entreat us to state the memory structure and/or the encoding and retrieval processes that mediate the item/relational distinction. Our rejoinder is that structure and process models can provide specific metaphors for the item/relational distinction but cannot replace it. Whether we think in terms of separate and joint traces (Begg, 1982, 1983), tagged items vs tagged associations (Anderson and Bower, 1972), distributed context-to-item vs interim associations (Humphreys *et al.*, 1986a) or differences in conversion operations (Tulving, 1983) is a matter of preference which, at this time, is largely independent of our methodology and data (Roediger, 1980; Watkins, 1981).

On the other hand, the item/relational distinction first introduced by Humphreys (1976) serves to summarize a large amount of data and leads to new predictions. Begg (1978b) for example has shown that whether a study emphasis on item or relational encoding is helpful to cued recall depends on whether the materials are already related—associated items benefit more from item encoding whereas unassociated items benefit more from relational encoding. Hunt and his colleagues (Einstein and Hunt, 1980; Hunt and Einstein, 1981; Hunt and Seta, 1984) have extended these results, showing in essence that organizational theories of free recall (e.g. Mandler, 1970) are inadequate because they ignore the learning of individual words, and reciprocally that the depth of processing approach (Craik and Lockhart, 1972) is insufficient because it ignores relational learning. Bain (1979) has demonstrated that final recognition and recall performances are dependent on the interaction of study encoding (item vs relational) and the intervening occurrence of different memory tests (plausibly differing in their call upon item and relational information). None of these results requires a specific structure or process model for its interpretation, but the communality of the studies is greatly aided by the item/relational distinction.

The primary disadvantage of our approach vis-à-vis explicit structure and process models is that it is not as easy to grasp and manipulate intuitively. That is, a structural difference (such as separate and joint traces), or a process difference (in conversion operations) seems to be easier to conceptualize than a cue-information relationship. On the other hand, the distinct advantage of the information level of discourse is that it is not as susceptible to changing preferences in memory metaphors. In short it is much closer to a functional analysis of the memory domain (Watkins, 1981).

## APPENDIX

Proof that under the meaning selection hypothesis (Figure 6.3 in the text) the probability of missing both words in a pair is less for intact that for rearranged pairs whenever the probability of selecting the correct meaning is greater for intact than for rearranged pairs and the probability of recognizing a correctly selected meaning is greater than zero.

Assume: $\rho(\overline{RgA}) \cap (\overline{RgB})|\text{Intact} < \rho(\overline{RgA}) \cap \rho(\overline{RgB})|\text{Rearranged}$

Then from equations (8) and (9) in the text, and using the expressions for item $A$ as the general case for items $A$ and $B$:

$$[\alpha(1 - E_{A(b)}) + (1 - \alpha)]^2 < [a(1 - E_{A(b)}) + (1 - a)]^2 \qquad \text{(i)}$$

(a)  Assume $E_{A(b)} = 1$, then

$$(1 - \alpha)^2 < (1 - a)^2$$

which holds whenever $\alpha < a$.

(b)  Alternatively, assume $E_{A(b)} < 1$. Rearranging, factoring and simplifying the inequality in (i) results in:

$$[(1 - E_{A(b)})(\alpha - a)]^2 < (\alpha - a)^2 \qquad \text{(ii)}$$

This inequality will hold if and only if $\alpha > a$ and $E_{A(b)} > 0$, the two conditions to be proved.

## AUTHOR NOTE

This research was supported by grants from the Australian Research Grants Scheme (A28115223 and A28315560) and from the University of Queensland. Some of the data were reported at the Australian Experimental Psychology Conference in Hobart, May 1983, and at the Conference of the Midwestern Psychological Association in Chicago, May 1985.

# REFERENCES

Anderson, J.R. (1983). A spreading activation theory of memory. *Journal of Verbal Learning and Verbal Behavior*, **22**, 261–295.

Anderson, J.R. and Bower, G.H. (1972). Recognition and retrieval processes in free recall. *Psychological Review*, **79**, 97–123.

Anderson, J.R. and Bower, G.H. (1974). A propositional theory of recognition memory. *Memory and Cognition*, **2**, 406–412.

Anderson, R.C. and Hidde, J.L. (1971). Imagery and sentence learning. *Journal of Educational Psychology*, **62**, 526–530.

Anderson, R.C. and Ortony, A. (1975). On putting apples into bottles: a problem of polysemy. *Cognitive Psychology*, **7**, 167–180.

Bain, J.D. (1979). Item and relational information in recognition and recall. Unpublished Doctoral Thesis, University of Queensland.

Bain, J.D., Humphreys, M.S., Tehan, G. and Pike, R. (1986). Is context involved in episodic recognition? Unpublished manuscript, University of Queensland.

Baker, L. and Santa, J.L. (1977). Semantic integration and context. *Memory and Cognition*, **5**, 151–154.

Beales, S.A. and Parkin, A.J. (1984). Context and facial memory: the influence of different processing strategies. *Human Learning*, **3**, 257–264.

Begg, I. (1978a). Imagery and organization in memory: instructional effects. *Memory and Cognition*, **6**, 174–183.

Begg, I. (1978b). Similarity and contrast in memory for relations. *Memory and Cognition*, **6**, 509–517.

Begg, I. (1979). Trace loss and the recognition failure of unrecalled words. *Memory and Cognition*, **7**, 113–123.

Begg, I. (1982). Imagery, organization and discriminative processes. *Canadian Journal of Psychology*, **36**, 273–290.

Begg, I. (1983). Imagery instructions and the organization of memory. In J.C. Yuille (Ed), *Imagery Memory and Cognition*, Hillsdale NJ: Erlbaum, pp. 91–115.

Bower, G.H. (1970). Imagery as a relational organizer in associative learning. *Journal of Verbal Learning and Verbal Behavior*, **9**, 529–533.

Bower, G.H. (1981). Mood and memory. *American Psychologist*, **36**, 129–148.

Bower, G.H. and Mayer, J.D. (1985). Failure to replicate mood-dependent retrieval. *Bulletin of the Psychonomic Society*, **23**, 39–42.

Craik, F.I.M. and Lockhart, R.S. (1972). Levels of processing: a framework for memory research. *Journal of Verbal Learning and Verbal Behavior*, **11**, 671–684.

Dempster, R.N. and Rohwer, W.D. (1974). Component analysis of the elaborative encoding effect in paired-associate learning. *Journal of Experimental Psychology*, **103**, 400–408.

Einstein, G.O. and Hunt, R.R. (1980). Additive effects of individual item and relational processing. *Journal of Experimental Psychology: Human Learning and Memory*, **6**, 588–598.

Estes, W.K. and Da Polito, F. (1967). Independent variation of information storage and retrieval processes in paired-associate learning. *Journal of Experimental Psychology*, **75**, 18–26.

Fernandez, A. and Glenberg, A.M. (1985). Changing environmental context does not reliably affect memory. *Memory and Cognition*, **13**, 333–345.

Flexser, A.V. and Tulving, E. (1978). Retrieval independence in recognition and recall. *Psychological Review*, **85**, 153–171.

Friendly, M., Franklin, P.E., Hoffman, D. and Rubin, D.C. (1982). The Toronto word pool: norms for imagery, concreteness, orthographic variables, and grammatical usage for 1080 words. *Behavior Research Methods and Instrumentation*, **14**, 375–399.

Geiselman, R.E. and Bjork, R.A. (1980). Primary versus secondary rehearsal in imagined voices: differential effects on recognition. *Cognitive Psychology*, **12**, 188–205.

Graf, P. and Mandler, G. (1984). Activation makes words more accessible but not necessarily more retrievable. *Journal of Verbal Learning and Verbal Behavior*, **23**, 553–568.

Gillund, G. and Shiffrin, R.M. (1984). A retrieval model for both recognition and recall. *Psychological Review*, **91**, 1–67.

Hintzman, D.L. (1984). Minerva 2: a simulation of human memory. *Behavior Research Methods, Instrumentation and Computers*, **26**, 96–101.

Horowitz, L.M. and Manelis, L. (1972). Toward a theory of redintegrative memory. In G.H. Bower (Ed), *The Psychology of Learning and Motivation*, vol. 6, New York: Academic Press, pp. 193–224.

Humphreys, M.S. (1976). Relational information and the context effect in recognition memory. *Memory and Cognition*, **4**, 221–232.

Humphreys, M.S. (1978). Item and relational information: a case for context independent retrieval. *Journal of Verbal Learning and Verbal Behavior*, **17**, 175–188.

Humphreys, M.S. and Bain, J.D. (1983). Recognition memory: a cue and information analysis. *Memory and Cognition*, **11**, 583–600.

Humphreys, M.S., Bain, J.D. and Pike, R. (1986a). Different ways to cue a unitary memory system: a theory for episodic, semantic and procedural tasks. Manuscript submitted for publication.

Humphreys, M.S., Pike, R., Bain, J.D. and Tehan, G. (1986b). Global matching: a comparison of the SAM, Minerva and Matrix models. Manuscript under revision.

Humphreys, M.S. and Yuille, J.C. (1973). Errors as a function of noun concreteness. *Canadian Journal of Psychology*, **27**, 83–94.

Hunt, R.R. and Einstein, G.O. (1981). Relational and item-specific information in memory. *Journal of Verbal Learning and Verbal Behavior*, **20**, 497–514.

Hunt, R.R. and Ellis, H.C. (1974). Recognition memory and degree of semantic contextual change. *Journal of Experimental Psychology*, **103**, 1153–1159.

Hunt, R.R. and Seta, C.E. (1984). Category size effects in recall: the roles of relational and individual item information. *Journal of Experimental Psychology: Human Learning and Memory*, **10**, 454–464.

Jorm, A.F. and Bain, J.D. (1978). Fine-state recall revealed by backward learning curves constructed from confidence ratings. *Memory and Cognition*, **6**, 259–265.

Kintsch, W. (1970). Models of free recall and recognition. In D.A. Norman (Ed), *Models of Human Memory*, New York: Academic Press, pp. 331–373.

Kirsner, K. (1973). An analysis of the visual component in recognition memory for verbal stimuli. *Memory and Cognition*, **1**, 449–453.

Kuiper, N.A. and Paivio, A. (1977). Incidental recognition memory for concrete and abstract sentences equated for comprehensibility. *Bulletin of the Psychonomic Society*, **9**, 247–249.

Light, L.L. (1972). Homonyms and synonyms as retrieval cues. *Journal of Experimental Psychology*, **96**, 255–262.

Light, L.L. and Carter-Sobell, L. (1970). Effects of changed semantic context on recognition memory. *Journal of Verbal Learning and Verbal Behavior*, **9**, 1–11.

Mandler, G. (1970). Words, lists, and categories: an experimental view of organized memory. In J.L. Cowan (Ed), *Studies in Thought and Language*, Tucson: University of Arizona Press, pp. 99–131.

Mandler, G. (1980). Recognizing: the judgment of previous occurrence. *Psychological Review*, **87**, 252–271.

Marcel, A.J. and Steel, R.G. (1973). Semantic cueing in recognition and recall. *Quarterly Journal of Experimental Psychology*, **25**, 368–377.

Martin, E. (1972). Stimulus encoding in learning and transfer. In A.W. Melton and E. Martin (Eds), *Coding Processes in Human Memory*, Washington DC: Wiley, pp. 59–84.

Martin, E. (1975). Generation-recognition theory and the encoding specificity principle. *Psychological Review*, **82**, 150–153.

McGee, R. (1980). Imagery and recognition memory: the effects of relational organization. *Memory and Cognition*, **8**, 394–399.

Murdock, B.B. (1982). A theory for the storage and retrieval of item and associative information. *Psychological Review*, **89**, 609–626.

Paivio, A. (1971). *Imagery and Verbal Processes*, New York: Holt, Rinehart & Winston.

Paivio, A., Yuille, J.C. and Madigan, S.A. (1968). Concreteness, imagery and meaningfulness values for 925 nouns. *Journal of Experimental Psychology, Monograph Supplement*, **76**, (1,pt2).

Pellegrino, J.W. and Salzberg, P.M. (1975). Encoding specificity in cued recall and context recognition. *Journal of Experimental Psychology: Human Learning and Memory*, **1**, 261–270.

Pike, R. (1984). A comparison of convolution and matrix distributed memory systems. *Psychological Review*, **91**, 281–294.

Reder, L.M., Anderson, J.R. and Bjork, R.A. (1974). A semantic interpretation of encoding specificity. *Journal of Experimental Psychology*, **102**, 648–656.

Roediger, H.L. III (1980). Memory metaphors in cognitive psychology. *Memory and Cognition*, **8**, 231–246.

Slamecka, N.J. (1975). Intralist cueing of recognition. *Journal of Verbal Learning and Verbal Behavior*, **14**, 630–637.

Smith, S.M. (1985). Environmental context and recognition memory reconsidered. *Bulletin of the Psychonomic Society*, **23**, 173–176.

Smith, S.M., Glenberg, A. and Bjork, R.A. (1978). Environmental context and human memory. *Memory and Cognition*, **6**, 342–353.

Thomson, D.M. (1972). Context effects in recognition memory. *Journal of Verbal Learning and Verbal Behavior*, **11**, 497–511.

Thomson, D.M., Robertson, S.L. and Vogt, R. (1982). Person recognition: the effect of context. *Human Learning*, **1**, 137–154.

Tulving, E. (1968). When is recall higher than recognition? *Psychonomic Science*, **10**, 53–54.

Tulving, E. (1972). Episodic and semantic memory. In E. Tulving and W. Donaldson (Eds), New York: Adademic Press, pp. 381–403.

Tulving, E. (1983). *Elements of Episodic Memory*, New York: Oxford University Press.

Tulving, E. (1985). How many memory systems are there? *American Psychologist*, **40**, 385–398.

Tulving, E. and Thomson, D.M. (1973). Encoding specificity and retrieval processes in episodic memory. *Psychological Review*, **80**, 352–373.

Tulving, E. and Thomson, D.M. (1971). Retrieval processes in recognition memory: effects of associative context. *Journal of Experimental Psychology*, **87**, 175–184.

Underwood, B.J. and Humphreys, M.S. (1979). Context change and the role of meaning in word recognition. *American Journal of Psychology*, **92**, 577–609.

Watkins, M.J. (1974). When is recall spectacularly higher than recognition? *Journal of Experimental Psychology*, **102**, 161–163.

Watkins, M.J. (1981). Human memory and the information processing metaphor. *Cognition*, **10**, 331–336.

Wolford, G. (1971). Function of distinct associations for paired-associate performance. *Psychological Review*, **78**, 303–313.

Yuille, J.C. (1973). A detailed examination of mediation in PA learning. *Memory and Cognition*, **1**, 333–342.

## NOTES

1. A notable exception is the class of 'perceptual' contexts (setting, clothing, activity, demeanour) that has been varied in person recognition studies (Beales and Parkin, 1984; Davies, this volume; Thomson, Robertson and Vogt, 1982). Some implications of this form of context are considered later in the chapter.

2. As we have noted elsewhere (Humphreys and Bain, 1983), the estimation procedures used by Mandler (1980) and adopted in this paper assume that the two trace access processes initiated by the target and its relational cue not only occur independently of the presence or absence of the other cue, but also occur independently of the success or failure of the other process. It is now well established that this is approximately so (Flexser and Tulving, 1978; Tulving and Wiseman, 1975).

3. This possibility was suggested by Art Flexser when reviewing an earlier paper (Humphreys and Bain, 1983).

4. As we discuss in relation to Experiments 3a, 3b, and 3c it is possible to have some of these models mimic the general independent cues model given certain arbitrary restrictions. Thus some global matching models can accommodate the prediction given in equation (6), unlike the intuitive configural models considered above.

5. The independent cues model assumes that the trace access processes initiated by presented cues occur independently, hence hit rates should not vary across rearranged and mixed pairs, nor should false alarms vary across mixed and new pairs. For the meaning selection hypothesis we have assumed a constant average reduction in the probability of accessing the study meaning of a target when it is tested in the presence of some word or other than its study pair member. Although this may not be correct with some special materials, it seems reasonable for unrelated word pairs and weak associates.

6. Mandler's (1980) assumption that familiarity depends only on frequency and recency of presentation could be preserved if there was a difference in the number of item rehearsals encouraged by the two study conditions. To check this we conducted a small experiment in which subjects in two study conditions ($n = 10$) were required to rehearse aloud. Rehearsals were recorded on audio tape and subsequently counted. Although the basic findings of Experiment 1 were replicated, there was no significant difference in rehearsal rate between the two conditions (the mean number of rehearsals per study pair was 8.59 for the joint rehearsal condition, and 7.95 for separate rehearsal—$F(1, 16) < 1.0$, $MS_e = 5.71$).

7. We do not assume that item information will always be equally encoded across all study conditions; the levels of processing literature clearly indicate otherwise. Rather, we assume that intentional learning instructions like those for separate and joint rehearsal typically create equivalent levels of item information even though they may result in marked differences in relational encoding.

Memory in Context : Context in Memory
Edited by G.M. Davies and D.M. Thomson
© 1988 John Wiley & Sons Ltd.

CHAPTER 7

# Language Context and Context Language

GUY TIBERGHIEN

*University of Grenoble*

## ABSTRACT

This review presents experimental and theoretical research on contextual effects in language understanding. A taxonomy of linguistic context
effects is suggested: (a) lexical context effects between and within sentences
(reference processes); (b) lexico-semantic effects of context (sentence-word
and word-sentence relations); (c) semantic context effects within sentences;
(d) inference and logical context; (e) thematic context, background and foreground information; (f) syntactical context effects.

In a second section, contextualist theories of linguistic comprehension
are critically examined: (a) activation theories; (b) reference theories; (c)
coherence theories.

In conclusion it is claimed that language is a fundamentally context-
dependent activity the dynamics of which is a prerequisite for any general
theory of language.

Over the last ten years the theoretical importance of the concept of
context has been steadily increasing. This fact can be attributed to the
need to account for the remarkable plasticity of human psychological
activity. Indeed, one of the most striking properties of the central nervous
system is its capacity for permanent adaptation to unique situations and to
the most subtle fluctuations of the environment. Any psychological theory
which aims at attaining a minimum of general relevance needs to offer an
explanation for the origin and the properties of this astonishing capacity
to modulate the processing of perceptual information and the resulting
behavior in accordance with apparently minor but psychologically crucial
modifications in situations encountered. In other words, psychology must
be in a position to explain how it comes about that a given aspect of a situation acquires the status of relevant information for a particular individual at
a particular time. Or, to put it differently, cognitive psychology is perforce

an ecological or, as Jenkins advocated as early as 1975, a contextualist psychology. It is probably not possible to conceive the complexity of psychological activities on the sole basis of an immutable abstract system of representations and transsituational fundamental units. The interpretation of such representation units and their relationship at any particular level is necessarily dependent on contextual factors intervening at other reality levels (Jenkins, 1980; Hoffman and Nead, 1983; Hoffman, 1986; McGuire, 1983; Tiberghien, 1986a). The recent history of programs of research and development in the field of automatic translation and more generally of artificial intelligence has moreover amply proved the strategic importance of the processing of contextual information in 'artificial' systems for the representation and manipulation of linguistic information (Bierschenk, 1982; Charniak, 1983; Nagao, 1983; Tiberghien, 1986a).

Thus psychological description of linguistic context effects does not call for another frame of reference. It is certain that context effects which occur in the understanding of discourse (written or oral) and in its production are doubtless very complex. The comprehension of a sentence, even a simple one, is the outcome of the complex integration of external or internal situational context information (pragmatics has very rightly drawn attention to this dimension of the process) of referential context information available in immediate memory and inferential context information activated in long-term memory. Nonetheless linguistic context effects do have a property which gives them relative specificity. Indeed, in many sensory, perceptual or memory situations it is always relatively easy to make an operational distinction between focal stimulus and contextual information. This operation is much more complex in the process of understanding or production of discourse by reason of the importance of temporal relations which characterize it. Indeed in this case, the various elements which make up the sentence, whether read or heard, are each in turn, and successively, focal information and contextual from an unceasing back and forth movement between representational and perceptual levels on one hand and between the levels of focal and contextual information on the other. The result is a puzzle of extraordinary complexity precisely because of the permanent transformation of the bundles of interactions already defined.

As a first approximation linguistic context can be defined as the whole set of active representations in working or long-term memory; this representational context interacts with perceptually available information currently undergoing processing. In other terms, the comprehension of discourse results from this complex dynamic integration between perceptual and representational data. This general schema gives specificity to that suggested by Clark and Carlson (1981, p.318) in their definition of linguistic context. For them the context is information available to a given individual which comes into interaction with a specific process at a specific time. This point of view concurs with that of Townsend and Bever (1982, p.701) when they define context effects as analysis of discursive information generating a complete unit at a given level of representation and specifying its relation to units on other levels. But what are these different levels? Five levels of occurrence of linguistic effects can be distinguished: the phonemic and graphic level, the syntactic, the lexical, the semantic and the pragmatic. These levels are obviously not independent and there is no doubt a 'constructivist' conception is necessary here (Frederiksen, 1975a,b). This means that context effects occurring at certain levels may be affected by focal or contextual information from another level. The processing of certain phonemes (or their production) may thus be modified by their phonemic environment but also by semantic processing of a high level. Similarly it is difficult to separate semantic and syntactic determinants in negation effects (Wason, 1965) or the effect of passive or active voice in a sentence. It is also obvious that lexical context effects, which have received a great deal of attention in recent years, are probably largely modified when lexical units are no longer studied in isolation but are inserted into sentences. Interactions between semantic and pragmatic context are also obvious in sentence interpretation and in integration between and within sentences. If the referential or inferential processing of semantic propositions of discourse is influenced by memory representation of immediately prior propositions (Bransford and Johnson, 1972; Bransford, McCarrell and Nitsch, 1976) it is also influenced by long-term representations of time, place, speaker and of social relationships of which he or she is a part (Lakoff, 1972).

The global importance of context effects in the understanding of discursive propositions needs no further proof. It is today widely recognized and clearly intervenes on several levels of the process of linguistic communication (Winograd, 1978; Sanford and Garrod, 1982). In this review of the question we will restrict ourselves mainly to the study of semantic and semantico-pragmatic context effects in the comprehension of sentences. We will only incidentally refer to phonemic, lexical and syntactic context effects. Though it is true that 'in the beginning is the word' (Carr, 1981) we will nonetheless leave aside here the study of the contextual effects of inhibition and facilitation an isolated word can have on perception, categorization or comprehension of another isolated word. Research on the 'priming' effect and lexical decision has been largely covered elsewhere (see for example Pynte, 1984). Instead, I will give a good deal of space to possible semantic effects of a word on perception and understanding of a simple sentence, to semantic effects of a sentence on the understanding of a word and finally to semantic effects of one sentence on the understanding of another. In other words, lexical items are of concern only to the extent that they are parts of sentences or capable of modifying the perception and comprehension of sentence. I shall present a tentative taxonomy of the different context effects occurring within the specific linguistic procedures of reference, inference and thematization. This classification should make it possible to evaluate the relevance of the main contextualist theories of understanding based on the notion of spreading semantic activation, on psychological reference mechanisms or on the concept of coherence. An analysis of this sort should make it possible to pinpoint the crucial contextual factors which have to be controlled in order to enhance the cohesion of utterances, their coherence and their comprehensibility in an optimized process of linguistic communication.

## TOWARDS A TAXONOMY OF LINGUISTIC CONTEXT EFFECTS

Depending on choice of criteria, various classifications of linguistic context effects are possible. Generally speaking, it can be said there is a linguistic context effect when a piece of linguistic information occurring at a particular moment in discourse influences the understanding and integration of another later element of information. The first can then be called contextual and the second target or focal information. Context and target may of course be isolated words as in classic experiments in lexical decision. The context can also be a more or less complex sentence and the target a simple lexical unit as in the case of sentence completion situations. Conversely the context may be an isolated word and the target a sentence of more or less elaborated text (termed a 'title' effect). The context word and the target word can be in separate clauses or sentences as in the case of anaphoric reference situations. (Anaphor is a syntactic device: a word (or a group of words) refers to another word (or group of words) for which it is a substitute. For instance, indefinite or definite articles and pronouns are anaphors.) Finally the most complex form of contextualization, but also the closest to natural understanding activities, is that where semantic or conceptual representations of sentences or clauses constitute both context and target (clausal integration). We will examine in turn these different classes of situation, the nature of the resulting context effects and the theoretical problems raised by the latter.

### Lexical context effects between and within sentences

The study of the facilitation or inhibition effects in the understanding of a word when it is preceded by another is not entirely satisfactory. Though the computation of meaning begins with lexical items, these latter have no linguistic reality if they are not part of interconnected sentences. There are, however, intermediate situations where several isolated lexical items may serve as context for another item. In early but classical research work, Howes and Osgood (1954) presented their subjects with three context words and asked them to add an associated lexical item to the sequence. The probability of a given associative response showed a linear increase according to the number of contextual words normatively associated with a given lexical item. In other words the probability of an associative response depended on the semantic density of the foregoing lexical context.

Nevertheless, as a final aim is relevant theoretical representation of the process of understanding, we cannot afford to ignore context effects within sentences. The most favoured ground for the study of these is undoubtedly that of definite reference. The reference mechanism can make use of various lexical items of different syntactical status-demonstrative, definite article or personal pronoun. But in all cases, a particular lexical item either prefigures or refers back to another item of which it is either a substitute or a prefiguration.

Definite reference can obviously be either direct or indirect. Reference is direct when the same word, the same lexical item, appears more than once in the same discourse. Reference is indirect when computation is required in order to decide just which earlier lexical item is referred to. Indirect reference can moreover be achieved simply by characterization or generalization. Here we must make a distinction between reference and inference in the strict sense. In the reference process all or part of the preceding piece of information is included in the referent whereas inference requires a computation of meaning which includes information not carried directly by the sentence because it requires either logical derivation or empirical, that is to say pragmatic, reconstruction.

The greater or lesser degree of facility with which a definite reference is interpreted depends on three main classes of factors: syntactical factors, semantic and relational factors and spatio-temporal factors. The first class is given by the syntactical status of the lexical elements involved in the reference situation. Thus Clark (1978) compared understanding of anaphoric and pronominal references. He noted little difference between comprehension times of critical sentences which included a noun or a pronoun referring to an entity previously encountered in the discourse. Using a different procedure of sentence completion, Chapman and Stockes (1980) noted that an anaphor deleted from a text is more likely to be guessed than a pronoun. In any case it is markedly easier to find a missing reference to complete a text than a missing conjunction. It was noted moreover that linguistic reference operations are already remarkably efficient at age 8 and improve to age 14. Furthermore, the difference in efficiency between pronominal and anaphoric reference decreases with age. In a more recent experiment, Garrod and Sanford (1981) compared reading times for sentences containing an anaphor of which the indirect referent is a noun ('car... vehicle') or a verb ('drive... vehicle'). It appeared that reading time is significantly longer in the second case (1404 ms.) than in the first (1339 ms.). Finally Haviland and Clark (1974, experiments 2 and 3) noted that the speed of comprehension for sentences containing an anaphoric reference is modified by the nature of the articles accompanying the referents. The same writers also showed that the process of reference is profoundly modulated by adverbial forms modifying the referent.

These experiments are a perfect illustration of how difficult it is to separate syntactic aspects from semantic aspects in the strict sense when dealing with the reference mechanism. Indeed the foregoing references differed not only in kind (noun-noun vs verb-noun) but also relationally (object-object vs action-object) and in categorical specificity ('vehicle' is an element of a non-ambiguous class, but 'drive' is an action which can be applied to various objects belonging to numerous classes). These semantic properties probably constitute the main determinants of definite reference. Thus Garrod and Sanford (1981) did a comparison of direct and indirect references. To be precise, they studied reading time for a critical sentence (the beer was warm) preceded by a contextual sentence with the explicit referent (Mary took the beer from the kitchen) or a contextual sentence without explicit referent (Mary took the picnic out of the boot). Under these conditions the average reading time for the target sentences is 1287 ms. for direct reference and 1302 ms. for indirect reference. However, the difference observed was not statistically significant.

In another investigation, Garrod and Sanford (1977) also studied the effect of semantic relations between the anaphor and the referent. In the material they designed the anaphor can be a generic category of which the referent is merely an instance (the pear was a new variety. The fruit...) or the other way round (the vehicle came roaring round the corner. The bus...). Experimental data collated show that comprehension time for the sentence containing the anaphor is shorter for the reference of the 'instance-category' type than for the 'category-instance' type. The effect exists whatever the frequency of the exemplar. Frequency gives rise to an overall non-differentiated increase in comprehension time for the critical sentence containing the anaphor. It would obviously be most interesting to study the process of definite reference between an object and its various properties. It is indeed well known that the properties of an object may be associated wih it more or less specifically and hence affect the degree of comprehension of the definite references they form part of. Barsalou (1982) has shown that certain properties of a concept are independent of context and therefore always activated when the concept is presented whereas others are dependent on context and only activated in special circumstances (Barsalou and Medin, 1986).

We need to insist on the fact that because the referent of an anaphor is always part of a sentence, it has relationships with the other words of the sentence. Research done by Dell, McKoon and Ratcliff (1983) illustrates the importance of lexical companions of the anaphoric referent. In this investigation subjects read four successive sentences. The first contains the referent of the anaphoric associated with another word or 'companion' of the referent (a thief watches the garage), two other sentences develop the scenario. The last, critical sentence contains a synonym of the referent (the delinquent glides...) or introduces a new entity (the cat glides...). The anaphor (delinquent) or the neutral noun (cat) can appear at varying places in the critical sentence (250 ms., 50 ms., 700 ms. from the beginning). The subject's task is to decide as quickly as possible whether the word had appeared previously. In a first experiment, Dell *et al.* show that the decision time is always more rapid for the anaphor than for the neutral word, and tends to increase according to the position of the critical word in the sentence. In three other experiments by Dell and his collaborators the decision target can be the anaphor, the companion of the referent or a control word. It then appears that the companion is activated by the anaphor at the same time as the referent. This activation is at a maximum at 500 ms. from the beginning of the critical sentence. This fact provides a forceful argument against a strictly lexical interpretation of reference. At the moment of encounter with the anaphor, the referent is not activated alone but in all likelihood the representation of the whole preceding proposition is as well, to a certain extent.

Finally, the distance betwen anaphor and referent has been the subject of more and more research and controversy. In Clark's experiment (1978, already mentioned) the number of sentences separating referent from anaphor or pronoun was varied. There is a clear marked increase in comprehension time of the sentence containing the anaphor when the number of interpolated sentences is higher. Dutka (1980) obtained perfectly convergent results using a very different technique. He asked his subjects to try to recall the referent of an anaphoric expression. Using the multiple correlation method he showed that the distance between referent and substitute is the most important factor in text comprehension.

However, the methods of measurement used by Clark and Dutka can be criticized. The former gives no information about comprehension activity at the actual moment when the subject encounters the referent substitute. The latter is open to criticism because measurement is not done at the same time as comprehension occurs. From this point of view techniques of analysis of eye movements and fixations may be very useful heuristically. As early as 1977, Carpenter and Just noted that if a pronoun occurs in a sentence, there is back fixation in 50 per cent of cases. This observation inspired Ehrlich and Rayner (1983) to undertake an exact study of the reference mechanism through an examination of eye fixation points. They used systematic variation of the distance between referent and pronominal substitute (adjacent, a line away, three lines away). Further they measured the average duration of fixations on the word before the pronoun, on the pronoun itself and on the following word. Their results reveal a very complex relation between distance and reference. Indeed there is hardly any increase in average time of fixation of the pronoun in relation to the distance separating it from its referent. Moreover average fixation time for the word immediately following the pronoun is very markedly affected by the distance from the referent. It would seem therefore that the referent is determined as soon as its pronominal substitute is encountered. However, if the referent occurred some considerable time before, the determination lasts until the processing of the word following the substitute.

The results presented here suggest that definite reference is a linguistic operation in which it is difficult to separate the syntactic and semantic components. However, semantic determinants probably play a decisive part in it: direct or indirect nature of the reference, degree of specificity of the relations between referent and co-referent, nature of the reference relation (category-instance or instance-category) and concepts associated with the referent. Besides, the distance between referent and co-referent is indisputably a decisive factor in the greater or lesser degree of complexity of the integration of the different parts of speech. Reference makes it possible to link and integrate what is said at a given moment with what has just been said and this is essential to sentence cohesion. How can the psychological mechanism which makes this cohesion possible be explained? When a lexical item is encountered, it can be supposed that the reader forms a mental representation of it which remains available for the moment in working memory and activates (or preactivates) a set of associated representations in long-term memory. When the reader later comes across a pronominal or anaphoric referent, for instance, it can be supposed that he regards it as a 'variable', the value of which he has to compute in order to preserve the discourse cohesion. Such computation can be direct if the representation of the co-referent is available in working memory at the time the reader encounters the referent. The computation can be done indirectly and in several different ways:

(a) the representation of the co-referent is no longer available in working memory and the reader has to search backward for perceptual information (back fixation) in order to reactivate it;

(b) the representation of the co-referent is no longer available in working memory but the reader can revive it by transferring an earlier preactivated representation from long-term to working memory;

(c) the representation of the co-referent is available in working memory but its semantic relation with the referent is such as to oblige the reader to transform an additional representation preactivated in long-term memory into one in working memory.

Such mechanisms obviously assume that reader or listener does more than construct a literal interpretation of the sentence (Fodor, 1974) and brings to bear a good deal of information from his semantic memory and his perceptions of the intentions of the speaker (Clark, 1978; Bransford *et al.*, 1976; Dutka, 1980).

The context effect of this linguistic mechanism of co-reference is obvious because facility of comprehension and integration of the referent depend both on the distance from the co-referent and the semantic relation between them. It can be seen that it would be incorrect to take the anaphor as a mere back reference. The backward fixation triggered by the encounter with the anaphor denotes a partial breakdown in integration of the discourse. A successful reference is one that makes it possible to activate the relevant units of meaning in working or in long-term memory and keep them available until the occurrence of the referent. Thus it is the forward context effects of reference which durably ensure cohesion of discourse.

This hypothetical analysis does, however, leave some questions pending. First, though the concept of activation is central in the explanation of contextual reference effects one can ask what is actually activated when the reader encounters the referent: is it merely the representation of the co-referent? Is it the representation of the co-referent plus that of one or more associated representations ('companion' of the referent)? Finally, is it an abstract propositional representation of the sentence or sentences read or heard just before? We shall not attempt to answer these questions yet but their theoretical importance is quite obvious.

There is yet another problem here which we cannot ignore. If reference makes it possible to verify semantic overlap (Garrod and Sanford, 1977) and is therefore one of the major determinants of sentence cohesion and integration, the exact time and place of such integration are still subject to controversy (Segui, 1986). It is well known that there are two broad classes of theories of understanding. Some researchers think that understanding is perfectly synchronized with the dynamics of eye fixation: the length of fixation of a word covers all the cognitive processes of understanding and integration of the word in the sentence ('process monitoring hypothesis'). The second class postulates that the reader can postpone or complete cognitive processing beyond the eye fixation period ('cognitive lag hypothesis'). Experimental results obtained by Ehrlich and Rayner (1983) show it is not easy to decide between the two. Indeed when the co-referent immediately precedes the referent fixation time alone is affected which is evidence in favour of the first hypothesis and seems to indicate that the reference process is triggered when the referent is encountered and ends as soon as the reader fixes the next word. However, as the distance between co-referent and referent increases, the average fixation time on the following work is higher than that on the referent itself, which is evidence in favour of the hypothesis of partly delayed cognitive processing of discourse information.

## Lexico-semantic effects of context within and between sentences

Experimental study of definite reference is mainly concerned with relations between lexical items within the sentence. Basically therefore it is concerned with the problem of relations between words and is probably a particular case of sentence context effects. Besides, the relation between the anaphor and its antecedent has attracted much more attention than the converse relation between antecedent and anaphor. In other words, definite reference is in all likelihood merely a particular case of intra-sentence context effects. We should therefore now examine more complex relations which may arise between overall meaning induced by any given clause and some of the lexical items which follow (sentence-word relation) and the symmetrical relations between any given lexical item and the 'computed' meaning of a clause coming after it (word-sentence relation).

### Sentence – word relations

Relations between the general meaning of a sentence and the understanding of a subsequent lexical item have been studied on the basis of extremely varied paradigms: sentence completion, word recognition or reading time, interpretation of ambiguous words, error detection and word-by-word reading. We shall examine in turn the results obtained with the help of these various study paradigms and shall outline the main theoretical problems they raise.

Sentence completion situations involve presenting a sentence containing a gap and asking the subject to complete the sentence, that is, to predict or guess the missing word. The word may of course be more or less predictable from sentence context. The degree of predictability is usually likened to the number of subjects capable of predicting a given lexical item in a given sentence context. Such predictability is to be distinguished from contextual constraint imposed by the sentence (number of words compatible with the target-gap). Perfetti (1982) showed there is an inverse relation between degree of predictability of target from context and identification time for the target in the sentence and also between the degree of contextual coherence and identification time. Though speed of identification is lower for poor than for good readers, there is no apparent interaction between identification time and reading capacity assessed by other means. However, if the target word is highly degraded good readers have more trouble identifying it than poor readers. It does not seem therefore that the degree of reading skill has any marked effect on strategies of utilization of contextual information (see also Potter, 1982). However, the influence of sentence context on probability of identification of a word is indisputable and Potter (1982) showed, moreover, that the context sentence only has a facilitating effect on the probability of guessing a target word if it comes before, not after, the latter. If the correlation between the different factors likely to affect comprehension is assessed (non-verbal IQ, richness of vocabulary, letter discrimination, etc.) it is observed that it is mainly general intellectual ability and richness of vocabulary which are correlated with the probability of completion in sentence completion situations.

Recognition time for a word in a sentence has been systematically studied by Stanovich and West (1983a,b). They had their subjects read sentences ending in a word to be recognized as rapidly as possible. The sentence context was either congruous with the target (example: 'the train came into a huge station'), neutral with respect to target ('he said it was a huge station'), or incongruous with the target ('the train went into a huge trunk'). Their data show that a congruous context raises comprehension speed whereas an incongruous context lowers comprehension speed. The effect is, moreover, amplified according to the lexical difficulty of the target word but is not affected by length of sentence, degradation of target word, context probability or the level of processing. This result is confirmed moreover by Tabossi and Johnson-Laird (1980, p.598) since they showed experimentally that reading time for a sentence which affects the meaning of one of its words is significantly longer than a sentence which does not affect the meaning of any of its words.

The above investigations all dealt with the influence of sentence context on the anticipation, perception or comprehension of a non-ambiguous lexical item. But many words in the language are polysemic and it can reasonably be supposed that the context effects studied here would be even more marked in the case of ambiguous words. An investigation done by Reder (1983) illustrates this way of posing the problem. Subjects were asked to decide if a sentence had a meaning or not. The critical sentence included an ambiguous target word (example: 'pipe') which was rendered non-ambiguous by the preceding verb. The critical sentence was preceded by a context sentence with a structure of the 'subject-relative clause-predicate' type. In this contextual sentence, the subject, the relative clause, or both, activated one of the meanings of the predicate. In a third of the cases the meaning of the expected target word was activated, in the second third the other irrelevant meaning of the target word was activated, and finally, in the last third a neutral meaning without relation to the target word was activated. Reder showed a context effect which reduced comprehension time for the sentence containing the target word. Moreover, the contextual effect of the subject term combined additively with the contextual effect of the term defined by the relative clause.

Using a paradigm of phoneme detection, Swinney and Hakes (1976) also examined the influence of a context on the understanding of a critical sentence containing an ambiguous word or not. This contextual sentence defined a meaning without any relation, either close or distant, to the ambiguous word in the target sentence. The writers did not note any ambiguity effect for the target word but did find a very marked context effect. The interaction between the two factors is significant since the context effect is observed only if there is an ambiguous word in the critical sentence. The specifically semantic effects of the contextual sentence do not, moreover, exclude effects of syntactic nature as shown in research by Townsend and Bever (1982). These writers presented ambiguous or non-ambiguous sentences including an English verb ending in 'ing'. For each sentence two contexts biased the meaning towards interpretation of the adjectival or present participle type. The subject's task was to decide as quickly as possible if the verb was a continuation of the sentence. The contextual effects observed were modulated by morphological and non-morphological marks, they also depended on the causal ('if') or restrictive ('although') nature of the contextual clause and their amplitude was greatest at the boundary between clauses. Townsend and Bever concluded that contextual information and local structure interact, the interaction depending on the nature of contextual information, of local structure and of the semantic relation between context and target (1982, p.698).

Finally, a few experimenters have attempted to study the effects of the semantic and syntactic construction of a sentence on the understanding of words in a way that is more dynamic than those of the foregoing paradigms. French (1983) used a technique of rapid serial visual presentation (or RSVP). In this technique the different words of a sentence are presented in succession at tachistoscopic speed. The writer varied both the syntactic complexity and semantic complexity of the sentences. Semantic and syntactic complexity were decisive at slow presentation speeds but at higher speeds semantic complexity alone appeared decisive and the average number of words perceived was a function of the predictability of semantic relations between subject, verb and predicate. Daneman and Carpenter (1983) used a somewhat different technique from that of French, one which had some real likeness to a listening situation. The subjects followed the ongoing presentation of words of a sentence and reading time per word was recorded. The contextual sentence contained an ambiguous word, in a specified meaning, followed by a target sentence containing a critical word either contradicting or conforming to the preceding interpretation. Thus, for example, the contextual sentence might introduce the ambiguous word 'bat' in its games meaning and be followed by a contradictory sentence introducing the other interpretation (nocturnal flying mammal). The writers showed an average increase of 230 ms. in reading the last word of the target sentence when it induced relative incoherence with respect to the meaning of the preceding sentence.

### Relations of the word-sentence type

If a sentence context is likely to have an influence on perception and comprehension of a target word inserted in a sentence, there are also some experimental data available which show the converse effect of a lexical context on the understanding of a sentence. A classic experiment by Dooling (1972) showed that the presentation of a semantically contextual word in connection with a target sentence raised comprehension time for the latter.

In another experiment, Dooling asked the subject to decide if the target sentence had a meaning or not or if the target sentence following the context word seemed appropriate. Comprehension time for the sentence turned out to be shorter when it was a matter of judging the semantic relation between target and context (920 ms. on an average) than if the meaning of the target sentence itself was to be judged (980 ms. on average). Furthermore, a contextual word with a semantic link to the target sentence had a facilitating effect on comprehension time (980 ms.) compared to a control situation without context word (1140 ms.); a semantically inappropriate word resulted in a considerable increase in comprehension time for the target sentence (1240 ms.). These results were given even greater precision by the work of Doll and Lapinski (1974) who manipulated the relationship between the contextual word and the target (direct or indirect referential relation, irrelevant relation, duplication of contextual word in target sentence). Whatever the type of relation, the context word always had a facilitating effect and the amplitude of this was maximal for a relation of direct reference. It is to be noted that the facilitation effect of the mere repetition of the context word in the target sentence was not particularly strong. These results are in contrast with those obtained by Dooling who, however, did not record comprehension time but time of meaning or compatibility judgment. Thus it may be that context effects have differential impact according to the type of processing required of the subject.

Thus, whatever the paradigm used, meaning induced by a sentence has indisputable influence on the anticipation of a word (completion situations), on speed of recognition and, although this conclusion is only inference, on understanding. It is a matter of a context effect since this influence is not observed unless the contextual sentence comes before the critical word. It is absent if the contextual sentence comes after it. The greater the ambiguity of the word, the greater such contextual influence and this also increased with the degree of predictability of the critical word on the basis of the contextual sentence and even with the degree of contextual coherence of the same critical word. Contextual information contributed by the sentence is, moreover, not only facilitating but can also be inhibiting when it induces a contradictory interpretation of the target word. This contextual influence is mainly semantic in origin since it is affected by the degree of congruency between the contextual sentence and target word, by their semantic closeness, the lexical difficulty of the target word and the density of contextual information in the sentence. But it is also affected by morphological features related to syntax in the contextual sentence, in particular when it is ambiguous (context effects are more marked with restrictive than with causal sentences). However, some factors do not influence this particular class of context effects. They are not affected by the length of the contextual sentence, the degree of degradation of the target word and the processing level of the contextual sentence. Finally, though good readers are more affected by context effects, no differential strategies between the two groups of subjects have come to light. Everything seems to indicate that the facilitating or inhibiting effects of context are not restricted to lexical information alone.

All in all, these recent experimental results relating to contextual effects of a sentence on perception and understanding of a word give more general extension to some of the questions raised in connection with the mechanism of definite reference. First of all it seems we must distinguish between a theoretical conception of moderate interaction and highly interactive models. The former supposes that contextual information and graphic properties of the target word affect probability of identification but do not necessarily interact (Morton, 1964; Perfetti and Roth, 1981). The latter suppose both classes of factors interact strongly (Rumelhart, 1977; McClelland, 1979; Rumelhart and McClelland, 1981). The interaction observed by Perfetti between contextual constraint and degree of degradation of the target word to be detected is experimental evidence in favour of the second class of models. French's observation (1983) that the relationship between syntactic and semantic complexity is not the same when the speed of tachitoscopic presentation of words of a sentence is increased, tends to prove the same: in this case semantic complexity becomes the major determinant of the probability of word identification. But how do the various levels of processing of linguistic information combine? Two points of view can here be contrasted.

According to a non-differentiated model, all levels of contextual information whether semantic or syntactic, may interact during processing and consequently a word in a sentence context may be recognized even before enough acoustic and phonetic information has accumulated for the selection of a particular word (Tyler and Marslen-Wilson, 1977). According to a more differential model, levels of contextual information interact only at certain specific points in the stream of discourse (Norris, 1982).

The results obtained by Townsend and Bever (1982) support the second hypothesis in that they showed the interaction to be maximum at clause boundaries, which is what Daneman and Carpenter also noted (1983). In fact the debate cannot be dissociated from that on the ongoing or postponed processing of linguistic information. The research by Daneman and Carpenter referred to above, by showing the importance for sensitivity to contextual influence of the position of the target word with respect to the clause boundary, is probably a solid argument in favour of the second hypothesis and it brings out the basic role played by working memory in linguistic integration procedures. It is obvious that the hypothesis of immediate processing of linguistic information is not particularly consistent with the hypothesis of direct contextual facilitation in terms of expectation. It is of prime importance to know whether interpretation of a target word is biased by the prior context event before it occurs (Foss and Jenkins, 1973; Schvaneveldt, Meyer and Becker, 1976) or affected only when it occurs. The results obtained by Swinney and Hakes (1976) support the second hypothesis as they show that the effect of a prior context is the same whether there is an ambiguity or not. This obviously diverges from Perfetti's explanation that context adds to activation of the localization of the word in memory, resulting in a reduction of the amount of data required at the level of the grapheme (1982, p.572). But it may be necessary to distinguish between two categories of context effects:

(a) automatic context effects based on spreading semantic activation, having facilitating influence only;
(b) context effects derived from conscious and deliberate predictions determined by the orientation of the reader's attention, his strategies and intentions and which may have inhibiting as well as facilitating influence.

A hypothesis of this sort would enable us to account for a general increase in context effects as a function of the perceptual difficulty of the target word. Moreover, the inhibiting effect of an incongruous context is the same whatever the difficulty of the target word (automatic inhibition) whereas the facilitating effect of a congruous context increases with the degree of difficulty of the target word (Stanovich and West, 1979, 1981, 1983). Thus the shift from lexical contextual relation (reference) to semantico-lexical contextual relations definitely makes the theoretical picture more complex.

### Semantic context effects within sentences

Up to now we have mainly studied contextual relations between lexical items on the one hand and between lexical items and sentences on the other. However, these experimental paradigms offer only highly specific, not to say artificial, situations and are not really representative of normal speech. The fact is that any conversation is a process over a certain period of time, implying the continual construction, on the basis of sentences, of high-level semantic representations which are inseparable from the speaker's knowledge of the world and the inferences he is in a position to draw. The cohesion and coherence of a text or a conversation are the result of a complex inferential activity of this sort, based both on syntactic and semantic relations of discourse and on their logical and pragmatic implications.

Such semantic context effects are very widespread as McCloskey and Glucksberg's research (1979) shows. They showed that verification time for the veracity of the sentence depends on the degree of difficulty of the sentences surrounding it. It takes 100 ms. more to check the veracity of a sentence among difficult sentences than for a sentence among easy sentences. This fact was confirmed by Kiger and Glass (1981) in a situation of verification of simple equations presented either in numeric ($8 + 2 = 10$?) or verbal form (eight plus two equals ten ?). It does not seem possible to explain this fact completely by the mere modification of decision criteria. These recent results can be compared with earlier data which also point to the generality of semantic context effects. Morton (1964), for example, had subjects read texts in language of varying degrees of approximation to English. He noted that reading speed of these pseudo-texts increased up to the fifth order for slow readers and the sixth for fast readers. Raising the degree of approximation of language obviously raises the predictability of discourse and it is no surprise that the number of back eye fixations decreases regularly up to the fifth and sixth order of approximation of language. It is also known that re-reading is always faster than a first reading and this facilitation is probably not only semantic but also graphemic in nature. The generality of context effects was also shown by Mitchell and Green (1978). In their experimental paradigm, the subjects read a text which could be run through a 'window' on a video screen at a pace that suited them. The dependent factor here was reading time of the contents of each window: the writers showed that reading time increased according to the number of words contained in the window and the position of these words at the end of a clause or a sentence. It decreased, on the other hand, with the frequency of the words and the consistency of the passage with prior contexts.

Even if we restrict our remarks to the semantic aspects of the integration process involved in understanding, we should first inquire how certain elementary contextual processes such as co-reference may be modified when they occur as part of a complex structure of dependence between parts of speech. First of all it would seem that the number of anaphoric references in a text is a decisive factor for comprehension.Rosenberg and Lambert (1974) have shown that reading time increases as the number of anaphoric relations contained decreases. It is clear that the subject uses 'contextual connectiveness' in the comprehension process. However, a co-reference is not processed by itself and its interpretation also depends on the background of discourse. Carpenter and Just (1978) showed that the resolution of pronominal references depends on the content of working memory and the concepts associated with what they call the discourse 'pointer'. They had their subjects read a proposition with two actors (example: the warden calls to the prisoner); this was followed by a critical sentence containing a pronominal referent which may refer to either one or the other (e.g. he had been at the prison for three years); the critical sentence can come straight after the introductory sentence or be separated by an interpolated sentence specifying the relationship between the two actors (the one the warden called to was named Jim). Carpenter and Just recorded eye fixation points and paid particular attention to backward fixation points when the subject encountered the pronominal referent. They observed that when the critical sentence came straight after the introductory sentence back fixations were more frequent on the antecedent 'warden' than on the antecedent 'prisoner'; when the critical sentence came last, on the other hand, they noted a larger number of back fixations on the antecedent 'Jim' (or 'prisoner') than on the antecedent 'warden'. This shows that a pronominal reference is influenced by the linguistic context in which it occurs. The context determines a 'discourse pointer' or, if one prefers, 'foreground' information which influences the following integration process. As Carpenter and Just point out (1977,p.239): comprehension involves much more than the elaboration of an abstract semantic representation of the sentence. It involves relating words and clauses in the sentences to information elsewhere in the discourse or encoded from perceptual context.

A good deal of attention has also been given to the understanding of sentences and their integration with prior information. Experiments by Chase and Clark (1972) and Clark (1978) on direct and indirect requests are now considered classic ('the star is (or is not) above (below) the cross'). It takes longer to understand questions which contradict visual information and indirect requests are resolved more slowly than direct requests, though they present the same general pattern of data. Bransford and Johnson (1972) also showed that comprehension and retention of the text describing the actual and potential contents of the picture are better if the picture is presented before and not after the text. A similar result was obtained with the second and fifth grade children by Arnold and Brooks (1976). Carpenter and Just also compared the time taken to assess position of a character in a scene from a linguistic description of a cleft (object or subject) or pseudo-cleft (object or subject) form. For example, the subject saw a picture with two characters (Jane and John) and read the proposition 'the one who is ahead of Jane is John' and was required to answer as rapidly as possible the question 'Is John on the left or the right of Jane?' In such conditions they showed that responses were more rapid (nearly 190 ms.) when the critical character of the question, shown in the picture, actually corresponded to the presupposed character in the descriptive sentence. The syntactic structure had no modulating effect on the phenomenon.

The foregoing effect, observed by Carpenter and Just, was moreover symmetrical, since in another experiment they presented the descriptive sentence before the picture. The subject was asked to decide as rapidly as possible if the contextual sentence and target picture were in agreement. In this case, it was noted that decision time was shorter when the discordance concerned the 'asserted' character than when it concerned the 'presupposed' character of the sentence.

The linguistic operation of co-reference may also be strongly affected by thematic modification taking place between prior information and the anaphoric referent. For example, Garrod and Sanford (1983) showed that thematic change of this sort interfered with comprehension of a referential utterance. They crossed the kind of reference involved in discourse (direct or indirect) with scenario structure (unchanged or modified). They had their subjects read three sentences in succession: the introductory sentence contributed the prior information explicitly or implicitly (e.g. 'Mary was putting clothes on the baby' or 'Mary was dressing the baby'). The next sentence either preserved or not the scenario unity given by the preceding sentence (e.g. 'She always had trouble doing this' or 'When she had finished she went to the shops'); finally the critical sentence brought in an anaphoric reference (e.g. 'the clothes were made of pink wool'). It appeared that scenario change increased reading time by about 200 ms. for the critical sentence; it should be noted that this was much more than the effect of the nature of the anaphoric reference.

In another piece of research, the same writers also show that a modification of discourse which violates time limits of the scenario affects comprehension time of all references which come after the scenario although it does not affect later references to the main characteristics introduced in the discourse. This result has been confirmed by various methods of measurement, reading time, text completion or answers to questions (Anderson, Garrod and Sanford, 1983). This important investigation shows clearly that discourse cohesion does not depend solely on the linguistic operation of co-reference but basically on the content of working memory, that is, on the current discourse 'topic' or, in other words, on the temporary state of discourse pointers or on contextual 'background'. To put it differently, this means that the efficacy of co-reference cannot be assessed at the syntactic lexical level alone, it must involve complex propositional computation which relates the referent-antecedent system to the spatiotemporal characteristics of the general theme of discourse. The mechanism is obviously complex and a far cry from a mere general non-differentiated context effect.

Context effects between sentences (or clauses) thus complicate considerably the dynamics of context effects observed in the domain of language. But up to now we have been dealing only with context effects based on direct or indirect reference; in the latter case it is indeed sometimes possible to talk of inference, but such inference is in fact rather limited in scope since the antecedent always implies, though in an implicit way, the properties which will be activated by the referent (thus 'was dressing' necessarily implies the handling of 'clothes'). However, there exist logical or pragmatic inferences which are much more complex and can occur in assertion verification, in comprehension of suppositions or conditional sentences, of implications, of syllogisms, of ambiguities or incoherencies and in certain special linguistic forms such as metaphor and hyperbole, for example. The context made up of the discursive contents of working memory, the pragmatic characteristics of the situation and the knowledge elements represented in long-term memory is no doubt the motor of linguistic inference. One can distinguish between three large classes of inferences which may intervene in the understanding of discourse:

(a) logical inferences which introduce relations of physical or logical causality;
(b) situational inferences (semantic or pragmatic) based on the mechanism of co-reference;
(c) value inferences based on the depth and extent of knowledge of the world.

The study of the last mentioned is especially difficult since it obviously assumes that the researcher has access to sufficient information about the knowledge possessed by the subject. They can, nonetheless, be studied indirectly by comparing, for example, comprehension of expert and novice subjects. One can then assume that expert subjects' knowledge gives them much greater prediction potential than novice subjects in the comprehension of a specialized text. In conditions of this sort, a secondary task (detection of 'clicks') should inhibit the reading of expert subjects much less than that of novice subjects. This is in fact what Britton and Tesser (1982) observed though the difference between expert and novice subjects failed to reach conventional significance level. At a certain level of technicality, then, it would not seem that access to prior knowledge increases cognitive capacity as applied to the main task.

Singer (1976), for his part, did an in-depth study of information inferences of semantico-pragmatic nature. He recorded the latency of verification responses to questions concerning information implied in earlier propositions (example: 'the little girl spent the bright penny' followed by an assertion to be checked 'the penny was bright (dull) ''or'' the penny was new (old)'). He showed that when context and target are presented close together (less than 2,5 s. interval) there is no difference between the verification time for an inference and for that of a synonymous assertion; it is only after a 7 s. interval that subjects need more time to check the veracity of an inference than that of a synonymous assertion. The fact seems therefore to indicate that certain inferences are computed on presentation of the context, are rapidly forgotten and have to be recomputed if the time lapse between context and sentence to be checked is too long. On the basis of this earliest research, Singer (1981) worked out a model of verification of language assertions and implications ('Vail'). According to this model, the subject encodes old and new information of the sentence to be verified in a propositional form, searches next for prior information and then verifies compatibility between new information and prior information which may, in some cases, require search for additional information in long-term memory in order to work out certain inferences, finally deciding whether to respond affirmatively or negatively. In the latter case, the subject modifies his initialized response index on the response 'yes'.

Singer's 'Vial' model predicts that the latency of the verification response is a compound formed by addition of various partial latencies of these sub-processes. It can be fairly generally predicted that true responses will in general be more rapid than false responses and that the verification of implicit propositions will take more time than the verification of explicit propositions. In one of his investigations Singer (1984) presented a descriptive sentence immediately followed by a sentence to be verified which could be either explicitly true, explicitly false, implicitly true or implicitly false. These implications were all pragmatic and could concern instrument, agent or subject. It was noted that the predictions from this model were perfectly verified. An important problem is that of the exact locus of the formation of the inference: during comprehension of the antecedent (forward inference) or at the time of verification or question (backward inference).

In order to decide between these two opposed hypotheses, Singer and Ferreira (1983) asked their subjects a question (example: 'did the spy burn the report?') by referring back to an earlier sentence either explicit, synonymous or inferential (example: 'the spy burned the report in the fire'; 'the spy incinerated the report in the fire'; 'the spy threw the report in the fire'). Singer and Ferreira observed in one of their experiments that it takes more time to respond to a question linked to an earlier synonymous sentence than to respond to a question linked inferentially to the earlier sentence (the difference not being significant). In a second experiment, the results were reversed. This second experiment was confirmed by the work of Carpenter and Just (1978) who showed also that the cumulative duration of back eye fixations is significantly larger in cases of indirect inferences than in the case of direct inferences. The empirical data obtained by Singer and his collaborators are thus ambiguous, but they do admit that the possibility of forward inference must depend not only on the inferential properties of speech elements but also on wider thematic relationships.

### Inference and logical context

Comprehension is not only biased by the computation of referents and the production of semantic or pragmatic inferences, it also implies references of a logical kind. The role of context and of order of presentation of information is thus a determining factor in the comprehension of the logical structure of discourse. The interpretation of suppositions ('if ... then') consists in devising a supposition from prior information and checking the supposition against specific knowledge. The syllogism is probably one of the best prototypical realizations of the supposition. Rips and Marcus (1978) were able to show that syllogistic inferences are more easily drawn when the second premise is identical to the antecedent of the condition.

Johnson-Laird (1982) has probably done the most precise study to date of the process of comprehension of syllogisms. He moreover integrated his research into a theory of mental logic which postulates that the human subject can be characterized by a variable rationality and confronts mental or cognitive models (as distinct from strictly logical ones) of the situations which correspond to the sentences he encounters, models which lend themselves to verbalization. Psychologists found quite some time ago that the content of the data of a syllogistic problem could bias the subject's response erroneously towards certain conclusions. To be more exact, this 'atmosphere effect' (Sells and Koob, 1937) is a manifestation of the experimental fact that the overall cognitive impression gained from the premise in most cases incites the subject to provide the syllogism with a conclusion in the same terms as those of the premise. In the same way, Johnson-Laird describes a figural bias which leads the majority of subjects to conclude the syllogism 'some A are B' and 'all B are C' by 'some A are C' whereas the conclusion 'some C are A' is also valid. In this view, the subject constructs a model of the first premise, possibly recalls this interpretation of the first premise at the moment of comprehension of the second, may invert the earlier interpretation and recalls the interpretation of the second premise. Depending on type of premise therefore, the conclusion necessitates more or less complex operations mainly determined by the contextual order in which elements of information are communicated to the subject. A series of experiments done by Johnson-Laird confirms this analysis.

Johnson-Laird believes his findings could have some practical implications. He points out, not without humour, that certain bureaucratic information would doubtless be better understood if it were communicated in logic-tree form instead of in a purely, and often obscure, linguistic form (see also: Wason, 1968; Jones, 1968). It is true that directions and instructions often come in the forms of suppositions and conditional sentences. The linguistic form can affect the speed of comprehension. It might be that a sentence is better understood when it follows the 'natural' or social order of the operations involved and that the mental model for a procedure is first established in a direct affirmative form. A highly original piece of research by Dixon (1982) seems to confirm this. He confronted his subjects with a simulation of an electronic apparatus on which they were to carry out certain manipulations in response to requests, the linguistic form of which was systematically manipulated. Dixon's first experiment showed that if the consequence is linked to an action, a request is understood faster than when the action is stated before the consequence. In a second experiment the writer compared action/consequence or consequence/action type requests; (example: 'keep pressing button A because dial X is at 20') with action/antecedent or antecedent/action type requests (example: 'keep pressing button A if dial X is at 20'). His findings were that if the action is presented first, the most rapidly understood request is the action/consequence type but if the action is presented second the antecedent/action type request is understood faster.

It is obvious that information relative to the action or to the logical subject has special status in mental representations of plans of action and procedures. Highly convergent results have been obtained in a very different situation with 10-year-old children who placed objects in a given spatial arrangement in response to request (example: 'the red car hits the blue one'). Huttenlocher and Strauss (1968) and Huttenlocher and Weiner (1971) have shown the importance of correspondence between the logical structure of movement and the grammatical structure of the sentence in the choice of the object first shifted. To sum up, it is the order of presentation of objects in the sentence which is decisive, not the position of the grammatical subject. In a related study with children, Presson (1980) also showed that the syntactical structure of the sentence (passive, active, cleft or pseudo-cleft), in so far as it modifies the identity relation between logical subject and grammatical subject, has a significant effect on the object first shifted.

The importance of logical relations between parts of speech is also confirmed in research done on the relation between the propositional structure of texts and their comprehension. In a continuous discourse or narrative, we can distinguish various propositional types (state, event, action, cognition, emotion, goal) associated by various types of logical connectors (motivation, physical cause, psychological cause, possibility, succession in time, co-ocurrence in time). Several analysis models of the propositional structure of context have moreover been based on the predicate-argument distinction (Kintsch, 1976) or on the conceptual dependency relationship (Schank, 1972). These logical factors produce very strong contextual dependencies as shown in research by Fredericksen (1975a). He had his subjects read a text of 503 words including 30 independent clauses and 25 declarative clauses linked by conditional and identity relations. He asked them to do a series of recalls of the text which they might either have simply read or might have read while trying to solve a logical problem. In the latter case, he found the proportion of inferred or overgeneralized recalls was definitely higher. In other words, the pragmatic and logical context of the ongoing action affects the encoding of propositions and their relationships. These results are moreover consistent with those obtained by Greeno and Norren (1974). These researchers constructed various paragraphs on the basis of Kintsch's propositional analysis, made up of information either in strictly hierarchical arrangement, in hierarchical arrangement with exceptions and in either general to specific order or in specific to general order. The writers found that more time is needed to read sentences on the lowest level of the propositional hierarchy. Moreover, the earlier expectations raised by the propositional structure of the text reduce reading time. Manelis and Yekovich (1976) also observed that the repetition of the same proposition in two succeeding sentences reduces comprehension time and improves later recall, and this even when the critical sentence is more complex than the earlier sentence. Such inference capacity changes with age as Johnson and Smith's work (1981) shows. They had subjects memorize a narrative containing transitive and causal inferences (implicit or explicit). The older children (fifth grade) were found to be superior to the younger (third grade) not only with respect to the number of inferences they could make but also to their complexity (distance between inference terms). They concluded that the crucial difference between the older and younger children is their ability to integrate propositions and compute their implications when there is a semantic and not just a time link (1981).

The processing of polysemic information contained in sentences is also based on inference activity. Anderson and Ortony (1975) showed that a retrieval cue, even if it is associated with a polysemic word in a sentence, does not make for efficient recall of the sentence meaning unless it evokes the meaning actually construed at the time of encoding. The reading of ambiguous sentences whose meaning becomes clear later in the sentence is also a good revealer of context effects. Frazier and Rayner (1982) show that in the case of ambiguous meanings the reader only determines one of the possible meanings with respect to the context and that he changes meaning later if it proves irrelevant. This fact is shown in the marked rise in mean reading time per letter at the moment when the ambiguity is detected and just afterwards. Nonetheless Holmes, Arwas and Garrett (1977) were not able to show any context effect on recall probability for words in ambiguous sentences and they concluded that the context does not diminish the complexity of processing for ambiguous sentences. But this negative result is doubtless due to the 'off-line' paradigm used by the writers since generally speaking context effects are evident when comprehension time is recorded and even more obvious when eye fixation points are taken into consideration. Finally, the role of context is decisive in the interpretation of metaphoric expressions. This is clearly shown by Ortony, Schallert, Reynolds and Antos (1978). These writers established the comprehension time for a target sentence for which a prior context of varying length determined either the literal or the metaphorical meaning. Their results revealed an effect of context-induced meaning the extent of which depends precisely on the length of the context. The writers conclude that the longer or shorter time taken to understand a sentence is a function of the ease with which it can be interpreted in the light of given contextual expectations. Literal language is processed in the same way as figurative. It is the relation with the context that determines the difficulty of processing.

### Thematic context, background and foreground information

Whether the linguistic operation of inference realization be semantic, pragmatic or logical, it seems dependent on both local and overall constraints. Linguistic context effects result, therefore, from the interaction between local context effects (reference, inference, ambiguity) and overall context effects (knowledge of the world, general theme of discourse). We have already mentioned contextual effects of thematization as modulators of co-reference mechanisms (Anderson *et al.*, 1983; Garrod and Sanford, 1983). But the theoretical importance of the concept in psycho-linguistics means we must pay it particular attention.

The simplest way to obtain a representation of a theme is to precede the critical passage with a passage or title which attracts the subject's attention to the general theme of the discourse. The paradigm has been widely used. Thus Bransford and Johnson (1972) compare the absence of introduction of the theme to its presentation before or after the critical passage. Comprehension judgment of critical material is always significantly better when the theme is introduced initially, whether the comprehension test intervenes immediately or a minute after presentation of the critical material. An effect of the same sort was observed by Gardner and Schumacher (1977) in a situation where the subject had to recall the critical material. Schallert (1976) confirms this effect of thematic representation on later memory recognition of a target text whatever the depth of encoding processing.

However, thematic facilitation only occurs if the target text is highly coherent semantically and if the semantic context is strongly associated with it (see Kieras, 1980; Townsend, 1983). Garrod and Sanford (1983) studied the effect of the degree of semantic compatibility between the associated theme (example: 'learning to ski') and a target sentence (example: 'the snow was cold') on comprehension time for the latter. An inappropriate title definitely increases comprehension time for the target sentence especially if it is connected to another sentence in the narrative by indirect reference.

However, the dynamics of these context effects need to be made clear. It is obvious that the degree of specificity of the theme or the scenario introduced is a decisive factor in the process of comprehension. Sentences are read faster if they are preceded by a sentence introducing a scenario in a specific manner than if they are preceded by a sentence introducing a scenario in a general manner (Sanford, Garrod and Bell, 1978). However, still further clarification of the situation is needed since the introduction of a context may involve both focal elements (new information) and presupposed (old) information. This has an undeniable psychological reality because most often old information tends to precede new information (Clark and Haviland, 1974, 1977) and the tendency is to answer questions by putting old information before new (Bock, 1977). The comprehension of a sentence could be expected to be facilitated when the information it contains is presupposed in it although it was focal in the context. This is in fact what Yekovich, Walter and Blackman showed (1979). In their research, one of the words of the target sentence appeared as presupposed whereas it was focal in the context (FP), focal in target and context (FF), presupposed in target and context (PP) or focal in target and presupposed in context (PF). (For example, in the context sentence 'Peter broke the glass', 'glass' is focal. This last word is presupposed in the following target sentence 'The glass was beautiful' (FP).) The writers noted a significant gradient on comprehension times for the target sentence as a function of the particular relation between the target and the context (FP was the best condition). Tiberghien and Audeguy (1985) have shown, moreover, that the focalization-presupposition arrangement interacts with the memory status of information: the reading time of impersonal semantic information is affected by this arrangement, but the reading time of personal semantic information is not modified by the relation of focalization-presupposition.

It was probably a similar finding that led Chafe (1972) to distinguish between foreground and background information, the former being available in working memory while the latter is at best reactivated in long-term memory. In the sequence 'yesterday the dog bit a little girl. She was frightened' it can be assumed that the concept 'little girl' is still available in working memory when the reader encounters the referent 'she' (foreground). But in the sequence, 'yesterday a black dog bit a little girl. He ran away and I am still trying to find him. She was very frightened'; it is likely that the information 'little girl' is no longer in working memory when the subject encounters the referent 'she', and to find it he has to refer to long-term memory (background).

Research on co-reference has been mainly concerned with discourse foreground and that on thematization with background. Little research work has included an attempt to control simultaneously both time facets of context effects. However, Lesgold, Roth and Curtis (1979) have attempted to separate them by distinguishing between two discursive structures; one concerning background (prior-new, theme-target) and the other foreground (prior-commentary-target). They showed that comprehension time for the target sentence was longer when the context was of the background than when it was of the foreground type, but the number of commentaries of new discursive themes introduced did not modify this overall effect. Foss and Ross (1983), using a different technique of phoneme detection, obtained strongly convergent results. They think that the best way to account for the data is to consider that the reader computes very general expectations at a high level of semantic integration ('great expectations').

### Syntactical context effects in comprehension

The semantic structure of sentences modifies the scope of semantico-pragmatic context effects. Some sentence structures have more functional completeness than others. Carroll, Tanenhaus and Bever (1978) have shown that detection time for a click superimposed on the terminal word of a sentence structure of the noun-verb-noun type was faster than that for a click superimposed on the terminal word of a functionally incomplete syntactic structure (initial gerund noun-phrase). A prior semantic context can moreover modify the very segmentation of a sentence. This can be shown by getting the subject to read an ambiguous sentence which could be segmented in various ways (example: 'Smith who Ford asked to remain in Vermont, for political reasons, decided to resign his post'). This critical sentence can be followed by contextual information in question form (example: 'why did Smith resign?' or 'why did Ford ask Smith to stay in Vermont?'). The paraphrases of the target sentence turn out to be different according to the type of preliminary questions. Thus semantic context can have a considerable effect on organization and syntactic segmentation of speech (Carroll *et al.*, 1978). Finally, it can be seen that the range of semantic context effects varies considerably with the structure of the target sentence. In particular such effects are more marked if the target sentence has a structure of the object relative clause type (example: 'the girl whom the boy kissed, blushed') rather than of the subject relative clause type (example: 'the girl who kissed the boy, blushed'). Using a technique of segmented self-presentation, Noizet (1983) also showed that times of exposure to a target sentence were longer when it was preceded by a contextual sentence which gave it the status of determinative relative than when it was preceded by a contextual sentence giving it the status of appositive relative subordinate. Thus listeners use contextual information when they organize sentences syntactically and contextual and inferential clues seem to be highly valid indicators of the functional completeness of discourse (Carroll *et al.*, 1978).

The compatibility between syntactic structure of the context and syntactic structure of the target sentence is also a factor which facilitates integration between sentences. For example, Vasquez (1981) studied the latency of verification for propositions of the type: 'It is true (it is not true, it is false, it is not false) that the dots are (are not) red (green) in colour' in the presence of an appropriate stimulus or not. She showed that processing of the final sentence is modified by the complexity of processing of the earlier clause. Carpenter and Just (1977) controlled the nature of segmentation of target and contextual sentences (example: 'The one who cries is John'; 'It is John who cries'). They showed that comprehension time for the target sentence was shorter when the syntactical structure was appropriate to that of the contextual structure, and this was so for any number of interpolated sentences. Moreover syntactic structure *materializes the relations* between new and old information: consequently discourse integration was facilitated when information that was new in the contextual sentence reoccured as old information in the target sentence. This fact was confirmed by the work of Hupet and Le Bouedec (1977) who found that 'the way propositions are arranged strongly determines the subject's capacity to construct a coherent organisation of information communicated in the sentence' (p.73). To be more precise, when the elementary ideas which make up the main ideas are arranged so that each idea provides a context for the next, this makes it possible to match prior information against given information.

But sentences in discourse are made up of interconnected clauses and the question is what might be the optimal contextual relations between different clauses on the one hand and clauses and sentences on the other?

Using a technique of delayed judgment of meaning, Townsend and Bever (1978) showed that the integration of the final clause was always more rapid than that of the first clause and that the integration of a subordinate clause in any position in the sentence was always slower than that of a principal clause. In a series of fourteen experiments Jarvella (1981) made a systematic examination of the role of discourse segmentation on context effects. He presented his subjects with two sentences one of which might be short (one clause) and another long (two clauses). Either could be presented first:

(a) short-long condition: (Sentence A) (Clause B—Clause C);
(b) long-short condition: (Clause A—Clause B) (Sentence C).

Depending on the experiment, the subject might undergo various retention tests after studying the two sentences: written or oral free recall, cued recall or recognition. It was found that recall for the last sentence (or clause) was the same whatever the syntactical structure of the foregoing discourse: on the other hand, recall for Clause B was always better when it was part of the last sentence (79 per cent on 4 experiments) than when it was part of the first sentence (49 per cent on 4 experiments). These results suggest that the boundary between sentences is the best predictor of success or failure of later recall of information.

Inter-sentence boundaries also affect the extent of contextual inference (co-reference, pronominalization, subordination). Tyler and Marlsen-Wilson (1977) have contributed (symmetrical) evidence in favour of the hypothesis that syntactical decisions can be modified by semantic factors before the end of the sentence. Finally Cairns, Cowart and Dablon (1981) noted strong context effects which were not modified by the fact that context and target were inserted in the same clause or in two different clauses. This result confirms that the distance between contextual and focal information is not a necessary condition of discourse coherence, but it is rather semantic and pragmatic relations and discourse segmentation that play the decisive role.

## TOWARDS A CONTEXTUALIST THEORY OF LINGUISTIC COMPREHENSION

The research reviewed above is striking in its diversity: diversity of material (sentences, words, texts); of paradigms (word-sentence, sentence-word, sentence-sentence, contextual relations); of experimental procedures and behavioral indicators (on-line measures: reading or comprehension time, analysis of eye fixation and movement; off-line measures: memory retention tests, incoherence or ambiguity detection, latency of verification judgment, decision, response to questions, judgment of meaning, similarity or compatibility, paraphrase association; added tasks: phoneme processing, click detection). We must now examine the different theories proposed with a view to unifying this vast field of empirical research and explaining how context influences sentence comprehension.

First of all, it is possible to enumerate the situational factors producing the integration of discourse information which makes possible continuous coherent discourse: understanding what one reads or hears requires a link to be established with what one has just read or heard. The co-reference operation is here a determinant condition for comprehension and though it is often explicit, it can also be indirect or implicit. Comprehension also supposes the frequent use of more or less complex inference procedures and processes. Whereas co-reference depends exclusively on inter-lexical relations, discourse inferences involve the whole set of propositions and meanings computed from sentences read or heard. Thus, they mobilize complex semantic conceptual representations; knowledge of the world and various pragmatic implications. These inferences cannot be dissociated from the speakers' activities, aims and intentions and cannot be separated from the current scenario and the general theme of discourse. Context effects are therefore basically semantic in nature even though they may, as we have seen, be modified by syntactical factors. Finally, what account can be given of the dynamics of the semantic context effects? First, have we any justification for speaking of context effects? The fact is there exist two broad classes of comprehension models:

(a) models based on strict interpretation of ongoing discourse ('interpretative models');
(b) models based on complex reconstruction of the meaning of ongoing discourse ('constructive models').

The former have always been worked out on the basis of experimental study of the comprehension of isolated sentences and strongly influenced by models and theories derived from generative grammar. This class of models postulates that sentence meaning is 'computed' on the basis of more or less automatic syntactic analysis of the sentence ('parser') followed by a semantic analysis. Such models, more or less explicitly, assume relative contextual invariance (Woods, 1970; Simmons, 1973; Walker, 1983; Fodor, 1974; for an overview: Fredericksen, 1975a,b). On the other hand, a constructivist approach supposes that the interpretation of each sentence necessitates construction of a high-level structure of mental representations integrating contextual information of a semantic nature and the individual's knowledge of the world (Bartlett, 1932; Bransford and Franks, 1971; Bransford et al., 1976; Fredericksen, 1972, 1975; Schank, 1972). In view of the experimental data we analyzed earlier this class of interactionist models is probably the one that deals with the experimental facts with the greatest realism. The degree of interactivity is, however, highly variable from one model to another. There are weakly interactive models in which context and graphic properties of words both affect identification but in virtually independent ways (Morton, 1964; McClelland, 1979; Perfetti and Roth, 1981). Perfetti (1982) defends a model of this class when he maintains that context does not directly affect the process of word identification but rather adds activation to the localization of the word in memory, reducing the quantity of data required at the graphic level (p.572). Such models are therefore not at all the same as strongly interactive models for which identification of words in the sentence results from active combinations of contextual properties derived from prior information and perceptually available graphic properties (Rumelhart, 1977; Rumelhart and McClelland, 1981). Both constructivist and interpretative theories, however, underestimate the role of pragmatic information in comprehension. A third class of constructivist theories could be proposed if we cared to insist on the intentional determination of comprehension. Sentence integration would then result from permanent interaction between syntactic, semantic and intentional information (Clark, 1978). Finally Fredericksen (1975a, p.140) defines constructivist models by reference to a high-level interaction between a subject's prior knowledge, his intentions, the context, the constraints of the task and the structure of linguistic input itself.

However, though constructivist models seem more valid to us than the interpretative ones, the former consider that context intervenes only at the level of lexical retrieval. In these conditions what we call context effects are perhaps only the result of memory retrieval of earlier lexical information at the time the subject processes a given lexical item. Context effects would then be backward and not forward in nature. But if we are to speak of genuine context effects these have to be forward in nature. Backward context effects are perfectly compatible with 'immediacy strategy' in which processing time for a word reflects the time needed for encoding, choice of meaning of syntactical function, computation of referents and inferential integration in discourse. A model of this sort is not particularly differentiated since all levels of contextual information may interact at any moment of linguistic processing (Tyler and Marlsen-Wilson, 1977). In this case, it should be noted that the individual, who finds himself in a situation of polysemy and ambiguity, completes only one sentence meaning which can be corrected by the rest of the following discourse in accordance with the 'garden-path' model (Frazier and Rayner, 1982).

Forward context effects are much more compatible with the opposite strategy, called cognitive 'buffer'. According to this hypothesis, the subject fills his working memory before carrying out all the linguistic processing, which might explain the special role played by the boundary between clauses and sentences. We have here a differentiated model since the levels of semantic and syntactic contextual information interact at certain sensitive points of discourse such as prepositions, word or morpheme groups, for example (Townsend and Bever, 1982). In the case of ambiguity, all interpretations of the sentence would be computed up to a point where ambiguity is dispelled (Marcus, 1980) or until the end of the sentence (Fodor, 1974). Analysis of eye fixations during reading seems on the whole to support this latter hypothesis (Swinney and Hakes, 1976; Carpenter and Just, 1978; Daneman and Carpenter, 1983; Ehrlich and Rayner, 1983). Finally it is possible that context effects do not result from the facilitation of a mere lexical process, but occur at a higher level. This is the point of view advanced by Cairns *et al.* (1981) when they maintain that all context effects originate at the message processing level rather than at the initial level of lexical access (p.450). Finally, the current debate bears on general questions which I can attempt to summarize briefly:

(1) Does discourse comprehension necessitate taking context into consideration? It seems to me the reply is affirmative.
(2) Do context effects occur on the lexical or the conceptual level?
    It seems that both types of process can exist: context most often facilitates access to the lexicon by reducing the number of lexical candidates to be chosen or by reducing the amount of phonemic information needed to select a candidate, but in some more complex inference situations context can create a mental structure which facilitates integration of later high-level propositions (here the classic opposition 'top-down' versus 'bottom-up' can be recognized).
(3) Is the mode of action of the context of the backward or forward type?

In the former case contextual information would be reactivated by computation of current meaning at the moment of the perceptual encounter with the critical word; in the latter the context would give rise to an activation or expectation biasing interpretation of subsequent information. In my opinion we should only talk of context effects in the strict sense in the latter case. So the current debate is about the exact locus of manifestation of context effects (before, at the moment of, or after the reading of focal information, at the end of the clause or the sentence?) and about the lexical or propositional nature of the effect. These questions are far from being satisfactorily answered and it is understandable that theoretical difficulties arise when an attempt is made to explain the inner workings and dynamics of these context effects. At this level of analysis, three classes of theories can be distinguished:

(a) activation theories;

f the 'given-new' contract;

textual coherence.

## Activation theories

These originated in the work of Quillian (1968, 1969). According to his theory the memory representation system is made up of concepts corresponding to words and sentences. These concepts are 'nodes' and are connected to other conceptual representations by labelled associations (super-ordination, subordination, co-occurrence, description). When a word or sentence is presented to the subject the corresponding concept or concepts are activated and the activation spreads gradually to nodes associated with the initial concept ('spread of activation'). All conceptual nodes reached by this activation are indexed by a 'tag' which specifies the concept initially activated. When a node already has a marker from the spread of activation from another node, interaction between the two initial concepts is detected, which may bring about a memory recognition or a conceptual integration. Activation spread lessens gradually as it gets further from the initial concept. Furthermore the range of activation spread is directly proportional to the processing time for the initial concept, inversely proportional to the time left after the end of processing and to the number of other interfering events. Finally Collins's model postulates that action due to different sources of activation accumulates at the interconceptual intersection and has to reach a given threshold to be effective (Collins and Loftus, 1975; Loftus, 1973). The hypothesis of a process of this sort is perfectly adequate to account for forward context effects in the comprehension of linguistic utterances. Indeed, in reading, when the subject encounters a particular word there is an activation of the corresponding concept which gradually spreads through the representational structure. If later the reader encounters a word which has been activated (or preactivated if the critical threshold was not reached) it can be recognized and understood more rapidly.

Numerous models have been based on this idea of a facilitation due to the spread of semantic activation (Meyer and Schvanaveldt, 1971; Forster, 1979). All these models assume, of course, some representational organization of the lexicon, but the structure of this varies from writer to writer (associative networks, list structures, mental dictionary). Very recently J.R. Anderson (1983) proposed a formalization of the principles of the spread of activation linked to a system of production rules to account for 'priming' effects. As a general rule these models are used mainly to explain context effects of lexical nature and two different sorts of criticisms have been levelled at them. First of all, it can be asked whether the model of spreading semantic activation can be used to explain all linguistic context effects.

Posner and Snyder (1975) think that the principle of semantic activation can only explain facilitating context effects: spread of activation is for them a very rapid automatic process which cannot do other than facilitate later perception and comprehension. In other words, the process of spread of activiation is not under the subject's intentional control. Therefore Posner and Snyder propose, in addition to this activation process, a much slower attentional component which develops semantic or conceptual expectations which may be appropriate or not. Only this attentional component could, in their view, explain the inhibiting context effects often observed in literature. Numerous experimental findings are compatible with a theoretical interpretation of this sort (Neely, 1977; Fischler and Bloom, 1979; Stanovich and West, 1979, 1983a,b).

The second criticism is aimed mainly at the empirical evidence advanced in support of spreading activation models ('priming' and lexical decision). They are, in fact, above all, lexical activation models. When a subject reads a sentence, the semantic and conceptual interpretation of it may very well be different from that of the words that make it up. If afterwards the subject encounters a given word in a sentence, it may very well be compatible with the words of the earlier sentence but not with the high-level semantic interpretation that has been constructed: 'the effect of the semantic relation between lexical items depends on the linguistic context in which the words occur' (Foss and Ross, 1983,p.173). In other terms, lexical and semantic activation do not necessarily obey the same laws. We have seen, for instance, that it is not so much the distance between words nor even the number of intervening words which are critical for the greater or lesser facility of linguistic integration: so long as the general theme of discourse and the spatio-temporal aspects of the scenario are preserved, semantic activation can operate effectively.

This empirical fact is not particularly compatible with the postulate that there should be gradual relative deterioration over time. Likewise lexical information semantically associated with later lexical information does not necessarily bring about facilitation of identification or comprehension. The principle of activation accounts for facilitation of lexical access much better than for facilitation or inhibition of high-level semantic integration, integration which can be studied only in relatively complex situations of comprehension of interconnected sentences and not in the relatively artificial situations of priming or lexical decisions. Such criticisms justify the approach adopted by Kintsch and Van Dijk (1978) who consider a text to be represented in memory as a set of propositions structured by explicit or inferred semantic relations. The meaning of sentences is thus attributed not only on the basis of their lexical components, but also on that of their relations with other sentences, each sentence or clause undergoing contextual interpretation involving not only connections between lexical items but, above all, connections between conceptual representations, including those on a very high level (macrostructure of discourse). Here again it is not so much access to semantic representations which is facilitated or inhibited, but rather the integration between high-level conceptual representations available in working memory and the representations elaborated on the basis of current perceptual information (see also Kieras, 1980; Singer, 1981, 1984).

## Reference theories

Theories of semantic activation have a high degree of generality and basically describe an evaluation procedure for the degree of semantic match of two concepts. Certainly this procedure plays an important part in linguistic comprehension but this latter raises much more specific problems. The co-reference situation, for example, can be described simply as an activation of the referent concept by the antecedent concept but a view of this sort does not take into consideration the specific linguistic status of both terms involved in the co-reference. More specific theories of reference have therefore been developed, theories all more or less inspired by that proposed by Clark and Haviland (1974). This postulates that the integration of linguistic information is based on the strategy known as 'given-new'. According to this, any sentence can be broken down into 'given', that is, old or presupposed, and 'new', that is, asserted, information. A given-new structure can arise in different ways: by the order of propositions (the presupposed generally precedes the asserted proposition), by the use of definite articles, of adverbial forms, of sentence caesura. In more practical terms, information can be considered to be 'given' if it has an antecedent in memory (which antecedent may be in a state of activation in working memory or of preactivation in long-term memory). As Haviland and Clark (1974) make clear, the listener does not feel he has fully understood a sentence unless he has integrated it with earlier knowledge stored in memory (p.514).

To speak of strategy implies of necessity, and in contradiction with theories of semantic activation, an activity which is not entirely automatic and may therefore include situations involving complex and deliberate inference. Confronted with a sentence, the reader has first to encode it, then to dissociate given from new information, use the given information to search for earlier information which may be stored in memory ('given' information here serves as a 'pointer' towards prior information) and finally to try to associate 'new' with prior information. If the subject does not find the prior information in memory, he can still construct or reconstruct it by inference which, in this case, amounts to considering the whole of the initial sentence information as being 'new'.

The theory devised by Haviland and Clark makes it possible to predict the now classic experimental finding that direct reference is more rapidly understood than indirect. Indeed, in the former case there is a literal match between given and earlier information, whereas in the latter matching requires a further inferential stage. Moreover, Rayner (1978) has brought forward a good deal of experimental evidence to the effect that backward eye fixations are very frequent when the reader encounters a referent and that eye fixation times are significantly longer on 'new' than on 'given' information.

However, reference theory, if restricted to lexical reference as such, is much too narrow to explain how context intervenes to ensure linguistic cohesion and integration. For example, very little is known about the part played by familiarity in the reference function. Also, it is hard to conceive that the 'given-new' classification is not affected by prior sentences as a whole, that is to say by the general theme of discourse and the succession of various scenarios (Kieras, 1978). These difficulties explain why attempts to make the reference theory more general have been numerous and varied. When first formulated, the 'given-new' theory applied to lexico-semantic relations only, that is, to relations between mental representations corresponding to definite lexical units.

Carpenter and Just (1977) very rapidly admitted that this conception was too narrow and they produced the concept of a 'discursive pointer' capable of activating not only an isolated concept but also a complete conceptual structure. Thus, they recognized the importance of working memory and the decisive role of certain linguistic devices ('cleft' structure in which new information comes at the beginning of the sentence and pseudo-cleft in which new information is at the end of the sentence; the role of 'topical' sentences at the beginning of a paragraph). They showed experimentally that performance is facilitated when the given-new structure corresponds to what is conceptually new and old for the reader. It is the earlier context of discourse which defines the new or old status. And what is old and new cannot be defined solely by the immediate contents of discourse. Certain inferences are 'allowed' and others not, depending on the contents of earlier sentences, on the situational context in which discourse is produced and on various conversational conventions (Clark, 1977). Reference theory has therefore to account not only for semantic but also for pragmatic reference. Hupet and Costermans (1982) speak here of 'socio-communicational contexts' and consider that 'context is also taken to refer to that which is of the order of convictions, beliefs and guesses relating to the exchange situation, including relations between the exchange partners' (p.762).

Finally it is obvious that the reference theory may be understood in two theoretically very different ways. We can consider first of all that at the time he encounters the referent, the listener/reader undertakes a memory search to obtain confirmation from relevant earlier information. This would be a backward pseudo-context effect. To this idea ('text-mapping hypothesis', Yekovich *et al.*, 1979) we can compare the hypothesis of genuine (forward) context effects ('model-mapping hypothesis'). In the latter case (A. Anderson *et al.*, 1983) the reader attempts, for example, to construct a representation or mental model of the text which is then collated with the new information encountered afterwards. This means then, that discourse representation is not worked out on the basis of references between lexical entities explicitly mentioned in the discourse. The matching between old and new information (via given information) takes into account the subject's knowledge, the textual background (theme) and the succession of scenarios. In other words, new information is not simply related to old information, but this latter makes it possible to develop expectations and predict the former. Only a conception of this sort can explain the relative independence of comprehension of an anaphor with respect to the distance between referent and its antecedent or to the amount of intervening information between referent and study. In co-reference, elements are not all processed in the same way: the existence or not of a 'companion' to the antecedent may complicate discourse comprehension; the main (thematic) subjects are probably not processed in the same way as subjects which depend on a particular scenario; time modifications and scenario sequence are by no means negligible.

All of which implies therefore that the mental representation of the text in memory is determined by the episodic structure of the text. Therefore text comprehension depends basically on long-term memory structure and on current contents of working memory (Tiberghien and Audeguy, 1985). Sentence sequence does not merely contribute a relational structure between referents and antecedents, but something more in the nature of a 'reference space' continuously modulated by the background and the subject's knowledge, which give it wider range, and by the focalization on a topic or a particular scenario, which narrows its scope (Sanford *et al.*, 1982). In other words, standard reference theory probably gives a good explanation of discourse cohesion, but cohesion does not necessarily mean coherence and reference theories are not entirely satisfactory from this point of view.

## Coherence theories

The cohesion of discourse is almost exclusively based on the sequence of textual co-relations. But although cohesion is a necessary condition for coherence it is by no means a sufficient one. Take the example of the following sentence sequence: 'The President of the Republic has just taken an important economic decision. He loves vanilla ice-cream'. It is obvious that the discourse is lacking in coherence although referential cohesion is perfectly maintained and there is no ambiguity as to the antecedent of the pronominal referent of the second proposition. This shows that a simple theory of co-reference probably cannot suffice to account for linguistic context effects. Coherence presupposes referential identity, of course, but depends also on the characteristics of the distribution of the information (introduction, continuity, expansion, topicalization), on the compatibility between order of facts and order of sentences, on knowledge of the world and on inference possibilities (Keenan, Baillet and Brown, 1984). Coherence is thus based essentially on reference (Van Dijk, 1980). Context cannot therefore be derived simply from syntactic and semantic aspects of preceding discourse: 'the common ground' of speakers must also be taken into consideration. This common ground is derived from various contextual origins:

(a) linguistic co-presence (linguistic, syntactic and semantic context of earlier discourse);
(b) physical co-presence (extra-linguistic perceptual context);
(c) cognitive context defined by knowledge of the speaker and his frame of reference.

Briefly, for a listener who is trying to understand what a speaker is saying to him at a given moment, intrinsic context (linked to ongoing comprehension) is the common ground the listener believes he shares with the speaker at that given moment (Clark and Carlson, 1981,p.319).

It is not particularly surprising that these problems of coherence have turned out to be particularly acute in the field of artificial intelligence. Indeed artificial comprehension or production of natural language requires more than mere syntactic and semantic analysis. Artificial systems of man – machine dialogue in natural or near-natural language may mask the importance of contextual determinants of linguistic comprehension. Now, the 'given-new' theory does not always ensure coherence because it is not always easy to decide which information is new and which old or, in other terms, which is the topic and which the commentary. Many examples show that coherence is more than the dialectics of antecedent and referent or 'given' and 'new', that coherence cannot be reduced to the use of explicit connectors, it is not of the rhetorical order and not the same thing as mere 'readability'. Hobbs (1979,1982) distinguishes three types of coherence:

(a) global coherence of a pragmatic nature (illocutionary acts) which is determined by the background of communication;

(b) thematic coherence defined by the relation to the whole set of sentences (paragraphs, texts, narratives) of the discourse;

(c) local coherence determined by relations between the proposition being read or heard and immediately prior propositions.

Hobbs (1979) considers local coherence is defined by four classes of relations:

(a) occurrence relations which determine inter-propositional causal structure (initial state-final state; initial state-action-final state);

(b) evaluation relations;

(c) explanation relations (paragraph, repetition, checking);

(d) expansion relations (parallel, generalization, example, contrast).

L. Vezin (1982), for example, studied the effect of this type of expansion relations on the comprehension and memorization of linguistic utterances taken from technical fields. She shows that the presentation of examples facilitates comprehension of general utterances but reduces capacity to generalize and to make inter-conceptual relations. Adding more general contextual utterances only has a facilitating effect if there is a relation of super-ordination between the various utterances. Finally, according to the theory of linguistic coherence, cohesion relations (such as co-reference) are derived from a higher causal order which integrates knowledge representation, processes of inference and co-reference, of resolution of syntactic and semantic ambiguity and the conversational aims and intentions of the speaker.

Hobbs's theoretical analysis and the practical aims he puts forward are of a very high level of generality, and up to now, there have been only a few attempts at implementation or simulation. In this area, Hobbs (1982) has constructed a discourse analysis program (Diana) which he claims is capable of recognizing most of the coherence relations identified by him. Grosz (1977) has also studied numerous dialogues between a learner and a computerized expert system capable of solving highly specific problems (repair of a compressor). The system includes general representation of knowledge which permits detection of focal information (local and global focus) and relevant contexts needed to interpret the discourse. This dialogue system makes it possible to resolve numerous co-references and to interpret some elliptical forms of discourse. But the contribution made by Charniak (1978, 1982, 1983) to the analysis of contextual problems involved in the process of comprehension is probably the most systematic to date.

In Charniak's view, sentence interpretation implies construction of hypotheses of a very high level of integration from low-level cues. Take for instance the following sentence: 'the young woman walked down the alley and took a can from the shelf and put it in her shopping basket'. It is obvious that the interpretation of the sentence is progressively worked out as reading progresses and a 'frame' is little by little activated, suggested and completed. In the foregoing example the 'frame' is obviously a 'supermarket' (alley—can—shopping basket—supermarket). The context functions as a frame of reference, more or less rapidly activated by the discourse and which selects its probable follow up. Here we see the close conceptual relationships between 'frame', 'script', 'scenario' and the more general concept of context which subsumes them all (Minsky, 1975; Schank and Abelson, 1977; Charniak, 1978; Schank and Birnbaum, 1980).

This suggestion of a frame of reference which allows for diverse expectations is obviously referential in nature. A system of knowledge representation should therefore take this into account and provide rapid access to the data base, activation and selection of appropriate frames. It can be seen that the problem we have here is highly important for natural language dialogue systems developed by artificial intelligence. Most of these confine themselves to doing syntactic analysis followed by a semantic analysis and in some cases by inferential decisions. A paradigm of this sort raises numerous difficulties of which the relations between the syntactic 'parser' and semantic interpretation is, however, probably the most serious. Indeed, though many tentative applications provide for interaction between syntactic and semantic levels, almost all syntactic analyses reject a-grammatical sentences whereas the human subject, in an appropriate context, accepts and understands them perfectly. To lessen the difficulty, Charniak proposes associating syntactic analysis with a transfer system for 'marker parsers' which on encountering a predicate will transfer markers to all predicates associated with the first one (such as super-ordinated concept, possible action) along the classic lines of spreading activation. Such a system could influence semantic analysis by specifying the meaning of certain words and, above all, by making 'contextual suggestions' ('frames') which would then intervene in final-stage interpretation deductions.

Charniak has not implemented his conception but this analysis shows that some AI researchers have understood that realistic man – machine dialogue in natural language can in no case ignore contextual information. Whether the technological aims can be reached before the theoretical solution is, of course quite another matter. We can even question the 'feasibility' of a program of this sort in the present state of our knowledge in logic, psychology and linguistics. One thing is, however, quite clear, the notion of context marks the frontier between artificial and natural systems of linguistic information processing that cannot be ignored. As Winograd recalled recently (1982): 'If you look at language in its context, every meaning is interpreted in connection with a prior knowledge about the context and the conversational goal ... . A meaning is always an ''open'' meaning;

it is not possible to build an *a priori* model including the exhaustive set of contexts and goals' (pp. 78–79).

## CONCLUSIONS

The set of facts we have studied in this review of the question shows the crucial role of the concept of context for an explanation of the mechanisms of linguistic comprehension. The comprehension of a word or a sentence cannot be reduced to the syntactic and semantic analysis of information at the moment undergoing processing. As Iser (1973) recalls: 'each sentence contains an anticipatory view of the following' (p.284). By context effects are meant, in the linguistic field, interaction between information perceptually available at the time, active representations in working memory and representations in long-term memory of a degree of availability which makes it possible to consider them as being in a state of pre-activation (Shebilske, 1980). Such context effects can obviously occur at various levels of linguistic processing (phonemic, lexical, logical, syntactic, semantic, pragmatic) but there is no point in separating them and considering that the psychological processes they involve are qualitatively different. These context effects all contribute to the preservation of discourse coherence by making possible various local, global or socio-communicative inferences (thus bringing into play the speaker's/listener's knowledge, beliefs, intentions and aims). Discourse coherence is thus the product of the interaction of reference and of inference processes.

It can be considered, in a very general way, that there are three classes of determinants for context effects. We saw first of all that syntactic structure could modulate context effects. There is a relation between the clause order structure and the logical natural or social structure of events. Compatibility between these two levels facilitates integration of discourse. Here we need only remind ourselves of the spectacular effects of such factors as different syntactical arrangements on sentence comprehension of passive vs active voice, supposition relation, implication or subordination relation, relation between actions, consequence and antecedent, role of negation.

The second level of occurrence of context effects is semantic. Co-reference plays a critical role in the preservation of discourse cohesion. Naturally it is conceivable that the computation of prior information is only done at the moment the referent is encountered and is not inhibited or facilitated by the actual properties of the co-reference structure. But the role played by the structure of this relation (for example a relation of particular to general), by the distance separating reference from antecedent or by the relation between the antecedent and its lexical 'companion' shows that co-reference is not merely a backward process but is also a forward interpretation process. Of course, context effects occurring in co-reference situations probably result most often from rapid automatic activation associated with the antecedent of the referent. But as soon as we reach the semantic level numerous inferential activities intervene to reinforce and complete the textual cohesion produced by the co-reference process. The complex dialectics we analyzed between 'given' and 'new' information, the opposition between topic and commentary, gives us a semantic and conceptual foreground which makes it possible to integrate what is said with earlier expectations. We know that the interaction between this foreground and the background of discourse which is gradually developed is a decisive factor of semantic integration. Discourse activates various plans, scripts and scenarios, the continuity sequence or discontinuity of which can help, facilitate or activate the functioning of referential devices.

Finally, though this aspect of the problem is still not well understood, the coherence of discourse read, heard or produced, depends also on the quantity and organization of the speaker's knowledge, including his episodic representations as well as the whole set of his pragmatic determinants (conversational postulates, intentions, goals).

In conclusion, coherence results from optimal interaction between the strength and the locus of spreading lexical and semantic activation in the stream of discourse and from the development of conscious and relevant expectations of what is to come. This description obviously has practical implications for all those whose task is to work out texts or dialogues in such a way as to ensure optimal comprehensibility. This optimum cannot be reached without special attention to the processing of contextual information which is one of the principal components of the readability or, more exactly, the comprehensibility of the message. The question here is one of text engineering, of composing a message so as to ensure optimal comprehension and to induce the consequent behaviour. Functional utilization of a message necessarily implies identifying its meaning, integrating it with memory contents and producing an appropriate act. The designer of messages and dialogues can use the various linguistic devices identified so far in order to ensure the best possible referential cohesion and inferential coherence. Though the former can be achieved by manipulation of textual characteristics (as such), the second involves of necessity taking into consideration the reader's or listener's knowledge, aims and intentions: 'producers of written information must have some idea of the user's aims' (Wright, 1980a;b,p.184) or again 'for a particular content, a given public and reading aims, the most efficient presentation of the information depends on the context in which the information is used' (Wright, 1980b).

It is true that it is especially difficult to design a text in view of the supposed knowledge of a potential reader; such knowledge is extremely variable and can only be inferred by the producer of written information.

It is nevertheless possible to obtain useful information by comparing expert readers in a field with beginners (errors, reading time, eye fixations) or by studying frequency of use and the degree of knowledge of the various elements of information implicit in a dialogue. For instance the planning of an access dialogue for an administrative data base would certainly be improved if normative information on the frequency of possession or use of various official papers were taken into account. Be that as it may, it is clear that the study of context effects linked to the speaker/listener or reader's knowledge and to the pragmatic aspects of the communication situation raise particularly tricky problems for which approaches and solutions can only be modal.

Though the difficulties involved in the study of textual cohesion and coherence are considerable, they are of a different nature and probably better suited to experimental investigation. It should, however, be noted that the study of referential or inferential context effects within the limits of a given linguistic corpus and of a specific dialogue drastically reduces the possibilities of manipulation and control of relevant factors. It is, however, the only way in which results of fundamental research can be extended to situations the ecological validity of which is more obvious.

Which factors, under these particular conditions of application and development, really need to be studied and controlled by the designer of interactive dialogues and messages? To begin with and as far as the co-reference mechanism is concerned, several variables can already be considered to be critical: expansion or restriction (particular – general), relations between prior information and the referent, distance from referential information, relations between referential antecedents and possible lexico-semantic 'companion', finally relations between the co-reference process and the structure of the various scenarios of the message. Then with respect to inferential mechanisms special attention should be paid to the logical, natural or social structure of events and to compatibility with the discourse structure supposed to express them; in view of the force of interactions between syntactic structure and context effects it should be arranged with care (passive – active, subordination, implication, negation); relations between foreground and background of discourse are also a major determinant of understanding; lastly, the producer of messages should take account of the complex relations existing between the structure of contextual presupposition/focalization and that of focal information. These questions have been carefully examined in the laboratory and should now be studied in more realistic situations, taking into account both the strong constraints linguistic material imposes in a particular field of knowledge and utilization, and those of the specific technological environment of the man – machine dialogue.

Last of all, there is one problem many specialists (linguists, psychologists, computer scientists, knowledge engineers) have in common and it is this: what are the function and aims of language and what exactly is meant by understanding language? Today the theoretical scope of the problem is indistinguishable from its technological impact: how can an artificial information processing system understand and produce the language and how can the interface between such systems and their human users be improved? In the 1970s, there was a real burgeoning of such systems, often much too ambitious in view of their concrete results. Today the lesson has been learned (conclusions have been drawn from the experiences of that period: Waltz, 1982) and it is clear that in order to understand coherent language, an artificial system must be capable of inference. This finding points to one research avenue only: how is knowledge to be formalized and represented? This is the central problem for artificial intelligence, and also for linguistics, psycho-linguistics and cognitive psychology. I can wager that the answers to the question will have to take account of the central problem of indexation and retrieval of contextual information in memory and of their utilization in the understanding of discourse.

## ACKNOWLEDGEMENTS

This research was financially supported by a grant from the French 'Centre National d'Etude des Télécommunications' (CNET) under convention 837BD29007909245/TSS/SEF. Preparation of this chapter was helped by assistance from Patricia Fogarty, Marie Guillet-Caillau, Viviane Mendelsohn and Danièle Le Taillanter.

## REFERENCES

Anderson, A., Garrod, S.C. and Sanford, A.J. (1983). The accessibility of pronominal antecedents as a function of episode shifts in narrative texts. *Quarterly Journal of Experimental Psychology*, **35A**, 427–440.

Anderson, J.R. (1983). *The Architecture of Cognition*, Cambridge MA: Harvard University Press.

Anderson, R.C. and Ortony, A. (1975). On putting apples into bottles: a problem of polysemy. *Cognitive Psychology*, **7**, 167–180.

Arnold, D.J. and Brooks, P.H. (1976). Influence of contextual organizing material on children's listening. *Journal of Educational Psychology*, **68**, 711–718.

Barsalou, L.W. (1982). Context-independent and context-dependent information in concepts. *Memory and Cognition*, **10**, 82–93.

Barsalou, L.W. and Medin, D.L. (1986). Concepts: static definitions or context-dependent representations. In G. Tiberghien (Ed), *Context and Cognition*, *Cahiers de Psychologie Cognitive*, **6**, 187–202.

Bartlett, F.C. (1932). *Remembering: a Study in Experimental and Social Psychology*, Cambridge: Cambridge University Press.

Bierschenk, B. (1982). An ecological model for the processing of symbolic information. *Perceptual and Motor Skills*, **54**, 663–674.

Bock, J.K. (1977). The aspects of a pragmatic presupposition on syntactic structure in question answering. *Journal of Verbal Learning and Verbal Behavior*, **16**, 723–734.

Bransford, J.D. and Franks, J.J. (1971). The abstraction of linguistic ideas. *Cognitive Psychology*, **2**, 331–350.

Bransford, J.D. and Johnson, M.K. (1972). Contextual prequisites for understanding: some investigations of comprehension and recall. *Journal of Verbal Learning and Verbal Behavior*, **11**, 717–726.

Bransford, J.D., Carrell, M.C. and Nitsch, K.E. (1976). Contexte, compréhension et flexibilité sémantique: quelques implications théoriques et methodiologiques. *Bulletin de Psychologie*, in No special, S. Ehrlich and E. Tulving (Eds), *La Mémoire Sémantique*.

Britton, B.K. and Tesser, A. (1982). Effects of prior knowledge on use of cognitive capacity in three complex cognitive tasks. *Journal of Verbal Learning and Verbal Behavior*, **21**, 420–436.

Broadbent, D.E. (1961). Principes communs à la réaction perceptive et à la décision de caractère intellectuel. *Bulletin du Centre d'Etudes et de Recherches Psychotechniques*, **10**, 145–156.

Bruner, J.S. and Goodman, C.C. (1947). Value and need as organizing factors in perception. *Journal of Abnormal and Social Psychology*, **42**, 33–44.

Cairns, H.S., Cowart, W. and Dablon, A.D. (1981). Effect of prior context upon the integration of lexical information during sentence processing. *Journal of Verbal Learning and Verbal Behavior*, **20**, 445–453.

Carpenter, P.A. and Just, M.A. (1977). Integrative processes in comprehension. In D. Laberge and S.J. Samuels (Eds), *Basic Processes in Reading: Perception and Communication*, Hillsdale, NJ: Erlbaum.

Carpenter, P.A. and Just, M.A. (1978). Reading comprehension as eyes see it. In P.A. Carpenter and M.A. Just (Eds), *Cognitive Processes in Comprehension*, Hillsdale, NJ: Erlbaum.

Carr, T.H. (1981). Research on reading: meaning, context effects, and comprehension. *Journal of Experimental Psychology: Human Perception and Performance*, **7**, 592–603.

Chapman, L.J. and Stockes, A. (1980). Developmental trends in the perception of textual cohesion. In P.A. Kolers, M.E. Wrolstad and H. Bouma (Eds), *Processing of Visible Language, Vol. 2*, New York: Plenum Press, 615 pp.

Charniak, E. (1978). On the use of framed knowledge in language comprehension. *Artificial Intelligence*, **11**.

Charniak, E. (1982). Context recognition in language comprehension. In W.G. Lehnert and M.H. Ringle (Eds), *Strategies for Natural Language Processing*, Hillsdale, NJ: Erlbaum.

Charniak, E. (1983). Passing markers: a theory of contextual influence in language comprehension. *Cognitive Science*, **7**, 171–190.

Chase, W.G. and Clark, H.H. (1972). Mental operations in the comparison of sentences and pictures. In L. Gregg (Ed), *Cognition in Learning and Memory*, New York: Wiley.

Chafe, W.L. (1972). Discourse structure and human knowledge. In J.B. Carroll and R.O. Freedle (Eds), *Language Comprehension and the Acquisition of Knowledge*, Washington, DC: Winston.

Clark, H.H. (1977). Inferences in comprehension. In D. Laberge and S.S. Samuels

(Eds), *Basic Processes in Reading: Perception and Communication*, Hillsdale, NJ: Erlbaum.

Clark, H.H. (1978). Inferring what is meant? In W.J. Levelt and G.A. Flores d'Arcais (Eds), *Studies in the Perception of Language*, New York: Wiley.

Clark, H.H. and Carlson, T.B. (1981). Context for comprehension. In J. Long and A. Baddeley (Eds), *Attention and Performance, Vol. IX*, Hillsdale, NJ: Erlbaum.

Clark, H.H. and Haviland, S.E. (1974). Psychological processes as linguistic explanation. In D. Cohen (Ed), *Explaining Linguistic Phenomena*, Washington, DC: Hemisphere.

Clark, H.H. and Haviland, S.E. (1977). Comprehension and the given-new contract. In R. Freedle (Ed), *Discourse Production and Comprehension*, Norwood, NJ: Alex.

Collins, A.M. and Loftus, E.F. (1975). A spreading-activation theory of semantic processing. *Psychological Review*, **82**, 407–428.

Daneman, M. and Carpenter, P.A. (1983). Individual differences in integrating information between and within sentences. *Journal of Experimental Psychology: Learning, Memory and Cognition*, **9**, 561–584.

Dell, G.S., McKoon, G. and Ratcliff, R. (1983). The activation of antecedent information during the processing of anaphoric reference in reading. *Journal of Verbal Learning and Verbal Behavior*, **22**, 121–132.

Dixon, P. (1982). Plans and written directions in complex tasks. *Journal of Verbal Learning and Verbal Behavior*, **21**, 70–74.

Doll, T.J. and Lapinski, R.H. (1974). Context effect in speeded comprehension recall of sentences. *Bulletin of the Psychonomic Society*, **3**, 342–344.

Dooling, D.J. (1972). Some context effects in the speeded comprehension of sentences. *Journal of Experimental Psychology*, **93**, 56–62.

Dutka, J.T. (1980). Anaphoric relations, comprehension and readability. In P.A. Kolers, M.E. Wrostad and H. Bouma (Eds), *Processing of Visible Language, Vol. 2*, New York: Plenum Press.

Ehrlich, K. and Rayner, K. (1983). Pronoun assignment and semantic integration during reading: eye movements and immediacy of processing. *Journal of Verbal Learning and Verbal Behavior*, **22**, 75–87.

Fischler, I. and Bloom, P.A. (1979). Automatic and attentional processes in effects of sentence contexts on word recognition. *Journal of Verbal Learning and Verbal Behavior*, **18**, 1–20.

Fodor, J.A. (1974). *The Language of Thought*, New York: Crowell.

Forster, J.I. (1979). Levels of processing and the structure of language processor. In W.E. Cooper and E.C. Walker (Eds), *Sentence Processing*, Hillsdale, NJ: Erlbaum.

Foss, D.J. and Jenkins, J.J. (1973). Some effects of context on the comprehension of ambiguous sentences. *Journal of Verbal Learning and Verbal Behavior*, **12**, 577–589.

Foss, D.J. and Ross, J.R. (1983). Great expectations: context effects during sentence processing. In G.B. Flores D'Arcais and R.J. Jarvella (Eds), *The Processes of Language Understanding*, New York: Wiley.

Frazier, R. and Rayner, K. (1982). Making and correcting errors during sentence comprehension: eye movements in the analysis of structurally ambiguous sentences. *Cognitive Psychology*, **14**, 178–210.

Frederiksen, C.H. (1972). Effects of task-induced cognitive operations on comprehension and memory processes. In R.O. Freedle and J.M. Carroll (Eds), *Language Comprehension and the Acquisition of Knowledge*, Washington: Winston.

Frederiksen, C.H. (1975a). Effects of context-induced processing operations on semantic information acquired from discourse. *Cognitive Psychology*, **7**, 139–166.

Frederiksen, C.H. (1975b). Representing logical and semantic structures of knowledge acquired from discourse. *Cognitive Psychology*, **7**, 271-458.

French, P. (1983). *Semantic and Syntactic Factors in the Perception of Rapidly Presented Sentences*. Pre-print, Los Angeles: University of California.

Freud, S. (1904). *Psychopathologie de la vie Quotidienne*, Paris: Payot.

Gardner, E.T. and Schumacher, G. (1977). Effects of contextual organization on prose retention. *Journal of Educational Psychology*, **69**, 146–151.

Garrod, S. and Sanford, A. (1977). Interpreting anaphoric relations: the integration of semantic information while reading. *Journal of Verbal Learning and Verbal Behavior*, **16**, 77–90.

Garrod, S. and Sanford, A. (1981). Bridging inferences and the extended domain of reference. In J. Long and A. Baddeley (Eds), *Attention and Performance, Vol. IX*, Hillsdale, NJ: Erlbaum.

Garrod, S. and Sanford, A. (1983). Topic dependent effects in language processing. In G.B. Flores d'Arcais and R.J. Jarvella (Eds), *The Processes of Language Understanding*, New York: Wiley.

Greeno, J.G. and Norren, D.L. (1974). Time to read semantically related sentences. *Voir Original*, **2**, 117–120.

Grosz, B.J. (1977). *The Representation and Use of Focus in Dialogue Understanding*, Technical Note 151, Memlo Park, CA: SRI International.

Haviland, S.E. and Clark, H.H. (1974). What's new? Acquiring new information as a process in comprehension. *Journal of Verbal Learning and Verbal Behavior*, **13**, 512–522.

Hobbs, J.R. (1979). Coherence and co-reference. *Cognitive Psychology*, **3**, 67–90.

Hobbs, J.R. (1982). Towards an understanding of coherence in discourse. In W.G. Lehnert and M.H. Ringle (Eds), *Strategies for Natural Language Processing*, Hillsdale, NJ: Erlbaum.

Hoffman, R.R. (1986). Context and contextualism in the psychology of learning. In G. Tiberglien (Ed), *Context and Cognition, Cahiers de Psychologie Cognitive*, **6**, 215–232.

Hoffman, R.R. and Nead, J.M. (1983). General contextualism, ecological and cognitive research. *The Journal of Mind and Behavior*, **4**, 507–560.

Holmes, V.M., Arwas, R. and Garrett, M.F. (1977). Prior context and the perception of lexically ambiguous sentences. *Memory and Cognition*, **5**, 103–110.

Howes, D. and Osgood, L.E. (1954). On the combination of associative probabilities in linguistic contexts, *American Journal of Psychology*, **67**, 241-258.

Hupet, M. and Costermans, J. (1982). Et que ferons-nous du contexte pragmatique de l'énonciation? *Bulletin de Psychologie*, **35**, No 356, 759–766.

Hupet, M. and Le Bouedec, B. (1977). The given-new contract and the constructive aspect of memory for ideas. *Journal of Verbal Learning and Verbal Behavior*, **16**, 69–75.

Huttenlocher, J. and Strauss, S. (1968). Comprehension and a statement's relation to the situation it describes. *Journal of Verbal Learning and Verbal Behavior*, **7**, 300–304.

Huttenlocher, J. and Weiner, S. (1971). Comprehension of instructions in varying contexts. *Cognitive Psychology*, **2**, 369–385.

Iser, W. (1973). The reading process: a phenomenological approach. In A. Bradford (Ed), *Teaching English to Speakers of English*, New York: Harcourt.

Jarvella, A.J. (1979). Immediate memory and discourse processing. In G.H. Bower (Ed), *The Psychology of Learning and Memory (Vol 13)*, New York: Academic Press.

Jenkins, J.J. (1974). Remember that old theory of memory? Well, forget it! *American Psychologist*, 11, 785–795.

Jenkins, J.J. (1980). Can we have a fruitful cognitive psychology? In H.E. Howe (Ed), *Nebraska Symposium on Motivation*, Lincoln: University of Nebraska Press.

Johnson, H. and Smith, L.B. (1981). Ninth Bartlett memorial lecture: thinking as a skill. *Quarterly Journal of Experimental Psychology*, 34A, 1–25.

Johnson-Laird, P.N. (1982). Ninth Bartlett memorial lecture: thinking as a skill. *Quarterly Journal of Experimental Psychology*, 34A, 1–25.

Jones, S. (1968). Instructions, self-instructions and performance. *Quarterly Journal of Experimental Psychology*, 20, 74–78.

Keenan, J.M., Baillet, S.D. and Brown, P. (1984). The effects of causal cohesion on comprehension and memory. *Journal of Verbal Learning and Verbal Behavior*, 29, 115–126.

Kieras, D.E.S. (1978). Problems of reference in text comprehension. In P.A. Carpenter and M.A. Just (Eds), *Cognitive Processing in Comprehension*, Hillsdale, NJ: Erlbaum.

Kieras, D.E.S. (1980). Initial mention as a signal to thematic content in technical passages. *Memory and Cognition*, 8, 345–353.

Kiger, J.I. and Glass, A.L. (1981). Context effects in sentence verification. *Journal of Experimental Psychology: Human Perception and Performance*, 7, 688–700.

Kintsch, W. (1976). Bases conceptuelles et mémoire de texte. *Bulletin de Psychologie*, No special: *La Mémoire Sémantique*, S. Ehrlich and E. Tulving (Eds), 327–334.

Kintsch, W. and Van Dijk, T.A. (1978). Toward a model of text comprehension and production. *Psychological Review*, 85, 363–394.

Lakoff, R. (1972). Language in context. *Language*, 48, 907–927.

Lesgold, A.M., Roth, S.F. and Curtis, M.E. (1979). Foregrounding effects in discourse comprehension. *Journal of Verbal Learning and Verbal Behavior*, 18, 291–308.

Loftus, E.F. (1973). Activation of semantic memory. *American Journal of Psychology*, 86, 331–337.

McCarroll, J., Tanenhaus, M.K. and Bever, T.G. (1978). The perception of relations: the interaction of structural, functional and contextual factors in the segmentation of sentences. In W.J. Levelt and G.B. Flores d'Arcais (Eds), *Studies in the Perception of Language*, New York: Wiley.

McClelland, J.L. (1979). On the time relations of mental processes: an examination of systems of processes in cascade. *Psychological Review*, 86, 287–330.

McCloskey, M. and Glucksberg, S. (1979). Decision processes in verifying class inclusion statements: implications for models of semantic memory. *Cognitive Psychology*, 11, 1–37.

McGuire, W.J. (1983). A contextualist theory of knowledge: its implications for innovation and reform in psychological research. In L. Berkowitz (Ed), *Advances in Experimental Social Psychology*, New York: Academic Press.

Manelis, L. and Yekovich, F.R. (1976). Repetitions of propositional arguments in sentences. *Journal of Verbal Learning and Verbal Behavior*, 15, 301–312.

Marcus, M. (1980). *A Theory of Syntactic Recognition for Natural Language*, Cambridge, MA: MIT Press.

Meyer, D. and Schvaneveldt, R. (1971). Facilitation in recognizing pairs of words: evidence of a dependence between retrieval operations. *Journal of Experimental Psychology*, 90, 227–234.

Minsky, M. (1975). A framework for representing knowledge. In P. Winston (Ed), *The Psychology of Computer Vision*, New York: McGraw-Hill.

Mitchell, D.C. and Green, D.W. (1978). The effects of context and content on immediate processing in reading. *Quarterly Journal of Experimental Psychology*, **30**, 609–636.

Morton, J. (1964). The effects of context upon speed of reading, eye movements and eye–voice span. *Quarterly Journal of Experimental Psychology*, **16**, 340–354.

Nagao, M. (1983). La traduction automatique. *La Recherche*, **14**, 1530–1541.

Neely, J.H. (1977). Semantic priming and retrieval from lexical memory: roles of inhibitionless spreading of activation and limited-capacity attention. *Journal of Experimental Psychology*, **106**, 226–254.

Noizet, G. (1983). Effet du contexte sur le déroulement temporel du processus de lecture. *L'Année Psychologique*, **83**, 395–408.

Norris, D. (1982). Autonomous processes in comprehension: a reply to Marlsen-Wilson and Tyler. *Cognition*, **11**, 97–101.

Ortony, A., Schallert, D.L., Reynolds, R.E. and Antos, S.J. (1978). Interpreting metaphors and idioms: some effects of context on comprehension. *Journal of Verbal Learning and Verbal Behavior*, **17**, 465–477.

Perfetti, C.A. (1982). Contexte discursif, identification de mots et capacité de lecture. *Bulletin de Psychologie*, **35**, 571–578.

Perfetti, C.A. and Roth, S. (1981). Some of the interactive processes in reading and their roles in reading skill. In A.M. Lesgold and C.A. Perfetti (Eds), *Interactive Processes in Reading*, Hillsdale, NJ: Erlbaum.

Posner, M.I. and Snyder, C.R.R. (1975). Facilitation and inhibition in the processing of signals. In P.M.A. Rabbitt and S. Dornic (Eds), *Attention and Performance*, New York: Academic Press.

Potter, F. (1982). The use of the linguistic context: do good and poor readers use different strategies? *British Journal of Educational Psychology*, **52**, 16–23.

Presson, C.C. (1980). Understanding sentences in varying contexts. *Journal of Child Language*, **9**, 217–228.

Pynte, J. (1983). *Lire... Identifier, Comprendre*, Lille: Presses Universitaires de Lille.

Pynte, J. (1984). Pour une approche psycholinguistique du dialogue homme-machine. *Cahiers de Psychologie Cognitive*, **4**, 127–149.

Quillian, M.R. (1968). Semantic memory. In M. Minsky (Ed), *Semantic Information Processing*, Cambridge, MA: MIT Press.

Quillian, M.R. (1969). The teachable language comprehension. *Communication of the ACM*, **12**, 459–476.

Rayner, K. (1978). Eye movements in reading and information processing. *Psychological Bulletin*, **85**, 618–660.

Reder, L.M. (1983). What kind of pitcher can a catcher fill? Effects of priming in sentence comprehension. *Journal of Verbal Learning and Verbal Behavior*, **22**, 189–202.

Rips, L.J. and Marcus, S.L. (1978). Suppositions and the analysis of conditional sentences. In P.A. Carpenter and M.A. Just (Eds), *Cognitive Processes in Comprehension*, Hillsdale, NJ: Erlbaum.

Rosenberg, S. and Lambert, W.E. (1974). Contextual constraints and the perception of speech. *Journal of Experimental Psychology*, **102**, 178–180.

Rumelhart, D.E. (1977). *Introduction to Human Information Processing*, New York: Wiley.

Rumelhart, D.E. and McClelland, J.L. (1981). Interactive processing through spreading activation. In A.M. Lesgold and C.A. Perfetti (Eds), *Interactive Processes in Reading*, Hillsdale, NJ: Erlbaum.

Sanford, A.J. and Garrod, S.C. (1982). Towards a processing account of reference. In A. Flammer and W. Kintsch (Eds), *Discourse Processing, Advances in Psychology, Vol 8*, Amsterdam: North Holland.

Sanford, A.T., Garrod, S. and Bell, E. (1978). Aspects of memory dynamics in text comprehension. In P.E. Morris and R.N. Sykes (Eds), *Practical Aspects of Memory*, New York: Academic Press.

Schallert, D.L. (1976). Improving memory for prose: the relationship between depth of processing and context. *Journal of Verbal Learning and Verbal Behavior*, **15**, 621–632.

Schank, R.C. (1972). Conceptual dependency: a theory of natural language understanding. *Cognitive Psychology*, **3**, 552–631.

Schank, R.C. and Abelson, R. (1977). *Scripts, Plans, Goals and Understanding*, Hillsdale, NJ: Erlbaum.

Schank, R.C. and Birnbaum, L. (1980). *Memory, Meaning, and Syntax*, Research report No 189, Department of Computer Science, Yale University.

Schebilske, W.L. (1980). Structuring an internal representation of text: a basis for literacy. In P.A. Kolers (Ed), *Processes of Visible Language, Vol 2*, New York: Plenum Press.

Schvenaveldt, R.W., Meyer, D.E. and Becker, C.A. (1976). Lexical ambiguity, semantic context and visual word recognition. *Journal of Experimental Psychology: Human Perception and Performance*, **2**, 243–256.

Segui, J. (1986). The role of context in language processing: when and how? In G. Tiberghien (Ed), *Context and Cognition, Cahiers de Psychologie Cognitive*, **6**, 175–186.

Sells, J.B. and Koob, H.B. (1937). A classroom demonstration of atmosphere effect in reasoning. *Journal of Educational Psychology*, **38**, 514–518.

Simmons, R.F. (1973). Semantic networks: their computation and use for understanding English sentences. In R. Schank and K. Colby (Eds), *Computer Models of Thought and Language*, San Francisco: Freeman.

Singer, M. (1976). Context inferences in the comprehension of sentences. *Canadian Journal of Psychology*, **30**, 39–46.

Singer, M. (1981). Verifying the assertions and the implications of language. *Journal of Verbal Learning and Verbal Behavior*, **20**, 46–60.

Singer, M. (1984). Mental processes of question answering. In A. Grasser and J. Black (Eds), *The Psychology of Questions*, Hillsdale, NJ: Erlbaum.

Singer, M. and Ferreira, F. (1983). Inferring consequences in story comprehension. *Journal of Verbal Learning and Verbal Behavior*, **22**, 437–448.

Stanovich, K.E. and West, R.F. (1979). Mechanisms of sentence context effects in reading: automatic activation and conscious attention. *Memory and Cognition*, **7**, 77–85.

Stanovich, K.E. and West, R.F. (1981). The effects of sentence context on ongoing word recognition. *Journal of Experimental Psychology: Human Perception and Performance*, **7**, 658–672.

Stanovich, K.E. and West, R.F. (1983a). On priming by a sentence context. *Journal of Experimental Psychology: General*, **112**, 1–36.

Stanovich, K.E. and West, R.F. (1983b). The generalizability of context effects on word recognition: a reconsideration of the roles of parafoveal priming and sentence context. *Memory and Cognition*, **11**, 49–58.

Swinney, D.A. and Hakes, D.T. (1976). Effects of prior context upon lexical access during sentence comprehension. *Journal of Verbal Learning and Verbal Behavior*, **15**, 681–689.

Tabossi, P. and Johnson-Laird, P.N. (1980). Linguistic context and the priming of semantic information. *Quarterly Journal of Experimental Psychology*, **32**, 595–603.

Tiberghien, G. (1985). Mais òu sont les stimulus d'antan? *Psychologie Française*, **30**, 177–184.

Tiberghien, G. (1986a). Context and cognition: Introduction. In G. Tiberghien (Ed), *Context and Cognition, Cahiers de Psychologie Cognitive (European Bulletin of Cognitive Psychology)*, **6**, 105–121.

Tiberghien, G. (1986a). Intelligence, mémoire et artifices. In C. Bonnet, J.M. Hoc and G. Tiberghien (Eds), *Psychologie, Intelligence Artificielle et Automatique*, Bruxelles: Mardaga.

Tiberghien, G. and Audeguy, N. (1985). La planification du dialogue dans les systèmes de communication automatisés. In *Proceedings of the Meeting Cognitiva*, 85, Paris: Centre d'Etudes des Systèmes et des Technologies Avancées.

Townsend, D.J. (1983). Thematic processing in sentences and texts. *Cognition*, **13**, 223–261.

Townsend, D.J. and Bever, T.G. (1978). Interclause relations and clausal processing. *Journal of Verbal Learning and Verbal Behavior*, **7**, 509–521.

Townsend, D.T. and Bever, T.G. (1982). Natural units of representation interact during sentence comprehension. *Journal of Verbal Learning and Verbal Behavior*, **21**, 688–703.

Tulving, E. (1983). *Elements of Episodic Memory*, New York: Oxford University Press.

Tyler, L.K. and Marslen-Wilson, W.D. (1977). The on-line effects of semantic context on syntactic processing. *Journal of Verbal Learning and Verbal Behavior*, **16**, 683–692.

Van Dijk, T.A. (1980). *Text and Context: Explorations in the Semantics and Pragmatics of Discourse*, New York: Longman.

Vasquez, C.A. (1981). Sentence processing: evidence against the serial independent stage assumption. *Journal of Psycholinguistic Research*, **10**, 363–374.

Vezin, L. (1982). Compréhension d'énoncés et indices contextuels. *Bulletin de Psychologie*, **33**, No 341, 845–854.

Walker, D.E. (1983). Automated language processing. *Annual Review of Information Science and Technology*, **8**, 69–119.

Waltz, D.L. (1982). The state of art in natural language understanding. In W.G. Lehnert and M.H. Ringle (Eds), *Strategies for Natural Language Processing*, Hillsdale, NJ: Erlbaum.

Wason, P.C. (1965). The context of plausible denial. *Journal of Verbal Learning and Verbal Behavior*, **4**, 7–11.

Wason, P.C. (1968). The drafting of rules. *New Law Journal*, **118**, 548–549.

Winograd, T. (1978). A framework for understanding discourse. In P.A. Carpenter and M.H. Ringle (Eds), *Cognitive Processes in Comprehension*, Hillsdale, NJ: Erlbaum.

Winograd, T. (Mar. 1982). Des machines savantes mais incultes. *Science et Vie*, No spécial:*La Science des Robots*, 76–83.

Woods, W.A. (1970). Transition network grammars for natural language analysis. *Communication of the A.C.M.*, **13**, 591–606.

Wright, P. (1980a). Usability: the criterion for designing written information. In

P.A. Kolers, M.E. Wrolstad and H. Bouma (Eds), *Processing of Visible Language, Vol 2*, New York: Plenum Press.

Wright, P. (1980b). Textual literacy: an outline sketch of psychological research on reading and writing. In P.A. Kolers, M.E. Wrolstad and H. Bouma (Eds), *Processing of Visible Language, Vol 2*, New York: Plenum Press.

Yekovich, F.R., Walter, C.H. and Blackman, H.S. (1979). The role of presupposed and focal information in integrating sentences. *Journal of Verbal Learning and Verbal Behavior*, **18**, 535–548.

APPLICATIONS TO APPLIED ISSUES

Memory in Context : Context in Memory
Edited by G.M. Davies and D.M. Thomson
© 1988 John Wiley & Sons Ltd.

CHAPTER 8

# Amnesia and Memory for Contextual Information

A.R. MAYES

*University of Manchester*

## ABSTRACT

Nature of the organic amnesic syndrome: critical lesions responsible for it, main psychological deficits related to it, possible heterogeneity, and outline of the major hypotheses about the underlying functional deficit. Amnesia as a specific memory deficit for interactive context. Amnesia as a specific memory deficit for independent context. Conclusions.

## INTRODUCTION

Brain damage to limbic system structures of the medial temporal lobes or to midline structures of the diencephalon can cause a selective and often severe deficit in recalling and recognizing semantic and episodic information, either acquired pre-traumatically or experienced post-traumatically. The deficit is known as organic or global amnesia. Identification of the lost function(s) that underlie the memory impairment of organic amnesics should therefore shed light on processes critical to the exercise of good memory. Furthermore, identification of the brain regions, damage to which is sufficient to cause the syndrome, and knowledge of the inputs, outputs and physiology of these regions, should help the development of a hypothesis about how the intact brain mediates semantic and episodic memory.

In organic amnesia poor recall and recognition of recently presented episodic and semantic information (anterograde amnesia) is accompanied by poor recall and recognition of pre-traumatically acquired episodic and semantic information, provided such information has not been massively rehearsed (retrograde amnesia). The severity of these deficits varies along a continuum from the very mild, where only a patient's relatives may notice that there has been a deterioration in memory, to the cripplingly severe, where a patient may be completely disoriented, unable to retain anything after attention has been distracted from it, and unable to remember great tracts of his personal history. Even in the severest cases, however, other cognitive functions as assessed by standard intelligence tests may be preserved and short-term memory as assessed by digit span performance may be normal. It is therefore unlikely that organic amnesia is caused by a gross deficit in the encoding and retrieval of meaningful information because such an impairment would also compromise intelligence. Nevertheless, as will be discussed later, similar hypotheses have been defended (see, for example, Butters and Cermak, 1975).

Although direct evidence is lacking, the weight of circumstantial evidence indicates that the sensory information, which forms the core of episodic and semantic memories, is processed and stored largely in the association neocortex, particularly that of the parieto-occipito-temporal cortex. It is therefore slightly puzzling that the lesions responsible for organic amnesia are not neocortical. The precise location of these lesions is still controversial. Within the medial temporal lobes damage probably to the hippocampus and possibly to the amygdala contributes to amnesia (see Squire, 1986) whereas within the diencephalon lesions to the mammillary bodies in the hypothalamus and to the dorsomedial and anterior nuclei in the thalamus have been implicated (Von Cramon, Hebel and Schuri, 1985). There is also evidence that lesions of the cholinergic neurons of the basal forebrain can cause amnesia (Damasio, Graff-Radford, Eslinger, Damasio and Kassell, 1985). These three groups of structures are closely interconnected and it has been argued by Mishkin (1982) that severe and permanent amnesia only results when there has been damage to both a hippocampal circuit, projecting from the hippocampus via the fornix to the mammillary bodies and thence to the anterior nucleus of the thalamus, and an amygdala circuit, projecting from the amygdala to the dorsomedial or other midline thalamic nuclei. Modulation of activity in both circuits can be disrupted by basal forebrain lesions because cholinergic neurons from this region project to hippocampus, amygdala and probably dorsomedial thalamus (see Crosson, 1986). Why should lesions to these structures disrupt the kinds of memory that are largely stored in the neocortex? Both hippocampus and amygdala receive processed sensory information from association neocortex and return projections to the neocortex as well as influencing the midline diencephalic structures, discussed by Mishkin (1982). The structures, damaged in amnesics, are therefore well placed to be influenced by and to influence the neocortical regions where episodic and semantic information is mostly processed and stored.

Any hypothesis about the functional deficit(s) that underlie amnesia must consider first, the neuroanatomy of amnesia, second, the pattern of memory and cognitive performance found in patients, and third, whether this pattern is a single disorder or whether it results from the chance concomitance of several memory dysfunctions. Anatomical factors do not currently provide many constraints for theories of amnesia except in so far as they make clear that most of the episodic and semantic information for which memory is so poor is likely to be stored neocortically. Even this likelihood has been challenged by Teyler and Discenna (1986), however, who have proposed that, at least for recently formed memories, the hippocampus stores a record of the neocortical modules, the activation of which represents the remembered information. This hypothesis does not require neocortical memory changes in the period shortly after learning. Although they may well be incorrect, plastic changes are produced in the hippocampus by neocortical inputs, so this structure and, possibly, some of the others that can be damaged in amnesia may store certain kinds of information important for episodic and semantic memory.

Organic amnesia is commonly regarded as a global disorder of memory, but, more correctly, it is a global disorder for all those kinds of information that can be recalled or recognized. Amnesics show preservation of other kinds of memory. There is good evidence that they can acquire and retain certain motor and perceptual skills, and some support for the view that they show normal ability to acquire and retain some cognitive skills although this is more problematic (see Squire and Cohen, 1984). There is also evidence that patients can show classical conditioning despite being unable to recognize the apparatus used to train them (Weiskrantz and Warrington, 1979). It remains to be proved that such conditioning is completely normal although this seems likely. Amnesics have, however, been shown to be totally normal at several priming tasks (see Shimamura, 1986; Schacter and Graf, 1986). Priming is a form of item-specific memory and occurs when an item is processed more efficiently or differently as a result of having been recently perceived. For example, when amnesics are asked to complete the opening three letters of a range of possible words with the first word that comes to mind, they show a normally enhanced tendency to produce words they have just studied even though they are not able to recognize these words as ones they have just seen (see Shimamura, 1986 for a review). Memory for skills, conditioning and priming does not require the rememberer to recall or recognize the stored information. Encoding, storage and retrieval of these kinds of memory cannot normally depend on the limbic-diencephalic structures, damaged in amnesics. But patients also seem to have preserved recall and recognition of much rehearsed, overlearnt semantic and episodic information, such as the kind of language used more or less every day. Recall and recognition of these well-established kinds of memory may be mediated within the neocortex and not involve the regions affected by amnesia.

Not only must hypotheses about the functional deficit(s), underlying amnesia be able to explain why the above kinds of memory are preserved in patients, they must also be able to explain why certain kinds of memory are disproportionately affected and why patients show any cognitive deficits. There are two problems that must be allowed for in assessing such claims. First, many amnesics also have damage to neocortex and brain stem structures, that cause symptoms unrelated to the basic syndrome, but which may inadvertently be confused with it. For example, some Korsakoff patients, who have an aetiology of chronic alcoholism, suffer from atrophy of the frontal association cortex. These patients often confabulate, that is, they fill out their impoverished memories with unrelated intrusions, but this confabulation is probably caused by their frontal lobe atrophy and is incidental to their core amnesic symptoms (Kapur and Coughlan, 1980). Second, it is very hard to establish a claim that one kind of memory is more impaired than another in patients. If patients are poor at memory tests A and B, then performance on A may appear to be worse affected because test B is generally less sensitive. Very few memory tests have been matched for sensitivity. Therefore, to demonstrate that performance on A is more disrupted than performance on B, patients must be equated with their controls on test B either by testing the controls after a much longer delay or after they have been given less opportunity to learn. If under similar conditions patients are worse at test A, then a disproportionate deficit will have been established. Claims for these kinds of deficit are discussed in the next two sections.

Even if the pattern of memory and cognitive ability can be clearly mapped in amnesics, their various deficits may be distinct and caused by a smaller lesion than that associated with the global syndrome. For example, it is well known that lesions of the left medial temporal lobe or medial diencephalon selectively impair verbal memory whereas right-sided lesions of these regions impair memory selectively for difficult-to-verbalize material. Three other more controversial claims have been made about the heterogeneity of the syndrome. First, it has been argued that medial temporal lobe lesions cause a form of amnesia which is characterized by poor learning and pathologically fast forgetting whereas diencephalic lesions cause a form of amnesia characterized by poor learning, but normal forgetting (see Squire and Cohen, 1984). The reality of the distinction is disputed (for example, see Weiskrantz, 1985). Second, retrograde amnesia has been reported in isolation from anterograde amnesia (see Kapur, Heath, Meudell and Kennedy, 1986) although it remains to be proved that this syndrome is caused by a smaller lesion of the kind that causes global amnesia. Also, no convincing case of isolated anterograde amnesia has ever been demonstrated even though in many global patients there is a poor correlation between the severity of anterograde and retrograde amnesia

(Butters, 1985; see Squire and Cohen, 1984). The third claim derives from Mishkin's (1982) hypothesis about the anatomy of amnesia. It is that lesions of the hippocampal and amygdala circuits affect distinct functions either of which alone may be sufficient for the display of a moderate degree of memory.

Hypotheses about the functional deficit(s) that cause amnesia may be classified as varying in two distinct ways. First, the postulated deficit may be one of encoding, storage, retrieval or some combination of these. Second, the postulated deficit may primarily affect memory for only a subset of those kinds of information for which recall and recognition is deficient, memory for the other kinds of information being poor because it depends on the initial retrieval of information primarily affected. Alternatively, it may affect memory for all kinds of information for which recall and recognition is poor in the same kind of way. With respect to the first kind of variation every type of hypothesis has been advanced, but the current *Zeitgeist* favours the view that where information is processed (encoded and retrieved) it is also stored (see Squire, 1986). If correct, this means that a lesion disrupting processing will disrupt storage, and vice versa. The paradox is that most of the processing of the kinds of information which amnesics cannot remember must be carried out in the neocortex. It is possible, however, that in amnesia there is impaired facilitatory modulation of neocortical storage as this is normally performed by the affected limbic-diencephalic structures. The amnesic deficit therefore is most likely either to affect all stages of memory or that of storage alone.

More central to the focus of this chapter is the second way in which hypotheses can vary. At present, the most influential kinds of hypothesis about the functional deficit in amnesia propose that patients only have a primary deficit for some of the information that they cannot remember. There are two variants of such hypotheses. The first proposes that amnesics have a special problem remembering those kinds of semantic information that require the sort of elaborative processing that is mediated by the prefrontal association neocortex (Butters and Cermak, 1975; Warrington and Weiskrantz, 1982). This kind of semantic information corresponds approximately to what Baddeley (1982) called interactive context because it forms the meaningful background to the event or item that falls at the focus of attention and influences the way in which this event or item is interpreted. The other variant of such hypotheses proposes that amnesics have a specific deficit in remembering background contextual information that relates to an event's or item's spatiotemporal position and the way in which it is presented (see Huppert and Piercy, 1978; Hirst, 1982; Mayes, Meudell and Pickering, 1985). This kind of contextual information corresponds to what Baddeley (1982) called independent context because it is unlikely to affect the interpretation of the target event or item. It is possible to argue that amnesics suffer from a specific memory deficit for both kinds of contextual information as perhaps was done by Kinsbourne and Wood (1982). The next section assesses the evidence relevant to the view that amnesics have a specific difficulty remembering interactive context and the third section examines evidence relevant to the view that they have a specific memory deficit for independent contextual information.

## AMNESIA AS A SPECIFIC MEMORY DEFICIT
## FOR INTERACTIVE CONTEXT

If amnesia is caused by a selective deficit in remembering interactive context two things must be true. First, interactive context must, at least to some extent, be processed by different brain mechanisms from those involved with the other kinds of information that can be recalled and recognized. Second, failure to retrieve interactive context must have a devastating effect on memory for recently experienced semantic and episodic information. With respect to the first requirement, it can plausibly be argued that the prefrontal cortex is pre-eminently involved with mediating elaborative semantic processing because of its critical role in planning (Duncan, 1986). Even unilateral lesions of this region have been shown to impair semantic categorization of pictures and words (Hirst, 1985; Rocchetta, 1986). This kind of semantic impairment can be distinguished from the basic semantic interpretation of stimuli, which Hasher and Zacks (1979) have argued is performed with the minimal expenditure of attentional effort. If semantic information that needs to be processed with planning and effort can be regarded as interactive context and semantic information that is more automatically encoded can be regarded as target information, then it can be argued that only the former depends vitally on the pre-frontal cortex. The distinction between interactive context and target information is, however, a somewhat blurred and arbitrary one that is perhaps best characterized by the experimental manipulations, used initially by Tulving and his colleagues. In such experiments, contextual stimuli are presented as background and indicated to be of secondary importance by the experimenters. Nevertheless, some target information is likely to require effortful processing and therefore the offices of the frontal cortex. At present, therefore, it cannot be concluded that there is any brain region solely concerned with processing interactive context. The frontal cortex does, however, probably play a more important role in processing interactive context than it does in processing target information.

Evidence relevant to the second requirement is slightly more compelling. Since Craik and Lockhart's (1972) formulation of the levels of processing framework, many studies have shown that reduced semantic encoding of stimuli leads to poorer recall and recognition. Further, work by Tulving and his colleagues (see Tulving, 1983) indicates that if the availability of interactive context cues is reduced at retrieval, then recognition is worsened as well as recall. It has not been demonstrated, however, that these impairments are as drastic as those seen in severe amnesia. If they are not, the view that organic amnesia is caused by a selective failure to remember interactive context may not necessarily be wrong. This is because manipulations of semantic processing in normal people may not have disrupted memory for interactive context as greatly as is found in severe amnesia.

The two main variants of the hypothesis that amnesics have a specific deficit in remembering those kinds of semantic information that have been effortfully processed do not explicitly claim that amnesics have a selective impairment in remembering interactive context. The likelihood that it is particularly interactive contextual information that requires elaborative processing does, however, make plausible the interpretation that the hypotheses do posit what is mainly a deficit in memory for interactive context. The first variant proposed originally that amnesics have poor memory because they have a habitual tendency not to encode semantic information (Butters and Cermak, 1975). More recent versions of this view suggest that the deficit extends to the retrieval of semantic information as well (Butters, 1984). As the view clearly applies only to those kinds of processing that are voluntary and planned, its main postulate is that amnesics fail to encode and retrieve interactive context normally. In the second variant of the hypothesis, Warrington and Weiskrantz (1982) deny that amnesics have an encoding problem and instead, they propose that patients either fail to store but, more likely, to retrieve those kinds of elaborated semantic information the processing of which is mediated by the frontal cortex. In their view, amnesics can still encode elaboratively as well as normal people, but because their frontal association cortex is subcortically disconnected from their posterior association cortex, cannot store or retrieve this normally encoded information. An alternative possibility, not excluded by Warrington and Weiskrantz's formulation, is that the disconnection prevents the integration of information processed by the frontal cortex with that processed by more posterior regions so that the integrated product is either not stored or not retrievable.

How do these hypotheses cope with available evidence about amnesia? First, with respect to the indirect evidence, they can explain normal amnesic performance on short-term memory tasks, such as digit span, if it is supposed, as it has often been, that these tasks do not depend on encoding and retrieving semantic information. The preserved intelligence of some amnesics, on the other hand, poses a serious problem, particularly for the Butters and Cermak (1975) hypothesis, which posits an encoding problem. It is difficult to see how a deficit, of whatever provenance, in encoding the semantic information, constituting interactive context, can be compatible with a preserved ability to solve the kinds of problem found in intelligence tests. As the patients on whom Butters and Cermak base their hypothesis are Korsakoff amnesics, whose aetiology of chronic alcoholism is often associated with frontal cortex atrophy (see Butters, in Moscovitch, 1982), it is plausible to argue (and shortly will be) that if their patients have problems encoding semantic information this is incidental to their amnesia and is caused by their frontal cortex atrophy. It should be pointed out that there has been a long controversy about whether direct lesions of the pre-frontal cortex cause decreases in intelligence. The probable answer is that they do not affect crystallized intelligence where performance depends on established strategies, but do disrupt fluid intelligence where performance depends on the planned execution of novel strategies. If Warrington and Weiskrantz's hypothesis is taken to postulate a retrieval deficit, then it also has difficulty explaining amnesics' preserved intelligence because the solution of novel problems is likely to need effortful retrieval of much semantic information. On the other hand, taken as a storage deficit hypothesis, it is compatible with preserved amnesic intelligence.

The second kind of evidence with which the hypotheses must cope is that concerning the preserved kinds of memory in amnesics. If the hypotheses are correct, then priming, the acquisition of skills and conditioning, should not depend in any way on the processing and storage of interactive context. Although this is plausible for memory of skills and conditioning, little relevant research has been done. The situation with priming is different. Schacter and Graf (1986) have argued that there are two distinct kinds of priming, which may be preserved in amnesics. The first kind, which should be preserved in all amnesics, depends on the activation of well-established memories, such as those for particular words. Studies by Schacter and Graf, in which normal subjects were encouraged to process either the semantic or physical features of single words or strong associates, found that semantic encoding improved recognition and recall, but had little or no effect on the kind of priming that depends on activation of well-established memories. The other kind of priming, which Schacter and Graf argue is only preserved in patients who are mildly amnesic, depends on newly formed memories. For example, if unrelated word pairs, such as 'mountain-reason' are presented, the likelihood that with 'word completion' instructions the second word will be produced, when its opening three letters are given as a cue, is increased if the cue is provided in the context of the first word (for example, 'mountain – rea – ?) rather than with another word. This kind of priming is only found if the word pairs are semantically encoded at their presentation and may not occur in severely amnesic patients. Although more elaborative semantic encoding (generating meaningful sentences linking the unrelated words as opposed to rating the meaningfulness of presented sentences that linked the unrelated words) improved cued recall in normal subjects, however, it had no effect on performance when 'word-completion' instructions were given. It is therefore possible that even the priming that depends on formation of new memories does not require the retrieval of interactive context, or at least of more effortfully encoded semantic information. Even so, the issue is unresolved and needs more research into the effects of semantic processing on priming and on whether the more recently found kind of priming only occurs in mild amnesics.

The third kind of evidence, most directly relevant to the interactive context-memory deficit hypotheses of amnesia, concerns the nature of the memory deficit for interactive context shown by patients. Whereas both hypotheses predict that amnesics should have disproportionately poor recall and recognition for interactive context relative to more automatically processed target information only the view of Butters and Cermak predicts that patients will show impoverished encoding of semantic information. The hypotheses also differ in their predictions about the mnemonic effects of getting patients to engage in elaborative semantic encoding. According to Butters and Cermak, amnesics do not spontaneously engage in such processing, but can do so if encouraged. Memory following a semantic orienting task, relative to memory following spontaneous learning, should therefore be more improved in amnesics than in normal subjects. In contrast, according to Warrington and Weiskrantz, amnesics should fail to remember the semantic information that they have elaboratively encoded. Unlike normals, they should therefore not benefit mnemonically from increased amounts of semantic encoding. On the whole, none of these predictions are well supported by current evidence.

Although Butters and Cermak (1975) have accumulated considerable evidence that amnesics do not show normal encoding of semantic information, this evidence is based on studies of Korsakoff patients. It seems most probable that these patients' deficits are caused by incidental frontal lobe damage, which results from their chronic alcoholism. For example, Korsakoff patients fail to show release from proactive interference in the Brown–Peterson task when there is a shift from one semantic category to another. Subjects were shown four successive lists comprising words drawn from a single semantic category and were then shown a list of words from a different semantic category. Recall decreased in all subjects across the first four list presentations, but whereas control recall improved on the fifth presentation that of the Korsakoff patients did not. This was originally interpreted as showing that amnesics do not spontaneously encode the meanings of words and so fail to benefit mnemonically when words from a new semantic category are given. It has been found, however, that only amnesics with an aetiology of chronic alcoholism fail to show release under these conditions, and that patients with frontal lobe lesions have a similar problem, provided they have mild recall deficits (Moscovitch, 1982; Freedman and Cermak, 1986). Other evidence indicates that frontal lobe lesions impair elaborative semantic processing, disturb recall more than recognition, and disrupt memory in other ways as well (see Mayes, 1987). It is most likely that some amnesics show deficient encoding of semantic information because they have incidental damage to their frontal lobes.

There have been several studies of amnesics, comparing the effects on memory of semantic orienting tasks and spontaneous learning. In a series of such studies with Korsakoff patients and using learning materials that included words, nonsense shapes, faces and cartoon pictures, it was found that both amnesics and their controls showed improved recognition when encouraged to process stimuli semantically and that the degree of improvement was the same in both groups (see Meudell and Mayes, 1982, for a review). These studies matched amnesic and control memory in the spontaneous learning condition by testing controls at a longer delay, so as to eliminate floor and ceiling effects. Although other studies have found both no improvement and greater improvement in some amnesics (see Butters, 1984), these results probably arose either from floor or ceiling effects or because tested patients had incidental frontal lobe damage. The weight of the evidence suggests that amnesics can engage in elaborative semantic encoding as effectively as normal people and that their later recognition of such encodings is no worse than that for any other kind of encoded information.

To demonstrate convincingly that amnesics are particularly bad at remembering material that requires elaborative semantic encoding it is necessary to match their memory with that of normals on other material that does not need such encoding, otherwise the results can be interpreted as floor or ceiling effects, or simply as consequences of the amnesics' poor memory. The best available evidence is drawn from the Brown–Peterson task. Recall of random word triplets, such as 'black, visit, tongue', was found to be normal in amnesics after a short, filled delay, but the recall of triplets, such as 'clock, slow, wind', related by semantic association, was impaired (see Warrington, 1985). This result is interesting, but requires replication with more amnesics because many patients fail to show normal recall even with random word triplets and the determinants of task performance are very poorly understood. Other demonstrations are much less convincing. Good amnesic performance with related paired associates, such as 'soldier—rifle', and terrible performance with unrelated pairs, such as 'germ—house', are confounded because the former almost certainly depends on priming whereas the latter cannot. As priming seems to be independent of recall and recognition (Schacter and Graf, 1986), its preservation in amnesics does not reveal whether patients' recall is worse for semantic than for other kinds of information. A study, claiming that amnesics cannot use weak semantic cues, presented during learning with target words (for example 'claw' as a cue for 'dog') to aid their recall of the target words (Cermak, Uhly and Reale, 1980), is more plausibly interpreted another way. The patients' recall was far worse than that of their controls, so because of their poor memory they treated all cues as strong semantic associates of possible target words. This interpretation is supported by the finding that patients' recall was even worse when given weak cues at encoding and retrieval than when they were given no cues at all.

It must be concluded that available evidence does not support the view that amnesia is caused by either a selective deficit in memory for all those kinds of elaborative semantic processing that encode both targets and their interactive contexts or a selective deficit in memory for interactive contexts alone. There does need to be more research, however, on whether amnesics have particularly severe problems with what is normally regarded as an interactive context. Even if not applicable to amnesia, a deficit in processing interactive context as well as some target-related kinds of semantic information may be the cause of the memory problems found in patients with frontal lobe lesions.

## AMNESIA AS A SPECIFIC MEMORY DEFICIT
## FOR INDEPENDENT CONTEXT

It is widely believed that amnesia is caused by a specific deficit in remembering independent context (see Mayes *et al.*, 1985). Despite its popularity the view is not usually formulated in an explicit and clear way, and much of the evidence cited in its favour is of dubious value. Minimally, the hypothesis claims that amnesics cannot process and store, or merely cannot store, the background spatiotemporal context of an event or item (background context), and also the mode of that event's or item's presentation (format context). Contextual features like these do not typically affect the way in which target events or items are interpreted and so can be regarded as independent context. Failure to retrieve background and format context leads to poor recall and recognition of the target information that is the focus of attention during learning. Like interactive context-memory deficit hypotheses this view must satisfy two main desiderata. Independent context must be processed differently from target information and by somewhat different structures that include the limbic-diencephalic regions lesioned in amnesics, and retrieval of independent context must be vital for target recognition and recall.

Hasher and Zacks (1979) postulated that memory for event recency, frequency and spatial location depends on automatic encoding and Lehmann (1982) has supported a similar claim about memory for the modality in which information is presented. By this they did not simply mean that normal people habitually encode such contextual features with minimal attentional effort so that context is later quite well remembered, but that context can only be encoded automatically. Their evidence for this claim was that getting people to focus their attention on context did not improve their memory for it. This stronger claim is strongly disputed by many researchers (see Jackson, Michon, Boonstra, De Jonge and De Velde, 1986), but even if independent context is only habitually encoded automatically and encoding of target information is a more effortful activity (but perhaps not as effortful as the encoding of interactive context!), there are some grounds for thinking that encoding independent context is mediated by somewhat different brain regions from those that encode target information.

The view that retrieving independent context plays some role in normal memory is suggested by studies of context- and state-dependent forgetting (see Baddeley, 1982; Smith, Davies, this volume). But Baddeley and others have argued that changing context or state between learning and test reduces recall, but not recognition. In contrast, amnesics may show severely impaired recall and recognition. Several comments about this contrast are in order. First, changing context or state between learning and test in normal subjects only slightly reduces the availability of contextual cues. Indeed, the forgetting effect can be greatly reduced if subjects are asked to imagine the learning context during recall (see Chapter 2, this volume, by Smith). The selective deficit in context-memory in amnesics, if it exists, is likely to be much more extreme and not reversible by appropriate instructions. Second, there is some evidence that changing the temporal order of items between presentation and test can impair recognition (Leonard and Whitten, 1983) and similar effects have been reported when an item's mode or modality of presentation is changed between learning and test (see Morton, Hammersley and Bekerian, 1985). Further, in this book (Chapter 3), Davies discusses evidence that recognition of faces or face photographs is impaired when they are perceived in a different background context from that in which they were originally experienced. This effect is probably caused by the reduced availability of the background context present when the stimuli were first learnt, a context that is unlikely to affect greatly the interpretation of the stimuli. Evidence from context- and state-dependent forgetting therefore suggests that retrieval of independent context is important for both recall and recognition although it may be more important for the former.

This tentative conclusion is compatible with a recent observation of the relative severity of recall and recognition deficits in a group of amnesics with mixed aetiologies (Hirst, Johnson, Kim, Phelps, Risse and Volpe, 1986). It was found that when amnesic and control recognition of recently shown words was equated by giving the control subjects much reduced learning exposures that the patients still had significantly worse recall. This disproportionate recall deficit could not easily be explained as a result of incidental damage to the frontal lobes because it occurred in patients who showed none of the cognitive signs of frontal lobe lesions. This finding needs confirmation with more amnesics, using different methods of equating recognition between amnesics and controls, but, if correct, is consistent with the independent context deficit hypothesis. Patients with frontal lesion show a similar deficit pattern, but in them the effect is probably caused by their reduced semantic processing, which impairs their ability to form associative links between words. Such links are more important for recall than they are for recognition. In other words, as Warrington (1985) argues that amnesics cannot retrieve such associations either, both variants of the context-memory deficit hypothesis predict this pattern of impairment.

On an *ad hoc* basis the independent context-memory deficit hypothesis provides quite convincing explanations of why certain functions are preserved in amnesics. The problem-solving abilities that constitute intelligence are unlikely to be disrupted by an impairment in the automatic processing of independent context, and even less so, by the impaired storage of such information. It might also be argued that a major characteristic of short-term memory tasks, such as digit span, is that they do not depend on the retrieval of the contextual markers of remembered items whereas this is a critical feature of long-term memory tasks. Similarly, to defend the hypothesis, it has to be supposed that conditioning, skills and priming are context-independent forms of memory unless they depend on representations of context radically different from those required for recall and recognition. If so, these forms of memory should not be susceptible to context-dependent forgetting. Although no relevant evidence exists for skill memory, Mackintosh (1985) has cited data that suggest conditioning does not show context-dependent forgetting. In priming, no explicit reference is made to the context in which an item was presented but, in recent unpublished work, we have found evidence that priming may be reduced both when background context is changed between presentation and test and when format context is similarly changed (Mayes and Hargreaves, in preparation). Normal subjects were shown words in one of two presentation formats and in one of two rooms, then later performed a priming task either in a different room with the cues presented in the same or a different format, or in the same room with the cues presented in the same or a different format. Priming was most reduced when both format and background context were changed, but was reduced to an equivalently lesser extent when either was changed alone. At present, there is one published study showing a reduction in priming when sensory modality of presentation was changed between presentation and test (see Shimamura,

1986). If these results are reliable they provide a problem for the context-memory deficit hypothesis as applied to independent context. It can only be defended in an *ad hoc* fashion by arguing that priming must depend on a different kind of representation of independent contextual information than is required for recognition and recall. Currently, there is no evidence to support this claim.

If amnesics show disproportionately poor memory for the format and the background context of events and items, this would be strong support for the independent context-memory deficit hypothesis. Several studies have found disproportionately poor context-memory, using designs in which amnesic and control memory for target material was matched by testing control subjects after a much longer delay and showing that certain aspects of amnesic contextual memory were still worse. First, it has been shown that amnesics' judgements about event recency can be impaired even when their target memory is equated to that of controls (Squire, 1982; Hirst and Volpe, 1982). For example, Squire (1982) found that under conditions when Korsakoff patients could recognize sentences as well as their controls, they were far worse at identifying in which of two lists they had appeared. This exceedingly poor ability of Korsakoff patients to make recency judgements is compatible with Huppert and Piercy's (1978) report that these patients base their judgements of both recency and frequency on the degree of a memory's familiarity rather than on specific contextual information as normal subjects usually seem to do. This qualitative difference between Korsakoff and normal memory cannot be explained as a result of the patients' poor memory because normal subjects do not behave in this way even when their memory is similarly weakened (Meudell, Mayes, Ostergaard and Pickering, 1985).

Second, a mixed group of amnesics has been shown to have impaired memory for the source of recalled information (source amnesia) even when conditions have been manipulated so that their recall of the information is as good as that of their controls (Schacter, Harbluk and McLachlan, 1984). Specifically, two experimenters took turns to read subjects obscure 'facts'. Tested immediately and unlike the controls who were tested a week later, the amnesics erroneously identified several of the facts they had recalled as having been acquired in an outside context, such as television. Third, a group of Korsakoff patients were impaired at identifying whether words had been presented to them visually or auditorily even when controls were tested under much harder conditions, so that recognition of the words was matched between the groups (Pickering, Mayes and Fairbairn, submitted). As yet, there have been no similar published demonstrations of disproportionately impaired amnesic spatial memory. Kohl (1984), in a study of target memory for words and abstract forms and also recency, frequency and spatial memory judgements, reported that Korsakoff patients showed greater spatial as well as frequency and recency memory deficits. Although a systematic matching procedure was not used, in one condition when the learning of items' spatial positions was incidental, patients were not worse than their controls at recognizing recently seen words, but were markedly worse at identifying where those words had been located. In my laboratory, we have found some evidence that Korsakoff patients' memory for words' spatial positions is impaired even when their recognition of the words is matched to that of their controls. Hirst and Volpe (1984) have also obtained preliminary evidence that amnesic spatial memory is worse than their memory for target material.

These findings of disproportionate amnesic deficits in memory for independent context should be regarded as tentative and need replication with larger groups of patients with different aetiologies, and preferably using several means of equating target memory between patients and their controls. At present, most of the results have been drawn from Korsakoff patients, who frequently have frontal lobe atrophy as well as damage to other non-limbic-diencephalic brain areas. This raises the serious possibility that the effects observed have nothing to do with the core amnesia. It has indeed been reported that patients with frontal lobe lesions are impaired at judging the recency and frequency with which items have been presented although their recognition of the items is normal (see Milner, Petrides and Smith, 1985). This deficit may seem puzzling if all memory problems caused by frontal lobe lesions result from failures of elaborative processing because of Hasher and Zacks' (1979) claim that temporal features are automatically encoded. Frontal lobe lesions have therefore been reported to impair memory processes like recall, believed to depend particularly on effortful processing, and also temporal memory, which is believed to depend on automatic processing. There are several possible views about the relationship between these reported deficits. First, they may be independent and caused by distinct frontal lobe lesions. Second, frontal lobe lesions may only impair temporal memory and other automatically processed forms of context-memory with deficits in recall and other forms of memory resulting from damage extending into other brain regions as has been suggested by Schacter (1987). Third, both kinds of memory deficit may result from deficient effortful processing caused by frontal lobe lesions. The first and third possibilities are supported by evidence that frontal lobe lesions do not impair memory for objects' spatial locations—something supposed depend on automatic processing (see Milner *et al.*, 1985)—although frontal lobe lesions in monkeys do impair spatial memory when temporal discrimination is also required (see Schacter, 1987). The notion of automaticity itself may, however, need revision. Contextual memory may indeed depend to some extent on effortful processing. It is unknown what features need to be encoded to make recency judgements and interestingly it has been found by Jackson *et al.* (1986) that normal subjects' recency judgements about words were more accurate when the words had been encoded in an elaborative semantic fashion. If correct, context-memory deficits found after frontal lobe lesions could, like recall deficits, result from failures of effortful processing. More work is needed, however, to decide between these three possibilities.

It remains uncertain whether amnesic contextual memory problems are exacerbated by incidental frontal lobe lesions. Hirst and Volpe (1982) reported disproportionate deficits in recency judgements in amnesics, who did not show cognitive signs of frontal lobe atrophy although their study has been criticized for other reasons (Schacter, 1987). Squire (1982), however, only found such deficits in Korsakoff patients, who tend to have such atrophy or at least to show cognitive signs typical of such atrophy, but not in other amnesics, who were less likely to have had frontal lobe atrophy. If the effects are caused by incidental frontal lobe damage, then there should be a correlation between the severity of the contextual memory deficit and the degree of impairment on cognitive tests, sensitive to frontal lobe lesions. Schacter *et al.* (1984) found such a correlation between memory for the source of information and 'frontal test' performance. They did not, however, find source amnesia in patients with lesions confined to the frontal lobes. We also found a significant correlation between 'frontal test' performance and memory for modality of item presentation. But memory for an item's presentation modality also correlated with recognition ability for target information, and partial correlations suggested that this latter relationship was stronger. Contextual and target memory needs to be examined in more amnesics and patients with frontal lobe lesions. Poor context-memory may occur in both groups for the same or different reasons, and different kinds of context-memory may be poor in the two groups. Some support for the former position exists, albeit weak, as Bowers, Verfaellie and Rapscyk (1987) have reported that amnesics with frontal damage were poor at temporal memory tasks whether they involved new learning or remote memory whereas an amnesic without frontal lobe damage was only poor at such tasks if they involved new learning.

## CONCLUDING COMMENTS

The view that amnesia is caused by a selective deficit in memory for events' or items' independent contexts is the best supported of the two variants of the context-memory deficit hypothesis. Even so, it lacks convincing support and may turn out to be false. In concluding, several issues, relevant to the testing and elaboration of the hypothesis will be briefly discussed.

First, the hypothesis must explain retrograde amnesia whether this has precisely the same cause as anterograde amnesia or an independent one. Most objective tests of retrograde amnesia indicate that there is relative sparing of older pretraumatic memories (Squire and Cohen, 1984) although the reason for this is problematical. One possibility, compatible with existing evidence, is that older memories only survive if they are rehearsed, and that memories achieve protection from limbic-diencephalic lesions to the extent that they are rehearsed. This rehearsal may reorganize the memories so that they can be recalled and recognized without first retrieving any of the contexts in which they were encoded and re-encoded. Cermak (1984) has argued that retrograde amnesia affects only episodic memories, and that the spared memories are semantic. This is not strictly correct because retrograde amnesia affects both episodic and semantic information, but it does capture the idea that autobiographical memories may become reorganized over time, so that they can be retrieved like well-rehearsed facts without accessing the contexts in which they were first experienced. Acquisition of both episodic and semantic information may initially require normal contextual memory but with rehearsal both kinds of information may be recalled without accessing any contextual markers.

Second, if amnesics can process and store target, but not contextual information, there may be circumstances where the target information can be recalled without accessing its context of acquisition. This may be what occurs when mildly amnesic patients show the kind of priming that depends on the acquisition of new information (Schacter and Graf, 1986). Tranel and Damasio (1985) have also reported that an amnesic showed discriminative autonomic responses to recently perceived faces that she was unable to recognize. It needs to be determined whether this form of memory occurs in severe amnesics. This phenomenon relates to a third point, which concerns the bases of recognition. The context-memory deficit hypothesis assumes that recognition, like recall, depends, to some extent on retrieval of an event or item's context. Mandler's (1980) two-process view of recognition allows for one process like this, but postulates another more direct one that depends on the increased fluency with which a recently perceived item is processed. If amnesic priming and 'autonomic discrimination' memory depend on this fluency mechanism, then it is unlikely to be sufficient for conscious recognition.

Fourth, amnesics should be more susceptible to proactive interference in A – B, A – C paradigms because the distinction between A – B and A – C items depends on the contexts in which they were initially embedded. Exactly such increased susceptibility to interference has been reported in studies that match amnesic and control memory on A – B memory (Warrington and Weiskrantz, 1974; Winocur and Weiskrantz, 1976). This matching on A – B memory is important because otherwise it could be argued the amnesic interference sensitivity results from their poor recall of the items. Unfortunately, in the above studies matching probably occurs because A – B memory in both groups depends largely on priming whereas A – C memory in controls depends much more on recall with amnesics still having to rely on priming. Mayes *et al.* (1985) have, in fact, shown that even normals show amnesic levels of proactive interference when they are made to rely on priming alone. Schacter and Graf (1986) have reported an enhanced sensitivity to proactive interference in some amnesics, using a task in which performance was unlikely to depend on priming. Patients could retrieve objects hidden at an initial location after a short delay, but when the objects were hidden elsewhere they tended to return to the initial location. Amnesics and their controls were not matched on memory for the initial placement so it is possible that the amnesic effect resulted from their poor memory rather than the other way around. There is also evidence, however, that this phenomenon of mnemonic precedence results from frontal lobe lesions (see Schacter, 1987). It is therefore still unknown whether amnesics without frontal lobe pathology are more susceptible to interference when priming is not involved, and whether such a susceptibility, if it exists, reflects the deficit that causes amnesia.

Finally, the context-memory deficit hypothesis may fruitfully be explored through the use of primate models of amnesia. Such models suggest that lesions of the hippocampal and amygdala circuits may disrupt different aspects of contextual memory. Thus, Parkinson and Mishkin (1982) have found that hippocampal, but not amygdala, lesions severely impair spatial memory in monkeys. In contrast, Murray and Mishkin (1985) found that amygdalectomy, but not hippocampectomy, impairs the ability of monkeys to make cross-modal memory judgements and that the former lesion also has a greater disruptive effect on the ability to make recency judgements. If these two circuits process and store different kinds of contextual information and Mishkin's (1982) dual circuit hypothesis of amnesia is correct, then damage to one circuit alone may leave the ability to retrieve sufficient contextual information to allow a modest degree of target recognition and recall.

In severe amnesics memories of recent experiences fade as do those of dreams on awakening. So drastic is this loss, that if the context-memory deficit hypothesis is true, a central role for the retrieval of contextual markers in episodic and semantic memory is implied. Alternatively, disproportionate memory problems for independent context may be caused by the incidental occurrence of particular frontal lobe lesions in some amnesics. If so, the study of patients with only these frontal lobe lesions may illuminate the role that retrieval of independent context plays in normal memory. It remains unknown whether the frontal lobe lesions that cause deficits in effortful processing are distinct from those that cause deficits in memory for independent context, but the study of such deficits should also throw light on normal memory processes.

## REFERENCES

Baddeley, A.D. (1982). Domains of recollection. *Psychological Review*, **89**, 708–729.
Bowers, D., Verfaellie, M. and Rapscyk, S. (1987). Different forms of temporal amnesia following basal forebrain vs retrosplenial-fornix lesions in man. *Journal of Clinical and Experimental Neuropsychology*, **9**, 15.
Butters, N. (1984). Alcoholic Korsakoff's syndrome: an update. *Seminars in Neurology*, **4**, 226–244.
Butters, N. (1985). Alcoholic Korsakoff's syndrome: some unresolved issues concerning etiology, neuropathology, and cognitive deficits. *Journal of Clinical and Experimental Neuropsychology*, **7**, 181–210.
Butters, N. and Cermak, L.S. (1975). Some analyses of amnesic syndromes in brain damaged patients. In R. Isaacson and K. Pribram (Eds), *The Hippocampus*, Vol. 2. New York: Plenum, pp. 377–409.
Cermak, L.S. (1984). The episodic-semantic distinction in amnesia. In L.R. Squire and N. Butters (Eds), *Neuropsychology of Memory*, New York: Guilford, pp. 55–62.
Cermak, L.S., Uhly, B. and Reale, L. (1980). Encoding specificity in the alcoholic Korsakoff patient. *Brain and Language*, **11**, 119–127.
Craik, F.I.M. and Lockhart, R.S. (1972). Levels of processing: a framework of memory research. *Journal of Verbal Learning and Verbal Behavior*, **11**, 671–684.
Crosson, B. (1986). On localization versus systemic effects in alcoholic Korsakoff's syndrome: a comment on Butters 1985. *Journal of Clinical and Experimental Neuropsychology*, **8**, 744–748.
Damasio, A.R., Graff-Radford, N.R., Eslinger, P.J., Damasio, H. and Kassell, N. (1985). Amnesia following basal forebrain lesions. *Archives of Neurology*, **42**, 263–271.
Duncan, J. (1986). Disorganization of behaviour after frontal lobe damage. *Cognitive Neuropsychology*, **33**, 271–280.
Freedman, M. and Cermak, L.S. (1986). Semantic encoding deficits in frontal lobe disease and amnesia. *Brain and Cognition*, **5**, 108–114.
Hasher, L. and Zacks, R.T. (1979). Automatic and effortful processes in memory. *Journal of Experimental Psychology: General*, **108**, 356–388.
Hirst, W. (1982). The amnesic syndrome: descriptions and explanations. *Psychological Bulletin*, **91**, 435–460.
Hirst, W. (1985). Use of mnemonic in patients with frontal lobe damage. *Journal of Clinical and Experimental Neuropsychology*, **7**, 175.
Hirst, W., Johnson, M.K., Kim, J.K., Phelps, E.A., Risse, G. and Volpe, B.T. (1986). Recognition and recall in amnesics. *Journal of Experimental Psychology: Learning, Memory and Cognition*, **12**, 445–451.
Hirst, W. and Volpe, B.T. (1982). Temporal order judgments with amnesia. *Brain and Cognition*, **1**, 294–306.
Hirst, W. and Volpe, B.T. (1984). Automatic and effortful encoding in amnesia. In M.S. Gazzaniga (Ed), *Handbook of Cognitive Neuroscience*, New York: Plenum, pp. 369–386.
Huppert, F.A. and Piercy, M. (1978). The role of trace strength in recency and frequency judgements by amnesic and control subjects. *Quarterly Journal*

*of Experimental Psychology*, **30**, 346–354.

Jackson, J.L., Michon, J.A., Boonstra, H., De Jonge, D. and Harsenhorst, J. de V. (1986). The effect of depth of encoding on temporal judgement tasks. *Acta Psychologica*, **62**, 199–210.

Kapur, N. and Coughlan, A.K. (1980). Confabulation and frontal lobe dysfunction. *Journal of Neurology, Neurosurgery and Psychiatry*, **43**, 461–463.

Kapur, N., Heath, P., Meudell, P. and Kennedy, P. (1986). Amnesia can facilitate memory performance: evidence from a patient with dissociated retrograde amnesia. *Neuropsychologia*, **24**, 215–222.

Kinsbourne, M. and Wood, F. (1982). Theoretical considerations regarding the episodic-semantic memory distinction. In L.S. Cermak (Ed), *Human Memory and Amnesia*, Hillsdale, NJ: Erlbaum, pp. 195–218.

Kohl, D. (1984). An automatic encoding deficit in the amnesia of Korsakoff's syndrome. Unpublished Ph.D. dissertation, John Hopkins University, Baltimore, M.D., U.S.A.

Lehmann, E.B. (1982). Memory for modality: evidence for an automatic process. *Memory and Cognition*, **10**, 554–564.

Leonard, J.M. and Whitten, W.B. II (1983). Information stored when expecting recall or recognition. *Journal of Experimental Psychology: Learning, Memory and Cognition*, **9**, 440–445.

Mackintosh, N.J. (1985). Varieties of conditioning. In N.M. Weinberger, J.L. McGaugh and G. Lynch (Eds), *Memory Systems of the Brain*, New York: Guilford, pp. 335–350.

Mandler, G. (1980). Recognizing: the judgement of previous occurrence. *Psychological Review*, **87**, 252–271.

Mayes, A. (1987). Human organic memory disorders. In H. Beloff and A.M. Colman (Eds), *Psychology Survey, Vol. 6*, The British Psychology Society, pp. 170–191.

Mayes, A.R., Meudell, P.R. and Pickering, A. (1985). Is organic amnesia caused by a selective deficit in remembering contextual information? *Cortex*, **21**, 167–202.

Meudell, P. and Mayes, A. (1982). Normal and abnormal forgetting: some comments on the human amnesic syndrome. In L.A. Ellis (Ed), *Normality and Pathology in Cognitive Function*, London: Academic Press, pp. 203–238.

Meudell, P.R., Mayes, A.R., Ostergaard, A. and Pickering, A. (1985). Recency and frequency judgements in alcoholic amnesics and normal people with normal memory. *Cortex*, **21**, 487–511.

Milner, B., Petrides, M. and Smith, M.L. (1985). Frontal lobes and the temporal organization of memory. *Human Neurobiology*, **4**, 137–142.

Mishkin, M. (1982). A memory system in the monkey. *Philosophical Transactions of the Royal Society, London*, **298B**, 85–95.

Morton, J., Hammersley, R.H. and Bekerian, D.A. (1985). Headed records: a model for memory and its failures. *Cognition*, **20**, 1–23.

Moscovitch, M. (1982). Multiple dissociations of function in amnesia. In L.S. Cermak (Ed), *Human Memory and Amnesia*, Hillsdale, NJ: Erlbaum, pp. 337–370.

Murray, E.A. and Mishkin, M. (1985). Amygdalectomy impairs crossmodal association in monkeys. *Science*, **228**, 604–606.

Parkinson, J.K. and Mishkin, M. (1982). A selective mnemonic role for the hippocampus in monkeys: memory for the location of objects. *Society for Neuroscience Abstracs*, **8**, 23.

Pickering, A.D., Mayes, A. and Fairbairn, A.F. (submitted). Amnesia and memory for modality of presentation.

Rocchetta dell, A.I. (1986). Classification and recall of pictures after unilateral frontal or temporal lobectomy. *Cortex*, **22**, 189–211.

Schacter, D.L., Moscovitch, M. Tulving, E., McLachlan, D.R. and Freedman, M. (1986). Mnemonic precedence in amnesic patients: an analogue of the AB error in infants? *Child Development*, **57**, 816–823.

Schacter, D.L. (1987). Memory, amnesia and frontal lobe dysfunction. *Psychobiology*, **15**, 21–36.

Schacter, D.L. and Graf, P. (1986). Preserved learning in amnesic patients: perspectives from research on direct priming. *Journal of Clinical and Experimental Neuropsychology*, **8**, 727–743.

Schacter, D.L., Harbluk, J.L. and McLachlan, D.R. (1984). Retrieval without recollection: an experimental analysis of source amnesia. *Journal of Verbal Learning and Verbal Behavior*, **23**, 593–611.

Shimamura, A.P. (1986). Priming effects in amnesia: evidence for a dissociable memory function. *Quarterly Journal of Experimental Psychology*, **38A**, 619–644.

Squire, L.R. (1982). Comparisons between forms of amnesia: some deficits are unique to Korsakoff's syndrome. *Journal of Experimental Psychology: Learning, Memory and Cognition*, **8**, 560–571.

Squire, L.R. (1986). Mechanisms of memory. *Science*, **232**, 1612–1619.

Squire, L.R. and Cohen, N.J. (1984). Human memory and amnesia. In G. Lynch, J.L. McGaugh and N.M. Winberger (Eds), *Psychobiology of Learning and Memory*, New York: Guilford Press, pp. 3–64.

Teyler, T.J. and Discenna, P. (1986). The hippocampal memory indexing theory. *Behavioral Neuroscience*, **100**, 147–154.

Tranel, D. and Damasio, A.R. (1985). Knowledge without awareness: an autonomic index of facial recognition. *Science*, **228**, 1453–1454.

Tulving, E. (1983). *Elements of Episodic Memory*, Oxford: Oxford University Press.

Von Cramon, D.Y., Hebel, N. and Schuri, U. (1985). A contribution to the anatomical basis of thalamic amnesia. *Brain*, **108**, 993–1008.

Warrington, E.K. (1985). A disconnection analysis of amnesia. *Annals of the New York Academy of Sciences*, **444**, 72–77.

Warrington, E.K. and Weiskrantz, L. (1974). The effect of prior learning on subsequent retention in amnesia patients. *Neuropsychologia*, **12**, 419–428.

Warrington, E.K. and Weiskrantz, L. (1982). Amnesia: a disconnection syndrome? *Neuropsychologia*, **20**, 233–248.

Weiskrantz, L. (1985). On issues and theories of the human amnesic syndrome. In N.M. Weinberger, J.L. McGaugh and G. Lynch (Eds), *Memory Systems of the Brain*, New York: Guilford Press, pp. 380–415.

Weiskrantz, L. and Warrington, E.K. (1979). Conditioning in amnesic patients. *Neuropsychologia*, **17**, 187–194.

Winocur, G. and Weiskrantz, L. (1976). An investigation of paired associate learning in amnesic patients. *Neuropsychologia*, **14**, 97–110.

Memory in Context : Context in Memory
Edited by G.M. Davies and D.M. Thomson
© 1988 John Wiley & Sons Ltd.

CHAPTER 9

# Here Today, Gone Tomorrow: The Appearance and Disappearance of Context Effects

MERRILL D. McSPADDEN, JONATHAN W. SCHOOLER,
and ELIZABETH F. LOFTUS

*University of Washington*

## ABSTRACT

Evidence is reviewed examining whether guided memory techniques can improve recollections when subjects have previously received misleading information. A series of three studies are reported which examined the impact of context reinstatement on the recall of inaccurately described details. Overall, these three studies suggested that guided memory could sometimes facilitate retrieval in the face of misleading information but the effects were rather fragile and unpredictable.

For many years we have been studying techniques for making memory worse. We have assaulted memory by making subjects feel stressed (Loftus and Burns, 1982), by exposing subjects to erroneous post-event information (Greene, Flynn and Loftus, 1982; Schooler, Gerhard and Loftus, 1986), and by interrogating subjects with leading questions (Loftus, 1979). It was natural that at some point we would want to stop and think instead about ways of improving memory. This interest was fueled by a call from a leading law firm in our city requesting some help with a problem. It seems that the only copy of an important medical X-ray had been sent to the firm by mail. It was critical because it provided proof of the cause of death of a party in litigation. It disappeared, and the lawyers were desperate to find it. A secretary was the last person to have seen the X-ray. Was there anything we could do, the head of the firm asked, to help her remember where she may have put the X-ray?

One of the most promising approaches for improving memory to appear in the recent literature involves a class of techniques loosely tied together by the term 'context reinstatement'. The basic idea underlying these techniques is that a person's ability to remember information is heavily influenced by the relation between the storage of that information and the retrieval context (e.g. Smith, Glenberg and Bjork, 1978; Thomson, 1972; Tulving and Thomson, 1973).

In the domain of memory for natural events, a number of studies have attempted to reinstate event context at the time of retrieval, and superior memory performance has resulted. Malpass and Devine (1981), for example, used a technique for reinstating context called 'guided memory'. Their subjects viewed a staged vandalism and were interviewed five months later. Some of the subjects were reminded of the vandalism in a detailed guided memory interview in which their feelings, their memory for details of the room, and their initial reactions were elicited. Following this guided memory manipulation, subjects tried to identify the vandal. Compared to control subjects, those whose memory had been guided were more accurate.

Another successful demonstration of the power of context-reinstatement was reported by Krafka and Penrod (1985). Store clerks served as subjects and were exposed to an 'unusual' interaction with a 'customer'. Two or 24 hours later they tried to identify the customer from a photo-array. Context was reinstated by asking the subject mentally to recall the event and by giving physical cues from the event. Compared to control subjects, those who had been exposed to context cues were more accurate. It is these and other results that have led Shapiro and Penrod (1986) to conclude that context-reinstatement is one of the most powerful influences on memory.

Against this promising background, we were anxious to see context-reinstatement at work. In particular, we were interested in determining whether context-reinstatement techniques would also benefit subjects who had been exposed to erroneous post-event information as well as subjects who had not. In fact, Bekerian and Bowers (1983) demonstrated that a type of context could reverse the effects of erroneous post-event information. In this study, subjects saw a series of 24 slides depicting a traffic accident (from Loftus, Miller and Burns, 1978) that included a traffic sign (e.g. a stop sign) as the critical item. Some subjects received misleading information about the sign (e.g. that it was a yield sign). In the test phase, 15 pairs of slides were shown and subjects had to indicate for each pair which slide they had seen originally. Some subjects received the test items in random order while others received the items in the order in which they occurred in the original sequence. A major finding was that subjects who received the sequential ordering, which presumably reinstated the event context, were not influenced by the misinformation.

Despite this observation, subsequent research by Bowers and Bekerian (1984) and by others (Geiselman, Cohen and Surtes, 1985; McCloskey and Zaragoza, 1985) revealed that the conditions under which context can reverse a misinformation effect are at best limited. Geiselman *et al.* used a powerful retrieval mnemonic called the cognitive interview (which involved some context reinstatement) and found it reduced the effects of misinformation, but only minimally. McCloskey and Zaragoza found that the misinformation effect was just as strong in the face of a context reinstatement manipulation as it was without it. Given these mixed results, one goal of our research was to learn more about the conditions, if any, under which context might be sufficiently powerful to circumvent misinformation.

## EXPERIMENT 1

One previously successful technique for improving memory for complex events involved a guided memory manipulation (Malpass and Devine, 1981). This was used in Experiment 1. We predicted that guided memory would enhance recall of information except, perhaps, in the case where misleading post-event information had been given. This expectation was based on the fact that most efforts to undo the misinformation effect have been unsuccessful.

### Method

#### Subjects

Subjects were 193 introductory psychology students from the University of Washington who participated for class credit. Subjects were tested in groups of 6 – 10.

#### Design and procedure

The experiment was a 3 × 2 factorial design. On day 1 all subjects viewed a video tape depicting a bank robbery. On day 2, subjects were assigned to one of three different post-event information conditions: misinformation, neutral information, or no information. Subjects were subsequently assigned to one of two context reinstatement conditions; they heard either an auditory tape instructing them to reinstate context, or they heard music.

On day 1 all subjects were met by Experimenter A and escorted to room A. Room A was rich in stimuli (cluttered, posters on wall). Subjects spent 20 min. engaging in an easy filler activity that left them ample time to look around the room. They then viewed a 30 sec. video tape depicting a bank robbery prepared by John Yuille at the University of British Columbia. The robbery was filmed from behind the counter; the face of the single customer was in full view, however, only the backs of two tellers were visible. A man entered from the left, walked behind a customer and approached the woman teller. He pulled a gun and ordered the tellers to put the large bills on the counter. He put the bills in a paper sack and backed out of the bank.

After viewing the video, subjects engaged in another 20 min. filler activity, and then they were asked to write down the events of the robbery in as much detail as possible.

On day 2, subjects were met by Experimenter B and escorted into room B, which was quite different in size and appearance from room A. At this time, subjects participated in one of three post-event conditions. Two-thirds of them read a narrative, under the belief that it was written by a police cadet. Subjects were asked to rate the narrative on clarity of writing, etc.

Two versions of the narrative were used. Misleading information was introduced in one version of the narrative. Five critical details were inaccurately reported. For example, one of the statements was, 'The male customer wore a gray sport coat and a green shirt'. The customer was in fact wearing a gray sport coat and a blue shirt. The robber was described as having straight hair when actually his hair was wavy. The robber supposedly put the money in a cloth sack when actually it was a paper bag. Approximately one-third of the subjects received this misinformation version.

A second version of the narrative, given to one-third of the subjects, contained the same information as the misleading narrative, except that no reference was made to the inaccurately reported details. For example, 'The customer wore a gray sport coat', or 'The robber had brown hair'. The remaining subjects did not read a narrative, but instead they read a Thurber fable that occupied the same amount of time.

For testing purposes, subjects were assigned to one of two conditions. In the guided memory condition, subjects listened to an audio tape designed to recreate the context under which the initial event was viewed. The tape asked subjects to relax, close their eyes and image as strongly as they could a sequence of images. During four pauses, subjects were asked to write down their images: (1) 'What was your first impression of the room as you walked in the door?'; (2) 'What part of the room did you notice first?'; (3) 'Visualize the parts of the room you found most interesting'; (4) 'Are there other parts of the room which you can visualize?'. The audiotape contained no information about the room or video tape. We used an audio tape to minimize the experimenter – subject interaction that was so prominent in the Malpass and Devine (1981) method. Control subjects listened to ten minutes of music instead of the guided memory tape.

Finally, subjects were tested with a 24-item, short-cued recall test. Eighteen questions asked about non-critical details, that is details that were not inaccurately referred to in the misleading narrative. For example, two questions were 'How many tellers were visible in the bank?' and 'What instructions did the robber give the tellers after they put out the money?'. Five questions concerned the critical details that were inaccurately reported in the misleading narrative. For example, subjects were asked 'In what type of container did the robber place the money as he took it off the counter?'. One of the questions asked about posters hanging on the wall of the experimental room. Subjects were to respond based upon their own memories.

Table 9.1   Data from experiment 1.

**Noncritical correct**

|  | Neutral | Misleading | Fable |
|---|---|---|---|
|  |  | Post-event condition |  |
| Music | 10.59 | 9.97 | 10.53 |
| Guided memory | 10.52 | 9.68 | 11.07 |

**Critical correct**

|  | Neutral | Misleading | Fable |
|---|---|---|---|
|  |  | Post-event condition |  |
| Music | 2.86 | 2.27 | 2.74 |
| Guided memory | 3.10 | 3.05 | 3.50 |

**Misinformation acquired**

|  | Neutral | Misleading | Fable |
|---|---|---|---|
|  |  | Post-event condition |  |
| Music | 0.65 | 1.46 | 0.61 |
| Guided memory | 1.10 | 1.55 | 1.39 |

## Results

We examined the performance of three dependent variables: non-critical correct (number of correct answers to all but the critical questions, maximum = 19); critical correct (number of correct answers to the critical items, maximum = 5); misinformation acquired (number of times a subject responded with the inaccurate information contained in the misleading narrative, maximum = 5). The influence of misleading information should be evident in a lower 'critical correct' score and/or a higher 'misinformation acquired' score. The data are presented in Table 9.1.

Did guided memory affect performance? A 2 × 3 Analysis of Variance (Guided memory/music vs Post-event condition) was performed for each of the three dependent variables. Subjects receiving guided memory did not differ significantly from music controls in the number of non-critical items answered correctly, $F > 1$. However, compared to music controls, guided memory subjects correctly recalled significantly more critical items $F(1,187) = 6.075$, $p > 0.01$. But, guided memory subjects were also significantly more likely than music controls to recall the misinformation $F(1,187) = 5.65$, $p > 0.02$. A simple main effects contrast between misled subjects who received guided memory and who listened to music yielded no significant differences for misinformation acquired, $t > 1$. The significant differences found in misinformation acquired were found in subjects who had no exposure to the misleading information. So, while guided memory improved the recall of critical items, it had no effect on the number of times misled subjects responded with the misinformation.

Did misinformation affect memory? Subjects who received the misleading narrative reported the inaccurately described information more often than those who received the neutral narrative or fable, $F(2,187) = 4.7$, $p > 0.01$. Type of narrative did not affect subjects' recall of the non-critical items $F(2,187) = 1.62$. Also type of narrative did not affect the number of accurately recalled critical details, $F(2,187) = 1.97$, although misled subjects did perform somewhat worse than the other two groups.

Did guided memory undo the misinformation effect? There was no interaction between type of narrative and the use of guided memory for any of the three dependent measures ($F > 1$). Guided memory did make misled subjects perform slightly more accurately on the critical items than music controls (3.05 vs 2.27 items correct). On the other hand, guided memory and music controls acquired the same amount of misinformation (1.55 vs 1.46 items). Thus, guided memory apparently shifted some of those who would have made a miscellaneous error into making a correct response.

### Discussion

The results of Experiment 1 were unexpected. On the non-critical items, where we expected to see an effect of guided memory, there was none. On the critical items, guided memory subjects were more likely to answer correctly than were music controls. There is no evidence to support the contention that guided memory can undo the negative effects of misinformation.

Because of the unusual effect of guided memory, we were anxious to conduct another experiment that would hopefully use a stronger context reinstatement technique. With this goal, we decided to combine the guided memory of Experiment 1 with another 'proven' context reinstatement technique—environmental context. Smith (1979) had found that subjects who physically or mentally reinstated the original environmental context performed better than subjects who were tested in a different environmental context. (It was only later that the fragility of the environmental context effect was brought to our attention, Fernandez and Glenberg, 1985). Our idea was to combine the two context reinstatement methods to produce a more powerful manipulation, a kind of multiple context reinstatement. Hence Experiment 2.

## EXPERIMENT 2

Experiment 2 was similar in many respects to Experiment 1 with the addition of a new variable, same or different environmental context.

## Method

### Subjects

The subjects were 142 introductory psychology students from the University of Washington who participated for class credit. Subjects were tested in groups of 6 – 10.

### Design and procedure

The experiment was a 3 × 2 × 2 factorial design. Two factors were identical to those investigated in Experiment 1: (1) post-event condition (misleading narrative, neutral narrative, or no narrative); (2) music or guided memory. The third factor was room-tested. Subjects were randomly assigned to be tested either in the room where they read the misinformation (room B) or in the room where they saw the video tape bank robbery (room A).

The procedure used on day 1 was identical to the procedure on day 1 in Experiment 1. Subjects spent 20 min. engaging in a filler activity, and then watched a 30 sec. video tape—all in room A.

On day 2, subjects were met by Experimenter B, escorted to room B, and read one of three narratives. Half the subjects were then escorted to room A; half remained in room B. Within each room, half the subjects heard the guided memory tape, and half heard ten minutes of music. Finally subjects were tested with the 24 item test.

## Results

As before, three dependent measures were computed: non-critical correct, critical correct, and misinformation acquired. The data are reported in Table 9.2.

Did context affect memory? A 2 × 2 × 3 Analysis of Variance was performed for each of the three dependent variables. Subjects receiving guided

Table 9.2   Data from experiment 2.

Noncritical correct
Subjects tested in Room 'A'

|  | Neutral | Misleading | Fable |
|---|---|---|---|
| Music | 12.08 | 11.43 | 10.07 |
| Guided memory | 11.93 | 10.31 | 11.00 |

Subjects tested in Room 'B'

|  | Neutral | Misleading | Fable |
|---|---|---|---|
| Music | 10.60 | 9.55 | 10.73 |
| Guided memory | 11.20 | 10.70 | 12.67 |

Critical correct
Subjects tested in Room 'A'

|  | Neutral | Misleading | Fable |
|---|---|---|---|
| Music | 2.46 | 2.14 | 2.43 |
| Guided memory | 2.33 | 1.38 | 2.00 |

Subjects tested in Room 'B'

|  | Neutral | Misleading | Fable |
|---|---|---|---|
| Music | 2.90 | 2.18 | 2.45 |
| Guided memory | 2.30 | 2.20 | 2.44 |

Misinformation acquired
Subjects tested in Room 'A'

|  | Neutral | Misleading | Fable |
|---|---|---|---|
| Music | 0.31 | 1.21 | 0.36 |
| Guided memory | 0.40 | 1.23 | 0.25 |

Subjects tested in Room 'B'

|  | Neutral | Misleading | Fable |
|---|---|---|---|
| Music | 0.20 | 1.91 | 0.36 |
| Guided memory | 0.20 | 1.10 | 0.44 |

memory did not differ significantly from music controls on non-critical correct, critical correct or misinformation acquired, $F > 1$, $F = 2.6$, $p = 0.11$, $F > 1$, respectively. Nor did the room in which subjects were tested affect any of the three performance measures, $F > 1$, $F = 1.7$, $F > 1$, respectively. One interesting comparison is between subjects who received both guided memory and environmental context reinstatement compared to subjects who received neither. On non-critical correct there was a slight advantage for the multiple context subjects (11.93 vs 10.60; 10.31 vs 9.55; 11.00 vs 10.73). One significant *post hoc* contrast was found: subjects in the multiple context reinstatement conditions (original room and tape) answered significantly more non-critical items correctly than the others, $t = 1.76$, $p > 0.05$.

On the critical correct there was a slight *disadvantage* of multiple context over no context (2.33 vs 2.90; 1.38 vs 2.18; and 2.00 vs 2.45).

For misinformation acquired, there was a slight trend for subjects to acquire less given multiple context reinstatement (1.23 misleading details vs 1.91).

Type of narrative yielded a significant difference on misinformation acquired, $F = 15.6$, $p = 0.001$. However, neither non-critical correct nor critical correct were affected by type of narrative, $F = 1.4$ and $F = 2.4$, $p = 0.09$, respectively.

## Discussion

Subjects in the context-reinstatement conditions recalled more of the non-critical items than the control groups. However, they also recalled fewer of the critical items, exactly the opposite of the results obtained in Experiment 1.

It occurred to us that the effects of guided memory might be obscured if the control subjects were spontaneously engaging in some private form of context reinstatement. By controlling exposure to the original context, this hypothesis could be tested. The assumption here is that longer exposure to the original context would result in greater availability of contextual cues. If subjects normally use context-reinstatement as a retrieval strategy, then subjects in both the guided memory and the music control groups should perform equivalently as more contextual-cues are available. If context-reinstatement is used only after instruction, then changing the amount of exposure to the original context might have a differential effect on the music and guided memory subjects.

## EXPERIMENT 3

The design of this experiment was similar to that of Experiment 1. The major innovation was the introduction of a new variable—time spent in the original environment.

## Method

### Subjects

Subjects were 72 psychology students from the University of Washington who participated for class credit. Subjects were tested in groups of 6–10.

### Design

The experiment was a 3 × 2 × 2 factorial design. On day 1, subjects were exposed for either 3, 9 or 15 minutes to the original context. On day 2 subjects were assigned to either the misinformation or neutral

Table 9.3  Data from experiment 3.

Noncritical correct

Number of minutes in original context

Music

| | | 3 | 9 | 15 |
|---|---|---|---|---|
| | Neutral | 6.80 | 8.17 | 7.80 |
| | Misleading | 8.75 | 8.33 | 7.71 |

Guided memory

| | | 3 | 9 | 15 |
|---|---|---|---|---|
| | Neutral | 7.50 | 9.17 | 8.67 |
| | Misleading | 8.83 | 8.70 | 9.71 |

Critical correct

Number of minutes in original context

Music

| | | 3 | 9 | 15 |
|---|---|---|---|---|
| | Neutral | 3.40 | 3.67 | 3.40 |
| | Misleading | 3.25 | 3.50 | 3.00 |

Guided memory

| | | 3 | 9 | 15 |
|---|---|---|---|---|
| | Neutral | 3.75 | 4.67 | 3.00 |
| | Misleading | 3.67 | 4.00 | 3.71 |

Misinformation acquired

Number of minutes in original context

Music

| | | 3 | 9 | 15 |
|---|---|---|---|---|
| | Neutral | 1.80 | 1.83 | 0.60 |
| | Misleading | 3.00 | 2.83 | 3.00 |

Guided memory

| | | 3 | 9 | 15 |
|---|---|---|---|---|
| | Neutral | 1.00 | 1.33 | 1.67 |
| | Misleading | 2.83 | 2.30 | 2.14 |

information condition and to hear either music or the guided memory tape.

*Procedure*

On day 1, subjects were met by Experimenter A and escorted to room A. Subjects were asked to listen to directions for approximately 1.5 min. Then, the experimenter pretended to adjust the video tape player until 2.5 min. had elapsed. In the 3-min. condition, the experimenter then immediately played the video tape of the robbery. In the 9-min. condition, the experimenter pretended to adjust the tape player and then left the room without speaking to the subjects. He returned after 8 total min. had elapsed (instruction time plus the time the experimenter was out of the room), and played the video tape. In the 15-min. condition, the experimenter left the room until 14 min. had elapsed. In all conditions, the subjects left the room immediately after viewing the video tape.

Day 2 proceeded exactly as in Experiment 1. Subjects were met by Experimenter B and escorted to room B to participate in one of two post-event conditions. Half the subjects read the narrative containing inaccurate information, and half read the neutral narrative. The narratives used in this experiment were similar to those used in Experiment 1, and identical to each other, except that 8 inaccurate items were reported in the misleading narrative.

Finally subjects were tested. Their test consisted of 8 critical items and 17 non-critical items. Prior to testing half listened to music and half listened to the guided memory tape used in Experiment 1.

## Results

Performance in each of the 12 conditions was scored for the three dependent variables. The data are presented in Table 9.3.

A $3 \times 2 \times 2$ Analysis of Variance was performed for each of the three dependent variables.

Did context affect memory? Subjects receiving guided memory did not differ significantly from controls on non-critical items correct, critical correct or misinformation acquired, $F = 3.379$, $p = 0.07$, $F = 2.035$, $p = 0.16$, $F > 1$, respectively. Nor did time in original room yield a significant difference on any of the performance measures, $F > 1$, $F = 1.77$ and $F > 1$, respectively.

We had thought that time in the original room might interact with the effects of context. Although not significant, there were some trends. If shorter duration of exposure to context reduces the effectiveness of contextual-temporal cues then the condition with the shortest exposure to the original context should perform worse on the recall test. If subjects in both control and guided memory groups are using context reinstatement as a retrieval strategy, then the improvement in performance should be the same for both groups of subjects. However, if only the guided memory subjects are making use of the available contextual cues then improvement should only be seen in the guided memory group. While the results were not significant the expected trends in the data appeared. In fact, sixteen of the eighteen cells have trends in the expected direction. For non-critical correct, the data can be collapsed across both post-event conditions. The differences are 0.63, 0.63, 1.48 as time in the original context increases. For critical correct and misinformation acquired, only the subjects who read the misleading narrative are of interest. Notice that the differences for critical correct are 0.08, 0.37, and 2.0; the differences for misinformation acquired are 0.42, 0.50, and 0.71. In each case the subjects who were exposed to the original context longer and had guided memory instruction performed better on the recall tests.

Did misinformation affect memory? Subjects who read the inaccurate narrative reported significantly more misleading details, $F = 10.33$, $p < 0.002$. However, neither non-critical correct nor critical correct differed as a result of type of narrative, $F < 1$ for both variables.

## Discussion

Neither guided memory nor time yielded a significant difference in performance. There was, however, a suggestive trend for guided memory to improve accuracy in recalling critical items ($p > 0.07$), and also a trend for the benefit of guided memory to be larger as a function of initial exposure time in the original environmental context.

## GENERAL DISCUSSION

These three experiments painted a rather messy picture of context reinstatement. In Experiment 1, guided memory improved performance on critical items, but not on non-critical ones. In Experiment 2, there was no significant effect of guided memory alone; however, when combined with environmental context reinstatement a small improvement in performance for non-critical items emerged. In Experiment 3, guided memory produced a slight but non-significant improvement in performance on critical items. In short, although context effects were observed, they were small and unreliable.

How can our present results be reconciled with context research conducted in other laboratories? Some researchers have had considerable success with context reinstatement. For example, in the present volume both Geiselman (Chapter 11), and Cutler and Penrod (Chapter 10) observed reliable context effects over a series of experiments. Other researchers have not been so successful; Fernandez and Glenberg (1985) in a series of valiant efforts, failed to obtain reliable benefits of context reinstatement. We believe that the inconsistent effects of context reinstatement observed both here and in the literature may be the result of a number of different factors including differences in experimental designs, individual differences, and publication bias.

There are a number of respects in which our study differed from those of Geiselman, and Cutler and Penrod. Firstly, these researchers used an interviewer in a one-on-one setting. We used a tape to reinstate context in order to avoid possible demand characteristics generated by an interviewer motivated to establish the success of context reinstatement. It is possible that using a tape recording reduced the relative effectiveness of our procedure either because it eliminated demand characteristics or because it served as a less stimulating source of context reinstatement. Secondly, both Geiselman, and Cutler and Penrod, used multiple techniques for improving memory while we primarily used only one context technique (in one condition in Experiment 2 we used multiple reinstatement techniques and observed an effect of context). Geiselman used the four-stage cognitive interview that includes mental context reinstatement, reporting everything, recalling the events in different orders, and changing perspective. Cutler and Penrod used three techniques: mnenonic instructions, exposure to snapshots of the crime, and exposure to the witness's own written descriptions. Since these researchers did not test each technique individually, it is possible that their reliable results were either due to the use of different techniques or else to the additive effects of using multiple methods of context reinstatement. Thirdly, the stimuli used by these researchers were different from ours. Cutler and Penrod convincingly demonstrate that the effectiveness of context techniques varies dramatically depending on the degree to which the target serves as a contextual cue. It is possible that either our items or our test questions provided sufficient contextual cues to reduce/eliminate our contextual effect.

While procedural differences may account for why we observed substantially smaller context effects than the others reported in this volume, they do not immediately explain why our effect was so unreliable. Our effect was not just small, it was also quite erratic. Moreover, context reinstatment affected different items in different experiments. Any situation which produces inconsistent effects across experiments strongly implicates individual differences. Accordingly, some subjects may be more responsive to context reinstatement than others and, additionally, subjects may vary with regard to the types of items for which context reinstatement is most effective. Such an interpretation seems particularly likely in light of Cutler and Penrod's observation that differences in target items can influence the magnitude of the effect; that is, optimal items for context reinstatement may vary from subject to subject and thus magnify the influence of individual differences. Individual differences may also account for the apparent benefits of using multiple context techniques; each subject is more insured of receiving at least one suitable technique. Clearly more research is necessary to explore the potential role of individual differences in context reinstatement.

We concede that the above considerations may account for our small and unreliable results; nevertheless we are still left with a slightly bitter aftertaste. We considered entitling this paper 'Three context reinstatement experiments that never would have been published in a journal'. It was not the experimental design that would have hampered our publishing efforts, but rather our results. Editors are notoriously unwilling to publish experiments with null or inconsistent results. This publication bias may have produced exaggerated estimates of the significance of context effects. After conducting a meta-analysis of 128 eyewitness research articles, Shapiro and Penrod (1986) concluded that context reinstatement was one of the most powerful variables to influence performance. Context reinstatement was as powerful a variable as exposure time and retention interval, two classics from memory literature. Publication bias may have particularly favoured context reinstatement in this meta-analysis. Context manipulations are typically the main purpose for a study and only get published if the effects are significant. Other variables, for example gender, are often secondary variables that appear in the literature even when not significant if there is some other independent variable that did produce significant results. Thus finding null gender effects in the literature is common; finding null context effects is not. The only circumstance likely to warrant the publication of a failure to find that context benefits memory is a vigorous failure to replicate a well-known result (e.g. Fernandez and Glenberg, 1985) or a reverse finding—context reinstatement produces significantly worse memory (Loftus, Manber and Keating, 1983). Thus cognitive psychologists who read only the published literature may have been presented with a biased view of the power of context effects.

Returning to the secretary for the law firm who desperately needed to find the critical missing X-ray, we tried to help her. We used guided memory technique to try to reinstate the context of her initial exposure to the item. When we failed to pluck the much-needed but recalcitrant memories from her mind, we should have known how our experiments might turn out.

This work was supported by grants from NIMH and NSF.

## REFERENCES

Bekerian, D.A. and Bowers, J.M. (1983). Eyewitness testimony: were we misled? *Journal of Experimental Psychology: Learning, Memory, and Cognition*, **19**, 139–145.

Bowers, J.M. and Bekerian, D.A. (1984). When will postevent information distort eyewitness testimony? *Journal of Applied Psychology*, **69**, 466–472.

Greene, E., Flynn, M.B. and Loftus, E.F. (1982). Inducing resistance to misleading information. *Journal of Verbal Learning and Verbal Behavior*, **21**, 207–219.

Fernandez, A. and Glenberg, A.M. (1985). Changing environmental context does not reliably affect memory. *Memory and Cognition*, **13**, 333–345.

Geiselman, R.E., Cohen, G. and Surtes, L. (1985). Eyewitness responses to leading and misleading questions under the cognitive interview. Unpublished manuscript, UCLA.

Krafka, C. and Penrod, S. (1985). Reinstatement of context in a field experiment on eyewitness identification. *Journal of Personality and Social Psychology*, **49**, 58–69.

Loftus, E.F. (1979). *Eyewitness Testimony*, Cambridge, MA: Harvard University Press.

Loftus, E.F. and Burns, T.E. (1982). Mental shock can produce retrograde amnesia. *Memory and Cognition*, **10**, 318–323.

Loftus, E.F., Manber, M. and Keating, J.P. (1983). Recollection of naturalistic events: context enhancement versus negative cueing. *Human Learning*, **2**, 83–92.

Loftus, E.F., Miller, D.G. and Burns, H.J. (1978). Semantic integration of verbal information into visual memory. *Journal of Experimental Psychology: Human Learning and Memory*, **4**, 19–31.

Malpass, R.S. and Devine, P.G. (1981). Guided memory in eyewitness identification. *Journal of Applied Psychology*, **3**, 343–350.

McCloskey, M. and Zaragoza, M. (1985). Misleading postevent information and memory for events: arguments and evidence against memory impairment hypothesis. *Journal of Experimental Psychology: General*, **114**, 3–18.

Schooler, J.W., Gerhard, D. and Loftus, E.F. (1986). Qualities of the unreal. *Journal of Experimental Psychology: Learning, Memory and Cognition*, **12**, 171–181.

Shapiro, P.N. and Penrod, S. (1986). A meta-analysis of facial identification studies. *Psychological Bulletin*, **100**, 139–156.

Smith, S.M. (1979). Remembering in and out of context. *Journal of Experimental Psychology: Human Learning and Memory*, **5**, 460–471.

Smith, S.M., Glenberg, A. and Bjork, R.A. (1978). Environmental context and human memory. *Memory and Cognition*, **6**, 342–353.

Thomson, D.M. (1972). Context effects in recognition memory. *Journal of Verbal Learning and Verbal Behavior*, **11**, 497–511.

Tulving, E. and Thomson, D.M. (1973). Encoding specificity and retrieval processes in episodic memory. *Psychological Review*, **80**, 352–373.

Memory in Context : Context in Memory
Edited by G.M. Davies and D.M. Thomson
© 1988 John Wiley & Sons Ltd.

CHAPTER 10

# Context Reinstatement and Eyewitness Identification

BRIAN L. CUTLER

*Florida International University*

and

STEVEN D. PENROD

*University of Wisconsin*

## ABSTRACT

A meta-analysis, laboratory experiment, and a field study showed that context reinstatement improves eyewitness identification accuracy. The laboratory experiment also revealed that context reinstatement is most effective when memory for the to-be-identified person is impaired. Practical applications of these findings are discussed together with theoretical implications.

There is a considerable body of literature documenting the unreliability of eyewitness identifications (Brigham, Maas, Snyder, and Spaulding, 1982; Clifford and Bull, 1978; Loftus, 1979; Penrod, Loftus, and Winkler, 1982; Yarmey, 1979); however, few studies examine procedures designed to enhance the reliability of eyewitness identifications. In our own program of research we have been interested in two primary questions: What factors reliably and strongly affect identification accuracy and to what extent can the effects of these factors be moderated by procedures that reinstate the context surrounding an event?

## VARIABLES THAT INFLUENCE EYEWITNESS IDENTIFICATION ACCURACY

We have addressed the question of which variables reliably affect identification accuracy from two perspectives. First, we have conducted a

231

meta-analysis of 128 separate facial identification and facial recognition experiments (Shapiro and Penrod, 1986), and second, we have conducted a factorial experiment to examine the main effects and interactive effects of thirteen separate variables on identification accuracy (Cutler, Penrod, and Martens, 1987a).

### A meta-analysis

In examining the effects of independent variables on recognition and identification accuracy across experiments, Shapiro and Penrod (1986) computed $d$ (a measure of effect-size indexing the number of standard deviations difference between the means of two experimental conditions) for both hits and false alarms, $d'$ (a signal-detection measure of sensitivity), and $b''$ (a signal-detection measure of criterion). Two examples can illustrate the meta-analytic findings. Among the variables shown to reliably and strongly affect facial recognition accuracy was transformation of the target's facial features. Transformations refer to either disguises or differences in facial characteristics from encoding to retrieval sessions, such as the addition or loss of a mustache, beard, or eyeglasses. The average effect-size for transformations was 1.05 on hits (manipulated across 19 conditions) and 0.40 on false alarms (manipulated across six conditions), both of which were significant. Signal detection measures further supported the contention that facial transformations affect recognition accuracy. For non-transformed faces, the average $d'$ was 0.74, whereas for transformed faces, the average $d'$ was only 0.32. This finding indicates that sensitivity declines with facial transformations. Facial transformations did not affect the decision criterion, however. Average $b'$ was 0.06 for non-transformed faces and 0.09 for transformed faces.

The meta-analysis also showed that retention interval significantly affected recognition accuracy. Across all experiments included in the meta-analysis, the average retention interval was 108 hours. For purposes of analysis, the retention interval variable was dichotomized into short and long. The average effect-size of retention interval was 0.43 on hits (manipulated across 18 conditions) and 0.33 on false alarms (manipulated across 14 conditions), both of which were significant. Analysis of signal detection measures indicated that the long retention interval reduced sensitivity: the average $d'$ was 0.47 for the short retention interval and 0.15 for the long retention interval. Retention interval also produced a small effect on criterion. Average $b''$ was 0.14 for the short retention interval and 0.06 for the long retention interval, indicating the subjects more less likely to report recognizing a face in the long retention interval condition. In conclusion, the meta-analysis showed that facial transformations and retention interval both have appreciable effects on the accuracy with which people report recognizing faces.

## A laboratory experiment

In order to substantiate the findings of the meta-analysis in a more applied setting, we conducted a fractional factorial experiment (Cutler *et al.*, 1987a). Fractional factorial designs (Cochran and Cox, 1957; Kenny, 1985) are those in which some main effects are perfectly confounded with higher-order interactions. In our experiment we confounded main effects with four- and five-way interactions. The benefit is that we can examine all main effects, two-way interactions, and some three-way interactions in a relatively condensed design with relatively few subjects. The cost is that we cannot assess four- and five-way interactions, as they are fully confounded with main effects. These four- and five-way interactions, however, are unlikely to be interpretable and are even less likely to replicate. Generally, a $2^{a + b}$ fractional factorial design refers to a design in which 'a' factors are fully crossed and 'b' factors are confounded with higher-order interactions between 'a' factors.

In the Cutler *et al.* (1987a) experiment subjects viewed a videotaped re-enactment of an armed robbery and later attempted an identification from an offender-present or an offender-absent line-up parade. Characteristics of the videotaped robbery and of the line-up procedures were systematically varied. The variables manipulated included stimulus videotape (liquor store robbery vs armed mugging), disguise of the robber, weapon visibility, exposure time (30 vs 75 seconds), arousal level of robbery (high vs low), whether or not there was a distractor task during viewing, type of semantic elaboration (non-facial vs facial), whether or not subjects expected a line-up test, and the number of additional distractors appearing in the videotape (2 vs 5) all of which were expected to affect the witness' ability to encode information from the robbery. Variables that were expected to affect eyewitness memory by acting upon stored information were exposure to mugshots and retention interval (immediate vs one week). Finally, line-up instructions (biased vs unbiased), a variable associated with the retrieval of information, was expected to affect identification accuracy. The full design was a $2^{7 + 7}$ fractional factorial in which there were $2^7 = 128$ experimental cells that encompassed fourteen variables—seven of which were intentionally confounded with four- and five-way interactions. (One variable, whether or not subjects wrote down reasons that contradicted their decisions, was expected to affect only eyewitness confidence and is therefore not discussed here.)

Among the 165 subjects who participated, 43 percent correctly identified the robber from offender-present line-ups, and 32 percent correctly rejected the offender-absent line-ups, thus yielding an average correct identification rate (proportion of hits + the proportion of correct rejections) of 0.36. The number of significant two-way interactions among the 13 variables examined (4 out of 78) was approximately what one might expect by chance alone at the 0.05 level of significance. We therefore discuss the analysis of main effects only. Given that line-up type (offender-present vs -absent) did not interact significantly with the other predictor variables, it was concluded that in this study all other independent variables influenced hit-rate and correct rejection-rate equivalently. All findings are therefore described in terms of correct identification-rate.

Weapon visibility had a significant influence on identification accuracy. Subjects who witnessed a robbery in which the robber outwardly brandished a handgun were less likely to correctly identify the robber from the line-up than were subjects who witnessed a robbery in which the handgun was hidden. It is presumed that the handgun draws the witness's attention and the characteristics of the robber are therefore less effectively encoded; consequently, performance on the line-up test is impaired. The average correct identification rate was 0.46 in the low weapon visibility condition but only 0.26 in the high weapon visibility condition ($d = 0.52$).

The instructions given to the subject-witnesses also significantly affected their subsequent abilities to identify the robber. Half of the subjects were given instructions that pressured them to choose a suspect from the line-up parade; these instructions did not explicitly offer the option of rejecting the line-up, although rejection of the line-up was an acceptable judgment. We refer to these instructions as 'biased instructions'. The remaining subjects were given 'neutral instructions', or instructions that explicitly offered the option of rejecting the line-up. The biased instructions significantly reduced identification accuracy. Among subjects given unbiased instructions, the correct identification rate was 0.48, but among subjects given biased instructions, that correct identification rate was only 0.24 ($d = 0.62$). This finding was not too surprising, as the effect of biased line-up conditions is perhaps one of the most reliable findings in experiments on eyewitness identification (Buckhout, Alper, Chern, Silverberg, and Slomovitz, 1974; Buckhout, Figueroa, and Hoff, 1975; Cutler, Penrod, and Martens, 1987b; Malpass and Devine, 1981a; Warnick and Sanders, 1980).

In support of the finding that facial transformations affected recognition accuracy in the meta-analysis, disguise of the robber also significantly influenced identification accuracy. In the high-disguise condition the robber wore a pull-over knit hat which covered most of his hair, and in the no-disguise condition, the robber wore no hat. Correct identification rate was 0.45 in the no-disguise condition but only 0.27 in the high-disguise condition. The effect-size for disguise ($d$) was 0.47, which is similar in magnitude to the effects of facial transformations on false alarms in the meta-analysis (0.40). In contrast to the meta-analysis, however, retention interval (immediate vs one week) did not affect identification accuracy in the predicted direction. In fact, the correct identification rate was significantly higher in the one-week condition (0.42) than in the immediate condition (0.30). Although such 'reminiscence effects' are unusual, they are not altogether uncommon (e.g. Deffenbacher, Carr, and Leu, 1981).

Although the issue of what variables reliably affect identification accuracy is far from settled (McCloskey and Egeth, 1983), the results of the experiment confirm that disguise, weapon visibility, and biased line-up instructions indeed influence identification accuracy, and the effects of these factors withstood qualification by (i.e. no interactions with) numerous other variables. Unfortunately, this research, along with many other eyewitness experiments, tells us little about how to improve the reliability of eyewitness identification; instead, it helps to identify and assess the magnitude of effects of variables that reduce identification accuracy. Nonetheless, it is obvious that one way to increase the reliability of eyewitness identification is to reduce the impact of factors such as disguise, weapon visibility, and retention interval on identification accuracy.

## IMPROVING EYEWITNESS IDENTIFICATION ACCURACY THROUGH CONTEXT REINSTATEMENT

One plausible procedure for reducing the effects of variables such as retention interval and disguise is to provide subject-witnesses with contextual cues that might enhance their ability to recognize the target. In a later contribution to this volume Geiselman and his colleagues show that procedures that reinstate the context surrounding events improve recall of details of the event, and similar procedures may enhance recognition abilities, as well. In fact, the effects of context reinstatement procedures on facial recognition accuracy were examined in Shapiro and Penrod's (1986) meta-analysis. Context reinstatement procedures had an enormous effect on hits ($d = 1.91$ across the 23 conditions in which it was manipulated) and a moderate, though undesirable, effect on false alarms ($d = -0.44$ across the 18 conditions in which it was manipulated), both of which were significant. Overall, the average $d'$ was 0.77 among subjects who received context reinstatement procedures but only 0.39 among subjects who did not receive context reinstatement procedures. It is clear that context reinstatement procedures reduced criterion ($b''$ was -0.06 among subjects who received context reinstatement procedures and 0.25 among subjects who did not receive context reinstatement procedures).

The effectiveness of contextual cues in enhancing recall and recognition depends largely on the cues that are already available to the subject. It is unlikely that context cues produce unqualified main effects on improving memory (but see Krafka and Penrod, 1985; Malpass and Devine, 1981b). With recognition accuracy in particular, the stimulus itself provides a relatively strong context cue (in signal-present trials). We therefore predict in line with Smith's (this volume) reasoning, that contextual cues are most effective in enhancing identification accuracy in situations in which the target itself serves as a relatively ineffective contextual cue. Factors that reduce the witness's ability to encode characteristics of the target (e.g. disguise, weapon visibility), factors that affect the form in which the target's characteristics are stored in memory (e.g. retention interval), and factors that affect the retrieval of information about the target (e.g. line-up instructions) are all likely to influence the effectiveness of the target as a contextual cue. In general, we predict that providing subjects with additional context cues aids recognition accuracy in conditions such as high disguise, high weapon visibility, long retention interval, and biased line-up instructions, but does not affect identification accuracy when such degrading conditions are not present.

We have therefore embarked on a series of experiments in which we examine the interactions between contextual cues at the identification stage and other encoding, storage, and retrieval variables that have been shown to affect identification accuracy.

Before discussing our findings regarding the effects of context reinstatement, several points are worth noting. The first regards the choice of the context reinstatement procedures we employed. As noted elsewhere in this volume (see for instance, Smith's contribution) contextual cues can be quite diverse and can differ on a number of dimensions. Unfortunately, no type of context cue has been shown to be consistently superior to other types of context cues in improving recognition. Using aspects of the physical environment as context cues has shown mixed results in the laboratory with lexical stimuli (Fernandez and Glenberg, 1986; Smith, Glenberg, and Bjork, 1978; McSpadden, Schooler, and Loftus, Chapter 9, this volume) and has shown mixed results in facial recognition as well (Davies and Milne, 1985; Sanders, 1984). Some experiments have shown that environmental context cues improve facial recognition accuracy (Davies and Milne, 1985), while others show null results (Sanders, 1984). However, two experiments that reinstated both environmental and emotional context (i.e. emotions experienced during encoding), have both shown improvements due to context reinstatement (Krafka and Penrod, 1985; Malpass and Devine, 1981b).

Since one of our purposes is to develop techniques that can be used in a forensic setting, our choice of technique depends on the ease with which a technique can be incorporated into an existing set of procedures for interviewing witnesses, and of course, its effectiveness.

Police interrogators follow procedures that have been developed with an eye to cost-efficiency relationships. Interviewing techniques that are costly in terms of equipment and/or training and are of questionable effectiveness are likely to be ignored by the criminal justice system. The context reinstatement techniques we employ (some of which are adopted from the work of Geiselman and colleagues) are not costly and do not involve extensive training, they may therefore prove useful to the criminal justice system.

## A laboratory experiment

An experiment was carried out (Cutler, *et al*. 1987b) to examine the effects of two types of context reinstatement procedures on identification accuracy. In this experiment 290 subjects viewed a videotaped robbery and later (after either 2 days or 14 days) attempted identifications from offender-absent or offender-present line-ups. One technique was implemented before the line-up phase and consisted of (1) mnemonic instructions, (2) exposure to a series of snapshots taken from the scene of the crime (snapshots which, of course, did not contain the robber), and (3) exposure to the witness's own written description of the events of the robbery and of the robber's physical characteristics. Subjects had given these descriptions immediately after viewing the videotaped robbery. In order to control for the completeness of descriptions across subjects, all subjects were asked (in questionnaire form) both open-ended and pointed questions regarding the events preceding the robbery, the robber – victim interaction, and the physical characteristics of the robber. The mnemonic instructions were modeled after Geiselman and Fisher's Cognitive Interview. Subjects were instructed to think back through the event from beginning to end, in different temporal orders, and were instructed to imagine witnessing the event from different perceptual perspectives, as well. Subjects were also instructed to reminisce about whether the robber's physical characteristics resembled those of people they knew, and to recall any thoughts and emotions experienced while witnessing the event. In this experiment these mnemonic instructions were given in writing in order to ensure comparability across the 64 experimental sessions in which context reinstatement procedures were used. The snapshots were various pictures of the inside of the liquor store in which the robbery was filmed. Besides showing the store there were some photographs of the clerk (the victim of the robbery) standing behind the counter where she stood during the robbery, and a snapshot of the handgun brandished by the robber. The three types of context cues, mnemonic instructions, exposure to description, and exposure to snapshots, were manipulated concurrently and we will henceforth refer to them as interview procedures.

The second context reinstatement procedure involved using the target's physical features as contextual cues. When studying the target's physical characteristics, subject-witnesses encode a host of information such as facial and other physical characteristics, posture, gait, voice quality, and the information encoded may be dependent upon the position from which they view the target (e.g. front or profile view). Subjects' abilities correctly to identify the target from a line-up parade may therefore depend on the particular information given to them during the recognition task. Posture, gait, and voice features may all be considered separate context cues and may improve identification accuracy. Some such cues may be qualitatively more effective than others, or perhaps the quantitative aspect of such cues is relevant. Half of the subjects attempted identifications from a line-up consisting only of slides of each suspect's head and shoulders from a front and full profile pose. The remaining subjects attempted identifications from line-ups which consisted of the slides of each suspect's head and shoulders and full bodies in front, three-quarter, and full profile views and in addition received voice samples and videotaped segments showing the suspects walking in and out of the room in which the line-up was held. Thus, we systematically exposed subjects to contextual cues such as posture (by showing the full body views), gait (by showing the videotaped segments of suspects walking), voice, skin color, and a three-quarter view.

In addition to manipulating the two types of contextual cues, interview procedures and line-up cues, retention interval, and the presence of the offender in the line-up, we also manipulated disguise, weapon visibility, the instructions given the witness before viewing the crime (facial vs non-facial elaboration) line-up size (6 vs 12 suspects), the degree to which the line-up members resembled the target in physical appearance (high similarity vs low similarity), and line-up instructions (biased vs unbiased). The full design was a $2^{7+3}$ fractional factorial.

Of the 290 subjects 64 percent correctly identified the robber from an offender-present line-up, and 29 percent correctly rejected the offender-absent line-ups. The relative absence of interactions between predictor variables and line-up type (offender-present vs -absent) except where noted indicated that hits and correct rejections were effected equivalently; therefore, we present most of the results in terms of correct identification rate (proportion of hits + proportion of correct rejections), as we did for the Cutler, *et al.* (1987a) experiment. The average correct identification rate was 0.46.

Main effects on identification accuracy were found for disguise and for line-up instructions. The average correct identification rate was 0.51 in the low-disguise condition and 0.40 in the high-disguise condition ($d$ = 0.24). The average correct identification rate was 0.41 among subjects who received biased line-up instructions and 0.51 for subjects who received neutral line-up instructions ($d$ = 0.22; $p < .10$).

A series of two-way interactions revealed that context cues were in fact moderating the effects of variables that affect identification accuracy. Disguise significantly impaired eyewitness performance among subjects who did not receive the context reinstatement interview. Among these subjects those who viewed the robber in disguise had a correct identification rate of only 0.29, and those who viewed a non-disguised robber had a correct identification rate of 0.57 ($d$ = 0.62). The context reinstatement interview, however, brought the correct identification rate up to 0.51 among those who viewed the disguised robber. The correct identification rate for those who viewed the non-disguised robber and had the context reinstatement interview was 0.47 ($d$ = 0.09). In other words, the only group whose performance suffered was the no context reinstatement interview, high-disguise group.

A similar pattern of results emerged in a marginally significant line-up instruction by context reinstatement interview interaction ($p$ λ 0.10). Among subjects who received no context reinstatement interview biased line-up instructions significantly reduced identification accuracy. The mean correct identification rate was 0.54 for subjects who received neutral line-up instructions but only 0.32 for subjects who received biased line-up instructions ($d$ = 0.49). However, among subjects who received the context reinstatement interview, correct identification rate did not suffer from the biased line-up instruction. The correct identification rate among this group was 0.50 for subjects who received neutral instructions and 0.48 for subjects who received biased line-up instructions ($d$ = 0.04). The group that had the lowest correct identification rate was the no context reinstatement interview, high-bias group.

The context reinstatement interview by line-up instruction interaction is best understood in the context of choosing rates, or the proportion of times a suspect was chosen from a line-up. Among subjects who did not receive the context reinstatement interview, the choosing rates were 0.65 for subjects who received neutral line-up instructions and 0.99 for subjects in the biased line-up condition ($d$ = 0.96). The corresponding choosing rates for subjects who received the context reinstatement interview were 0.71 for subjects given neutral instructions and 0.89 for subjects given biased instructions ($d$ = 0.51). Context reinstatement significantly reduced the effect of biased line-up instructions on choosing rates.

Using additional physical characteristics as context cues within the line-up also produced a promising pattern of interactions with factors that affect identification accuracy. The added cues of voice features, three-quarter pose, full body view, and gait improved performance if line-ups contained a large number of suspects who resembled the robber in physical appearance. Among subjects shown such line-ups, the correct identification rate was 0.36 for subjects not given the additional context cues but 0.54 among subjects given the added context cues ($d$ = 0.40). Among subjects who were shown line-ups that contained few suspects who resembled the robber in physical appearance, the additional context cues provided in the line-up had a non-significant effect on correct identification rate. The correct identification rate was 0.50 for subjects who received no additional context cues and 0.44 for subjects who received additional context cues ($d$ = 0.13). This interaction shows that when line-ups contained suspects who resembled the robber in physical appearance, which any 'fair' line-up should, the context cues provided by voice, gait, three-quarter, and full body views were helpful in discriminating among targets and foils.

The above interaction is perhaps better understood if considered along with a significant interaction between line-up cues and similarity of line-up members in predicting choosing rates. When additional context cues were not given in the line-up, the choosing rate was 0.72 in low similarity line-ups but 0.89 in high similarity line-ups ($d$ = 0.48). Without the additional context cues, increasing the number of line-up suspects who resemble the target in physical appearance increased the likelihood that a line-up suspect was chosen. When the additional cues were given, however, increasing the number of similar looking suspects led to a significant shift in criterion in the opposite direction; the corresponding choosing rates were 0.88 and 0.76, respectively ($d$ = 0.34).

The additional context cues in the line-up parade also improved the identification rate in the two-week retention interval condition. Among the subjects who attempted identifications after two weeks, the correct identification rate was 0.37 among subjects who did not receive the additional context cues in the line-up, but 0.59 among subjects who received the additional context cues ($d$ = 0.49). Among subjects who attempted identifications after only two days, the additional context cues provided in the line-up had a non-significant effect on identification rate. The correct identification rate for these subjects was 0.49 among subjects who did not receive additional context cues and 0.39 for subjects who received additional context cues ($d$ = 0.22). It should be noted that although subjects in the two-week condition who received additional context cues in the line-up had higher correct identification rates than subjects in the two-day condition, the increase in correct identification rate from 0.49 (two-day, no additional context cue condition) to 0.59 (two-week, additonal context cue condition) was non-significant, even using the most lax criterion (simple comparison using Fisher's LSD test). This difference in performance is probably attributable to chance variation.

Finally, there was a significant interaction between contextual cues in the line-up parade and exposure to mugshots. Among subjects who were not shown mugshots, the added context cues in the line-up significantly improved identification accuracy. Among this group the correct identification rate was 0.35 among the subjects who did not receive additional cues but 0.51 among subjects who did receive additional cues ($d = 0.35$). The corresponding correct identification rates for subjects who searched mugshots were 0.51 and 0.47, respectively ($d = 0.09$).

In conclusion, the context reinstatement interview effectively offset the effects of disguise and biased line-up instructions on identification accuracy. The interaction between line-up instructions and the context reinstatement interview in the prediction of identification accuracy and choosing is particularly interesting. Unlike disguise, biased line-up instructions do not affect the encoding of information, but increase the pressure to choose a suspect from the line-up. It has been predicted that the effects of social pressure on judgements of perception increase as ambiguity of the object about which the judgment is being made increases (Asch, 1951). If the context reinstatement interview serves to improve the vividness of the witness' image of the target, then one might expect the effects of biased line-up instructions to be alleviated by the reinstatement of context. Our results support this conjecture. Further research will be needed (and is presently being conducted) to unconfound the effects of the three procedures that comprised this interview, mnemonic instructions, exposure to snapshots showing the environment in which the crime occurred, and exposure to the subject's own description of the robber's physical characteristics and of the environment.

Using additional context cues in constructing the line-up increased the reliability of identifications in the two-week retention interval condition and in the high-similarity line-up condition. Exposure to mugshots during the interim between witnessing the event and viewing the line-up reduced the effectiveness of the line-up contextual cues.

Until now we have only described the effects of context reinstatement procedures obtained in our laboratory and in the meta-analysis. It is therefore appropriate to inquire about the effects of context reinstatement procedures in more naturalistic settings. Experiments that involved staged incidents, for example, have shown positive effects for context reinstatement (Malpass and Devine, 1981b; Timm, 1981; Wagstaff, 1982), but such optimistic results are not universally obtained (Lindsay and Wallbridge, 1983).

### A field experiment

Krafka and Penrod (1985) examined the effects of context reinstatement procedures on identification accuracy in an applied, forensically-relevant context. The settings of the experiment were liquor stores, convenience stores, and small neighborhood groceries throughout Madison, Wisconsin and the surrounding area. The procedures of the experiment were as follows. An experimental 'confederate' entered a store and purchased a small item with a travellers' check. Either 2 or 24 hours later, an experimenter, posing as a law intern, entered the store and asked the clerk with whom the first target confederate interacted to identify the target from a six-person, target-present or target-absent photospread. The context reinstatement procedures, which half of the subjects received, consisted of (1) instructions to recall what occurred during the transaction and mentally to reconstruct the target's face, (2) exposure to a photocopied form of identification (non-photo) displayed by the target during the transaction, and (3) exposure to another travellers' check signed by the target. In all, 85 clerks participated in the experiment. Data from target-present and target-absent photospreads were analyzed separately.

In data from the target-present line-up condition the overall hit rate was 0.41. Among the subjects who received context reinstatement procedures, the hit rate was 0.55, but among subjects who received no context reinstatement procedures, the hit rate was only 0.29; this difference was significant ($d = 0.36$). No significant differences in hit rate were attributable to retention interval or to the interaction between context reinstatement procedures and retention interval. Analysis of data from the target-absent arrays showed that context reinstatement procedures did not affect the false identification rate.

## IMPLICATIONS FOR FORENSIC APPLICATION AND FURTHER RESEARCH

The fallibility of eyewitness identification presents the legal system with a perplexing problem. The courts must devise appropriate criteria for evaluating the reliability of identifications given specific circumstances and intuition alone is insufficient for developing these criteria (Wells and Murray, 1983). The legal system might profitably rely on the findings of social scientists to aid in determining appropriate criteria. The knowledge that social scientists gain from their experimentation may contribute not only to more informed decision-making on the part of factfinders, but perhaps to more effective factfinding on the part of the police. Our findings indicate positive effects on witness' abilities to correctly identify a perpetrator of a witnessed crime for procedures designed to reconstruct the context of a witnessed event. These findings complement those of Geiselman, who demonstrates that such procedures enhance the reliability of eyewitness recall.

We have discussed the results of studies that adopt a variety of methodologies including meta-analysis, laboratory experimentation, and experimentation in the field. Taken together our results show that procedures that reinstate the context surrounding an event can effectively increase the reliability of eyewitness identification. Although the findings of the meta-analysis (Shapiro and Penrod, 1986) and those of Krafka and Penrod (1985) and of Malpass and Devine (1981b) show that context reinstatement procedures may have main effects on identification accuracy, it is also the case that the meta-analysis allows for assessment of few two-way interactions, and the Krafka and Penrod (1985) and Malpass and Devine (1981b) experiments manipulated few variables. Results of our fractional factorial experiments indicate that the effects of context reinstatement are likely to be qualified by interactions with other variables, which probably explains the generally inconsistent findings regarding the effects of context cues on recognition accuracy (e.g. McSpadden *et al.*, this volume). Further research is needed to clarify the roles of various forms of context cues in affecting identification or recognition accuracy. Adding characteristics such as voice features, gait, and posture proved useful when used in combination with one another. Mnemonic techniques, reinstatement of emotions experienced at encoding, and mental reinstatement of environmental cues were effective in the Krafka and Penrod (1985), Malpass and Devine (1981b), and Cutler *et al.* (1987b) experiments. Further research in this area will increase our knowledge about how and which context cues affect the memory system generally, and might assist in developing procedures that will increase the reliability of eyewitness identifications.

## ACKNOWLEDGEMENT

This research was supported by National Science Foundation Grant SES-8411721 and National Institute of Justice Grant 84-IJ-CX-0010 to the second author.

## REFERENCES

Asch, S. (1951). Effects of group pressure upon the modification and distortion of judgments. In H. Guetzkow (Ed.) *Groups, Leadership, and Men*, Pittsburgh: Carnegie Press.

Brigham, J. C., Maas, A., Snyder, L. D. and Spaulding K. (1982). Accuracy of eyewitness identifications in a field setting. *Journal of Personality and Social Psychology*, **42**, 673–680.

Buckhout, R., Alper, A., Chern, S., Silverberg, G. and Slomovitz, M. (1974). Determinants of eyewitness performance on a lineup. *Bulletin of the Psychonomic Society*, **4**, 191–192.

Buckhout, R., Figueroa, D. and Hoff, E. (1975). Eyewitness identification: effects of suggestion and bias in identification from photographs. *Bulletin of the Psychonomic Society*, **6**, 71–74.

Clifford, B. R. and Bull, R. (1978). *The Psychology of Person Identification*, Boston: Routledge & Kegan Paul.

Cochran, W. G. and Cox, G. M. (1957). *Experimental Designs*, 2nd edn., New York: Wiley.

Cutler, B. L., Penrod, S. D. and Martens, T. K. (1987a). The reliability of eyewitness identifications: the role of system and estimator variables. *Law and Human Behavior,* 11, 233–258.

Cutler, B. L., Penrod, S. D. and Martens, T. K. (1987b). Improving the reliability of eyewitness identifications: putting context into context. *Journal of Applied Psychology*, 72, 629–637.

Davies, G. and Milne, A. (1985). Recognizing faces in and out of context. *Current Psychological Research*, 2, 235–246.

Deffenbacher, K. A., Carr, T. H. and Leu, J. R. (1981). Memory for words, pictures, and faces: retroactive interference, forgetting, and reminiscence. *Journal of Experimental Psychology: Human Learning and Memory*, 7, 299–305.

Fernandez, A. and Glenberg, A. (1986). Changing environmental context does not reliably affect memory. *Memory and Cognition*, 13, 333–345.

Kenny, D. (1985). Quantitative methods for social psychology. In G. Lindzey and E. Aronson (Eds.) *The Handbook for Social Psychology*, New York: Erlbaum.

Krafka, C. and Penrod, S. (1985). Reinstatement of context in a field experiment on eyewitness identification. *Journal of Personality and Social Psychology*, 49, 58–69.

Lindsay, R. C. L. and Wallbridge, H. (1983). Do the clothes make the man? An exploration of the effect of line-up attire on eyewitness identification. Unpublished manuscript.

Loftus, E. F. (1979). *Eyewitness Testimony*, Cambridge, MA: Harvard University Press.

Malpass, R. S. and Devine, P. G. (1981a). Eyewitness identification: lineup instructions and the absence of the offender. *Journal of Applied Psychology*, 66, 482–489.

Malpass, R. S. and Devine, P. G. (1981b). Memory in eyewitness identification. *Journal of Applied Psychology*, 66, 343–350.

McCloskey, M. and Egeth, H. (1983). Eyewitness identification: what can a psychologist tell a jury? *American Psychologist*, 38, 550–563.

Penrod, S., Loftus, E. F. and Winkler, J. D. (1982). The reliability of eyewitness testimony: a psychological perspective. In R. Bray and N. Kerr (Eds.), *The Psychology of the Courtroom*, New York: Academic Press.

Sanders, G. L. (1984). The effects of context cues on eyewitness identification responses. *Journal of Applied Social Psychology*, 14, 386–397.

Shapiro, P. and Penrod, S. D. (1986). A meta-analysis of the facial identification literature. *Psychological Bulletin*, 100, 139–156.

Smith, S. M., Glenberg, A. M. and Bjork, R. A. (1978). Environmental context and human memory. *Memory and Cognition*, 6, 342–353.

Timm, H. W. (1981). The effect of forensic hypnosis techniques on eyewitness recall and recognition. *Journal of Police Science and Administration*, 9, 188–194.

Wagstaff, G. F. (1982). *Context Effects in Eyewitness Reports*. Paper presented at the Law and Psychology Conference, Swansea, Wales.

Warnick, D. H. and Sanders, G. S. (1980). Why do eyewitnesses make so many mistakes? *Journal of Applied Social Psychology*, 10, 362–366.

Wells, G. L. and Murray, D. M. (1983). What can psychology say about the *Neil v Biggers* criteria for judging eyewitness accuracy? *Journal of Applied Psychology*, 68, 347–362.

Yarmey, A. D. (1979). *The Psychology of Eyewitness Testimony*, New York: Free Press.

Memory in Context : Context in Memory
Edited by G.M. Davies and D.M. Thomson
© 1988 John Wiley & Sons Ltd.

CHAPTER 11

# Improving Eyewitness Memory Through Mental Reinstatement of Context

R. Edward Geiselman

*University of California*

## ABSTRACT

Research is described on the Cognitive Interview. This new procedure incorporates (i) mental reinstatement of context, (ii) exhaustive recall, (iii) perspective changes, (iv) repeated retrieval using different starting points, all of which lend to improved recall under laboratory conditions. Studies involving both live and video incidents demonstrate the superiority of the cognitive interview over conventional techniques as provided by experienced police personnel.

A critical component of effective law enforcement is the ability of police investigators to obtain accurate and detailed information from witnesses (Rand Corp., 1975). Eyewitness testimony also can have a great impact on jury decisions in the courtroom (Loftus, 1974). However, eyewitness accounts are known frequently to be fallible and incomplete (Loftus, 1979). Fortunately, we can devise tools to improve the quality of eyewitness reports.

In the typical crime scenario, the events unfold rapidly under emotionally charged conditions. As a consequence, consciously controlled encoding strategies are unlikely to be used. Practically, eyewitness memory can be enhanced only by developing mnemonics that improve the retrieval or search phase of memory. The focus of the research described here, then, has been to develop mnemonics that can be used to facilitiate recollection at the time of retrieval.

One generally accepted principle of memory that is relevant to the eyewitness situation is that a memory trace is composed of several features (Bower, 1967; Underwood, 1969; Wickens, 1970) and the effectiveness of a

245

retrieval cue is related to the amount of feature overlap with the encoded event (Flexser and Tulving, 1978). This is a statement of encoding specificity (Tulving and Thomson, 1973). One way to maximize feature overlap is to reinstate the context that surrounded the incident. Smith, Glenberg, and Bjork (1978) found that recall performance was improved when subjects were taken back to the room where the information had been learned. In the eyewitness case, that is analogous to going back to the scene of the crime. Furthermore, Smith (1979) reported that recall performance also was improved if subjects simply imagined returning to the original room. In the eyewitness case, mental reinstatement of the context that surrounded a crime scene may be preferable to physical reinstatement because that would save valuable time for investigators with demanding case loads and because the crime scene may change markedly in appearance over time.

## THE COGNITIVE INTERVIEW

Based in part on this theoretical and empirical framework, Geiselman, Fisher et al. (1984) developed a memory retrieval procedure for eyewitnesses called the Cognitive Interview that consists of four general retrieval mnemonics. Of these, two attempt to increase the feature overlap between encoding and retrieval contexts: (1) mentally reinstating the environmental and personal (internal) contexts that existed at the time of the crime (Malpass and Devine, 1981; S. Smith, 1979): and (2) reporting everything, even partial information, regardless of the perceived importance of the information. The latter technique might be effective either because some witnesses do not know what information has investigative value or because the act of being complete can lead to recollection through feature overlap of information that is important. The other two mnemonics encourage using many retrieval paths: (3) recounting the events in a variety of orders (Burns, 1981; Loftus and Fathi, 1985; Whitten and Leonard, 1981): and (4) reporting the events from a variety of perspectives (Anderson and Pichert, 1978; Firstenberg, 1983).

In the experiments described in this chapter, interviewers using the Cognitive Interview technique read the following descriptions of the general mnemonics verbatim to the 'eyewitnesses' at the beginning of the interview:

(1) Reinstate the Context: try to reinstate in your mind the context surrounding the incident. Think about what the surrounding environment looked like at the scene, such as rooms, the weather, the lighting, any smells, any nearby people or objects. Also think about how you were feeling at the time and think about your reactions to the incident.

(2) Report Everything: some people hold back information because they are not quite sure that the information is important. Please do not edit anything out of your report, even things you think may not be important.

(3) Recall the Events in Different Orders: it is natural to go through the incident from beginning to end. However, you also should try to go through the events in reverse order. Or, try starting with the thing that impressed you the most in the incident and then go from there, going both forward in time and backward.

(4) Change Perspectives: try to recall the incident from different perspectives that you may have had, or adopt the perspectives of others who were present during the incident. For example, try to place yourself in the role of a prominent character in the incident and think about what he or she must have seen.

In addition to the four general mnemonics, a series of specific techniques was developed that could be used by an investigator to elicit specific items of information following the narrative phase of an interview. These specific mnemonics include the following:

(1) Physical Appearance: think about whether or not the suspect reminded you of anyone you know. If you were reminded of someone, try to think of why. Was there anything unusual about the physical appearance or clothing?

(2) Names: if you think that a name was spoken but you cannot remember what it was, try to think of the first letter of the name by going through the alphabet. Then, try to think of the number of syllables.

(3) Numbers: was the number high or low? How many digits were in the number? Were there any letters in the sequence?

(4) Speech Characteristics: think of whether the voice reminded you of someone else's voice. If you were reminded of someone, try to think of why. Was anything unusual about the voice?

(5) Conversation: think about your reactions to what was said and the reactions of others. Were there any unusal words or phrases used?

As described below, the Cognitive Interview has been found in several studies to be effective for enhancing eyewitness memory. The amount of correct information generated was significantly increased in comparison to the standard police interview. This result, which was evident even for the most critical items from the crime scenarios, was not accompanied by an increase in the amount of incorrect information generated.

While the Cognitive Interview is composed of several elements, each of the four general retrieval mnemonics has been observed to be effective in enhancing eyewitness recall when used in isolation (Geiselman, Fisher, MacKinnon and Holland, 1986a, Experiment 2). The mental reinstatement of environmental and personal (internal) context was especially effective in isolation, but none of the four general mnemonics was as effective as the full Cognitive Interview.

## REVIEW OF THE EXPERIMENTS

The Cognitive Interview was first evaluated positively in a preliminary experiment conducted by Geiselman *et al.* (1984). In that research, actors disrupted a classroom situation and the students were interviewed subsequently as eyewitnesses via questionnaire. Students who were instructed in the four memory retrieval mnemonics at the time of test recalled more correct information about the incident than did subjects who were told simply to keep trying to remember more information. Further, the Cognitive Interview showed none of the drawbacks sometimes found with other innovative interview techniques, such as hypnosis (M. Smith, 1983). It did not lead to more incorrect information being generated, nor did it lead to greater eyewitness confidence in the incorrect information. While the results of that study were encouraging, one major limitation was that the conditions of the experiment were somewhat dissimilar to those found in a real crime and police interview. The ecological validity of the tests was increased in the experiments described below.

### Experiment 1

This study (Geiselman, Fisher, MacKinnon, and Holland, 1985) was designed to maximize the ecological validity of the results: the stimulus materials were emotionally arousing films of simulated crimes; the eyewitness recall protocols were collected using interactive interviews rather than fixed questionnaires; and the interviews were conducted by experienced law enforcement personnel. The present study also extended the earlier work of Geiselman *et al.* (1984) by comparing the Cognitive Interview to the forensic hypnosis interview and to the standard (control) police interview. The data from the hypnosis condition are not directly relevant to the topic of this chapter, and therefore they will not be discussed here.

### Method

The subjects were 89 undergraduate students recruited from introductory classes at the University of California, Los Angeles.

The interviewers were 17 law enforcement professionals who represented a variety of specialties: police detectives, CIA investigators, polygraph specialists, and private detectives. To ensure homogeneity among the interviewers, each interviewer had compleed a 40-hr course on forensic hypnosis and had subsequent field experience on hundreds of cases.

The four films used in this experiment were borrowed from the training academy of the Los Angeles Police Department (LAPD). The academy utilizes these films as part of a computerized training process in which police officers are exposed to simulated, life-threatening situations (Decision Evaluation Firearms Trainer). Each film presents an audio-visual scenario of a violent crime or crime situation that lasts approximately four minutes. The scenarios of the four films include: a bank robbery, a liquor store holdup, a family dispute, and a search through a warehouse. In each film, at least one individual is shot and killed. The scenarios are realistic in that monitored physiological reactions of officers in training have been found to be comparable to reactions that would be expected in similar street situations (LAPD). The films are rich in quantifiable information including person descriptions, mannerisms, weapons, and sequences of events.

Approximately 48 hrs after viewing the film, the subjects were interviewed by the law enforcement personnel. Before each interview, the interviewer was told only the title of the crime scenario that had been witnessed by the subject (e.g. bank robbery). All interviews were audio-recorded.

Three weeks prior to the interviews, each interviewer received instructions for one, and only one, of the following interview procedures.

(1) *Standard Interview.* These interviewers were told to use the questioning procedures that they normally would use without an hypnotic induction procedure. The only restriction was that each 'witness' was to be asked first to describe in their own words what they remembered (open-ended report). Then, and only then, were the interviewers to ask any specific questions about the film based on the witnesses' account.

(2) *Cognitive Interview.* In this condition, the interviewers were to describe the four general memory retrieval techniques of the Cognitive Interview to the subjects before the questioning began. A four-item list of the techniques was placed in full view of the witness during the entire interview as a reference guide. Otherwise, the format of this interview was the same as that for the standard interview.

*Analysis and results*

Each tape-recorded interview was transcribed and the information contained in the transcriptions was categorized into three exhaustive lists for each film: persons, objects, and events. The persons category included

Table 11.1  Facts recalled with the three types of interview.

|                       | Type of interview | |
|-----------------------|-----------|----------|
|                       | Cognitive | Standard |
| Number correct        | 41.15     | 29.40    |
| Number incorrect      | 7.30      | 6.10     |
| Number confabulated   | 0.70      | 0.40     |

physical appearance, clothing, mannerisms, and speech characteristics. The objects category included guns, knives, cars, and carried articles. The events category included movements, number of shots, interperson contacts, conversation, and general sequencing. These exhaustive lists were compiled and matched against the information contained in the four films for accuracy. This catalogue of information then was used to score each subject's transcribed report for (1) the number of correct bits of information recalled, (2) the number of incorrect bits of information generated (e.g. the wrong hair color of a suspect), and (3) the number of confabulated bits of information generated (e.g. a description of a suspect's face when the face was not shown in the film).

The results are presented in Table 11.1. The Cognitive Interview elicited approximately 35 percent more correct items of information than the standard (control) interview, but the two types of interview did not differ on the number of incorrect items generated or on the number of confabulations.

To determine whether the extra information generated by the Cognitive Interview had investigative value, 20 facts from both the bank robbery and liquor-store holdup films were chosen for selective scoring as the most important items of information from those crime scenarios. As in the overall analysis, the Cognitive Interview led to the recall of more correct items than did the standard interview. Thus, the Cognitive mnemonics were successful in the enhancement of eyewitness memory even for the most critical facts, not simply for ancillary facts.

## Discussion

The major finding of this study was that cognitive retrieval mnemonics are effective for the enhancement of eyewitness memory retrieval in the police interview. We believe the observed effects to lie in the guided memory search components of the Cognitive Interview. The standard police interview, as observed here, consists mainly of repeated attempts to recall the target information, each time in the same way without supplemental memory retrieval guidance. The effectiveness of the Cognitive Interview could not be attributed to differential questioning time, the number of questions asked, or to heightened subject or interviewer motivation (see Geiselman *et al.*, 1985 for a discussion of these issues).

As part of the technique, the Cognitive Interview encourages the eyewitness mentally to reinstate the environmental and personal context that surrounded the crime. As an example, one 'witness' was asked if she had anticipated that the suspect who was hiding in the trashbin was going to shoot at the officer. (This question served to reinstate internal context.) When she answered that she was surprised by the shooting, she was asked to explain her surprise. She said that the suspect had dropped a gun earlier and that she had assumed it to have been his only weapon. That the suspect had dropped a second gun was not elicited previously in this interview.

**Experiment 2**

This study (Geiselman *et al.*, 1986a, Experiment 1) was conducted to expand the generalizability of the effectiveness of the Cognitive Interview in an important way, to a non-student population. An argument could be made that the Cognitive Interview would be less effective with non-students because non-students are less practiced at using memory search strategies; all of the research on the retrieval mnemonics used in the Cognitive Interview has been carried out with college students. A competing argument could be made that the Cognitive Interview would be more effective with non-students either because: (1) students are poorer observers due to their 'preoccupation with competing thoughts' (McCarty, 1960), and thus much information is not stored for later retrieval in any case; or (2) students are more likely to know about and use retrieval mnemonics without being instructed to do so, and thus control subjects carry out their own version of the Cognitive Interview.

*Method*

Fifty-one subjects were recruited from advertisements placed in a local paper and announcements posted at various locations at the University of California, Los Angeles. College students were excluded from the study. The participants were from a variety of occupations, such as custodian, secretary, laboratory assistant, and maintenance man. The demographic characteristics of the subjects accurately reflected the population of California, as per available census data, with the exception of

Table 11.2   Recall performance as a function of type of interview
and level of education.

|                     | College | | No college | |
|---------------------|-----------|----------|-----------|----------|
|                     | Cognitive | Standard | Cognitive | Standard |
| Number correct      | 42.23     | 35.33    | 40.50     | 35.86    |
| Number incorrect    | 8.14      | 8.22     | 9.90      | 8.86     |
| Number confabulated | 1.59      | 3.33     | 1.79      | 1.29     |

education. However, the level of education in the present sample ranged between tenth grade and college Masters degree. Thus, we were able to analyze the potential influence of level of education on the memory performance variables.

The interviewers were recruited from various police departments in southern California. The final group of interviewers consisted of nine male police detectives. Each interviewer had considerable field experience with hundreds of cases. Three weeks prior to the interviews, each interviewer received instructions for one, and only one, of the following two interview procedures: The Cognitive Interview or the standard interview.

The two films used in this experiment were the bank robbery and liquor-store holdup scenarios that were also used in Experiment 1. Approximately 48 hrs after viewing the film, the subjects were interviewed by the police detectives. All interviews were audio recorded.

*Analysis and results*

Each tape-recorded interview was transcribed and scored as in Experiment 1. The results are presented in Table 11.2. The statistical analysis showed that the Cognitive Interview was effective in eliciting more correct items and it was as effective for less educated witnesses as for witnesses with a college education.

For number incorrect, neither the main effect of type of interview nor the Type of Interview × Level of Education interaction effect was significant. For number confabulated, the main effect of type of interview was not significant; but the Type of Interview × Level of Education interaction was significant. With college-educated witnesses, the number of confabulations was reduced when the Cognitive Interview was administered; but with lesser educated witnesses, the number of confabulations was not affected significantly by the type of interview. The reason for this interaction is not apparent.

*Discussion*

This study provided a second replication of the effectiveness of the Cognitive Interview in eliciting more correct information from eyewitnesses without an accompanying increase in errors. This study further demonstrated that the Cognitive Interview is as effective with non-student, lesser educated witnesses as it is with persons who are college-educated. Thus, the Cognitive Interview is effective for those who are most likely to be victims or witnesses of crime.

**Experiment 3A**

From a legal perspective, it is important that the Cognitive Interview be generally accepted as a reliable tool by the scientific community (*Frye vs US*, 1923). That is, it is important to demonstrate that not only is the Cognitive Interview an effective and reliable memory-enhancement device, but that it is free of technical problems potentially associated with memory retrieval.

One criticism of forensic hypnosis has been that it heightens the negative effect of misleading questions on eyewitness memory (Sanders and Simmons, 1983; Zelig and Beidleman, 1981; Sheehan, Grigg, and McCann, 1984 — but for evidence to the contrary, see Sheehan and Tilden, 1983). The aim of Experiment 3A (Geiselman, Fisher, Cohen, Holland, and Surtes, 1986b) was to assess the effect of the Cognitive Interview on eyewitness responses to misleading questions.

Although the interviewers in our previous studies asked few questions on their own that were clearly misleading or leading, Yuille (1984) reported that a significant percentage of Canadian police detectives believe that leading questions must be asked to produce reasonably complete reports. Thus, the effect of the Cognitive Interview on eyewitness responses to misleading questions should be assessed to establish more fully the usefulness of the technique as an investigative tool.

There are two possible ways in which the Cognitive Interview might influence the recollection of details about which misleading information has been presented. On the one hand, the interview might produce a strong bond between the interviewer and the witness, as is suspected with the hypnosis interview, and therefore the witness is more easily misled by the cognitive interviewer. On the other hand, arguments can be made that the Cognitive Interview should *reduce* a subject's susceptibility to misleading questions. First, if a misleading question serves to create a second memory that co-exists with the original one (Bekerian and Bowers, 1983) rather than replacing the original one (Greene, Flynn, and Loftus, 1982; Loftus, 1979), then reinstatement of the original context with the Cognitive Interview should lead the subject to retrieve the original (correct) episodic record. Or, because of more complete memory access with the Cognitive Interview, the Cognitive Interview might prevent the alteration or augmentation of the original (correct) memories in the first place, at the time the misleading questions are asked.

*Method*

The subjects were 42 undergraduate students recruited from introductory psychology classes at the University of California, Los Angeles.

A staged incident was carried out during the first meeting with the subjects by three research assistants from the Theater Arts Department at UCLA. A female played the role of an experimenter from the psychology department and two males played the roles of intruders. The experimenter greeted the students upon arrival and informed them that they would be expected to memorize a long list of words. The words were projected one at a time onto a screen at the front of the room. After approximately 20 slides had been presented, the two males entered the room and turned on the lights. One intruder pushed a cart that held a tape recorder and a typewriter. The other intruder carried a backpack with a yellow cord hanging out of it and stated that they were there to pick up the projector because it was scheduled to be used by a professor. A verbal exchange ensued between the intruders and the experimenter in which several bits of key information were presented. Despite objections by the experimenter, the intruders put the projector on their cart and left. The entire incident lasted between 45 sec. and 1 min.

Each subject returned 48 hrs after observing the incident and was assigned randomly to one of two groups. The two groups of subjects were taken to different rooms. At that time, both groups were asked to recall as much information as they could about the incident. Each subject in each group was given a printed test booklet that was to be used to record the information they recalled. The group that received the Cognitive Interview was first instructed in the use of the four memory retrieval mnemonics to aid their recall as described in Experiment 1.

At the beginning of the specific-questions phase of the interviews, which immediately followed the narrative phase, space was provided in the response booklets for the answers to three questions. For each subject, one of these questions contained misleading (incorrect)

Table 11.3 Proportion of subjects giving each type of answer
to the target questions in Experiment 3A.

| Type of question | Type of answer | | | |
|---|---|---|---|---|
| | Correct | Misleading alternative | Other alternative | 'Don't Know' |
| Leading | | | | |
| Cognitive | 0.55 | 0.09 | 0.05 | 0.31 |
| Standard | 0.65 | 0.05 | 0.10 | 0.20 |
| Control | | | | |
| Cognitive | 0.55 | 0.05 | 0.18 | 0.22 |
| Standard | 0.50 | 0.05 | 0.25 | 0.20 |
| Misleading | | | | |
| Cognitive | 0.15 | 0.49 | 0.05 | 0.31 |
| Standard | 0.05 | 0.60 | 0.10 | 0.25 |

information, another contained leading (correct) information, and the remaining question served as the control, containing no supplemental information. (The present distinction between leading and misleading questions has been labeled by other researchers as consistent versus inconsistent information questions — e.g. Loftus, 1979.) The target items were: a name (Dr Henderson) that was mentioned by one of the intruders; the nature of the trousers (tan slacks) worn by one of the intruders; and the color of a backpack (blue) carried by the other intruder. As an example, the three versions of the question referring to the backpack were as follows: leading version, 'Describe whether anything was hanging out of the blue backpack carried by the guy who talked the most'; misleading version, 'Describe whether anything was hanging out of the green backpack carried by the guy who talked the most'; control (no-information) version, 'Describe whether anything was hanging out of the backpack carried by the guy who talked the most.' Only one of the three versions of each question was asked of a given subject. Counterbalancing across subjects ensured that each target item was assigned to each type of question equally often within each of the two interview conditions. The misleading information for the name and trousers questions was Dr Davidson and brown corduroys, respectively.

Following those three questions, additional specific questions were presented in the test booklet as filler items. At the end of each of the interviews, space was provided for the answers of three questions designed to assess the impact of the leading/misleading questions manipulation. Immediately prior to asking these questions, the experimenter in the Cognitive Interview condition briefly reviewed the four general mnemonics for the subjects. Subjects in the standard interview condition waited for a comparable period of time (1 min.). Then, the questions were read as follows: 'What was the color of the backpack carried by one of the intruders?' 'What was the name of the doctor who was mentioned?' 'Describe the trousers worn by the intruder who pushed the cart'

*Results and discussion*

The results for the three target questions are presented in Table 11.3. The number-correct data illustrate the considerable influence of leading and misleading questions on the accuracy of eyewitness reports. However, the important aspect of the present data is that the Cognitive Interview did not increase the effects of leading and misleading questions as is sometimes reported with hypnosis, but rather the Cognitive Interview decreased both effects 0.10 each. The difference in the percentage correct between the leading and misleading conditions represents a numerical index of the overall influence of those questions on eyewitness memory performance. A difference score was computed for each of the two interview conditions; and the difference between these two difference scores was evaluated statistically. The difference in recall accuracy between the leading and misleading question conditions was 0.60 without the Cognitive Interview but 0.40 with the Cognitive Interview. (The difference between these two proportions did not achieve statistical significance at the standard 0.05 level, $p < 0.10$; but Experiment 3C, presented below, provided a replication of this pattern of results with a larger sample size, and statistical significance was achieved.)

The decrease in responses to the misleading questions with the Cognitive Interview was accompanied by an increase of 0.25 in the likelihood that the subjects would give unsolicited comments that the target information had been inserted in an earlier question. The comments appeared in two forms. Some subjects wrote 'The doctor's name was Henderson, but you said it was Davidson.' Others wrote 'I don't know what color the backpack was, but you said earlier that it was green.' The subjects who were not given the Cognitive Interview were unlikely to comment and were somewhat less likely to give 'don't know' responses. Instead, those subjects were more likely to respond with the information that had been inserted in the previous questions. This cannot be attributed to a relaxed response criterion because the subjects in the two groups did not differ on 'don't know' responses to the control questions.

The number-correct data with leading questions represent the first instance in all of our research where the Cognitive Interview led to a lower probability of recall than the standard interview, but this is as should be the case. This result is understandable when the 'don't know' data are considered. Some of the subjects who were given the Cognitive Interview searched for the original memory and found the target information to be unavailable or inaccessible. Some of these subjects, then, replied that they did not know the answer. The subjects who were not given the Cognitive Interview responded with the information that had been inserted (see Table 11.3), which happened in this case to be correct.

Thus, unlike what has been claimed by some researchers to be the case with forensic hypnosis, the Cognitive Interview did not heighten eyewitness responsiveness to misleading or leading information embedded in questions. To the contrary, the data suggest that the Cognitive Interview may insulate some subjects from the negative effects of misleading questions on accurate recall.

An important theoretical question is whether the Cognitive Interview sometimes prevents the replacement of the original episodic record in the first place (assuming that replacement would otherwise occur), or whether the Cognitive Interview sometimes guides the eyewitness to the original record that naturally co-exists with the memory created from the leading/misleading questioning. The greater incidence of unsolicited comments about the misleading questions in the Cognitive Interview condition suggests that the subjects were not simply guided back to an intact original memory record without accessing memories created by the interviewer. However, the data from the leading-question manipulation would appear to support the co-existence theory. Given that the information inserted in the leading questions happened to be correct, there was no inconsistency that the Cognitive Interview could have detected at the time the leading question was asked. The new information should have become part of any subject's record that did not yet contain the target information. Given that this did not occur with the Cognitive Interview, it is plausible that two memories sometimes were created.

### Experiment 3B

In this experiment, the locus of the effect of the Cognitive Interview was determined by delaying the cognitive training until after the leading/misleading questions had been asked. If the Cognitive Interview guides the subject to an intact, original memory record, then the Cognitive Interview should again reduce the effects of leading/misleading questions on subsequent witness recall. If the Cognitive Interview methods are ineffective with this revised procedure, then the Cognitive Interview either prevents the original (correct) memory from being altered, or it

Table 11.4   Proportion of subjects giving each type of answer
to the target questions in Experiment 3B.

| Type of question | Type of Answer | | | |
|---|---|---|---|---|
| | Correct | Misleading alternative | Other alternative | 'Don't Know' |
| Leading | | | | |
| Cognitive | 0.60 | 0.00 | 0.00 | 0.40 |
| Standard | 0.58 | 0.00 | 0.05 | 0.37 |
| Control | | | | |
| Cognitive | 0.60 | 0.00 | 0.05 | 0.35 |
| Standard | 0.46 | 0.00 | 0.22 | 0.32 |
| Misleading | | | | |
| Cognitive | 0.35 | 0.40 | 0.05 | 0.20 |
| Standard | 0.32 | 0.47 | 0.00 | 0.21 |

prevents a competing (incorrect) memory from being formed and stored as a correct memory.

*Method*

The subjects were 39 undergraduate students recruited from introductory psychology classes at the University of California, Los Angeles. The film used in this experiment was the bank-robbery scenario from Experiment 1. Immediately following the film, all subjects were asked to solve some unrelated mathematics problems for 5 min. Then they were given a printed test booklet and were asked a series of three questions. One of these questions contained misleading (incorrect) information, another contained leading (correct) information, and the remaining question served as the control, containing no supplemental information.

Following these three questions, the subjects in the standard interview (control) group were required to wait 6 min. and then were told to write down as much information as they could remember about the incident that they had just viewed. Those subjects receiving the Cognitive Interview were instructed in the use of the four memory retrieval mnemonics for 6 min., as described above in Experiment 1, before writing their narrative accounts.

After the narrative phase was completed, additional specific questions were presented as filler items in the test booklet. Then, the subjects in the Cognitive Interview condition were reminded of the four mnemonic techniques, while the control subjects waited for a comparable period of time (1 min.). Finally, all subjects were asked a set of three assessment questions to determine the effects of the prior leading/misleading questions.

*Results and discussion*

The results for the three assessment questions are presented in Table 11.4. Across both interview conditions, the number correct data again show the strong influence of leading and misleading questions on the accuracy of eyewitness reports. As in Experiment 3A, the difference in the percentage correct for leading versus misleading questions was computed for each of the two interview conditions. These difference scores reflect the combined magnitude of the leading/misleading question effects within each interview condition. The values were 0.26 for the standard condition and 0.25 for the cognitive condition. Thus, the Cognitive Interview did not affect the magnitude of the leading/misleading question effects in this experiment. In addition, the pattern of 'don't know' responses did not differ between the two types of interview; and none of the 39 subjects gave unsolicited comments that the interviewer had inserted information relevant to the assessment questions in earlier questions.

Comparing these results to those of Experiment 3A suggests that the Cognitive Interview affects witness susceptibility to leading/misleading questions only if the cognitive techniques are presented before the leading/misleading questions are asked, as would normally be the case in the field. Thus, either the Cognitive Interview prevents a second, new memory from being formed and stored as a correct memory (a memory incorporating leading/misleading information) or it prevents the original (correct) memory from being altered. In either case, the Cognitive Interview, as it is normally conducted, is useful. Not only does the Cognitive Interview not heighten witness responsiveness to misleading questioning, but it may serve to reduce, in some cases, the negative effects of leading/misleading questioning.

## Experiment 3C

The purpose for Experiment 3C was to replicate the results of Experiment 3A using the methodology from Experiment 3B. This was important for two reasons. First, the reduction of the leading/misleading question effects with the Cognitive Interview in Experiment 3A was rather small, and therefore those results should be replicated in a second experiment. Second, the comparison of results between Experiments 3A and 3B was somewhat tenuous because other methodological factors were varied between those experiments aside from the point in the interviews where the cognitive training was presented (e.g. stimulus materials, retention interval).

Table 11.5   Proportion of subjects giving each type of answer
to the target questions in Experiment 3C.

| Type of question | Type of Answer | | | |
|---|---|---|---|---|
| | Correct | Misleading alternative | Other alternative | 'Don't Know' |
| Leading | | | | |
| Cognitive | 0.53 | 0.00 | 0.06 | 0.41 |
| Standard | 0.63 | 0.00 | 0.09 | 0.28 |
| Control | | | | |
| Cognitive | 0.53 | 0.00 | 0.09 | 0.38 |
| Standard | 0.44 | 0.00 | 0.19 | 0.37 |
| Misleading | | | | |
| Cognitive | 0.44 | 0.18 | 0.00 | 0.38 |
| Standard | 0.28 | 0.50 | 0.00 | 0.22 |

*Method*

The subjects were 66 undergraduate, introductory psychology students, who volunteered to participate in this experiment in exchange for course credit. Thirty-four of the subjects were randomly assigned to the Cognitive Interview condition and 32 were assigned to the standard interview condition.

The materials and procedure were identical to those of Experiment 3B with the exception of the point in the Cognitive Interviews where the cognitive training was presented. Following the showing of the film and the 5-min. distractor task, the subjects in the Cognitive Interview condition received the 6-min. training on the cognitive methods as described in Experiment 3A. The subjects in the standard condition simply waited 6 min. Then, the interview procedures for the two groups mimicked those of Experiment 3A, but using the questions and response booklets from Experiment 3B.

*Results and discussion*

The results are presented in Table 11.5. As in the previous experiments, the difference in the percentage correct for leading versus misleading questions was computed for each of the two interview conditions. These difference scores reflect the combined magnitude of the leading/misleading question effects within each interview condition. The values were 0.35 for the standard condition and 0.09 for the cognitive condition. This pattern is consistent with Experiment 3A, and the difference between these two difference scores was significant.

The pattern of 'don't know' responses also mimicked that of Experiment 3A, with the subjects in the Cognitive Interview condition being more likely to use the 'don't know' option in response to the assessment questions for the leading/misleading items but not for the control items. Finally, some subjects in the Cognitive Interview condition again offered unsolicited comments when answering the assessment questions that the interviewer had inserted relevant information in previous questions. Of the subjects, 30 percent commented on misleading items and 20 percent commented on leading items. Only one of the subjects in the standard interview condition commented on the leading/misleading questioning.

In sum, subjects who received the Cognitive Interview as it normally would be administered were significantly less affected by leading/misleading questioning. The locus of the effect of the Cognitive Interview is at the point in the questioning where the leading/misleading questions are first asked.

## Experiment 4

The purpose of this most recent part of the research program (MacKinnon, O'Reilly, and Geiselman, 1988; Mende, MacKinnon, and Geiselman, 1986) is to extend the scope of cognitive interviewing to the important problem of witness memory for license plates. While most law-enforcement professionals would likely agree that a witness's recall of a license plate can be the backbone for case solution (e.g. for bank robberies), memory for license plates has received little attention in the eyewitness research literature. In fact, a computer search of the psychological and police-science literatures at UCLA produced no papers that directly addressed memory for license plates.

The research described here was designed to develop and test techniques to enhance the completeness and accuracy of eyewitness reports for license plate information. Among the techniques studied were an innovative questioning routine that includes mental reinstatement of contextual information, and a license plate simulation device that serves to aid the witness in visualizing plate characters. The questioning routine began with the following visualization instructions: 'Visualize the car in your mind. Did the car remind you of anyone else's car? Now visualize the back end of the car. Focus in on the trunk, the tail lights, now the bumper. Were there any stickers on the bumper? Now center in on the license plate.' The witness then was asked: 'Did the letters or numbers remind you of any words or things? Did the characters have lines, curves, or anything special about them? Did the characters appear to be close together? Etc.' The plate simulation device was constructed of colored paper and vinyl alphanumeric characters such that the characters could be inserted and interchanged in the plate shell upon the subject's command. The purpose of the device was to reinstate the visual context of a license plate and to provide an opportunity for the witness to generate candidate character configurations for inspection.

## Method

Over 300 subjects, in total, were shown slides that depicted what was described simply as a 'suspicious event.' The set of 10 slides presented a man who carried a television set, placed it in his car in a hurried manner, and drove the car down the street. Two sets of slides were used with a different car and plate appearing in each set. Immediately after the last slide, the witness was asked to write down the events they saw in the slides. After this unstructured narrative recall, the witness received one of four types of interview to recall the plate. The types of interview were created from two factors: (1) cognitive questioning or no cognitive questioning, and (2) plate simulator or no plate simulator. The control subjects were asked a series of questions that were generated from a poll of several detectives in the Los Angeles area regarding their interview techniques for license plates. For example, 'Was there a frame on the plate? Was it a personalized plate?'

## Results and discussion

Both the cognitive interviewing and simulation device resulted in a significant increase in correct plate information being generated from the subjects. While the control subjects improved throughout the interview by 1 percent additional correct characters relative to incorrect characters, the subjects with either cognitive interviewing or the plate simulation device improved by 10 percent additional correct characters relative to incorrect characters. Furthermore, the two effects were additive. Subjects who received cognitive interviewing plus the plate simulation performed best of all, with a 33 percent (or two-character) increase in additional correct characters. These results cannot be explained by more time spent with the witness because performance was unrelated to questioning time, and there is no evidence that motivation to try harder in itself can enhance the retrieval of memories (Weiner, 1966). Thus, the cognitive questioning and plate simulator were both useful for reconstructing witness memories for plate information. These data represent another instance where mental reinstatement of context is a powerful technique for enhancing witness memory retrieval.

While the techniques studied here rarely led to the recall of a complete plate (the average number of characters recalled was 3.85 out of 7), the two-character increase dramatically reduces the number of possibilities for investigation and computer search. For example, if the characters given by a witness were recalled in their correct order (only 10 percent of the errors observed were transposition errors), then recalling four characters instead of two on a California license plate would reduce the number of possibilities from 676,000 plates to 260 plates. These results are encouraging.

## GENERAL CONCLUSIONS

The purpose of this research was to identify and develop interview methods based on current memory theory to enhance the completeness and accuracy of eyewitness reports, and to test these methods empirically in controlled, yet ecologically valid, laboratory settings. The Cognitive Interview consists of four general methods for jogging memory, including the mental reinstatement of the environmental and personal, internal context that existed at the time of a crime scenario, and also a series of specific techniques for eliciting particular information such as names, numbers, license plates, and suspect characteristics. The Cognitive Interview was found to be effective with non-student, lesser educated witnesses as well as with college students. The cognitive procedures also are legally acceptable given that the Cognitive Interview did not lead to the generation of more incorrect information or confabulations.

Furthermore, the negative effect of asking misleading questions was reduced when the Cognitive Interview was used. In contrast, other researchers have reported that the misleading question effect is not reduced when context reinstatement instructions alone are used (McSpadden, Schooler, and Loftus, Chapter 9, this volume). However, in all three of their experiments, context reinstatement was attempted only after the misleading information had already been presented. Their results, then, are consistent with the results of the present Experiment 3B, where a procedure similar to McSpadden *et al.* was used. As noted above, the locus of the positive impact of the Cognitive Interview on the misleading question effect appears to be at the point where the misleading information is first presented (see Experiments 3A and 3C versus Experiment 3B). Thus, the effect of context reinstatement on misleading the witness in the present experiments does not bear on the issue of whether the original memories are replaced or whether they coexist with the misleading information in memory (however, see Bekerian and Bowers, 1983).

The Cognitive Interview techniques can be incorporated into the interviews of police investigators with little training, and eyewitnesses can learn the mnemonics quickly so as to save valuable time for the investigators, who often have demanding case loads. While the version of the Cognitive Interview studied here elicited as much as 35 percent more correct information than the standard police interview, a recently refined version of the Cognitive Interview was observed to be 50 percent more effective than before (Fisher, Geiselman, & Raymond, 1987). Current effort is to draw the program to its logical conclusion, namely to implement and evaluate the expanded and refined version of the Cognitive Interview in the field.

As for whether context reinstatement alone is useful for enhancing witness memory, McSpadden *et al.* point out that a number of studies published recently have failed to find significant context effects. While some researchers reliably observe positive context effects on memory performance (Cutler and Penrod, 1986, Chapter 10, this volume; Geiselman *et al.*, 1986a, Experiment 2; Shapiro and Penrod, 1986), others do not (Fernandez and Glenberg, 1985; McSpadden *et al.*, 1986). Determining whether this disparity reflects a fragility of the effect, as suggested by McSpadden *et al.*, or a not immediately apparent procedural difference, requires interpreting support for the null hypothesis theoretically. In this regard, very few researchers have reported *negative* effects of context reinstatement (Loftus, Manber, and Keating, 1983). From a practical perspective, mental context reinstatement may not always affect recall performance significantly, but it does not appear to hinder recall performance. Assuming that context reinstatement has no effect on recall and setting the alpha level at 0.05, it would be expected that for every 20 experiments showing a positive effect of context reinstatement (which there are), there should be 20 experiments showing a negative effect of context reinstatement (which, it appears, there are not) with 360 experiments supporting the null hypothesis (this figure excludes experiments with methods that are flawed). The present author's observations across experiments are vastly inconsistent with these odds. If more negative results are observed in the future, perhaps we will be in a position to unravel the conflicting pattern of results. Until then, some researchers will be reluctant to feel that we have been deluded into grandeur by our encouraging data on context reinstatement.

## ACKNOWLEDGEMENTS

The preparation of this chapter and the experiments that are described herein were supported by grants from the National Institute of Justice (USDJ-83-IJ-CX-0025 and USDJ-85-IJ-CX-0053). The author wishes to thank Dr Ronald P. Fisher who collaborated on the development of the Cognitive Interview and on the research reported herein, several law-enforcement professionals, and the UCLA research group of Heidi Holland, Lisa Hutton, Dr. David MacKinnon, Kim O'Reilly, and Teresa Panting.

## REFERENCES

Anderson, R.C., and Pichert, J.W. (1978). Recall of previously unrecallable information following a shift in perspective. *Journal of Verbal Learning and Verbal Behavior*, **178**, 1–12.

Bekerian, D.A., and Bowers, J.M. (1983). Eyewitness testimony: were we misled? *Journal of Experimental Psychology: Learning, Memory, and Cognition*, **9**, 139–145.

Bower, G. (1967). A multicomponent theory of the memory trace. In K.W. Spence and J.T. Spence (Eds.), *The Psychology of Learning and Motivation*, vol.1, New York: Academic Press, pp. 299–325.

Burns, M.J. (1981). The mental retracing of prior activities: evidence for reminiscence in ordered retrieval. Unpublished Doctoral Dissertation, University of California, Los Angeles.

Fernandez, A., and Glenberg, A.M. (1985). Changing environmental context does not reliably affect memory. *Memory and Cognition*, **13**, 333–345.

Fisher, R.P., Geiselman, R.E., and Raymond, D.S. (1987). Critical analysis of police interview techniques. *Journal of Police Science and Administration*, **15**, 177–185.

Firstenberg, I. (1983). The role of retrieval variability in the interrogation of human memory. Unpublished Doctoral Dissertation, University of California, Los Angeles.

Flexser, A., and Tulving, E. (1978). Retrieval independence in recognition and recall. *Psychological Review*, **85**, 153–171.

*Frye vs U.S.*, 293 ff. 1013 (1923).

Geiselman, R.E., Fisher, R.P., Firstenberg, I., Hutton, L.A., Sullivan, S., Avetissian, I., and Prosk, A. (1984). Enhancement of eyewitness memory: An empirical evaluation of the cognitive interview. *Journal of Police Science and Administration*, **12**, 74–80.

Geiselman, R.E., Fisher, R.P., MacKinnon, D.P., and Holland, H.L., (1985). Eyewitness memory enhancement in the police interview: Cognitive retrieval mnemonics versus hypnosis. *Journal of Applied Psychology*, **70**, 401–412.

Geiselman, R.E., Fisher, R.P., MacKinnon, D.P., and Holland, H.L., (1986a). Enhancement of eyewitness memory with the cognitive interview. *American Journal of Psychology*, **99**, 385–401.

Geiselman, R.E., Fisher, R.P., Cohen, G., Holland, H.L., and Surtes, L. (1986b). Eyewitness responses to leading and misleading questions under the cognitive interview. *Journal of Police Science and Administration*, **14**(1), 31–39.

Greene, E., Flynn, M., Loftus, E.F. (1982). Inducing resistance to misleading information. *Journal of Verbal Learning and Verbal Behavior*, **21**, 207–219.

Loftus, E.F. (1974). Reconstructing memory: the incredible eyewitness. *Psychology Today*, **8**, 116–119.

Loftus, E.F. (1979). *Eyewitness Testimony*, Cambridge, MA: Harvard University Press.

Loftus, E.F., and Fathi, D.C. (1985). Retrieving multiple autobiographical memories. *Social Cognition*, **3**, 280–395.

Loftus, E.F., Manber, M., and Keating, J.F. (1983). Recollection of naturalistic events: context enhancement versus negative cueing. *Human Learning*, **2**, 83–92.

MacKinnon, D.P., O'Reilly, K.E., and Geiselman, R.E. (1988). Memory for licence plates. Manuscript under review, University of California, Los Angeles.

Malpass, R.S., and Devine, P.G. (1981). Guided memory in eyewitness identification. *Journal of Applied Psychology*, **66**, 343–350.

McCarty, M. (1960). *Psychology and The Law*, Englewood Cliffs, N J: Prentice-Hall.

Mende, L., MacKinnon, D.P., and Geiselman, R.E. (1986). Memory for license plates as a function of exposure time. *Journal of Police Science and Administration,* 15(1), 68–71.

Rand Corporation. (October 1975). The Criminal Investigation Process, (vols 1–3), Research Reports Nos. R-1776-DOJ, R-1777-DOJ, Santa Monica, CA: Rand.

Sanders, G.S., and Simmons, W.L. (1983). Use of hypnosis to enhance eyewitness accuracy: does it work? *Journal of Applied Psychology,* 68, 70–77.

Shapiro, P.N., and Penrod, S. (1986). A meta-analysis of the facial identification studies. *Psychological Bulletin,* in press.

Sheehan, P.W., Grigg, L., and McCann, T. (1984). Memory distortion following exposure to false information in hypnosis. *Journal of Abnormal Psychology,* 93, 259–265.

Sheehan, P.W. and Tilden, J. (1983). Effects of suggestibility and hypnosis in accurate and distorted retrieval from memory. *Journal of Experimental Psychology: Learning, Memory and Cognition,* 9, 283–293.

Smith, M. (1983). Hypnotic memory enhancement of witnesses: Does it work? *Psychological Bulletin,* 94, 387–407.

Smith, S. (1979). Remembering in and out of context, *Journal of Experimental Psychology: Human Learning and Memory,* 5, 460–471.

Smith, S., Glenberg, A., Bjork, R.A. (1978). Environmental context and human memory. *Memory and Cognition,* 6, 342–353.

Tulving, E., and Thomson, D.M. (1973). Encoding specificity and retrieval processes in episodic memory. *Psychological Review,* 80, 352–373.

Underwood, B.J. (1969). Attributes of memory. *Psychological Review,* 76, 559–573.

Weiner, B.J. (1966). The effects of motivation on the availability and retrieval of memory traces. *Psychological Bulletin,* 65, 24–37.

Whitten, W., and Leonard, J. (1981). Directed search through autobiographical memory. *Memory and Cognition,* 9, 566–579.

Wickens, D. (1970). Encoding categories of words: an empirical approach to meaning. *Psychological Review,* 77, 1–15.

Yuille, J.C. (1984). Research and teaching with police: a Canadian example. *International Review of Applied Psychology,* 33, 5–23.

Zelig, M., and Beidleman, W.B. (1981). The investigative use of hypnosis: a word of caution. *International Journal of Clinical and Experimental Hypnosis,* 29, 401–412.

Memory in Context : Context in Memory
Edited by G.M. Davies and D.M. Thomson
© 1988 John Wiley & Sons Ltd.

CHAPTER 12

# Context, Memory and Education

MICHAEL J.A. HOWE

*University of Exeter*

ABSTRACT

Success at school depends on memory skills which many children do not acquire at home. Memory skills are to a considerable extent specific to particular contexts and domains of knowledge, and do not readily transfer to new areas of learning. Level of performance at one memory task does not provide a good basis for predicting the same individual's achievements at other tasks.

INTRODUCTION

Whenever people ask me whether I have a good memory (and they do) I try to imagine what kind of a conceptualization of a memory system might be behind such a question. I can only assume that, for many people, memory is still regarded as being some kind of instrument, like a kind of mental hammer, that can be applied more or less willy-nilly to any task that seems to necessitate information being retained in someone's brain. One of the consequences of facing up to the importance of contextual factors in memory is that one is forced to recognize that how well a person does in any memory task depends to a very large extent on the particular demands and circumstances of the task. The child who arrives at school will already be highly skilled at remembering certain kinds of information that need to be recalled in order to cope with the demands of everyday home life, but school will confront the child with demands to remember in circumstances where contextual influences are in various respects new or unfamiliar. Not surprisingly, performance at various kinds of memory tasks is powerfully affected by schooling (Cole, Gay, Glick and Sharp, 1971; Rogoff, 1981).

At school a child may for the first time experience a situation in which having to remember substantial amounts of information is a task in itself, not simply a means to an end, and in such circumstances there is likely to be a need for deliberate plans or strategies. Unless the classroom teacher is sufficiently aware of the ways in which success at school memory tasks depends on strategies which may not have been acquired at home, and can provide opportunites for the child to acquire them, the child will be at a real disadvantage. This point is nicely illustrated by the findings of some experiments by Flavell, Beach and Chinsky (1966) and Keeney, Cannizzo & Flavell (1967). They found that when children tried to remember a list of common objects, some children spontaneously rehearsed but others did not. Most of the older children in the study (aged ten years) did rehearse, but most of the youngest children (who were five years-old) did not. The suggestion that rehearsal contributed to the accuracy of recall was supported by the finding that not only did older children remember more objects than younger children, but that, at each age, those who did rehearse (as assessed by observing lip movements, which turns out to be a fairly reliable way of assessing rehearsal in young children) recalled considerably more items than those who did not rehearse. Moreover, when those children who did not spontaneously rehearse were taught to do so their performance improved abruptly, to match the level achieved by the spontaneous rehearsers. Findings such as these indicated that it is reasonable to conclude that on entry to school the child encounters memory tasks that make demands that will be unfamiliar, at least for some children, and that in order to succeed at such tasks it is necessary to gain memory skills (such as rehearsal) that may have been unnecessary for meeting pre-school demands on memory.

School tasks may make other kinds of unfamiliar demands, for which children need to be prepared in order to be successful. For example, a pre-school child may be experienced at those kinds of memory retrieval activities in which external memory cues can be counted upon (as, for instance, in discovering 'Where did you put your dolly?') but less experienced at kinds of activities that demand searching through one's knowledge, in the absence of substantial external cues (Flavell and Wellman, 1977). Generally speaking, memory tasks that involve the acquisition and retrieval of substantial bodies of knowledge are much more commonly encountered at school than beforehand, and such tasks call for various strategies and skills that are necessary for dealing with very large amounts of information. For example, adequate procedures for grouping and organizing knowledge are essential. Moreover, in those school tasks which involve the acquisition of new knowledge a major cause of success is the extent to which the child already possesses knowledge or skills to which the new information can be linked: thus the capacity to draw upon existing knowledge within the specific domain of the information to be acquired is often crucial. Throughout school, the child will frequently be in situations where one's capacity to deal with a new memory or learning problem largely depends upon what one already knows. It should be emphasized, however, that pre-school children are by no means lacking in memory skills, and their metamemory abilities may also be substantial (Kreutzer, Leonard and Flavell, 1975). What they may lack are the *particular* memory skills that are needed for the particular, and distinct, demands of school tasks.

## THE FRAGMENTARINESS OF CERTAIN SKILLS

Psychologists working in the field of education and school learning keep on being taken aback to discover just how closely human effectiveness at intellectual tasks is bound to particular circumstances. Just how context-bound human performance can be is illustrated by the case of a mentally retarded man who had been trained to work with a highly complex piece of machinery (Zigler and Seitz, 1982). His performance was perfectly adequate so long as the conditions in which he was required to work were identical to those in which he had learned to operate the machine. But if the workshop director changed things simply by turning the machine around the man became quite incapable of running it.

To illustrate the power of contextual influences, Bronfenbrenner (1979) tells an anecdote about the institution for 'feebleminded' people where his father worked as a neuropathologist. Occasionally,

> the New York City courts would commit to our institution, out of error or
> —more probably—sheer desperation, perfectly normal children. Before
> he could unwind the necessary red tape to have them released, it would
> be too late. After a few weeks as one of eighty inmates in a cottage with two
> matrons, their scores on the intelligence tests administered as a compulsory
> part of the discharge process proved them mentally deficient. (Bronfenbrenner, 1979, p.xii)

Amongst individuals who, unlike the unfortunate children in Bronfenbrenner's tale, are genuinely retarded, the fact that mental feats are closely tied to particular contexts may not seem particularly surprising. After all, it is widely accepted that lack of flexibility is to be expected in people who are mentally handicapped. Even so, the magnitude of contextual influences can surprise us. For example, Julia Smith and I (Smith and Howe, 1985) once examined an adolescent 'idiot savant' whose arithmetic skills appeared meagre. He could do simple subtraction tasks, but with difficulty: for instance, if asked to subtract 12 from 20 he would sometimes take half a minute to produce the correct answer. But since his special skill was calendar-date calculating we were interested to know how he would perform on a subtraction task that was based on calendar dates and involved the kinds of operations that might be necessary for solving a calendar problem. So we asked him some further subtraction questions, but this time they took the form 'If I was born in ——, how old would I be in ——?' When the questions were phrased like this, he was able to answer them all with great ease, even when spans of several hundreds of years were involved.

## HAVING MEANINGFUL GOALS

Before starting school, many children will have experienced memory tasks mainly in the context of goals and ongoing activities that are highly meaningful. (With a few exceptions, the existence of 'pure memory' tasks is confined to psychologists' laboratories. In most real life situations the cognitive activities that psychologists force into separate categories are untidily mixed up together, and in the classroom it is often difficult to make a non-arbitrary distinction between 'learning tasks' and 'memory tasks'.) The reason for having to remember something will usually have been clear: memory tasks as ends in themselves may have been unusual. That the contextual factors in different situations associated with a child's goals and purposes may be crucial, even when the physical environment remains unchanged and tasks are formally identical, was vividly demonstrated in a classic study conducted in the 1940s in the USSR (Istomina, 1975).

Istomina was interested in discovering how young children's memory performance would be affected by their perceptions of the task goals. There were essentially two experimental conditions in her study. In one, the children simply listened to lists of words. Each list contained five names of common objects, such as *carrot, milk* and *sock*. The children were told to remember as many items as they could, and one minute after they had heard the words they are asked to try to recall them. Few of the children did particularly well at this task, although the older children recalled more items than the younger ones. Average recall scores were 0.6 items (out of five) for the youngest children, who were three to four years of age, and 2.3 words for the eldest subjects, who were aged six to seven years.

Why did the children do so badly, particularly the younger ones? The task appears to be not unlike those that children often engage in at school, but it may have seemed very unfamiliar to young subjects who were unused to the kinds of memory demands that are encountered at school. Might the young children have performed better if the memory task had been one which made a more direct contribution to the children's own aims and activities? To investigate this possibility, some other children were given a memory task that required them to remember exactly the same words as those given to the subjects in the first group, but in which the instructions would have appeared more familiar and less strange. These children were given the task in the context of a game of shopping in which they were busily engaged. At one point in the game the experimenter recited to a child exactly the same list of words that the children in the other experimental group had heard. This time, however, the task instructions were different. The child had to go to the 'shop' (a play-counter at the other end of the room) and request the items he or she had been told about.

Note that although the instructions and the task contexts were different in the two conditions, the actual memory requirements were identical. In each condition the identical words were spoken, and in each condition (after an interval of time that was arranged to be equivalent) the child subject was to attempt recall by speaking them aloud. The difference between the two groups lay not in the formal demands of the task but in the familiarity and the meaning of the situation. For those young children who were playing at shopping there was an understandable reason for remembering the words. For the other children there was no equivalently meaningful goal. Since the task's formal memory demands were the same in both conditions, comparing performance provided a way of assessing the influence of the contextual factors that differed between the two conditions.

Istomina found that average recall scores were indeed substantially higher in the second condition. For example, amongst the three-to-four year-olds scores averaged 1.0 words, almost twice the average score of the youngest children in the other group, and in the oldest children average recall was 3.8 words, that is, about 60 percent higher than in similarly aged participants in the first condition. Hence the findings leave us in no doubt that the influence of contextual factors related to the purpose and familiarity of children's memory tasks can be extremely substantial.

## GENERAL ABILITIES AND PARTICULAR ACHIEVEMENTS

Why should psychologists be surprised to find that context exerts such a large influence on memory and cognition? I think that two broad intellectual influences on our understanding of human performance and development have encouraged us to believe that human performance is limited mainly by a person's relatively fixed abilities rather than the particular task and circumstances. The first influence is that of stage approaches to human development.

Piaget's theories appear to support the view that the form and level of a child's thinking are determined largely by the stage of intellectual development that has been reached. Although Piaget never denied the importance of context, some of the conclusions that were drawn from his experiments undoubtedly underestimated the importance of context-ual factors. For example, in research in the Piagetian tradition important deductions about children's broad ability to perceive from different per-spectives have been made from studies which tested young subjects' performance at tasks requiring them to imagine how modelled mountains would appear from alternative vantage points. However, later researchers questioned the appropriateness of this type of task for children who have never lived in a landscape with mountains, let alone model ones. When the original tests were replaced by ones involving situations and events that were more familiar to young children, performances indicating consider-ably more advanced stages of mental functioning were observed. Clearly, if the assessment of a child's stage of mental functioning is found to be seriously influenced by contextual aspects of the test situation, one has to accept that either the concept of fixed stages of intellectual development is inappropriate or that stage of development is by no means the only determinant of actual performance.

The second contributing factor to a mental climate which has given insufficient attention to the possibility that people's ability to remember is strongly influenced by context is our acceptance of the psychometric approach to human abilities. Basic to this tradition is the reasonable assumption that differences in human performance are largely caused by differences in basic abilities.

Undoubtedly there is a degree of truth in such a view, but it has encouraged psychologists to believe that they need look no further in order to explain individual differences. If Charlie's reading is better than Jimmy's, so the argument goes, the reason is that Charlie is a better learn-er, or a more intelligent one, or one with a higher level of reading ability. Charlie is seen as brighter, with greater potential to do well. Jimmy, on the other hand, may be labelled a slow learner, and may be placed in a 'low-ability' stream. In short, the observation that Charlie performs better in a particular situation is immediately translated into a pseudo-explanatory statement which purports to say *why* he performs better, and which does so by invoking some hypothesized broad mental attribute.

The absurdity of such deductions has been demonstrated many times. For example, the apparently plausible assumption that children who are more successful than others at school memory tasks possess superior memory abilities is clearly contradicted by the fact that many individuals who are extremely unsuccessful at remembering in school situations can nevertheless recall enormous amounts of information about sports, and may remember all the Saturday-afternoon scores in the main British football leagues after a single presentation (Morris, Gruneberg, Sykes and Merrick, 1981; Morris, Tweedy and Gruneberg, 1985). Similarly, the assumption that children who are successful at school and also perform well in intelligence tests inevitably have superior reasoning abilities to individuals who do badly in school and perform poorly on such tests is contradicted by the observation (Ceci and Liker, 1985) that some individuals with IQs as low as 80 and very little schooling are as capable as graduates with much higher measured intelligence (and having equivalent knowledge and experience relevant to the task) at the extremely intellectually-demanding task of mentally estimating odds and handicaps for horse-racing.

## PREDICTING PARTICULAR PERFORMANCES FROM GENERAL MEASURES

Although IQ scores make good predictors of performance at future tests of intelligence, which is hardly surprising, and provide reasonably accurate predictions of school success, the correlations between such test scores and other indices of mental competence are not at all impressive. Correlations with measures of everyday performance in post-school life are generally no higher than around 0.20, a level indicating too low a degree of relationship to permit useful predictions concerning individuals. Even among mentally retarded people, ability to function adequately in the real world is more closely related to personality than to tested intelligence, and the post-institutional adjustment of moderately retarded people has been found in a number of studies to be unrelated to IQ (Zigler and Seitz, 1982). It was also found that the ability of moderately retarded individuals to adjust to the demands of military life in the US Army was unrelated to IQ: again, personality was found to be far more important.

Even within school environments, there is little firm evidence to support the apparently commonsense notion that intelligence test scores provide an accurate indication of those basic abilities which determine a child's success. Correlations between test scores and school success appear to be reasonably high—around 0.7—but in fact a relationship of this magnitude only accounts for half the variance in performance. When one bears in mind the fact that many of those factors other than mental ability as such that contribute to success at school—attitude to school, competitiveness, familiarity with testing situations, and so on—also contribute to test scores, and therefore account for at least a substantial part of the above correlation, the link between basic intellectual abilities and school success begins to appear less firmly established than might have been expected.

The fact that measures of success at particular tasks of learning and memory are very weakly correlated with IQ scores provides another reason for questioning the centrality of the mental competence assessed by any global measure of mental competence. Furthermore, it is also significant that when measures of individuals' performance at a number of different memory tasks, or at a number of different learning tasks, are correlated, the relationships are found to be very low, correlations usually being less than 0.20.

Putting these findings together, it is hard to avoid concluding that particular mental skills and abilities are highly specific, and more strongly influenced by the precise nature of the task context and the detailed circumstances involved than by the kind of overall ability that tests of intelligence purport to measure. In short, it appears that people do well at particular tasks because those tasks are ones that they find interesting, or relevant to their needs, or familiar, or because they have acquired knowledge and skills that contribute to the level of performance, rather than because those people possess superior memory, reasoning or learning systems that can be applied to all tasks irrespective of the particular context.

All of us are more likely to remember those things that have personal significance for us (Rogers, Kuiper and Kirker, 1977). The activities at which we do well are usually ones which, over long periods of time, have been important to us. Thus competitive middle-class children who have been taught to value education do well in school, Moroccan carpet dealers who stand to make financial gains from having a detailed knowledge of the designs of different carpets come to possess what appear to us to be prodigious memories for carpet designs (Wagner, 1978); and farmers for whom it is necessary to know their animals impress other people by their ability to recall the names of numerous apparently similar cows or other animals.

Furthermore, cocktail-bar waitresses who know that they will make more money if they can remember large numbers of customers' orders are much better than other people at recalling drink orders (Bennett, 1983), as are waiters at remembering orders for meals (Ericsson and Polson, in press); football enthusiasts remember the scores obtained by those teams for which they have strong positive or negative feelings much more accurately than the scores of teams they do not care about; individuals who are paid to practise remembering sequences of digits, and given considerable encouragement, are eventually able to recall digit lists up to ten times as long as the length of lists recalled by people who have not been through the same experiences (Chase and Ericsson, 1981); and people such as the eminent nineteenth-century historian Thomas Macaulay, who devote a lifetime to interest in literature and the printed word, and for whom the ability to recall large passages of poetry and prose is useful, prestigious and highly valued, and greatly admired by one's friends, tend to devote enormous amounts of time and energy to such memorization tasks and, not entirely unexpectedly, are highly successful at them (Hunter, 1985). Even mentally retarded people, if they regularly devote many hours of their time to thinking about calendars and dates, eventually acquire a considerable body of remembered knowledge about dates. On the whole, people do well at those memory tasks which they perceive to be important, those for which they receive encouragement for doing well, and those on which they give themselves lots of practice. This is especially true for those memory-dependent skills and varieties of knowledge that are learned in school contexts.

Yet the view that differences in children's rate of success at school are mainly due to differences in basic (and perhaps innate) ability is so firmly entrenched that it is not easily modified by evidence showing that contextual modifications can lead to those individuals who generally do well performing very badly and those who normally fail at school doing extremely well. Evidence of high achievements by those children who are academic failures tends to be dismissed, either by denigrating the intellectual content of the task or by the suggestion that evidence of ability outside school merely reflects street-wisdom or other qualities that may be discounted as unimportant simply because they do not produce school success.

## THE UNEVENNESS OF PERSONAL ACHIEVEMENTS

At all levels of performance, competences at those skills and tasks in which memory has a central role can be remarkably specific: people may be highly skilled at one ability and yet totally lacking in competence at another skill that appears to be closely related to the first one. Conversely, people who are not at all competent at one skill may nevertheless be highly successful at other, ostensibly very similar feats. Such evidence of intellectual skills which are highly specific, context-bound and fragmentary appears to be clearly incompatible with a viewpoint in which particular abilities are seen as being under the control of broadly based intellectual ability, or intelligence. However, there has been a tendency to discount or ignore such evidence, partly since much of it comes from observations of mentally retarded people (the individuals known as 'idiots savants', for example) in whom striking intellectual feats of various kinds are seen to occur in people who are clearly retarded in other areas of mental activity. It is easy enough to dismiss such cases as being 'anomalous', implying that even if such a disparity between abilities is to be found among retarded individuals, the apparent absence of transfer between skills has little relevance to patterns of performance in normal people and is merely a symptom of the inflex-ibility and rigidity of mental functioning that is particularly characteristic of mentally handicapped individuals.

Less easy to ignore or discount is a body of evidence showing that performance at different memory-based skills and abilities that make apparently similar intellectual demands on the individual can be equally uneven and fragmentary even in people who are not at all mentally retarded. As it happens, it is by no means unusual for expertise in certain areas of intellectual competence to be unaccompanied by any evidence of exceptionality in other areas. There are expert chess players who fail to display superior mental skills at even those forms of reasoning and thought that appear to make intellectual demands that are highly similar to those involved in playing chess. Feldman (1982) noted that eight-year-olds who were extraordinarily good at chess were generally no better than average in other spheres. Biographical descriptions of extraordinarily talented individuals include numerous accounts showing that a gifted individual's skills outside the particular areas of special talent and expertise can be very mediocre. For example, Norbert Wiener, the brilliant mathematician who was a notable prodigy in early life, records in his autobiography that not until he had reached the age of seven did he become aware that Santa Claus was a fiction invented by the grownups. He adds:

> At that time I was already reading books of more than slight difficulty, and it seemed to my parents that a child who was doing this should have no difficulty in discarding what to them was obviously a sentimental fiction. What they did not realize was the fragmentariness of the child's world. (Wiener, 1953, p.81)

An autobiographical account by Francis Galton provides another illustration of the unevenness of a precocious child's achievements. Writing of his boarding school, where he started at the age of eight, Galton records that,

> In that room was a wardrobe full of schoolbooks ready for issue. It is some measure of the naïveté of my mind that I wondered how the books could have been kept so fresh and clean for nearly two thousand years, thinking that the copies of Caesar's commentaries were contemporary with Caesar himself. (Francis Galton, *Memories of My Life*, London: Methuen, 1908. Quoted by Forrest, 1974, p.8.)

In conclusion, there is little doubt that particular abilities are often much more fragmentary than people suppose, more separate from and independent of other abilities, dependent more upon particular contexts of knowledge, interests and attitudes and less upon the levels or stages of mental functioning that are often believed to exert a broad influence on performance across a wide range of tasks. I have already suggested that in schools there has been perhaps too much readiness to use ratings of performance at particular skills as a basis for classifying children and ranking them as having more or less ability, or as being fast or slow learners. In fact, as we have seen, such ratings are really far too specific and context-dependent to be legitimately used for making any more general assessment of a child's abilities, outside the particular task and the particular circumstances in which the ratings were used.

## STARTING SCHOOL: WHY SOME CHILDREN HAVE AN EDGE

Despite all that has been said in the above paragraphs, there is no denying either that some children do better in school than others or that the practical consequences of success or failure at school are considerable. Beginning at school is an important transition in a young child's life. It is widely acknowledged that children at school are expected to learn and remember things in circumstances and contexts which, for many, are very different from the contexts in which learning has occurred prior to school.

Of course, all children who arrive at school for the first time will already have mastered many skills, and they will already have demonstrated expertise at remembering some kinds of information and events. The acquired language skills of the average five-year-old, or example, are very considerable. What is unfamiliar about school, for some children more than for others, lies in the new circumstances and contexts in which memory and learning skills have to be exercised. Generally speaking, the ease of a child's transition to the new circumstances of school learning, and hence the likelihood of early successes at school (and, in consequence, subsequent successes as well) will be strongly influenced by the extent to which the child's home life has provided experiences of learning in circumstances that are similar to, and therefore provide adequate preparation for, the circumstances and contexts of school learning.

It has been common to speak of some children, usually ones whose school achievements are less than satisfactory, as coming from home environments that are educationally 'disadvantaged' or deprived, or inadequate, so far as remembering and learning are concerned. In reality, there is no overriding reason to suppose that, so far as learning in general is concerned, the home environments which have been thus labelled are necessarily less stimulating than others, or that the total amount of learning achieved by children reared in them is necessarily particularly small. What is less arguable is that the kinds of home environments to which these labels have been attached are ones in which the *match* between the forms, circumstances and contexts of learning with those to be encountered in school is relatively poor. In other words, so far as school learning is concerned these home environments are less than optimal not because the child fails to learn in them but because he or she does not have sufficient opportunities to become accustomed to the particular kinds of memory demands and forms of learning that will be encountered in school. It is interesting to note that the effectiveness of parents at helping their children to be successful at the mental skills needed for school appears to be as closely related to the amount of schooling received by parents as it is to parental intelligence. This suggests that a crucial factor is the extent to which the parent is 'school-wise' in the sense of being aware of the specific requirements of learning in the school, anticipating the demands on a child and preparing the child to deal with them.

## HELPING THE DISADVANTAGED CHILD

But even if the child from a so-called 'disadvantaged' environment is in fact not lacking expertise as a learner upon arrival at school, but simply lacking experience of learning in those particular contexts and circumstances that are necessary for school success and not inevitably encountered in pre-school life, the disadvantages are nonetheless real and important. For better or worse, lack of success at school is associated with relative lack of success in life afterwards. The fact that the root causes of failure may not lie in the absence of any basic abilities is little or no consolation if the child is failing. Therefore, it remains important to try to identify those particular qualities and skills that are needed if a child is to make the best of school experiences, and to ensure that those children whose home environments have not provided adequate preparation for the new demands of school can receive compensatory experiences that fill the need for such preparation.

So far as memory demands are concerned, there are a number of ways in which school learning differs from learning at home, and to varying extents most of the fairly numerous compensatory educational programmes that have been designed to help young children have involved considering and taking account of the differences (see, e.g. Glaser, 1984). Particular attention has been given to the fact that whereas before a child goes to school most situations demanding learning or remembering are ones in which the reasons for learning are fairly obvious, and form part of daily experiences, and the relationships between the learning activities and the reasons for performing such activities are straightforward or 'natural', at school it is often necessary to learn 'for its own sake', with no practical reason that is immediately obvious to the child. At school, compared with home, it is more likely to be necessary to make a deliberate effort to learn, and to have to make use of methods, techniques and strategies that are likely to be needed when what is to be learned takes the form of information or knowledge, rather than skills and activities as such. Learning and memory tasks at school also tend to appear more artificial, and abstract, as well as being more closely tied to knowledge, and to be more complex and highly organized. For example, subjects like mathematics and the physical sciences may require the sequential acquisition of skills that each depend on those skills that have already been acquired.

A matter that is currently being debated in educational psychology concerns the extent to which it is realistic to teach various skills that contribute to thinking, memory and other kinds of cognition, on the assumption that, once learned, they can be applied to a variety of different educationally important situations.

There is no doubt that it is possible to identify certain basic cognitive skills, subskills and other prerequisites that are necessary for the acquisition of cognitive abilities. It is clear that the lack of such skills renders many important educational achievements impossible. For example, Feuerstein (1980) points out that success in many school tasks necessitates the learner being able to reflect carefully, to make mental comparisons and groupings, and organize information, to delay responding to events until thought operations have been completed, to apply remembered information in order to interpret new information, to concentrate at length on a task, avoiding distractions, and so on. He argues that such abilities are best acquired through mediated learning experiences that are likely to occur when a child is involved in some kind of a dialogue with an older person, typically a parent. Any child who fails to acquire them will remain at a disadvantage so far as school learning is concerned. As a consequence, compensatory educational programmes that are intended to help educationally disadvantaged children or adolescents would do well to emphasize the provision of opportunities for helping young people to acquire those essential prerequisite learning skills they currently lack.

Up to this point such a diagnosis would meet fairly general agreement. The next step is the one where disagreement is encountered. On the one hand, many researchers and educators, including Feuerstein (1980) and others who have tried to teach 'memory skills' or 'thinking skills' or 'learning skills' to disadvantaged learners would argue that the best approach is to teach children such skills, so that they can then be applied whenever the child encounters a memorization, learning or thinking task to which they are applicable. On the other hand, others (Glaser, 1984) have argued that however plausible or attractive such a plan may appear, it is in fact unrealistic because the assumption that mental subskills function as widely applicable multi-purpose abilities that are detachable from the contexts (in particular the specific domains of knowledge) in which they have been acquired, is simply wrong.

The claim is that the knowledge and skills that are being acquired always go hand in hand: although they may be conceptually separate in the mind of the researcher they remain tightly linked in the learner (Chi and Koeske, 1983). Glaser (1984) argues that cognitive skills are in fact always acquired in the contexts of particular domains of knowledge, and that to a considerable extent their availability remains closely tied to that knowledge. If Glaser is correct, they cannot be simply applied or transferred whenever a situation arises for which they might be useful: the suggestion that a person's cognitive skills have such a general-purpose nature is simply wishful thinking. It may be true that in a highly successful learner skills eventually come to acquire such a nature, and thus become widely available for use in a variety of different circumstances, but such a state of affairs, however desirable, is not characteristic of the young or inexperienced learner. In the young, abilities remain to a large extent specialized, specific to particular tasks, contexts and knowledge domains, and inaccessible except via the particular contexts in which they were taught. It has been suggested that the context-specificity and lack of accessibility of cognitive abilities in the young may be not totally unlike the state of affairs where many 'lower' species possess adaptive specializations that are exceedingly complex and impressive, but are relatively unmodifiable and unavailable for use except in the particular circumstances for which they were designed (Rozin, 1976).

Clearly, the question of the extent to which memory skills and other cognitive skills are, on the one hand, transferable and widely applicable to a variety of different circumstances, or on the other hand, limited to particular contexts, is a matter of educational importance. Doubtless some skills are more transferable than others, and almost certainly transferability is more likely among skills that have become habitual, rather than among those that have been just acquired, and in mature learners rather than inexperienced ones. But a fuller understanding is needed of the extent to which memory skills can be applied to different educational contexts, and of the circumstances in which transfer to unfamiliar situations most readily occurs. If it is true, as it appears to be, that remembering and other mental achievements are more context-bound than has been admitted in the past, and less exclusively determined either by the extent of an individual's measured intelligence or by the achieved stage of mental development, we may need to modify our teaching, and we would be wise to place little faith in the exercise of trying to explain achievements by reference to abilities that are at all broadly based.

## REFERENCES

Bennett, H.L. (1983). Remembering drink orders: the memory skills of cocktail waitresses. *Human Learning: Journal of Practical Research and Applications*, **2**, 157–170.

Bronfenbrenner, U. (1979). *The Ecology of Human Development: Experiments by Nature and Design*, Cambridge, Mas: Harvard University Press.

Ceci, S.J., and Liker, J. (1985). Academic and non-academic intelligence: a framework. In R. J. Sternberg and R. K. Wagner (Eds.) *Practical Intelligence: Origins of Competence in the Everyday World*, New York: Cambridge University Press, pp. 119–142,

Chase, W.G. and Ericsson, K. A. (1981). Skilled memory. In J. Anderson (Ed.), *Cognitive Skills and their Acquisition*, Hillsdale, NJ: Erlbaum, pp. 141–189.

Chi, M. T. H., and Koeske, R. D. (1983). Network presentation of a child's dinosaur knowledge. *Developmental Psychology*, **19**, 29–39.

Cole, M., Gay, J., Glick, J. A., and Sharp, D. W. (1971). *The Cultural Context of Learning and Thinking*, New York: Basic Books.

Ericsson, K. A., and Polson, P. G. Memory of restaurant orders. In M. T. H. Chi., R. Glaser and M. J. Farr (Eds.), *The Nature of Experience*, In press.

Feldman, D. H. (1982). A developmental framework for research with gifted children. In. D. H. Feldman (Ed.), *Developmental Approaches to Giftedness and Creativity*, San Francisco: Jossey-Bass, pp. 31–46.

Feuerstein, R. (1980). *Instrumental Enrichment: an Intervention Program for Cognitive Modifiability*, Baltimore: University Park Press.

Flavell, J. H., Beach, D. R., and Chinsky, J. M. (1966). Spontaneous verbal rehearsal in a memory task as a function of age. *Child Development*, **37**, 283–299.

Flavell, J. H., and Wellman, H. M. (1977). Metamemory. In R. V. Kail and J. W. Hagen (Eds.) *Perspectives on the Development of Memory and Cognition*, Hillsdale, NJ: Erlbaum, pp. 3–33.

Forrest, D. W. (1974). *Francis Galton: the Life and Work of a Victorian Genius*, London: Elek.

Glaser, R. (1984). Education and thinking: the role of knowledge. *American Psychologist*, **39**, 93–104.

Hunter, I. M. L. (1985). Lengthy verbatim recall: the role of test. In A. Ellis (Ed.) *Progress in the Psychology of Language, Vol. 1*, London: Erlbaum, pp. 217–235.

Istomina, Z. M. (1975). The development of voluntary memory in pre-school-age children. *Soviet Psychology*, **13**, 5–64.

Keeney, T. J., Cannizzo, S. R., and Flavell, J. H. (1967). Spontaneous and induced verbal rehearsal in a recall task. *Child Development*, **38**, 953–966.

Kreutzer, M. A. Leonard, C., and Flavell, J. H. (1975). An interview study of children's knowledge about memory. *Monographs of the Society for Research in Child Development*, **40** (1, Serial No. 159).

Morris, P. E., Gruneberg, M. M., Sykes, R. N., and Merrick, A. (1981). Football knowledge and the acquisition of new results. *British Journal of Psychology*, **72**, 479–483.

Morris, P. E., Tweedy, M., and Gruneberg, M. M. (1985). Interest, knowledge and the memorizing of soccer scores. *British Journal of Psychology*, **76**, 415–425.

Rogers, T. B., Kuiper, N. A., and Kirker, W. S. (1977). Self-references and the encoding of personal information. *Journal of Personality and Social Psychology*, **35**, 677–688.

Rogoff, B. (1981). Schooling and the development of cognitive skills. In H. C. Triandis and A. Heron (Eds.) *Handbook of Cross-cultural Development Psychology*, vol.4, Boston: Allyn and Bacon.

Rozin, P. (1976). The evolution of intelligence and access to the cognitive unconscious. *Progress in Psychobiology and Physiological Psychology*, **6**, 245–280.

Smith, J., and Howe, M. J. A. (1985). An investigation of calendar calculating skills in an idiot savant. *International Journal of Rehabilitation Research*, **8**, 77–79.

Wagner, D. A. (1978). Memories of Morocco: the influence of age, schooling and environment on memory. *Cognitive Psychology*, **10** 1–28.

Wiener, N. (1953). *Ex-prodigy: My Childhood and Youth*, New York: Simon & Schuster.

Zigler, E., and Seitz, V. (1982). Social policy and intelligence. In R. J. Sternberg (Ed.), *Handbook of Human Intelligence*, Cambridge, Mass: Cambridge University Press, pp. 586–643.

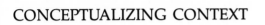

CONCEPTUALIZING CONTEXT

Memory in Context : Context in Memory
Edited by G.M. Davies and D.M. Thomson
© 1988 John Wiley & Sons Ltd.

CHAPTER 13

# Context and False Recognition

D.M. THOMSON

*Monash University*


## ABSTRACT

The effect of reinstated context on recognition errors is an underresearched problem. Four different uses of the term 'recognition' are defined: conceptual, previous occurrence, episodic memory, and identification. These different usages are related to different classes of context experiment all of which demonstrate context-related errors. It is concluded that context effects are multiply determined and that explanations of recognition error may be different from those required to explain facilitation.

In recognition memory, papers in the late 1960s and early 1970s by Light and Carter-Sobell (1969), Thomson (1970, 1972) and Tulving and Thomson (1971) were the forerunners of a veritable deluge of papers on the effects of context (e.g. Baddeley and Woodhead, 1982; Beales and Parkin, 1984; Memon and Bruce, 1983; Patterson and Baddeley, 1977; Watkins, Ho and Tulving, 1976; Winograd and Rivers-Bulkeley, 1977). For the most part, the focus of all the studies reported in these papers and the other chapters of this book has been the effect of context on recognition of previously presented objects or events, that is, the effect of context on correct recognition or hit rate. Almost uniformly the finding of reported studies has been that recognition of previously presented objects or events is impaired when the context of these objects or events is altered at the time of the recognition test. This finding has led writers to pose the question as to why available mnemonic information becomes inaccessible when contextual changes have occurred in the recognition test (see Lockhart, this volume).

The question of the role of context in the accessibility of mnemonic information is clearly important as an answer to this question will provide significant insights into the memory processes. However, there is another effect of context which has been largely ignored and which may illume the recognition processes and mechanisms of context: the effect of context on false recognition. It is the effect of context on false recognition which is the concern of this chapter.

The remainder of this chapter is divided into three sections. In the first of these sections, the nature of context and context effects are discussed, in the second section sources of false recognition are outlined, and in the final section the effect of context on false recognition is examined.

## CONTEXT AND CONTEXT EFFECTS

One problem which besets many areas of psychology is that central concepts have different meanings for different researchers. Such a situation exists with respect to context. The problem can be best illustrated by comparing and contrasting the meanings of words such as setting, environment and ground which are frequently used as synonyms for context. Context is defined in the *Shorter Oxford English Dictionary* as 'the parts which immediately precede or follow any particular passage or text and *determine* its meaning'. I have italicized the word 'determine' to emphasize the active role ascribed to context. The entry in the dictionary further notes that context may also be used in a figurative sense. For purposes of memory, I would define context as the events which immediately precede, accompany, or follow a target and which determine the meaning of that target. The meaning of context should be contrasted with that of setting. According to the dictionary setting refers to the manner or position in which a target is set, fixed or placed. Note that there is no necessary relationship between the setting of a target and the meaning of the target. It is only when setting determines the meaning of the target that the words setting and context become interchangeable.

The word environment is given two meanings in the *Shorter Oxford English Dictionary*, one meaning is synonymous with context and the other with setting. Because the word environment has these two different meanings great care should be exercised in its use. When Tulving and Thomson (1971) wished to use environment in its context meaning they referred to it as 'cognitive environment'.

The word ground also has these two distinct meanings. Thus on the one hand it refers to the foundation on which other parts are overlaid, or on which they rest for support or display. On the other hand ground frequently has a meaning similar to that given it by the Gestaltists (see Koffka, 1935; Kohler, 1941; Wertheimer, 1923). In Gestalt psychology figure and ground are fundamental concepts. Koffka (1935, p. 84) describes the relationship between figure and ground in the following fashion: 'The figure depends for its characteristics upon the ground on which it appears.

The ground serves as a framework in which the figure is suspended and thereby determines the figure.' It is only the latter sense of ground which is synonymous with context.

The distinction between setting and context is, however, blurred in experiments designed to explore context effects. These experiments have, in actual fact, often involved the manipulation of setting rather than context. As has been noted earlier, it is only to the extent that setting determines the meaning of the target that a setting becomes the context. What emerges from the findings of experiments which have manipulated settings is that some settings prove to be more effective contexts than others. Some settings may be contextually unimportant, for example, room settings when recognition of lists of words is being tested. Other settings may create pervasive and irresistible context, for example, activity settings when recognition of persons is being tested (Thomson, Robertson and Vogt, 1982).

There is yet another problem which bedevils research into context effects. While there may be little, if any, disagreement as to the distinction of context and target in the abstract for specific persons, objects and events, consensus as to what constitutes the context and what constitutes the target may be impossible to attain. What constitutes the context and target for one observer may be different from that of another observer (compare discussion of Kolers and Roediger, 1984, p. 440, on incidental and intentional learning).

In some situations, the distinction between context and target seems clear. For example, if the word strawberry accompanied the word jam few would dispute that the word strawberry serves as context for the word jam (see Light and Carter-Sobell, 1969; Thomson, 1972). However, it may be argued that the target is not jam but strawberry jam. The problem is more sharply focussed with the words head light (see Thomson, 1972; Thomson and Tulving, 1970; Tulving and Thomson, 1971, 1973). Is the word head context for the target word light or is the target part of the word headlight? Analysis of other situations suggests that even obvious context-target distinctions may become rubbery. For example, would alteration in the print-colour of a word be considered context or target?

Thus far I have confined my discussion of the distinction between context and target to recognition of words. For recognition of persons the question of what constitutes context and what constitutes target becomes even more problematical. Thomson *et al.* (1982) drew attention to this difficulty. In that paper, it was pointed out that location and clothing of persons may play a major role in how subjects identify or name persons depicted in slides. In the study reported by Thomson *et al.* one slide depicted a person digging a hole in a garden setting, another slide depicted that same person digging a similar hole in a setting which was clearly a cemetery. The first slide was described by subjects as a person digging a hole in the garden, the second slide, as a grave digger digging a grave. One slide depicted a person standing on a pedestrian crossing, his arm extended and hand pointing upward. Another slide depicted that same person in the same location in the same pose, but this time the person was dressed in police uniform. Subjects described the first slide as a man waving to a friend on the other side of the road, the second slide was described as a policeman directing traffic. Most people would be happy to classify location as context but would demur to clothing being classified as context. In the Thomson *et al.* paper it was argued that no distinction should be made between location and clothing, a position to which I still adhere.

## FALSE RECOGNITION

False recognition occurs whenever an item, be it a word, a person, object or event, is incorrectly adjudged as having been previously observed. However, before false recognition is considered further, four uses of the word recognition will be discussed. The first common use of the word recognition is when it is the structure or form of an item that is recognized by an observer. Thus, word-recognition may refer to a sequence of letters being recognized or identified as a word rather than a non-word, and face-recognition may refer to a particular shape or form being recognized or identified as a face rather than as some other shape. Used in this way, recognition is synonymous with perception.

Secondly, recognition is frequently used to refer to a person's judgment that a presently observed item has been observed sometime, somewhere previously. This meaning of recognition is to be contrasted with a third, very similar meaning where recognition is used to indicate that a presently observed item was observed previously at some specified place or time. This third meaning of recognition is the meaning of recognition when that word is used in relation to episodic recognition tasks or eyewitness identification.

The final meaning of recognition involves the elicitation of the name or equivalent of a particular individual when that individual is observed, for example, to be able to identify a particular person as being Ross Knight. This final meaning of recognition has much in common with the first meaning—both require the observer to identify the thing being observed. The difference between these two meanings is that the first meaning refers to identification of the class of the item or event being observed, the second to the identification of a specific individual.

A number of writers (e.g. Atkinson and Juola, 1974; Gillund and Shiffrin, 1984; Jacoby and Dallas, 1981; Mandler, 1980; Posner and Synder, 1975; Thomson, 1986; Tiberghien, 1976) have proposed that the different types of recognition may call into play two different processes or alternatively two different types of information. One process is automatic, fast, and unanalysable, the other analytic and inferential. Recognition of an item as a word or as a class of objects is likely to be derived from the automatic process, whereas recognition that a word, object or person was observed at a particular time or place is likely to require a greater contribution from analytic and inferential processes.

For each of the different but related meanings of recognition there are corresponding meanings for false recognition. Thus, a particular pattern can be misclassified, for example, a non-word may be incorrectly classified as a word, a particular shape, incorrectly classified as a face. Secondly, an observer may erroneously judge a never-been-observed-before item, as one which he or she had observed somewhere before. Thirdly, an observer may incorrectly decide that a previously observed item was observed at a particular time or place. Finally, an item may be wrongly identified or misperceived.

In this chapter, the relationship of context to three sources of false recognitions is examined: where misperceptions are the source of false recognitions, where ecphoric similarity is the source, and where localization is the source. Implications of research findings for memory theories are discussed.

## CONTEXT AND MISPERCEPTION

Misperception occurs whenever an observer perceives the occurrence of a particular item which in fact did not occur. Circumstances in which misperceptions occur range from items which are physically similar to other items through to the perception of an item in the absence of the physical presence of any item.

Most of the recent research relevant to the question of the effect of context on perception has concerned the perception of words. Numerous studies have shown that speed in making a lexical decision or naming a word is enhanced when that word is primed by an earlier occurrence of the same word (Forbach, Stanners and Hochhaus, 1974; Forster and Davis, 1984; Kirsner and Smith, 1974; Oliphant, 1983; Scarborough, Cortese, and Scarborough, 1977; Thomson, 1976) or an associatively related word (Becker, 1976; Marcel, 1980; Meyer, Schvaneveldt, and Ruddy, 1974; Shulman, Hornak, and Sanders, 1978). Findings from recent studies suggest that priming effects resulting from an earlier presentation of the same word and from an earlier presentation of an associatively related word do not derive from the same source (see Bradley, 1987). A similar finding that repeated and semantically related material have different effects is reported in the next section where ecphoric similarity is considered. What is not disputed is that context affects the identification of linguistic material. Jacoby and Kelley (in press) interpret this priming phenomenon in terms of Polanyi's (1958) classification of tool and object as an example of memory functioning as a tool.

What then is the relationship of context to misperception? There is extensive evidence which implicates context in misperceptions, when context is another word, a sentence, a shape or a face. McClelland and Mozer (1986) required subjects to report one of two words presented side-by-side. When the two words contained a number of common letters, McClelland and Mozer found that often the word reported was an amalgam of the two words, for example land would be reported when sand and lane were presented together.

A familiar experience pertinent to the role of context in misperceptions is proof reading. Haber (in Haber and Schindler, 1981) found that detection of a misprinted word was impaired if that misprinted word appeared in a semantic context which highly constrained the meaning of the misprinted word. Holbrook (1978) has reported a negative correlation between the predictability of completing a sentence with the 'right' word and detecting a misprint of that word. Ehrlich and Rayner (1981) have proposed these misperceptions can be attributed to context affecting eye movements and fixations.

Other studies also demonstrate the power of context to produce misperceptions. Broadbent and Broadbent (1981) required their subjects to identify words which were presented in a degraded form. Sometimes the degraded words were accompanied by other non-degraded words, the primes. These non-degraded words were associatively related to the degraded words or were associatively related to a word which had two letters in common with the degraded word. In comparison to non-primed words, priming resulted in significant misperception of degraded words which were not associatively related to the prime but which had two letters in common with a word associatively related to the prime.

A similar effect of context on speech perception was reported by Marslen-Wilson and Welsh (1978). Their subjects were required to listen to a passage read to them and then repeat the passage as it was being read. Some of the words were mispronounced. Marslen-Wilson and Welsh found that subjects, in repeating the passage, frequently gave the correct pronunciation of a mispronounced word, rather than repeating the mispronunciation of a mispronounced word. Similarly, in an oral reading task, Danks, Fears, Bohn and Hill (1978) found that subjects substituted words that were appropriate to the context for distorted or inappropriate words.

Misperceptions may produce false recognitions because, as far as the observer is concerned, the test item has previously occurred. The misperception may have occurred when a particular item was presented earlier in the study phase, or the misperception may occur in the test phase. The following examples illustrate the effect of context on perception in these two phases. Suppose the sentence 'The hunter shot quail and peasants' is read. Because of the context the reader or listener misperceives the word peasants as pheasants when the sentence is read. Thus, when the reader or listener is asked later whether he or she saw or heard the word pheasants earlier, he or she is likely to say yes. Alternatively, the sentence 'The hunters shot quail and pheasants' may be accurately read or heard but when the reader or listener is asked 'Did you see the word peasants?' he or she misperceives the word peasants as the word pheasants in the question.

Given that memory for orthographic or phonological features is likely to be extremely poor (see Craik and Lockhart, 1972; Sachs, 1967), the reader or listener would appear to have little or no way of checking or correcting his or her misperception when the misperception has occurred in the study phase. However, where the misperception occurs at the time of testing, the observer may be able to overcome the effect of context by being able to check each word in isolation and thus correct his or her misperception.

Context has been shown to play a significant role in the perception or misperception of objects and persons. One line of research which demonstrates the power of context in perception utilized ambiguous figures as the to-be-perceived material (Boring, 1930; Bugelski and Alampay, 1961; Dallenbach, 1951). In Boring's study, subjects who had been exposed to pictures of a young woman were much more likely to perceive that young woman in an ambiguous figure which contained some aspects of the young woman and some aspects of an older woman. The reverse was true for those who had previously seen pictures of the old woman.

Bruce (Bruce, 1983; Bruce and Valentine, 1985, 1986) has reported findings from face recognition (perception) studies which parallel the findings of word recognition studies. Speed in judging a well-known face as familiar was faster if that well-known face was preceded by the face of another well-known person who previously often accompanied the other person. Bruce did not explore the effect of priming on misperception.

Misperceptions create almost insoluble problems in the criminal justice system. The eyewitness who misperceives the offender at the scene of the crime as being somebody else is likely to select that innocent party in any subsequent identification parade. No matter how carefully the identification parade is conducted the misperception is unlikely to be corrected. The only avenue of the defence for the accused, in these circumstances, is to demonstrate that the context of the event would have induced a misperception, and to have a cast-iron alibi.

## ECPHORIC SIMILARITY

Ecphoric similarity, a term introduced into the memory literature by Tulving (1983), has to do with the similarity of the perceptual or conceptual characteristics of an item and the characteristics of some memory representations.

The effect of a variety of characteristics on false recognition has been reported in the literature. Some studies have explored the influence of phonological and orthographic similarity in word recognition (Bruder and Silverman, 1972; Cramer and Eagle, 1972; Kollasch and Kausler, 1972; Nelson and Davis, 1972; Raser, 1972; Underwood, 1965); other studies have examined the effect of similarity of imagery on word recognition (Underwood, 1965); others the similarity of pictures on picture recognition (J. Mandler and Parker, 1976); other studies, the similarity of photographs or slides of persons on the recognition of photographs or slides of persons (Memon and Bruce, 1983; Peris and Tiberghien, 1984; Thomson *et al.*, 1982; Watkins *et al.*, 1976; Winograd and Rivers-Bulkeley, 1977) and finally, other studies, the similarity of persons (Hilgendorf and Irving, 1978). In all these studies the rate of false recognition was higher for the similar items than the rate of false recognition for control items.

Studies which have assessed the effect of conceptual similarity on false recognition are largely confined to word recognition and sentence recognition. In word recognition studies researchers have investigated synonymity (Anisfeld, 1970; Anisfeld and Knapp, 1968; Bruder and Silverman, 1972; Cramer and Eagle, 1972; Fillenbaum, 1969), antonymity (Anisfeld 1970; Cramer and Eagle, 1972; Fillenbaum, 1969), associativity (Anisfeld, 1970; Anisfeld and Knapp, 1968; Cramer and Eagle, 1972; Goldfarb, Wirtz and Anisfeld, 1973; Grossman and Eagle, 1970; Hall and Crown, 1970; Mandler, Pearlstone, and Koopmans, 1969; Rabinowitz, Mandler, and Barsalou, 1977; Thomson, 1972, 1973, 1984; Tulving and Thomson, 1971; Underwood, 1965; Winograd, Karchmer and Russell, 1971) and category or prototype (Cantor and Mischel, 1977; Kintsch, 1968). The findings of all these studies showed that false recognition of conceptually similar words or ideas exceeded false recognition of words or ideas not conceptually similar. In sentence recognition studies, false recognition has been found to be higher for sentences which have similar meanings (Sachs, 1967) and for sentences which are consistent with a theme of a passage previously heard or read (Abelson, 1981; Bower, Black, and Turner, 1979; Graesser, Gordon, and Sawyer, 1979; Neisser, 1976; Woll and Graesser, 1982).

I have conducted a large number of experiments which were designed to investigate the role of context on false recognition as a function of retention interval. In one series of experiments word-recognition was tested. One experiment employed a continuous recognition task and retention interval was varied from a lag of 2 words through to 62 words. In the second experiment a study-test procedure was used and retention interval ranged from a short interval—testing occurred immediately after the study list—to an interval of one week. The list material comprised three instances for each of a number of categories. Thus, for example, in the study phase the words copper, zinc and iron were presented successively. In the test phase subjects would be tested successively with the words copper, zinc, iron, or sweep, wash, iron, or, copper, zinc, steel, or sweep, wash, mend. The third word in the triplet was the critical item; the first two members provided the context. In the continuous recognition task when context was reinstated hit rates of 99, 94, 92, and 85 were obtained for lags of 2, 5, 17, and 62 respectively, when a new instance such as steel followed the occurrence of previously seen context, corresponding false recognition rates of 18, 8, 19, and 32 were obtained. For control words—new words in a new context—the false recognition rate was 6 percent. In the study-test recognition task when context was reinstated recognition of previously presented items—61%, 67%, 74%, 73%, 64%, 61%, was much the same across the different retention intervals—0, $^{1}/_{2}$, 1, 3, 24, 168 hours, whereas false recognition of words presented in previously seen context increased from 22 percent at immediate testing to 32 percent at 3 hours to 47 percent at one week. The corresponding level of false recognition for new words presented in a new context at the three retention intervals was 16, 20 and 32 percent.

In another series of studies the effect of retention interval in recognition of repeated words was compared with the effect of retention interval on false recognition of words associatively related to previously presented words. A continuous recognition task was used in this experiment. As each word was presented subjects were required to indicate whether or not they recognized the word as having occurred earlier in the list. Included in the list were repeated words and pairs of associatively related words such as table and chair. The lag between repeated words and between the first member and second member of associatively related words ranged from 0, 1, 5, and 20. For some of the associatively related word pairs, the first member of the word pair was repeated. If the first member was repeated, the lag between the repetitions was varied. Other words, not associated to any other word in the list, were repeated three times, with the lag between first and second presentation, and second and third presentation being varied orthogonally.

The findings with respect to repetition are as follows: subjects' accuracy in recognizing the second presentation of a word declined as lag increased. Subjects' recognition of the third presentation of a word increased as a function of increasing lag between the first two presentations. These findings are consistent with those reported by numerous other researchers (see Greeno, 1970; Madigan, 1969; Peterson, 1963). As for the effect of lag between the second and third presentation, recognition tended to be higher at short lags. The pattern of correct yes responses contrasted with that of incorrect yes responses made to new, but associatively related words. The lag between associatively related pairs made no difference to the level of false recognition. Thus, a person was as likely to falsely recognize the word chair when it appeared immediately after table as when it appeared 1, 5, 10, or 20 items later (compare Raser, 1972). Further, repetition of the first word of the associatively related pair did not affect the level of false recognition of the second number of the pair. Lest it be thought that the failure to find a lag effect or a repetition effect on the level of false recognition was because false recognition was impervious to associative relationships, it should be noted that in all experiments the rate of false recognitions to associatively related words was double that of control words.

The effect of context on false recognition of persons has been reported by a number of researchers (Brutsche, Cisse, Deleglise, Sonnet, and Tiberghien, 1981; Klee, Leseaux, Malai, and Tiberghien, 1982; Memon and Bruce, 1983; Patterson and Baddeley, 1977; O'Hara, 1985; Thomson *et al.*, 1982; Watkins *et al.*, 1976; Winograd and Rivers-Bulkeley, 1977). The general finding of all these studies is that presenting a new person in a previously seen context increases the level of false recognition. Mostly the increased level of false recognition as a function of testing in an old context has been less than the increase in correct recognitions of items presented in their original context (see particularly, Thomson *et al.*, 1982).

Using both a continuous-recognition task and a study-test-recognition task I have investigated the effect of context on person recognition across different retention intervals. As in the Thomson *et al.* (1982) experiment, there were four person-context-test conditions: a previously seen person was tested in the context in which he or she previously appeared (same-person-same-context), a previously seen person in a new context (same-person-different-context), a new person in a previously seen context (different-person-same-context) and a new person in a new context (different-person-different-context). In the continuous recognition task, retention interval had little or no impact on recognition of previously seen persons presented in their previously seen context, recognition was uniformly high—hit rates ranging from 90 to 95 per cent. False recognition of new persons tested in previously seen contexts was higher at all retention intervals than those of new persons tested in new contexts, and the false recognition increased from 34 per cent at lag 0 to 54 per cent at lag 32. In the study-test task, level of false recognition of a new person presented in an old context was similar across the retention intervals of 0, ½, 1, 3, 24, and 168 hours—there was an average false recognition rate of 60 per cent across these conditions compared to 17 per cent for the control condition.

I have recently completed an experiment which examined the effect of context on person recognition as a function of age in a continuous recognition task. In these experiments subjects ranged in age from 5 years to 20+ years. There were no age differences in the same-person-same-context condition and in the different-person-different-context condition. However, in the other two conditions there were dramatic age differences. Young children had great difficulty in recognizing slides which depicted persons in a different context, the responses of 5-year-olds to these slides were indistinguishable from their response to different persons in different contexts. There was a dramatic increase in the number of persons recognized in different contexts by 6-year-olds as compared to 5-year-olds. By 8 years the children's performance was little worse than adults.

The different-person-same-context was the second condition where the performance of children diverged from that of adults. Children up to the age of 12 were heavily influenced by context, false recognition rates being in the order of 50 per cent. Teenage subjects were less seduced by context and were as accurate as adults who had a false recognition rate of 33 per cent (compare Diamond and Carey, 1977). This pattern contrasts with the control condition where 5-year-olds had a false recognition rate of 9 per cent which increased to 24 per cent by 8 years and remained at that level for all other ages.

A number of conclusions can be drawn from the findings of the studies reviewed in this section. First, context is clearly implicated in the mechanism which generates false recognitions. Secondly, the interactive effects of context and retention interval operate differently for false recognition and correct recognition. Thirdly, the effect of context on false recognition over time seems to depend on the type of context, for example, associately related context compared to synonymous context.

## LOCALIZATION CONFUSION

When a person is required to judge whether a particular item was one that had previously occurred at a particular time or place an error may be made in relation to its occurrence at the specified time or place. The item may be correctly recognized as having been observed previously but it was observed at a time or place other than the one specified. The typical laboratory recognition task and the task of the eyewitness in identifying an offender are susceptible to this type of false recognition.

In an episodic-recognition experiment subjects are exposed to a list of items and then their recognition for these items is tested. Typically, before the test phase commences subjects are informed that their recognition for items which appeared in the study phase is to be tested. The identification task of a witness of a crime is similar. The witness is required to view eight or nine persons in a line-up or in a photographic display and indicate which, if any, of the persons in the line-up or display he or she recognizes as the offender.

Localization confusion as a source of false recognition is a phenomenon which has received little attention. However, the importance of localization confusion is tacitly acknowledged in interference theory and in explanations of list-discrimination findings. In list discrimination experiments, subjects are shown a number of lists of items (the study lists) and then presented a test list which includes items drawn from both study lists. The subject's task is to indicate from which study list each item came or to identify all the items which belonged to a specified study list, (for example, Winograd, 1968; Winograd and Smith, 1966). Winograd (1968) found accuracy in list discrimination increased as a function of increasing the interval between the lists and decreased as a function of increasing retention interval.

Interference theorists (e.g. Barnes and Underwood, 1959; Postman, 1961; Underwood, 1945, 1949) attribute forgetting to two sources: unlearning and response competition. Typically, the paired-associate learning paradigm has been employed by interference theorists. Subjects study two lists of pairs of words. They are then presented with the left-side members of the pairs, the stimulus words, and required to recall the words which accompanied these stimulus words. In one variant of this task, the A B, A D paradigm, the same stimulus words are used in both lists. When subjects are required to recall right-side members of one particular list, recall is poor. The poor recall in these circumstances has been attributed to response competition, two responses are competing as the response to be evoked.

An alternative explanation, or at least an alternative emphasis, for the forgetting attributed to response competition in paired-associate learning is list recognition or identification difficulties. The two responses are available but subjects are unable to identify the list from which each comes. Therefore the more distinctive the lists are made, or the more distinctive the items of a list, the better the recall of items of a particular list. One way of making the lists more distinctive is to increase the inter-list interval as Winograd (1969) did. Another way of facilitating list-recognition would be to present lists in different distinctive locations. There is some weak evidence that lists studied in different rooms lead to better memory performance (Bilodeau and Schlosberg, 1951; Greenspoon and Ranyard, 1957; Strand, 1970).

Graham Davies and I have examined the role of context in localization in a series of unreported recognition experiments. In these experiments subjects studied two lists of slides of persons. Later, subjects were presented a third list of slides and asked whether the person depicted in the slide had appeared in either the first or second list and if the answer was yes, in which list. Context of persons in the test slides was manipulated in the manner outlined previously (see Thomson *et al.*, 1982). In addition, inter-list interval and retention interval were varied—in one condition the second list was presented 3 minutes after the first list with a 20-minute retention interval between the second list and the recognition test; in the other condition there was a 20-minute inter-list interval and a 3-minute retention interval. There were three main findings of this experiment. First, the pattern of subjects' recognition responses as a function of context was consistent with the pattern I have previously found, namely, reinstatement of context increased yes responses to old items and increased yes responses to new items presented in old contexts. There were hit rates of 86 and 46 per cent respectively for same-persons-in-the-same-context, and same-persons-in-different-context, and a false recognition rate of 51 and 21 per cent respectively for different-persons-in-the-same-context and different-persons-in-different-contexts.

The second main finding concerned the inter-list interval. Recognition was marginally higher when the two lists were separated by a 20-minute interval compared to a 3-minute interval, hit rates being 64 and 68 per cent, false recognition rates being 36 and 37 per cent respectively.

However, the finding of greatest relevance concerned the effect of context on accuracy in identifying the lists in which the persons appeared. When context was reinstated the proportion of those persons who were recognized as having been seen before and who were correctly assigned to their list was 69 per cent when the original context was reinstated but dropped to 57 per cent when persons were tested in a context different from what they had seen originally.

Even more germane and revealing are the false recognition data. Given that a person has been falsely recognized as appearing in either of the lists, when there was no inter-list interval, approximately 50 per cent of the persons were identified as having appeared in list 1 and 50 per cent in list 2. This equal distribution of false recognitions occurred regardless of the newness or sameness of the context in which a person appeared. This pattern is somewhat surprising as it might have been expected that, when a different person appeared in a context which had occurred in one of the lists and that person was falsely recognized, those persons would be identified with the study-list context in which they appeared. The pattern is quite different when a 20-minute interval is interpolated between the two lists. Of the persons tested in an old context who were falsely recognized as occurring in either list 1 or list 2, 82 per cent were identified as coming from the list in which the context had appeared. False recognition of persons in new contexts was distributed equally between the two lists.

False recognition data of this experiment suggest that context is used to establish not only that a person has been seen before but also when or where that person was previously observed. As such it may either facilitate accuracy in identifying the time or place at which an event is observed or it may be misleading and produce false recognitions.

## CONCLUDING COMMENTS

The thesis of this chapter is that the theoretical implications of the effects of context on false recognition are at least as important as the effects of context on correct recognition. To date, the role of context on false recognition has been largely neglected. The view which I have developed here is that there are three sources of false recognition, each source being sensitive to context. Evidence in support of this claim was drawn from findings in such diverse areas as form perception, speech perception, lexical and semantic decisions, face and word recognition, and list discrimination. In this final section, the implications of some of these findings for models of recognition are examined.

Current explanations about the effects of context on recognition focus on accessibility (e.g. Lockhart, this volume; Thomson, 1970, 1972). However, if it is assumed that the sources of context are the same for correct recognition as well as false recognition then explaining context effects in term of accessibility is too crude. There is an urgent need for greater precision in specifying the components of accessibility. Thus, for example, reinstatement of context may increase recognition performance by ensuring the same meaning is given to the test item, reinstatement of context may increase recognition performance by increasing the ecphoric similarity, and reinstatement of context may increase performance by the enhancement of localization. Recognition that a polysemous word has occurred earlier is likely to depend first on the appropriate meaning being given to the word and then on a comparison with a mnemonic representation. The first stage is variously called perception, implicit memory or, in Polanyi's (1958) terms, memory as a tool, the second stage, episodic memory, explicit memory, or once again, in Polanyi's terms, memory as object.

During the last twenty years many different models of recognition have been developed, for example, the logogen model (Morton, 1969, 1970, 1979), the activation model (Anderson, 1976, 1983; Collins and Loftus, 1975; Collins and Quillian, 1969; Dell, 1986; McClelland and Rumelhart,

1981; Meyer and Schvaneveldt, 1971), the retrieval model (Gillund and Shiffrin, 1984; Ratcliff and McKoon, in press), and the adaptive resonance model (Grossberg and Stone, 1986). While these models differ in a number of important aspects, they all predict that variables which affect recognition will effect false recognition in a similar way: a prediction which does not accord with findings which I have reviewed. Repetition of an item increases the probability that that item is subsequently recognized but does not increase the probability of falsely recognizing a similar or associatively related item. Spacing the presentations of an item increases the probability of subsequent recognition but not subsequent false recognition of similar or associatively related items. The probability a previously observed item is recognized declines as retention interval increases, but the level of false recognition either remains unchanged for associatively related items, or increases for similar items, as retention interval increases.

For many years now, the major use made of false recognition data has been in the calculation of recognition measures such as the $d'$ measure of signal detection. It is clear that false recognition has not been the subject of systematic research and it has therefore played little part in shaping recognition theories. As research so necessary in this area unfolds recognition theories will doubtless undergo significant changes.

## REFERENCES

Abelson, R.P. (1981) Psychological status of the script concept. *American Psychologist*, **36**, 715–729.

Anderson, J.R. (1976). *Language, Memory and Thought*, Hillsdale, NJ: Erlbaum.

Anderson, J.R. (1983). *The Architecture of Cognition*, Cambridge, Mass.: Harvard University Press.

Anisfeld, M. (1970). False recognition of adjective-noun phrases. *Journal of Experimental Psychology*, **86**, 120–122.

Anisfeld, M. and Knapp, M.E. (1968). Association, synonymity, and directionality in false recognition, *Journal of Experimental Psychology*, **77**, 171–179.

Atkinson, R.C. and Juola, J.F. (1974). Search and decision processes in recognition memory. In H. Krantz, R.C. Atkinson, R.D. Luce, and P. Suppes (Eds), *Contemporary Developments in Mathematical Psychology*, vol. 1, *Learning, Memory, and Thinking*, San Francisco: Freeman, pp. 243–293.

Baddeley, A.D. and Woodhead, M. (1982). Depth of processing, contexts and face recognition. *Canadian Journal of Psychology*, **36**, 148–164.

Barnes, J.M. and Underwood, B.J. (1959). 'Fate' of first-list associations in transfer theory. *Journal of Experimental Psychology*, **58**, 97–105.

Beales, S.A. and Parkin, A.J. (1984). Context and facial memory: the influence of different processing strategies. *Human Learning*, **3**, 257–263.

Becker, C.A. (1976). Allocation of attention during visual word recognition. *Journal of Experimental Psychology: Human Perception and Performance*, **2**, 556–566.

Bilodeau, I.M. and Schlosberg, H. (1951). Similarity in stimulating conditions as a variable in retroactive inhibition. *Journal of Experimental Psychology*, **41**, 199–204.

Boring, E.G. (1930). A new ambiguous figure. *American Journal of Psychology*, **42**, 444 – 445.

Bower, G.H., Black, J.B. and Turner, T.J. (1979). Scripts in memory for text. *Cognitive Psychology*, **11**, 177 – 220.

Bradley, D.C. (1987). Lexical and episodic representation. Paper presented at 14th Experimental Psychology Conference, University of New England, Armidale, Australia.

Broadbent, D.E. and Broadbent, M.H.P. (1981). Priming and the passive/active model of word recognition. In R.S. Nickerson (Ed.), *Attention and Performance VIII*, Hillsdale, NJ: Erlbaum, pp. 419 – 434.

Bruce, V. (1983). Recognizing faces. *Philosophical Transactions of the Royal Society, London*, **302B**, 423 – 436.

Bruce, V. and Valentine, T. (1985). Identity priming in the recognition of familiar faces. *British Journal of Psychology*, **76**, 373 – 383.

Bruce, V. and Valentine, T. (1986). Semantic priming of familiar faces. *Quarterly Journal of Experimental Psychology*, **38A**, 125 – 150.

Bruder, G. and Silverman, W. (1972). Effects of semantic and phonetic similarity on verbal recognition and discrimination. *Journal of Experimental Psychology*, **94**, 314 – 320.

Brutsche, J., Cisse, A., Deleglise, D., Finet, A., Sonnet, P. and Tiberghien, G. (1981). Effets de contexte dans la reconnaissance de visage non familiers. *Cahiers de Psychologie Cognitive*, **1**, 85 – 90.

Bugelski, B.R. and Alampay, D.A. (1961). The role of frequency in developing perceptual sets. *Canadian Journal of Psychology*, **15**, 205 – 211.

Cantor, N. and Mischel, W. (1977). Traits as prototypes: effects on recognition memory. *Journal of Personality and Society Psychology*, **35**, 38 – 48.

Collins, A. and Loftus, E. (1975). A spreading-activation theory of semantic processing. *Psychological Review*, **82**, 407 – 428.

Collins, A. and Quillian, M. (1969). Retrieval time from semantic memory. *Journal of Verbal Learning and Verbal Behavior*, **8**, 240 – 248.

Craik, F.I.M. and Lockhart, R.S. (1972). Levels of processing: a framework for memory research. *Journal of Verbal Learning and Verbal Behavior*, **11**, 671 – 684.

Cramer, P. and Eagle, M. (1972). Relationship between conditions of CRS presentation and the category of false recognition errors. *Journal of Experimental Psychology*, **94**, 1 – 5.

Dallenbach, K.M. (1951). A picture puzzle with a new principle of concealment. *American Journal of Psychology*, **64**, 431 – 433.

Danks, J.H., Fears, R., Bohn, L., and Hill, G.O. (1978). Comprehension processes in oral reading. Paper presented at Psychonomic Society Meeting, San Antonio, Texas.

Dell, G. (1986). A spreading-activation theory of retrieval in sentence production. *Psychological Review*, **93**, 283 – 321.

Diamond, R. and Carey, S. (1977). Developmental changes in the representation of faces. *Journal of Experimental Psychology*, **23**, 1 – 22.

Ehrlich, K. and Rayner, K. (1981). Contextual effects on word perception and eye movements during reading. *Journal of Verbal Learning and Verbal Behavior*, **20**, 641 – 655.

Fillenbaum, S. (1969). Words as feature complexes: false recognition of antonyms and synonyms. *Journal of Experimental Psychology*, **82**, 400 – 402.

Forbach, G.B., Stanners, R.F. and Hochhaus, L. (1974). Repetition and practice effects in a lexical decision task. *Memory and Cognition*, **2**, 337 – 339.

Forster, K.I. and Davis, C. (1984). Repetition priming and frequency attentuation in lexical access. *Journal of Experimental Psychology Learning, Memory, and Cognition,* 10, 680–698.

Gillund, G. and Shiffrin, R. (1984). A retrieval model for both recognition and recall. *Psychological Review,* 19, 1–65.

Goldfarb, C., Wirtz, J. and Anisfeld, M. (1973). Abstract and concrete phrases in false recognition. *Journal of Experimental Psychology,* 98, 25–30.

Graesser, A.C., Gordon, S.E. and Sawyer, J.D. (1979). Recognition memory for typical and atypical actions in scripted activities: tests of a memory pointer and tag hypothesis. *Journal of Verbal Learning and Verbal Behavior,* 18, 319–332.

Greeno, J.G. (1970). Conservation of information-processing capacity in paired-associate memorizing. *Journal of Verbal Learning and Verbal Behavior,* 9, 581–586.

Greenspoon, J. and Ranyard, R. (1957). Stimulus conditions and retroactive inhibition. *Journal of Experimental Psychology,* 53, 55–59.

Grossberg, S. and Stone, G. (1986). Neural dynamics of word recognition and recall: attentional priming, learning, and resonance. *Psychological Review,* 93, 46–74.

Grossman, L. and Eagle, M. (1970). Synonymity, antonymity, and association in false recognition responses. *Journal of Experimental Psychology,* 83, 244–248.

Haber, R.N. and Schindler, R.M. (1981). Error in proofreading: evidence of syntactic control of letter processing. *Journal of Experimental Psychology: Human Perception and Performance,* 7, 573–579.

Hall, J.W. and Crown, I. (1970). Associative encoding of words in sentences. *Journal of Verbal Learning and Verbal Behavior,* 11, 92–95.

Hilgendorf, E.L. and Irving, B.L. (1978). False positive identification. *Medicine, Science and the Law,* 18, 255–262.

Holbrook, M. (1978). Effect of subjective interletter similarity, and contextual variables on the recognition of letter substitutions in a proofreading task. *Perceptual and Motor Skills,* 47, 243–250.

Jacoby, L.L. and Dallas, M. (1981). On the relationship between autobiographical memory and perception learning. *Journal of Experimental Psychology: General,* 3, 306–340.

Jacoby, L.L. and Kelley, C.M. (in press). Unconscious influences of memory for a prior event. *Personality and Social Psychology Bulletin,*.

Kintsch, W. (1968). Recognition and free recall of organized lists. *Journal of Experimental Psychology,* 78, 481–487.

Kirsner, K. and Smith, M.C. (1974). Modality effects in word identification. *Memory and Cognition,* 2, 637–640.

Klee, M., Leseaux, M., Malai, C. and Tiberghien, G. (1982). Nouveaux effets de contexte dans la reconnaissance de visages familiers, *Revue de Psychologie Appliquée,* 32, 109–119.

Koffka, K. (1975). *Principles of Gestalt Psychology,* New York: Harcourt.

Kohler, W. (1941). On the nature of associations. *Proceedings of the American Philosophical Society,* 84, 489–502.

Kolers, P. and Roediger, H. (1984). Procedures of mind. *Journal of Verbal Learning and Verbal Behavior,* 23, 425–449.

Kollasch, S.F. and Kausler, D.H. (1972). Recognition learning of homophones. *Journal of Experimental Psychology,* 92, 432–434.

Light, L. and Carter-Sobell, L. (1969). Effects of changed semantic context on recognition memory. *Journal of Verbal Learning and Verbal Behavior,* 9, 1–12.

McClelland, J.L. and Mozer, M.C. (1986). Perceptual interactions in two-word displays: familiarity and similarity effects. *Journal of Experimental Psychology: Human Perception and Performance*, **12**, 18–35.

McClelland, J. and Rumelhart, D. (1981). An interactive activation model of context effects in letter perception: Part 1. An account of basic findings. *Psychological Review*, **8**, 375–407.

Madigan, S.A. (1969). Intraserial repetition and coding processes in free recall. *Journal of Verbal Learning and Verbal Behavior*, **8**, 828–835.

Mandler, G. (1980). Recognising: The judgement of previous occurence. *Psychological Review*, **87**, 252–271.

Mandler, J.M. and Parker, R.E. (1976). Memory for descriptive and spatial information in complex pictures. *Journal of Experimental Psychology Human Learning and Memory*, **2**, 38–48.

Mandler, G., Pearlstone, Z. and Koopmans, H.S. (1969). Effects of organization and semantic similarity on recall and recognition. *Journal of Verbal Learning and Verbal Behavior*, **8**, 410–423.

Marcel, A.J. (1980). Conscious and preconscious recognition of polysemous words: locating the selective effects of prior verbal context. In R.S. Nickerson (Ed.), *Attention and Performance VIII*, Hillsdale, NJ: Erlbaum, pp. 435–457.

Marslen-Wilson, W.D. and Welsh, A. (1978). Processing interactions and lexical access during word recognition in continuous speech. *Cognitive Psychology*, **10**, 29–63.

Memon, A. and Bruce, V. (1983). The effects of encoding strategy and context change on face recognition. *Human Learning*, **2**, 313–327.

Meyer, D. and Schvaneveldt, R. (1971). Facilitation in recognizing pairs of words: evidence of a dependence retrieval operation. *Journal of Experimental Psychology*, **90**, 227–234.

Meyer, D.E., Schvaneveldt, R.W. and Ruddy, M.G. (1974). Functions of graphemic and phonemic codes on visual word recognition. *Memory and Cognition*, **2**, 309–321.

Morton, J. (1969). The interaction of information in word recognition. *Psychological Review*, **76**, 165–178.

Morton, J. (1970). A functional model for memory. In D. Norman (Ed.), *Models of Human Memory*, New York: Academic Press, pp. 203–259.

Morton, J. (1979). Facilitation in word recognition: experiments causing change in the Logogen model. In P. Kolers., M. Wrolstal, and H. Bouma (Eds), *Processing Visible Language*, vol. 1, New York: Plenum, pp. 259–268.

Neisser, U. (1976). *Cognition and Reality: Principles and Implications of Cognitive Psychology*, San Francisco: Freeman.

Nelson, D.L. and Davis, M.J. (1972). Transfer and false recognitions based on phonetic identities of words. *Journal of Experimental Psychology*, **92**, 347–353.

O'Hara, J. (1985). The effects of context and depth of processing instructions on face and person recognition. Unpublished B.Sc. (Hons.) thesis, Monash University.

Oliphant, G.W. (1983). Repetition and recency effects in word recognition. *Australian Journal of Psychology*, **35**, 393–403.

Patterson, K.E. and Baddeley, A.D. (1977). When face recognition fails. *Journal of Experimental Psychology: Human Learning and Memory*, **3**, 406–417.

Peris, J.L. and Tiberghien, G. (1984). Effet de contexte et recherche conditionelle dans la reconnaissance de visage non familiers. *Cahiers de Psychologie Cognitive*, **4**, 323–334.

Peterson, L.R. (1963). Immediate memory: data and theory. In C.N. Cofer and

B.S. Musgrave (Eds), *Verbal Behavior and Learning: Problems and Processes,* New York: McGraw-Hill, pp. 336–353.

Polanyi, M. (1958). *Personal Knowledge: Towards a Post-Critical Philosophy,* Chicago: University of Chicago Press.

Posner, M. and Synder, C. (1975). Attention and cognitive control. In R. Solso (Ed.), *Information Processing and Cognition: The Loyola Symposium,* Hillsdale, NJ: Erlbaum, pp. 55–86.

Postman, L. (1961). The present status of interference theory. In C.N. Cofer (Ed.), *Verbal Learning and Verbal Behavior,* New York: McGraw-Hill, pp. 152–179.

Rabinowitz, J.C., Mandler, G. and Barsalou, L.W. (1977). Recognition failure: another case of retrieval failure. *Journal of Verbal Learning and Verbal Behavior,* **16,** 639–663.

Raser, G.A. (1972). False recognition as a function of encoding dimension and lag. *Journal of Experimental Psychology,* **93,** 333–337.

Ratcliff, R. and McKoon, G. (in press). A retrieval theory of priming in memory. *Psychological Review.*

Sachs, J. (1967). Recognition of semantic, syntactic and lexical changes in sentences. *Psychonomic Bulletin,* **1,** 17–18.

Scarborough, D., Cortese, C. and Scarborough, H. (1977). Frequency and repetition effects in lexical memory. *Journal of Experimental Psychology: Human Perception and Performance.* **3,** 1–17.

Shulman, H.G., Hornak, R. and Sanders, E. (1978). The effect of graphemic, phonetic, and semantic relationships on access to lexical structures. *Memory & Cognition,* **6,** 115–123.

Strand, B.Z. (1970). Change of context and retroactive inhibition. *Journal of Verbal Learning and Verbal Behavior,* **9,** 202–206.

Thomson, D.M. (1970). Context effects in recognition memory. Unpublished Ph.D. thesis, University of Toronto.

Thomson, D.M. (1972). Context effects in recognition memory. *Journal of Verbal Learning and Verbal Behavior,* **11,** 497–511.

Thomson, D.M. (1973). False recognition: a problem of memory and a problem for memory. Paper presented at ANZAAS, Perth, Australia.

Thomson, D.M. (1976). Episodic and lexical memory: two systems or one? Paper presented at Experimental Psychology Conference, Flinders University, Australia.

Thomson, D.M. (1984). Context effects in recognition memory: developmental aspects. Paper presented at the experimental Psychology Conference, Deakin University, Australia.

Thomson, D.M. (1986). Face recognition: more than a feeling of familiarity. In H.D. Ellis, M.A. Jeeves, F. Newcombe and A. Young (Eds), *Aspects of Face Processing,* Dordrecht: Nijhoff, pp. 118–122.

Thomson, D. M., Robertson, S.L. and Vogt, R. (1982). Person recognition: the effect of context. *Human Learning,* **1,** 137–154.

Thomson, D.M. and Tulving, E. (1970) Associative encoding specificity and retrieval: weak and strong cues. *Journal of Experimental Psychology,* **86,** 255–262.

Tiberghien, G. (1976). Reconnaissance á long term, pourquoi ne pas chercher? In S. Ehrlich and E. Tulving (Eds), *La mémorie semantique,* Paris: Bulletin de Psychologie, pp. 188–197.

Tulving, E. (1983). *Elements of Episodic Memory,* New York: Oxford University Press.

Tulving, E. and Thomson, D.M. (1971). Retrieval processes in recognition memory: effect of associative context. *Journal of Experimental Psychology,* **87,** 116–124.

Tulving, E. and Thomson, D.M. (1973). Encoding specificity and retrieval processes in episodic memory. *Psychological Review*, **80**, 352–373.

Underwood, B.J. (1945). The effect of successive interpolations on retroactive and proactive inhibition. *Psychological Monographs*, **50**, No. 3.

Underwood, B.J. (1949). Proactive inhibition as a function of time and degree of prior learning. *Journal of Experimental Psychology*, **39**, 24–34.

Underwood, B.J. (1965). False recognition produced by implicit verbal responses. *Journal of Experimental Psychology*, **70**, 122–129.

Watkins, M.J., Ho, E. and Tulving, E. (1976). Context effects in recognition memory for faces. *Journal of Verbal Learning and Verbal Behavior*, **15**, 505–517.

Wertheimer, M. (1923). Untersuchungen Zur Lehre von der Gestalt, II. *Psychologische Forschung*, **4**, 301–350.

Winograd, E. (1968). List differentiation as a function of frequency and retention interval. *Journal of Experimental Psychology, Monograph Supplement*, Pt. 2, 1–18.

Winograd, E. and Smith, W.S. (1966). List differentiation with varied trials on both lists. *Science*, **152**, 1101–1102.

Winograd, E., Karchmer, M.A. and Russell, I.S. (1971). Role of encoding unitization in cued recognition memory. *Journal of Verbal Learning and Verbal Behavior*, **10**, 199–206.

Winograd, E. and Rivers-Bulkeley, N.T. (1977). The effects of changing context on remembering faces. *Journal of Experimental Psychology: Human Learning and Memory*, **3**, 397–405.

Woll, S.B. and Graesser, A.C. (1982). Memory discrimination for information typical or atypical of person schemata. *Social Cognition*, **1**, 287–310.

Memory in Context : Context in Memory
Edited by G.M. Davies and D.M. Thomson
© 1988 John Wiley & Sons Ltd.

CHAPTER 14

# Everyday Contexts

D.A. Bekerian and M.A. Conway

*MRC Applied Psychology Unit, Cambridge*

ABSTRACT

A distinction is drawn between molecular and everyday contexts. Molecular contexts relate to internal (mood, state-dependent effects) or external (environmental, spatial cues) contexts. Such contexts, which may be linguistic or extra-linguistic, are assumed to be automatically activated and not capable of conscious control. Everyday contexts, on the other hand, relate to 'scripts' or 'frames' for action and prime the individual to expect subsequent events and to anticipate particular outcomes. The relationship between molecular and everyday contexts is unclear but both may be subsumable within a 'headed-records' framework.

The notion that every experienced event has associated with it something called 'context' has long been with psychology, particularly in the study of memory. Over a century ago Galton (1883) suggested that the recollection of everyday events could be facilitated if individuals recalled memories in the same environment (context) in which events had originally been experienced. More recent research has demonstrated that context influences many aspects of memory. For example, context has been found to effect memory for verbal materials (e.g. Anderson and Bower, 1973; Bransford, 1979; Tulving and Thomson, 1973), encoding of objects and scenes (e.g. Bartlett, 1932; Anderson and Ortony, 1975; Brewer and Treyens, 1982), and retention of text (e.g. Bower, Black, and Turner, 1979; Bowers, 1986).

The notion of context and contextual elements has never been rigidly specified, however. Typically, context is operationally defined in terms of the experimental materials employed in a study, such as word lists, texts, pictures, or specific environments. In this article we shall distinguish between two different approaches to context and argue that these approaches reflect different aspects of context. One approach defines context in terms of specific elements present within a single event being experienced by the subject. The elements can be either external to the subject, that is, perceptual details, or internal to the subject, that is, mood of the subject and we will refer to this as molecular contexts. The second approach to context defines context in terms of general characteristics of classes of situations which either are being experienced by the subject, or are anticipated to occur. Typically, this approach is concerned with the knowledge people have about classes of situations. This knowledge includes such things as rules about social behaviour, actors involved, likely appropriate actions and reactions, and underlies beliefs, attitudes and expectations that an individual brings to situations (cf. Harr//e, Clarke, and DeCarlo, 1985). This approach to context is typified by research dealing with the types of knowledge people display about social situations and social behaviour, and emphasizes what will be referred to as everyday contexts.

The molecular and everyday approaches have focussed on different characteristics of contexts and have emphasized different underlying processes. This has had the consequence of making the two approaches diverge in their interests and overall aims. However, it will be argued here that one must consider both approaches to context, if we are to understand the role of context in memory. After briefly outlining each, we will consider what requirements each might impose on memory models.

## THE MOLECULAR APPROACH TO CONTEXT

In order to characterize what we mean by the molecular approach to context, we will first describe a number of studies which exemplify this approach. Characteristics of molecular aspects of context will then be discussed in detail.

Many studies of memory manipulate specific features of the external environment at encoding followed by partial or whole reinstatement of these features at retrieval. In a seminal study, Tulving and Thomson (1973) demonstrated a high level of recognition for previously presented words when those words were cued by weakly associated words with which they had been previously paired. A comparatively lower level of recognition was found when the to-be-recognized words were cued with highly associated words that had not been previously seen. Thus, reinstatement of specific features previously present at encoding (weakly associated words) proved to be a more powerful memory cue than highly associated cues not presented at encoding. Tulving and Thomson account for this finding in terms of the 'encoding specificity' principle (ESP). ESP proposes that a cue must reinstate information present in the original memory trace to be effective at retrieval. Central to ESP is the notion of context, which Tulving and

Thomson refer to as the 'cognitive milieu'. The phrase cognitive milieu refers to features present at the time of encoding that become represented in the memory trace. These features encompass both external and internal elements present at the time a subject is encoding an event. Thus, the appearance of a word in a word pair would constitute an external feature of the encoding context and reinstatement of that word at test enables effective retrieval.

The manner in which context is referred to in ESP assumes that effects occur in rather an automatic fashion, to the extent that encoding and retrieval operations are automatic and not subject to conscious control. Thus, specific contextual elements of the encoding environment are represented in the memory trace and retrieval processes are facilitated when context is reinstated. Investigations in repetition priming lend further support to this view. In a repetition priming experiment a subject may be exposed to a set of words and asked to perform some task with those words. Later the subject may be exposed to a further set of words, which include the original set, and asked to perform an apparently unrelated task on this second set. For example, Jacoby and Dallas (1981) found that repetition priming improved word recognition. Clarke and Morton (1983) found facilitative effects of word repetition across modalities. In such studies whole or partial reinstatement of context led to the facilitation of performance across different tasks where subjects were not aware of the relation between the two tasks.

Studies investigating ESP and repetition priming effects provide examples of the influence external contextual elements can have on memory. However, as suggested by ESP, other aspects of the verbal environment could have a similar influence. Investigations by Bransford and his colleagues (cf. Bransford, 1979) have demonstrated that subsequent memory performance can be determined by the particular conceptual features emphasized in the encoding environment. In one experiment, Barclay, Bransford, Franks, McCarrell, and Nitsch (1974) presented subjects with nouns in different types of contexts. For example, a subject might read the sentence 'The man lifted the piano'. Recall was superior when subjects were cued with the appropriate conceptual feature, for example, 'heavy object' and 'something that makes nice sounds'. Bransford (1979, Ch.5), in a review chapter of work related to this type of effect, concludes that: 'Previous knowledge must be activated in order to facilitate one's current abilities to understand and learn' (p. 135). We would suggest that effects such as these demonstrate how aspects of the internal encoding environment provide a context that specifies conditions for effective retrieval, and that the effects are rather automatic in their operation (see Tiberghien's chapter in this volume for further examples and discussion).

So far we have described studies which have exclusively manipulated verbal features of encoding contexts. Other demonstrations of context effects with verbal materials have sought to reinstate non-linguistic aspects of context. Studies of environmental contexts have demonstrated strong context effects when encoding and recall are performed in the same environment. For example, Baddeley, Cuscaro, Egstrom, Weltmen, and Willis (1975) asked divers to learn passages either on land or under water. Memory performance was found to be far superior when the test environment matched the learning environment. Godden and Baddeley (1980) reported similar context dependency effects on recall of word lists. Smith, Glenberg, and Bjork (1978) investigated the effects of the experimental environment by manipulating the room subjects were in at the time of learning and test. They report that recall was superior when subjects were tested in the room where learning had taken place compared to test performance in a different room. In general these types of findings rely on a notion of context in terms of specific environmental features that are assumed to be conjointly encoded with the to-be-remembered materials by virtue of their faciliative effects at recall (see Smith's contribution to this volume for further discussion).

Other more specific environmental features of an encoding environment have also been found to influence subsequent memory performance. Bekerian and Bowers (1983) and Bowers and Bekerian (1984) demonstrated that order in which stimuli are experienced will effect the later recognition of those stimuli. In their studies subjects were presented with slide sequences depicting common scenes and later required to discriminate previously presented slides from similar but previously unseen slides. In between presentation and test subjects were exposed to misleading information concerning the content of the slides. In the test phase subjects performed a recognition task on pairs of slides. For some subjects, slide pairs were in random order with respect to the original presentation; for others, the order of slide pairs preserved the original ordering.

Subjects who saw the test sequence which preserved the original order of presentation were less likely to be misled by the new slides. Bowers (1986) has shown a similar advantage for recognition of sentences from a text when the test sentences are presented in an order matching that of original learning. These findings contrast with those of Godden and Baddeley (1980) who found context effects in recall but not in recognition. However, Baddeley and Godden employed word lists. It may be that with more complex materials, such as slide sequences and texts, recognition memory can be influenced by the reinstatement of external, contextual features.

Other investigations of molecular contexts have focussed on features that might be thought of as being primarily internal to the subject. Recent research into mood state dependency effects has established that mood may be a powerful determinant of memory (Bower, 1981; Teasdale, 1983; Guenther, this volume). Bower (1981) reported a series of studies which found that when a subject's mood at test was congruent with his/her mood at encoding, memory performance was facilitated. In contrast, when mood at test was incongruent, memory was impaired. Bower (1981) and Teasdale (1983) report studies demonstrating that memory for mood-related material is enhanced when the subject's mood at test is congruent with previously presented materials. Thus, memory for words with negative emotional connotations is enhanced if a negative mood is induced at test. Teasdale (1983), using clinically depressed individuals, has shown that the recall of autobiographical memories is similarly effected by mood state, with depressive or negative memories being recalled faster when the depressed patients were suffering a particularly severe bout of depression. Finally, Eich (1980, and in this volume) reviews the literature on induced physiological states, showing that congruence between learning and test states determines memory performance. Thus, it seems reasonable to conclude that the internal state of an individual serves as part of the context for an event.

Having briefly reviewed the above findings, we can now consider how these studies share assumptions about the nature of context and the role it plays in memory operations. All the studies outlined above clearly demonstrate that memory performance will be effected by manipulations of contextual features, be they external to the subject or internal to the subject. One common characteristic of these studies is that the experimental manipulations effect relatively automatic processes that do not rely extensively on the subject's phenomenal awareness. For example, a subject either cannot have, or does not have much, conscious control over the processes involved in reading, lexical decision or recognition memory. Nonetheless, each of these operations has been found to be sensitive to the reinstatement of contextual features. Cognitive operations of this type have been categorized by Harr//e *et al.* (1985) as belonging to the 'first domain': subroutines of cognition over which a person has little specific control and of which there is little phenomenal knowledge. Because of this, we suggest that one characteristic of the way in which molecular contexts have been studied is the emphasis on automatic operations. The idea we wish to capture is that studies of molecular contexts are generally concerned with the operation of relatively immutable processes. These processes can be assumed to be constant across different types of tasks, for example, visual recognition memory vs lexical decision tasks, and appear to respond automatically to the reinstatement of features of the encoding environment even when the subject has no phenomenal knowledge that such reinstatement has occurred.

The second common characteristic in the above studies is that context is defined with respect to the unique features of the particular session. For example, contextual elements are identifiable to the experimenter by virtue of their manipulation. Because of this, contextual elements are generally depicted as specific features of the environment that are made distinctive at the time of encoding, for example, words making up a word pair, environmental features, mood of the subject.

Thus, the molecular approach to context restricts its analyses to specific features present at the time the specific event is experienced. The effects that these features are assumed to have are confined to fairly immutable processes which automatically respond to manipulations of reinstatement at the time of retrieval.

It is perhaps unwise, but nonetheless interesting to speculate on what functions are served by retaining knowledge of molecular contexts. It would seem to be advantageous to retain some knowledge of the specific elements unique to a particular event. Such knowledge could help distinguish one event-member from a whole class of events, and provide the basis for our most detailed, intimate recollections (e.g. Morton, Hammersley, and Bekerian, 1985). On the other hand, there certainly are constraints that knowledge of molecular contexts can impose, such as failures to recognize or recall familiar situations when the seemingly unimportant features of the molecular context have changed. However, even these constraints can be argued to be beneficial, as in the case of 'adaptive' forgetting or repression (cf. Freud, 1957).

## THE EVERYDAY APPROACH TO CONTEXT

The everyday approach to context attempts to define classes of social situations people encounter in their day-to-day lives. Such social situations include, among other things, an external environment, actors involved and beliefs/expectations about how the various actors should interact. Although environmental features are present in everyday contexts, we shall suggest that they do not constitute the most important constituents. Rather, what are crucial in identifying everyday contexts are the expectations people hold about who is involved, what the likely sequence of events might be, and the rules governing social interaction. Because everyday contexts incorporate expectations concerning social episodes, one critical characteristic of everyday contexts is that they are socially dictated: socio-cultural factors serve to establish features of everyday contexts and what might be expected from them. An individual appropriates his/her knowledge about everyday contexts from the society as well as his/her own experiences. This knowledge enables the individual to anticipate likely interactions and allows the individual to respond with behaviours that are proscribed and appropriate for the social situation.

Everyday contexts will be crudely divided into two general types: those that are repeatedly and regularly experienced by the individual, for example, going to a restaurant; and those that are experienced infrequently by the individual but occur often within the society as a whole, for example, getting married. It should be noted that this latter type represents events that are highly predictable and well specified within a culture. For the present purposes, we will refer to these two types as repeated and infrequent everyday contexts, respectively.

Much psychological research has focussed on repeated contexts. Probably the most well known of such work is the research by Schank and his colleagues (cf. Schank and Abelson, 1977). The central concept to emerge from this work is the notion of a 'script'. The main feature of scripts is the representation of general and regular properties of events. These properties are abstract. They are not tied to any specific experience of an event, but rather are common to most experiences of the event. There is also the proviso that scripts may contain information quite unique to a specific experience of an event, but this generally occurs only to the extent that such information is either unanticipated or highly distinctive.

A common example used to illustrate scripts is that of a 'restaurant' script. A restaurant script contains general information which specifies what an individual may *expect* of a restaurant. For example, the restaurant script may contain information about booking a table, arrival at the restaurant, ordering the meal, eating the meal, paying the bill and leaving the restaurant. Scripts, then, specify information about likely props, actors, actions, outcomes, and ordering of actions, associated with a frequently experienced event (cf. Bower, Black, and Turner, 1979). As Schank (1982) points out, a script may also contain event-specific information relating to a past experience when script expectations were violated, for example, paying for a meal *before* the meal is served.

Cantor, Mischel, and Schwartz (1982) have also studied properties of repeated everyday contexts (e.g. parties, work). Across a number of paradigms featuring free descriptions, image generation times, and structured ratings, they found that people shared relatively standard and easily retrievable prototypes for common social situations. The social situations frequently contained information about likely actors and the types of social interactions which might be expected. In other words people appeared to have an elaborated, well-defined, and shared knowledge which characterized general properties of a range of social situations. Cantor *et al.* concluded that 'Categorical knowledge about situations includes a substantial amount of information about the typical people, behaviours and feelings associated with situations' (p. 70), and suggested that such knowledge is critical in the planning and regulating of social behaviour.

The work of Schank (1982), Abelson (1981) and Cantor *et al.* (1982) illustrates some basic characteristics of repeated everyday contexts. One is that our knowledge of these contexts is abstract. The information is not specific to any unique experience but rather common to most experiences. Another is that our knowledge of everyday contexts can take on what appears to be an habitual order. For example, violations of the order of occurrence of actions can sometimes be surprising, for example, getting your meal before you have ordered it. A third is that our knowledge spans different classes of information. Some may be perceptual, others emotional. This means that there is a multiplicity in the information we have about everyday contexts. The multiplicity of information present in everyday contexts is highlighted in Minsky's (1975) discussion of 'frames', which for present purposes are treated as analogous to scripts. Minsky comments that: 'Some of this information is about how to use a frame. Some is about what one can expect to happen next. Some is about what to do if these expectations are not confirmed' (p. 355).

As might be expected, abstract knowledge of repeated everyday contexts can have some profound effects on memory, since what we *expect* to see or hear in a given situation will determine what we remember seeing or hearing.

For example, Bower *et al.* (1979) found that when subjects were presented with some actions from a script and subsequently asked to remember those actions, subjects falsely remembered script-related actions which had not been previously seen. A study by Brewer and Treyens (1981) illustrates further the effect of repeated everyday contexts. In this study subjects arriving to take part in an experiment were asked to wait briefly in a graduate student's office. The subjects were then taken to a test area and unexpectedly asked to recall the contents of the room in which they had waited. The contents of the room had been carefully manipulated so that some were highly congruent with expectations concerning a graduate student's office (e.g. desk, typewriter, coffee-pot, etc.) and some were unexpected (e.g. a skull, a piece of bark, a rolling pin, etc). Memory performance for items congruent with individuals' expectations of the room was high, while memory for incongruent items was low. Further, subjects falsely remembered congruent items which had not been present. These findings clearly indicate that general knowledge of repeated everyday contexts can determine subsequent memory for a specific context.

Conway and Bekerian (1987) have demonstrated that knowledge of everyday contexts can facilitate the recognition of single words. They found that emotion words were recognized reliably faster when they were preceded by the presentation of a highly associated situation (e.g. 'the lovers walked along a moon-lit beach', followed by the word 'happy'). This finding reinforces the view that knowledge of everyday contexts includes expectations about likely emotions (Conway and Bekerian, 1987; Schacter and Singer, 1962). The data also suggest that rather automatic memory operations like word recognition can be primed by 'everyday' knowledge, in the way that semantic categories can prime exemplars of the category (see Conway, 1987).

So far we have considered repeated everyday events (going to restaurants, getting up in the morning, etc.). We now turn to a discussion of infrequent everyday contexts. Within these, we will focus on events that are generally considered to be significant life events. We shall refer to them as *personally significant events* (e.g. first day at school, first job, getting married, buying house, changing job, becoming a parent, etc.). Although personally significant events have not been frequently studied by cognitive psychologists, some recent research has examined the properties generally associated with them.

Most investigations of personally significant contexts have concentrated on autobiographical memory retrieval. The central finding from studies looking at memories of personally significant contexts is that they are rated as being recollected with great vividness (Brown and Kulik, 1977; Conway and Bekerian, 1986; Rubin and Kozin, 1984). Personal significance is not the only factor that influences the vividness of autobiographical memories (see Conway and Bekerian, 1986). However, memories of personally significant contexts seem differentially associated with specific factors: they are surprising, emotional, consequential, and frequently rehearsed.

How might our prior knowledge of infrequent everyday contexts influence autobiographical recollections? The suggestion is that we can anticipate the personal significance of many infrequent contexts and, in turn, prime our memories accordingly. A comparison of data from Bekerian (1986) and from Conway and Bekerian (1986) can illustrate the point. Bekerian (1986) asked subjects between 18 to 80 years of age to list contexts that would be likely to be experienced as personally significant by an average person. Other subjects from similar age groups were asked to produce contexts that would be likely to be well remembered by the average person. There was close concordance across age groups within both tasks, as well as concordance across tasks in the contexts listed. Thus, 18- and 80-year-olds were in agreement that 'birth of a child' was personally significant, and 18- and 80-year-olds believed 'birth of a child' would be well remembered. The vivid memories of personally significant events reported by Conway and Bekerian (1986) closely matched the most frequently listed contexts reported by Bekerian (1986). In short, the most vivid of all autobiographical memories an individual can recollect are linked to anticipations that certain everyday contexts will be personally significant and well remembered. Additionally, it seems that this knowledge (in the form of anticipations) need not be based on our direct personal experience of these contexts.

Our knowledge of repeated and infrequent everyday contexts could be serving many functions. For example, it is likely that the influence of cultural values on everyday contexts helps members of the same society remember similar contexts in a similar way (cf. Bartlett, 1932). Such knowledge can also cognitively prepare an individual for certain sorts of experiences. An advantage of cognitive preparation is that it minimizes the 'load' placed on an individual in everyday social situations. Cognitive preparation may also help to reduce some uncertainty in the environment. We know what to expect from a wide range of situations. We have compensating strategies that may come into play if our knowledge is violated and we can assume that other people we encounter share our expectations.

Let us summarize the characteristics of everyday contexts that distinguish them from molecular contexts. First, everyday contexts operate through our knowledge, beliefs, and expectations of general classes of experiences, not specific ones. Our knowledge can take on the characteristic of being orderly, to the extent that violations of order can serve to make a single event unique in memory. Everyday contexts and our knowledge of them are diverse. Knowledge includes what to expect, how to respond, how to compensate when expectations are disconfirmed, what typical emotional reactions are likely, and what personal significance can be expected. Some of this knowledge is accessible to conscious awareness, though it does not exclusively operate in the conscious domain. As such, our knowledge of everyday contexts may reduce the cognitive 'load', direct attention to specific features of a specific context, determine storage, and influence the nature of retrieval operations.

Finally, our knowledge of everyday contexts is largely consensual and, in some cases, externalized as beliefs within the culture. In this way, the knowledge resides within the society as well as the individual. This shared knowledge allows uniformity within the culture, and frees the individual from the prerequisites of personal experience in order to have such knowledge. Overall, then, the cognitive characteristics of everyday contexts appear to differ markedly from characteristics of molecular contexts.

## MOLECULAR CONTEXT AND EVERYDAY CONTEXT

The experience of naturally occurring events clearly entails the operation of knowledge associated with both molecular and everyday contexts. It is unclear how the two types of context operate in unison, however.

Perhaps suggestions can arise only after one lists some of the criteria that must be met.

From what we have said about everyday contexts, it is clear that there must be general information available that can prime the individual to anticipate actions, outcomes and emotional reactions. Such information must be phenomenally accessible on occasion. It is also the case that knowledge of everyday contexts can prime lower-level operations, such as response latencies in word recognition. In contrast, molecular contexts seem to have the greatest influence on automatic processes, with the information being either perceptual in nature or not extensively processed. It would seem that the minimal requirements of a model of memory incorporating both types of contexts are the following: provisions for different kinds of information, that is, highly processed vs relatively unprocessed; differential accessibility of such information, that is, phenomenally available vs unavailable for conscious introspection; differential levels of abstraction, that is, highly abstract and general vs highly specific to a unique experience; and different learning sources, that is, societal knowledge vs individually experienced knowledge. Any context, molecular or everyday, will fall along a continuum for any of these four characteristics.

We would suggest that there is no single model of memory that can accommodate both types of contexts. On the one hand, it could be argued that memory for everyday contexts is largely under the domain of theories stressing script-like properties of memory (e.g. Schank, 1982; Loftus, 1979). However, these types of theories do not address how learning takes place within a memory system that is largely schematic in nature (see Bowers, 1986, for a discussion of schema theories and learning). Further, these approaches cannot as readily accommodate findings from the study of molecular contexts.

In contrast, there are models that can easily discuss molecular contexts, but have little or nothing to say about the role everyday contexts play in memory. For example, a recent model of memory, called Headed Records (cf. Morton *et al.*, 1985) seems ideal for explaining effects of molecular contexts. In this model, memories are made up of two major components: a heading, which contains relatively unprocessed and unretrievable information; and a record, which is likely to contain processed information and information which is directly accessible to conscious inspection. Headings are used to access the information contained in the record, but cannot themselves be accessed. Descriptions (cf. Norman and Bobrow, 1979) are used to match headings and they are made of internal and external cues present at the time one is trying to retrieve information. Cues, that is, descriptions, must match information contained in a heading before any access of information in the record can be achieved. Thus, in encoding specificity (cf. Tulving and Thomson, 1973) the previous presentation of a word pair may result in one member of the pair being contained in the heading and the other member in the record. At the time of recall, presentation of the previously seen word may automatically access the heading and thereby ensure retrieval of the correct item. In cases where the cue fails to map onto any heading, two options are available. Either search is terminated, or a new memory description is formed, and the process of attempting to match a heading is iterated.

The Headed Records model provides a relatively straightforward account of how molecular contexts are realized in memory. However, the model does not state, explicitly, how everyday contexts may act to prime encoding processes, or may act cognitively to prepare the individual for an upcoming event. It could be that there are elements of the model which could be expanded for these purposes. For example, the formation of descriptions, that is, the process used to search memory initially, might be biased to retrieve a certain type of previously experienced memories, and might, as a consequence, bias the selection of certain features or bias attention towards certain features. However, such flexibility is not explicit in the model and awaits further development.

In this chaper we have drawn a distinction between *molecular* and *everyday* approaches to context and argued that the molecular approach has studied context effects upon memory which may be mediated by a comparatively automatic process responding to reinstated contextual features. Such automatic processes may be preceded by, or entail, conscious cue generation (cf. Williams and Hollan, 1981) or may respond directly to reinstated context. The molecular approach also emphasizes different components of a memory trace which represent both external and internal aspects of context at different levels of abstraction. The everyday approach to context has studied how people may be cognitively prepared to beliefs and attitudes externalized in society, by the social organization of specific events, and by implicit cultural demands relating to the structuring of experience, to encode naturally occurring contexts in certain ways and, subsequently, to recode memories. The effects of everyday contexts upon memory retrieval may be less direct than the effect studied within the molecular approach but, nonetheless, may be just as pervasive.

In conclusion, different levels of description characterize different aspects of context. Much is known about how molecular aspects of context affect memory. In comparison, little is known about how more abstract (everyday) aspects of context influence memory for naturally occurring events. Virtually nothing is known about how the knowledge of these different contexts interacts in the encoding and recoding of common experiences. It seems to us that in order to understand how naturally occurring contexts influence human behaviours, we must adopt an approach which combines both levels of contextual description.

## REFERENCES

Abelson, R. (1981). The psychological status of the script concept. *American Psychologist*, **36**, 715 – 729.

Anderson, J. and Bower, G. (1973). *Human Associative Memory*, Washington, DC: Winston.

Anderson, R. (1981). Psychological status of the script concept. *American Psychologist*, **36**, 715 – 729.

Anderson, R. and Ortony, A. (1975). On putting apples into bottles—a problem of polysemy. *Cognitive Psychology*, **7**, 167 – 180.

Baddeley, A., Cuscaro, W., Egstrom, G., Weltmen, C. and Willis, M. (1975). Cognitive efficiency of divers working in cold water. *Human Factors*, **17**, 446 – 454.

Barclay, J., Bransford, J., Franks, J., McCarrell, N. and Nitsch, K. (1974). Comprehension and semantic flexibility. *Journal of Verbal Learning and Verbal Behavior*, **13**, 471 – 481.

Bartlett, F. (1932). *Remembering*, London: Cambridge University Press.

Bekerian, D.A. (1986). *Predicting Autobiographical Memories*, MS submitted for publication.

Bekerian, D.A. and Bowers, J. (1983). Eyewitness testimony: were we misled? *Journal of Experimental Psychology: Human Learning and Memory*, **9**, 139 – 145.

Bower, G. (1981). Mood and memory. *American Psychologist*, **36**, 129 – 148.

Bower, G.H., Black, J.B. and Turner, T.J. (1979). Scripts in text comprehension and memory. *Cognitive Psychology*, **11**, 177 – 220.

Bowers, J. (1986). Schema theory and memory. Doctoral dissertation, University of Cambridge, England.

Bowers, J. and Bekerian, D.A. (1984). When will post-event information distort eyewitness testimony? *Journal of Applied Psychology*, **69**, 466 – 472.

Bransford, J. (1979). *Human Cognition*, Belmont, CA: Wadsworth.

Brewer, W. and Treyens, J. (1981). Role of schemata in memory for places. *Cognitive Psychology*, **13**, 207 – 230.

Brown, R. and Kulik, J. (1977). Flashbulb memories. *Cognition*, **5**, 73 – 99.

Cantor, N., Mischel, W. and Schwartz, J. (1982). Prototype analysis of psychological situations. *Cognitive Psychology*, **14**, 45 – 77.

Clarke, R. and Morton, J. (1983). Cross modality facilitation in tachistoscopic word recognition. *Quarterly Journal of Experimental Psychology*, **35a**, 79 – 96.

Conway, M.A. (1987). Verifying autobiographical facts. *Cognition*, **26**, 39 – 58.

Conway, M.A. and Bekerian, D.A. (1986). *Vivid Memories Encoding or Recoding?* Unpublished manuscript.

Conway, M.A. and Bekerian, D.A. (1987). Situational knowledge and emotions. *Cognition and Emotion*, **1**, 145 – 191.

Eich, J. (1980). The cue-department nature of state-dependent retrieval. *Memory and Cognition*, **8**, 157 – 173.

Freud, S. (1957). Repression. In J. Strachey (Ed.), *The Standard Edition of the Complete Psychological Works of Sigmund Freud*, vol. 14, London: Hogarth Press.

Galton, F. (1883). *Inquiries into Human Faculty and its Development*, London: Macmillan.

Godden, D. and Baddeley, A. (1980). Context-dependent memory in two natural environments. *British Journal of Psychology*, **71**, 99 – 104.

Harré, R., Clark, D. and DeCarlo, N. (1985). *Motives and Mechanisms*, London: Penguin.

Jacoby, L.L. and Dallas, M. (1981). On the relationship between autobiographical memory and perceptual learning. *Journal of Experimental Psychology: General*, **3**, 306–340.

Loftus, E. (1979). *Eyewitness Testimony*, New York: Harvard University Press.

Minsky, M. (1975). A framework for representing knowledge. In P. Winston (Ed.), *The Psychology of Computer Vision*, New York: McGraw-Hill.

Morton, J., Hammersley, R. and Bekerian, D.A. (1985). Headed records: a model of memory and its failures. *Cognition*, **20**, 1–36.

Norman, D. and Bobrow, D. (1979). Descriptions: a basis for memory acquisition and retrieval. *Cognitive Psychology*, **11**, 107–123.

Rubin, D. and Kozin, M. (1984). Vivid memories. *Cognition*, **16**, 81–95.

Schacter, S. and Singer, J. (1962). Cognitive, social and physiological determinants of emotional state. *Psychological Review*, **69**, 379–399.

Schank, R. (1982). *Dynamic Memory*, Cambridge: Cambridge University Press.

Schank, R.C. and Abelson, R.P. (1977). *Scripts, Plans, Goals and Understanding*. New York: LEA.

Smith, S., Glenberg, A. and Bjork, R. (1978). Environmental context and environmental memory. *Memory and Cognition*, **6**, 342–353.

Teasdale, J. (1983). Affect and accessibility. In D. Broadbent (Ed.), *Functional Aspects of Human Memory*, Cambridge: Cambridge University Press.

Tulving, E. and Thomson, D. (1973). Encoding specificity and retrieval processes in episodic memory. *Psychological Review*, **80**, 352–373.

Williams, M. and Hollan, J. (1981). The process to retrieval from very long term memory. *Cognitive Science*, **5**, 87–119.

Memory in Context : Context in Memory
Edited by G.M. Davies and D.M. Thomson
© 1988 John Wiley & Sons Ltd.

## CHAPTER 15

# Conceptual Specificity in Thinking and Remembering

ROBERT S. LOCKHART

*University of Toronto*

### ABSTRACT

A parallel is drawn between context effects in memory and those in problem-solving. It is argued that in both domains context controls accessibility to the extent that it influences stimulus conception. A general theory of accessibility should therefore incorporate the results from both domains.

### INTRODUCTION

This chapter will take the position that there is something to be gained in our understanding of context effects in memory if such effects are seen as a special case of a more general class of phenomena that might loosely be referred to as *the accessing of available information*. Context effects in memory—or any other cognitive process – are interesting precisely because of the extent to which context controls access to available knowledge and skills.

The general problem posed by context effects is that of establishing the conditions under which task-relevant information, previously acquired in one context, will be accessed in a different context. If it *is* accessed then the phenomenon to be explained is usually referred to by terms such as recognition, transfer of training, de-contextualization, stimulus generalization, lateral transfer, or insight. If the information is not accessed, but is known to be accessible in some other context, then we speak of recognition failure, or of the information being 'available but not accessible', of 'welding', of failure of transfer, or of *Einstellung*. In these latter cases the question to be answered is why contextual changes often lead to a failure to utilize knowledge or skills that are both available and relevant to the task at hand.

Described in these broad terms, context effects can be seen to be one of the oldest and most pervasive problems in psychology. The root issue is that the relationship between two stimuli (e.g. the relationship of identity or, more generally, of similarity) cannot be defined independently of the observer. In the modern era of psychology this fact has been acknowledged, if not always remembered, at least since H(o)ffding (1891). The very phrase *context effects* assumes that it is both possible and useful to distinguish a core stimulus from other aspects of the total stimulus configuration and that core and context can be varied independently.

The first step in the present analysis of context effects will be to state some theoretical underpinnings and to use this foundation to clarify what is meant by 'core invariance.' Following this background, three broad classes of context will be distinguished and applied to some representative experimental results.

## CONCEPTUALISM

A useful theoretical foundation for a discussion of context effects is to be found in the conceptualism of William James (1890). Especially relevant in *The Principles of Psychology* are Chapters 12 and 22. The difficulty confronting James was the same question that context effects pose for contemporary cognitive theory. Contextual change is the rule, not the exception. No two experienced events are ever identical. One must therefore ask how, in the constantly changing flux of experience, in the ever-moving stream of consciousness, does the mind register identity? In answering this question James advocates a version of conceptualism that emphasizes the mind's capacity to single out 'some one part of the mass of matter for thought that the world presents, and hold fast to it without confusion' (James, 1890, vol. 1, p. 461). It is this ability to conceptualize that is the basis for any recognition of sameness. 'A polyp would be a conceptual thinker if a feeling of "Hello! thingumbob again!" ever flitted through its mind,' (James, 1890, vol.1, p. 463). James's conceptualism has three central characteristics that are important for our present discussion of context effects.

First, conception is a function; it is an operation, or a set of operations, applied to reality; it denotes neither the mental state itself nor what the mental state signifies, but the relation between the two. According to James we should speak not of concepts, but 'of conceiving states of mind' or 'acts of conception.' Thus to claim that we possess concepts such as 'animal', 'dog' or 'courage' is to say that the mind is able to adopt towards objects or events a certain sustained point of view; it is able to conceive an object *as a pet*, or *as a dog*, or a given action *as courage*. This selection and adoption of a sustained point of view James terms a *mode of conceiving*. A mode of conceiving is not to be confused with the object of the conception, a confusion so disastrous yet so tempting that James advocated that the noun *concept* be avoided altogether. To have a concept of dog is not to have a mental replica of *canis familiaris*. We 'have' concepts only in the sense that we might say that we have a foreign language or a good tennis serve; that is, to refer to an ability or capacity, to indicate a potential for a certain kind of mental operation on physical action.

Second, any object or event has an indefinitely large number of ways in which it can be conceived, and our knowledge of the world *is* our way of conceiving the world. 'There is no property ABSOLUTELY *essential to any one thing*' (James, 1980, vol. 2, p. 33). Thus the same object may be conceived of as a pet, a source of protection, a retriever, a thing-to-be-walked, and so on, *without limit*. No one of these modes of conceiving constitutes the essence of the object. Even conceiving this object *as a dog* enjoys no special status. Such categorization serves the purpose of labelling and discrimination (one calls it a 'dog' and not a 'teddy bear') and perhaps other purposes as well, but such classification reflects just one of this infinity of ways of conceiving the object. It is interesting to compare James's position to the highly similar arguments of Nelson Goodman (Goodman, 1976, 1978). The notion of purpose leads to James's final point.

Third, conception is teleological. Whereas the number of potential ways of conceiving objects or events is essentially infinite, not all ways are equally useful. The mind conceives according to the purposes at hand. Thus (to use James's own example) the material on which I am writing is presently conceived as a surface for inscription, but under different circumstances (e.g. should I wish to light a fire) it might be conceived differently, as combustible material, or if I need to apply a verbal label then my conception serves the purpose of classifying and appropriate labelling. But the fact that the objects may warrant the label 'paper' is no more of its essence than is the fact that it may warrant the conception combustible material. Says James, '*the only meaning of essence is teleological, and that classification and conception are teleological weapons of the mind*. The essence of a thing is that one of its properties which is so *important for my interests* that in comparison with it I may neglect the rest,' (James, 1890, vol. 2, p. 335).

## CORE INVARIANCE AND THE CONCEPT OF 'SAMENESS'

As noted previously, the term 'context effects' presupposes a distinction between a core component that is invariant across presentations of a stimulus complex and other components that are designated context. The question most commonly addressed by psychologists is whether this invariance can be identified under changes in context. Thus, to take a well-known example, if the word JAM is presented on one occasion preceded by the word STRAWBERRY and on a second occasion preceded by the word TRAFFIC we might ask whether a subject can detect the repetition (invariance) of the letters JAM despite the change in the preceding word that is designated context.

Before proceeding further, the concept of invariance must be examined more closely. What does it mean to say that two objects or events are 'the same'? This seemingly innocent question is a major source of confusion, especially in discussions of context effects. If the letters D-O-G appear twice, in different parts of a list, it can be reasonably said that the same word has appeared twice. Or can it? The two events are not literally the same physical entity—they differ in a variety of physical parameters—we simply say that these differences are irrelevant; it is the *word* dog in both cases. If the word appeared in upper case letters on one occasion and lower case letters on the other, or if it appeared as *dog* on one occasion and *chien* on another, we might still claim that they are the same word. Yet clearly this sameness is conceptually dependent. There is a point of view or a *mode of conceiving* (roughly, what the words denote) that renders the stimuli dog, DOG, and chien 'the same' and there are conceptions (e.g. physical form) which render them different. Conversely, in the sentences *The boy has a playful dog* and *The boy ate a hot dog* the stimuli comprising the letters D-O-G invite the same point of view from the perspective of physical form but invite quite different conceptions in terms of what they denote. It is therefore by no means paradoxical to say that there are conditions under which *dog* and *chien* are conceptually equivalent, but *dog* and *dog* are not. Thus there can be no absolute answer to the question of whether or not stimuli are the same since the only form of identity is identity of conception. Tulving (1983, p. 270) quotes Hollingworth making essentially the same point.

In brief, physical identity does not imply a particular conceptual identity nor, in general, does a particular conceptual identity require physical identity or any degree of physical similarity. A specified form of physical identity is neither necessary nor sufficient to establish conceptual identity. Physical identity enjoys no priority of status, it reflects just one mode of conceiving, just one basis on which an equivalence relation might be established.

In stressing the conceptual relativity of equivalence it is important not to lose sight of James's first point that conception is a mental operation, not a mental entity. The importance lies in the fact that equivalence of conception does not mean identity of the operations that establish that equivalence. To say that *dog* and *chien* are equivalent is not to say that the equivalence-establishing operations that are applied to *dog* are the same as those applied to *chien*.

## TYPES OF CONTEXT

It is helpful to regard experimental manipulations of context as exerting their effects through induced changes in the mode of conceiving the target item, or more precisely, in the operations underlying the conception of the target item. However, the term context is notoriously vague. The vagueness is largely attributable to a confusion between experimental techniques for the manipulation of context on the one hand and, on the other, the mechanisms or processes that are initiated by such manipulations and are thought to be responsible for the observed effects. The former provides a clearer basis for distinguishing types of context. In terms of experimental manipulations, three broad classes of context can be usefully distinguished. We will term these *physical context, mental context,* and *surface context.* The first two correspond roughly to Tulving's (1983) distinction between the 'setting' and the 'cognitive environment' of a focal stimulus. In both these cases, from the viewpoint of physical form, the core remains invariant, or at least as invariant as possible. The third type of context, surface context, depends on a distinction between the abstract or deep structure of a stimulus and the physical means of its instantiation. Thus *dog* and *chien* might be said to represent the same core instantiated by a different surface context.

While the term context is most commonly taken to mean physical context, all three of the above uses share the same fundamental property. Each distinguishes between a core and its context and each exploits the experimental technique of varying one while holding the other constant.

### Physical context

The term context is most frequently taken to refer to the immediate physical surround of a target stimulus. Thus in a memory experiment the context may be defined as the word preceding, or the word paired with, a target word as in the experiments reported by Light and Carter-Sobell (1970) or Thomson (1972). Or the context may refer to more global features of the environment in which the stimulus is presented such as under water or on land (Godden and Baddeley, 1975) or, less exotically, in one room or another. The experimental manipulation of this form of context entails a change in the physical surround with the physical properties of the core stimulus remaining largely unchanged. Frequently a physical context is chosen because of its specific semantic properties, and the experimental manipulation is essentially an exploitation of the phenomenon of mental set. Thus the meaning assigned to, our mode of conceiving, the letters *jam* is likely to be different if preceded by the words *strawberry* from what it would be if preceded by *traffic.* On the other hand, changes to some general aspect of the environment (such as the room furnishings) are manipulations of context that typically have no specific hypothesis about the source of contextual influences. While such studies of non-specific context effects may answer certain practical questions about the impact of changes in certain real-world environments, they are of limited theoretical value. Since all context effects must occur via some induced change in the conception of the core stimulus, it is difficult to see what is gained by way of increased insight into basic mechanisms through manipulations that leave the source of this influence so poorly specified.

There is, of course, a large body of data documenting the effects of physical context on memory performance. These well-known results show clearly that context can control the accessibility of available information by inducing changes in the conceptual operations applied to a given stimulus. For present purposes it will be sufficient to make the obvious link between these results and corresponding effects in the area of problem-solving. Consider a very dramatic example from Levine (1971). Subjects were shown a sequence of cards, each containing two side-by-side circles, one large and one small. They were required to learn a simple discrimination rule (e.g. large) applied to these pairs of circles. Under normal conditions subjects learned such a rule in an average of three trials. If, however, this same problem is preceded by a set of problems in which the rules to be learned consist of positive sequences for which size was irrelevant (e.g. left, right, left, right ...) then an average of 62 trials was required and 28 of 60 subjects had not solved it after 115 trials.

Levine's experiment is fundamentally the same as one in which the word *jam* is presented preceded by *strawberry* and tested for recognition preceded by the word *traffic*. In the former, the context prevents subjects from applying a conceptualization consisting of a simple attribute that in another context would be applied almost immediately. In the latter example, in which subjects are asked whether the word *jam* has been seen previously, the change in physical context may lead to quite a different conceptualization of the letter sequence so that from one viewpoint the same word has *not* been previously presented. The task requirements, however, define identity in terms of physical properties (the letters J-A-M) so that a response 'new' is scored as an error. In both cases context inhibits that conception of the stimulus that is most likely to lead to a solution of the respective problems.

## Mental and pragmatic context

Conception is influenced not only by properties of the physical stimulus but also by a multitude of factors that have to do with mental states. Some of these states, such as mood, emotionality, or drug states have been studied in relation to remembering, but such investigations suffer the same shortcomings as do studies of non-specific physical context. In both cases the independent variable does not specify with any precision the sources responsible for any observed effect, a point explored by Eich and Birnbaum in an earlier contribution in this volume. There is, however, one class of mental states that can be manipulated with greater specificity. We will refer to this class as the pragmatic context.

Pragmatic context refers to the goal that conception serves. A single object or event, a piece of paper for example, might be conceived quite differently depending on whether the pragmatic context is that of needing to write or of needing to light a fire. Pragmatic context influences such elementary cognitive tasks as verbal labelling. Whether or not the label *dog* is appropriate will depend not only on the object to be labelled, but on the pragmatic context. If you ask an exhibitor at a dog show, 'What is that?' the response 'a border collie' but not 'a dog' is likely to be considered appropriate.

An example of manipulating the pragmatic context in recent memory research is the use of different incidental orienting tasks, an experimental paradigm that was emphasized in the development levels of processing (Craik and Lockhart, 1972; Lockhart, 1979). The essential purpose of orienting questions such as 'Does this word rhyme with ...?', 'Is this object a member of the category ...?' or 'How well are you described by the adjective ...?' is to establish a well-defined pragmatic context. The experimental facts are that memory can be strongly influenced by pragmatic context. That is, holding everything else constant, substantial difference in memory performance can be produced merely by changes in the goal underlying the conception of a word. Under a wide set of conditions, the word *dog*, conceived as a word rhyming with *fog* will be more poorly remembered than if it is conceived as an instance of the class 'domestic pets'. More precisely, memory performance is negatively influenced by a change in the pragmatic context between acquisition and retrieval (Fisher and Craik, 1977; Morris, Bransford, and Franks, 1977).

It is possible to interpret the phenomenon of recognition failure of recallable words (Tulving and Thomson, 1973), as being in large part a consequence of a change in pragmatic context. Although the item to be recognized is, under one conceptualization, the same as the item recalled, the pragmatic context within which recall occurs is very different from that in which recognition is tested.

The effects of pragmatic context are well documented in the domain of problem-solving, the classic example being, of course, the phenomenon of functional fixedness. Experiments reported by Perfetti, Bransford, and Franks (1983) provide a less obvious example of the influence of pragmatic context. In these experiments subjects were required to solve simple insight problems such as the following. 'A man who lived in a small town in the

U.S. married 20 different women of the same town. All are still living and he has never divorced one of them. Yet, he has broken no law. Can you explain?' In some conditions these problems were preceded by sentences containing information that essentially constituted a solution to each of the problems that followed. For example, the sentence corresponding to the above problem was 'A minister marries several people each week.' Subjects were given an orienting task that asked them to rate each of these prior sentences for truthfulness. Despite the seemingly obvious relevance of the content of these sentences to the problems, if subjects were not explicitly informed of this relevance, they performed little better on the problems than a control group who did not see the sentences. The question to be answered is why the problem failed to cue memory for the relevant, recently presented, sentence. One obvious line of explanation begins with an analysis of the change in pragmatic context between the orienting task and the problems and goes on to ask how this shift in context influences conception. The initial pragmatic context is one that demands little more than straightforward comprehension along with whatever accessing of a knowledge base is needed to rate the sentence for truthfulness. The problems on the other hand require a reconception of a word or phrase from a common conception to a less common one. For example, the word *man* must be reconceptualized as *clergyman*. It is the shift in conceptualization that produces insight or the 'aha' experience. The analytic operations demanded by the first pragmatic context are simply not relevant to those operations required to solve the problem.

A similar point is illustrated in the experiments reported by Weisberg, Dicamillo, and Phillips (1978) who had subjects learn a list of paired associates before solving Duncker's box-and-candle problem. The key to solving this problem is the ability to conceptualize the box as a platform to support the candle rather than as a container. Weisberg *et al.* found that having the word pair *candle-box* embedded in the paired-associate list did not facilitate solving the problem even when differences in surface context were minimized. Given the present analysis this failure of transfer is not surprising. The pragmatic context defined by the paired-associate task elicits conceptual operations that are likely to be quite different from those required in the problem-solving context. In the latter case the fundamental operation required is that of conceiving the box as a supporting platform, a conception unlikely to arise in a different pragmatic context.

It follows from this account that if the orienting task can be modified so that relevant reconceptualization is required then positive transfer should result. For example, if, in the Perfetti *et al.* (1983) study, sentences in the orienting task were presented in a problem-solving context rather than in the straightforward factual manner of Perfetti *et al.* then problem-solving should be facilitated. We have performed such an experiment (Lockhart,

Lamon, and Gick, 1988). In this experiment the procedure of Aubel, Franks, and Soraci (1979) was used to give subjects in one group sentences that posed a comprehension problem. That is, instead of seeing a sentence such as 'The clergyman married ten people each week' they received the sentence 'The man married ten people each week' followed by a 5 sec. pause at which point they were shown the word 'clergyman.' This 'aha' condition yielded substantial positive transfer to the problems whereas the straightforward sentences were of little help. Notice that both groups receive the same information; the only difference is that in the problem-solving context subjects were forced to engage in precisely those conceptual operations demanded by the problems. In the 'aha' condition, the noun *man* must be reconceptualized from its normal meaning to the less frequent meaning of clergyman and this, of course, is precisely the operation required to solve the problem. While presenting the word *clergyman* from the outset conveys the relevant information, it does not elicit the appropriate conceptual operation.

## Surface context

The third type of context depends on a distinction between the surface features and the 'deep structure' of a stimulus situation. The *object* strawberry may be represented by the word *strawberry* presented in any of a variety of auditory or printed forms, or by a picture, or by a botanical definition. As with the previous forms of context we can distinguish between an invariant core, the deep structure, and a variable context, the surface structure.

The manipulation of surface context is the basic paradigm of studies of concept attainment. Exemplars vary in their surface features while maintaining an invariant core that constitutes the defining characteristic of the concept. Whether, or under what circumstances, this core is to be thought of as a set of features, a prototype, a schema, a rule, or a theory is a matter that cannot be addressed here, although the issues involved are undoubtedly important for an understanding of context effects. Context effects in this case refer to the effect of changes in surface features on the recognition of invariance.

If the core of a concept is defined in terms of an invariant physical feature, as in Hull (1920), then the notion of surface context can be thought of as a special case of physical context. Hull used Chinese ideographs, a conceptual class being defined by the presence of an invariant figure hidden within the ideograph. The major difference is that unlike the previous examples of physical context, in a task with stimuli such as Hull's, the major difficulty confronting the subject is the physical partitioning of the stimulus into core and context.

There is one result from Hull's monograph that is particularly interesting for present purposes. In experiment E, subjects were presented with the defining common element without any context at all. That is, they were essentially given the answer. Granted that under normal conditions the identification of the defining component within the surface context is a major aspect of the task's difficulty, it might be expected that such a give-away condition would yield a substantial improvement in the rate of learning. Hull found that it produced no improvement at all. It would seem that being given a core without context does not facilitate performance on a task that entails identification of that same core within a context.

This conclusion seems also to hold when the core is an abstract schema rather than a physical component of the whole. In this case the core is the underlying structure of a problem while the surface features that instantiate the problem constitute the context. Thus the same problem can be presented in different contexts and one can ask whether subjects recognize them as the same, that is, as analogous, or to use the term of Simon and Hayes (1976), as problem isomorphs. In their study of analogical transfer, Gick and Holyoak (1983) examined this question. They used Duncker's radiation problem which requires for its solution the application of a 'convergence schema.' While most of their experiments are concerned with the effects of solving prior analogous problems, in Experiment 2 they attempted to teach subjects the convergence schema without any accompanying story. They found that this attempt to teach the schema directly had very little beneficial effect.

Both the Hull (1920) result and that of Gick and Holyoak (1983) can be understood in terms similar to those used to interpret the results from the Perfetti et al. (1983) study. The acts of conceptualization that underly the training or study phase are not those necessary to solve the problem. Being able to solve Duncker's radiation problem is not just a matter of 'having' a convergence schema any more than solving the insight problems of Perfetti et al. was simply a matter of 'having' the relevant information. Rather, it is a question of whether the surface context will cue the appropriate conceptualization. Being given context-free concepts would seem to be of limited value if the subsequent conditions of utilization are not context free.

It is possible to interpret in similar terms the large body of data demonstrating that reasoning is content dependent (see Johnson-Laird, 1983). Subjects may reason correctly in one surface context but make errors on a formally equivalent (isomorphic) problem presented in a different surface context. Such results pose difficulties for theories of reasoning that posit a content-independent mental logic. They pose no difficulty, however, for theories (such as Johnson-Laird's) that view reasoning and problem-solving as entailing a process whereby a given conceptualization (a mental model) is applied to, or constructed from, a given surface context.

In the area of human memory there are many studies examining the effects of changes in surface context. In this case the core is usually an invariant meaning and the changing context is the physical or syntactic form instantiating this meaning. Thus a given meaning may be denoted verbally or pictorially, undergo transformation of modality, typescript, language, etc. In studies of memory there are two quite different questions that might be asked. One might test memory for the core, or for the context as well. In the latter case one is interested in whether information about surface context is preserved and a given response (for example, a synonym or a translation of a presented word) might be scored an error although such a response clearly demonstrates memory for the core. Of greater relevance to the present discussion is the question of whether changes in surface context influence memory for the core.

The answer to this question would seem to be largely negative, even when memory for the surface context itself is quite good. That is, changing an item's modality or some other aspect of its surface context does not seem to have a strong influence on recognition of that item's core. The data reported by Kolers (1979) may be taken as an example. In these studies, changes in surface context consisted of transformations (e.g. inversion) of typography. Whereas memory for typography is long-lasting, the effect on recognition memory of changing typography is relatively small. In fact, text presented in inverted typography and tested in normal typography, is as well recognized as text that is both presented and tested in normal type.

The small effect on recognition memory of changes in surface context is probably to be understood in terms of the linguistic materials typically used in memory experiments. Because of well-practiced language habits, changes in surface context are unlikely to cause changes in the conception of the stimulus. Our conception of the stimulus *dog* is likely to be the same regardless of whether the word is spoken, written, printed upside down, or whatever, assuming, of course, that other forms of context are held constant. Our effective use of language demands that we are highly practiced at extracting invariant meaning under conditions of variable surface context. Although changes in surface context may entail different analytic operations in achieving a common conception, and although such differences may support accurate memory for surface context, they do little to prevent recognition of the invariant core.

## CONCLUSIONS

Although I have done no more than sketch an argument in broad outline, the picture that emerges from all three forms of context is that context controls accessibility to the extent that it influences a subject's mode of conception. Conception is the selective construction of meaning and is governed by habit and purpose, a point of view exemplified in the conceptualism of William James. These principles of constructivism and conceptual relativity have not always been readily accepted, especially among those who study memory for linguistic materials, a state of affairs that probably accounts for much of the resistance to ideas such as encoding specificity and related phenomena such as the recognition failure of recallable words (Tulving, 1983). Language habits are so strong and the conceptual processes underlying word meaning so overlearned that it takes strong experimental manipulations (such as large changes in pragmatic context or exploitation of ambiguities such as homographs) to make the point that the mental operation of conception must not be confused with the object of conception. Another way of making the point is to recognize that the same principles obtain in other areas of cognition, such as problem-solving, where context effects are much stronger. In such cases the effects are usually referred to by different names, but the experimental manipulations embody the same principles. If this argument is correct then it would seem plausible to set as a goal the construction of a general theory of de-contextualization (or of encoding specificity to express the same idea negatively) that would incorporate the results from both domains.

## REFERENCES

Aubel, P.M., Franks, J.J. and Soraci. S.A. (1979). Effort towards comprehension: elaboration or 'Aha'? *Memory and Cognition*, 7, 426–434.

Craik, F.I.M. and Lockhart, R.S. (1972). Levels of processing: a framework for memory research. *Journal of Verbal Learning and Verbal Behavior*, 11, 671–684.

Fisher, R. and Craik, F.I.M. (1977). The interaction between encoding and retrieval operations in cued recall. *Journal of Experimental Psychology: Human Learning and Memory*, 3, 701–711.

Gick, M.L. and Holyoak, K.J. (1983). Schema induction and analogical reasoning. *Cognitive Psychology*, 15, 1–38.

Godden, D.R. and Baddeley, A.D. (1975). Context-dependent memory in two natural environments: on land and underwater. *British Journal of Psychology*, 66, 325–332.

Goodman, N. (1976). *Languages of Art*, Indianapolis: Hackett.

Goodman, N. (1978). *Ways of Worldmaking*, Indianapolis: Hackett.

Höffding, H. (1891). *Outlines of Psychology*, New York: Macmillan.

Hull, C.L. (1920). Quantitative aspects of the evolution of concepts. *Psychological Monographs*, 28 (Whole no. 128).

James, W. (1980). *The Principles of Psychology*, New York: Dover.

Johnson-Laird, P.N. (1983). *Mental Models*, Cambridge, Mass.: Harvard University Press.

Kolers, P.A. (1979). A pattern-analyzing basis of recognition. In L.S. Cermak and F.I.M. Craik (Eds), *Levels of Processing in Human Memory*, Hillsdale, NJ: Erlbaum, pp. 363–384.

Levine, M. (1971). Hypothesis theory and nonlearning despite ideal S – R reinforcement contingencies. *Psychological Review*, **78**, 130 – 140.

Light, L.L., and Carter-Sobell, L. (1970). Effects of changed semantic context on recognition memory. *Journal of Verbal Learning and Verbal Behavior*, **9**, 1 – 11.

Lockhart, R.S. (1979). Remembering events. In L.S. Cermak and F.I.M. Craik (Eds), *Levels of Processing in Human Memory*, Hillsdale, NJ: Erlbaum, pp. 77 – 88.

Lockhart, R.S., Lamon, M. and Gick, M.L. (1988). Conceptual transfer in simple insight-problems. *Memory and Cognition*, **16**, 36 – 44.

Morris, C.D., Bransford, J.D., and Franks, J.J. (1977). Levels of processing versus transfer appropriate processing. *Journal of Verbal Learning and Verbal Behavior*, **16**, 519 – 533.

Perfetti, G.A., Bransford, J.D., and Franks, J.J. (1983). Constraints on access in a problem solving context. *Memory and Cognition*, **11**, 24 – 31.

Simon, H.A. and Hayes, J.R. (1976). The understanding process: problem isomorphs. *Cognitive Psychology*, **8**, 165 – 190.

Thomson, D.M. (1972). Context effects in recognition memory. *Journal of Verbal Learning and Verbal Behavior*, **11**, 497 – 511.

Tulving, E. (1983). *Elements of Episodic Memory*, New York: Oxford University Press.

Tulving, E. and Thomson, D.M. (1973). Encoding specificity and retrieval processes in episodic memory. *Psychological Review*, **80**, 352 – 373.

Weisberg, R., Dicamillo, M., and Phillips, D. (1978). Transferring old associations to new problems: a nonautomatic process. *Journal of Verbal Learning and Verbal Behavior*, **17**, 219 – 228.

# CONCLUSIONS

Memory in Context : Context in Memory
Edited by G.M. Davies and D.M. Thomson
© 1988 John Wiley & Sons Ltd.

CHAPTER 16

# Context in Context

GRAHAM DAVIES

*North East London Polytechnic*

and

DONALD THOMSON

*Monash University*

## ABSTRACT

The theoretical and practical implications of research reviewed in this book
are briefly considered. At a theoretical level, there is a need for a clear definition and classification of context effects. At a practical level, the conditions
need to be specified under which context reinstatement will improve memory and those where reinstatement will have either neutral or even negative
effects. Progress is evident on both theoretical and applied fronts.

In this brief concluding section, we attempt to bring out some common
themes and links between our different contributors and to highlight
continuing controversies and new avenues of research. We have divided
our comments between those which relate to the theory-driven laboratory
research and those which are more concerned with applied issues.

## CONTEXT IN THEORY

The most frequently quoted allegation regarding research on context is
that the term is a 'conceptual trash-can' covering a multitude of effects
with no clear linkage between them. There is clearly a need, first, for a
working definition of context and, second, for a typology of context which
subsumes the manifold effects discussed by our contributors.

As we emphasised in our introduction, we regard context not as an explanatory concept, so much as in functional terms: a phenomenon whose effects are sufficiently powerful and prevasive as to form an essential feature of any theory of memory. Bain and Humphries, Tiberghien and Davies have all emphasised how modern theories of memory have attempted to come to terms with context effects but have used the term in rather different ways. Given the looseness with which it is used, there may even be advantages in discarding the label 'context' altogether in favour of some more limited, but more tightly defined terms; but for the moment let us consider its generic usage.

All definitions of context assume a distinction between stimulus and setting, figure and ground. One of the major problems, highlighted by Thomson, is that of defining what constitutes setting and what are merely components of the total stimulus: is 'strawberry' the context for 'jam' or part of the stimulus? Thomson sharpens the distinction between 'setting' and 'ground' in an attempt to differentiate between the two situations. To develop the point further it is necessary to distinguish operationally between integrated compounds and juxtaposed elements. Such a distinction is clearly related to the interactive/independent view of context effects advanced by Baddeley (1982), though the problems of independently defining such terms remain formidable. One opening might be through examining the pattern of free recall, as argued originally by Horowitz and Prytulac (1969). Compound stimuli, they argued, will tend to be recalled as a single unit and rarely as isolated components. Recall will be by a process of re-integration, such that one element automatically gives access to the second; recall of one is inseparable from the other. This contrasts with the priming or cueing function of the independent elements where accesss to the accompanying element is not guaranteed. Horowitz and Prytulack in their own studies failed to find such a strong differentiation between the two classes of stimuli; it may well be that one is dealing with a continuum rather than a dichotomy. Be that as it may, the free recall test seems one way worth exploring for escaping from this conceptual cul-de-sac.

A second problem is highlighted in Lockhart's contribution. Lockhart emphasises the essentially subjective nature of context. It is the subject, the learner or perceiver, who determines what is stimulus and what is ground. The subject's perspective, argues Lockhart, will be determined by his goals or the object of the task as he or she perceives it. Lockhart's analysis contains the important truism that experiments which merely manipulate the physical setting of the learning task or its mode of presentation are at best using an indirect means of changing context. Implicit assumptions are being made about how the subject treats the task and setting. Lockhart's analysis is instructive in considering several much-discussed failures to obtain contextual facilitation which have appeared in the literature in recent years.

For instance, Saufley, Otaka and Baveresco (1985) repeatedly failed to find context effects in examination results where students either sat their exams in the same or a different room from that in which the information had been taught originally. As Smith points out in this book, context effects are unlikely in this setting as material will have been revised in a variety of different environments: the purpose of revision is precisely to free information from the context in which it was assimilated in order to ensure universal accessibility, a point made by Howe. Perhaps it is the most anxious students, those who must always sit in the same spot in the same room, who will show marked effects of learning context (Mueller, Lenhart and Gustavson, 1987).

Likewise, Bower and Mayer (1985) have reassessed their own earlier research which might have implied that improved retrieval was an inevitable consequence of mood reinstatement. Their later analysis emphasises the importance of the learner perceiving a link between his or her prevailing mood and the content of the material to be memorised. If the link between stimulus and context is absent, then context reinstatement will be ineffective (see also Fiedler and Stroehm, 1986).

Finally, Fernandez and Glenburg (1985) attribute their repeated failure to replicate Smith's work on environmental context and memory to differences in the way their subjects perceived the relationship between the learning materials and the room where learning took place. Echoing Bower and Mayer, they suggest that the room must interact with, or be seen as part of, the learning task by the subject for stable context effects to occur.

Clearly, these studies and Lockhart's analysis call for a greater emphasis upon manipulating subjects' conceptions of the learning process, either through instructions or task demands. If this is done, perhaps future studies will be more prescriptive in predicting under what conditions contextual facilitation will take place and when an apparent manipulation of context will be irrelevant to performance.

Another consideration is, that for all its ubiquity, context reinstatement may not always be the primary or most powerful retrieval technique available to the subject. Subjects who know they are to be asked subsequently to recall material may use other encoding strategies which, if they are sufficiently effective, may 'crowd out' any effects due to context. Such a view has been advanced by Smith (1986) who has demonstrated that context effects may even be found for recognition as well as recall, when verbal material is tested within an incidental learning paradigm. Such an hypothesis is also consistent with the findings of Harris (1980) who reported that mental reinstatement emerged as the single most frequently employed mnemonic aid in an everyday memory questionnaire where, of course, much of the material to be retrieved would involve incidental recall.

Do we have a theory to explain context effects in memory? Bain and Humphries, Thomson and Davies all offer synoptic views of how contemporary memory theory interfaces with context effects and all conclude that no single theory is sufficient to explain their operation even in one narrowly defined area, let alone the overall pattern. There is a clear need for a logically defensible classification of the major varieties of contextual phenomena. When this is established it may be possible to evolve mini-theories to cover the major groupings, from which more general principles may emerge.

Such classifications are offered by a number of contributors including Smith, Lockhart, Thomson and Tiberghien. Rather than reshuffle these well-thought-through distinctions, we can perhaps attempt to relate them to more general conceptions of memory function.

One dimension is the idea of automaticity versus strategic control or 'active' versus 'passive' context as Thomson terms them. Some of our contributors such as Mayes, Bekerian and Conway, see context effects as automatic and involving little or no degree of subject control. This certainly seems true of some contextual phenomena, particularly the linguistic contexts reviewed by Tiberghien. The environmental contexts, on the other hand, reviewed by Smith and Davies, seem to involve a much greater degree of subject control. The success of such procedures as Geiselman's 'cognitive interview' and the emphasis laid upon the subject as perceiver in producing such effects argues against automaticity for all contextual phenomena.

Mood presents some interesting anomalies. On the one hand, Guenther's analysis argues for the fragility of mood as state-dependent variable and for the subtle interaction between material and mood, a view also endorsed by Blaney (1986) in his commentary on the literature. On the other hand, drug studies involving state-dependency, particularly those with animals, argue for the minimum of cognitive modulation. Work of the kind described by Eich and Birnbaum will help us to understand more clearly the interplay between automatic and strategic processes in inducing mood effects.

A second dimension concerns the episodic and semantic poles in memory. The linguistic context discussed by Tiberghien and the everyday contexts of Bekerian and Conway veer strongly toward the semantic pole. They represent frameworks for understanding language and language function on the one hand, and familiar everyday events on the other. At the opposite pole are the environmental and mood-dependent context effects discussed by other authors; these are concerned with retrieval of specific incidents, rather than the comprehension of general classes of events; with retention rather than inference.

Ironically the one class of material which fails to fit neatly into either of these dimensions is the work which precipitated the current wave of interest in context effects: Tulving and Thomson's (1973) research on cued recall. On the question of automaticity, it seems to contain elements of both automatic and subject control. Effects of changed semantic context on memory are consistent and replicable, yet moderated by instructional sets and encoding instructions as Bain and Humphries' contribution illustrates. Likewise, while being firmly in the episodic domain, the origins of such studies seem closer in some respects to the linguistic contexts of Tiberghien. Unlike the mood and environmental context studies, verbal studies have limited ecological relevance: they remain an abstraction of events which have their origins in linguistic processes. Charting the relationships between the two realms of knowledge described by Tiberghien and Bain and Humphries is a project worthy of another book. For now, we turn to the applications of these theoretical notions to the problems of everyday remembering.

## CONTEXT IN PRACTICE

Two contrasting perspectives are offered in this book on the impact of context on cognition: context as a facilitator and as an inhibitor of performance in the real world. In its role as a facilitator, contextual cueing is seen as facilitating memory at retrieval or priming task-appropriate behaviour. When cast as an inhibitor, context is seen as constraining what should be generalised problem-solving strategies or imbueing novel events with a false sense of familiarity. What evidence is there for these contractory processes and how can their opposing effects be reconciled?

On the facilitatory side, both Geiselman and Cutler and Penrod provide evidence for the view that reinstatement of context can be a practical aid to the recovery of memories not initially accessible to an observer. Context reinstatement may take the form of actual physical reinstatement of cues or mental exercises designed to instantiate the circumstances of the original incident. Both see an immediate application to witness interrogation procedures. Both acknowledge, however, that memory enhancement is not a necessary or inevitable consequence of contextual reinstatement, echoing the new-found caution of more laboratory-oriented researchers. Cutler and Penrod focus on line-up identification. They argue that contextual reinstatement is most likely to be effective when a disparity exists between the original memory of the person and their appearance at the line-up. Supportive evidence is provided from their studies which demonstrates that variables such as delay, disguise, or the presence of a weapon, all of which serve to reduce recognition under normal instructions, are sensitive to contextual reinstatement procedures. While their data are internally consistent, their finding of enhanced contextual impact with delay may be contrasted with the results from the laboratory studies of face recognition reviewed by Davies which have generally failed to find any greater impact of context with delay. Cutler and Penrod's argument might also lead them to predict much larger influences on memory where the copy cue is absent, as in the case of recall. As Davies and Milne (1985) note, where recall and recognition measures have been employed in the same experiment, this has not always been the case. Nevertheless, as Geiselman's studies illustrate, substantial effects of witness recall can be demonstrated for contextual reinstatement under forensically realistic conditions.

Geiselman's Cognitive Interview procedure incorporates an element of mental reinstatement as well as other cognitive strategies designed to improve retrieval. In the applied context, the great strength of this work is the demonstration in realistic settings that interviewers given a brief training in the use of the Cognitive Interview can elicit more information than seasoned police officers using normal procedures: a true base-level for assessing the effectiveness of the technique. Geiselman and Fisher are currently developing and refining the Cognitive Interview so as to yield even greater amounts of information. In a recent experiment, high school pupils trained in the revised procedure were again more successful than experienced police officers in interrogating witnesses to a filmed crime. Moreover, the levels of information elicited with the revised Interview, both central action and peripheral detail, were greater than with the original version (Fisher and Geiselman, in press). While it is tempting to credit such successes to context alone, it must be born in mind that it forms but one of four components of the Interview and the weighting of this component relative to the other strategies embodied in the Interview remains to be determined.

Both Geiselman and Cutler and Penrod incorporate features into their design to counteract the effects of response bias: the possibility that contextual procedures will produce spurious improvements in performance due to a greater tendency to respond under conditions of contextual reinstatement. Both Davies and Thomson discuss evidence that demonstrates that this can occur, but both dismiss response bias as the sole explanation of context effects. Similarly, Cutler and Penrod are able to reject such a view as accuracy is improved even for line-ups from which the target is absent. Likewise Geiselman examines recall not merely of correct information but also of erroneous or fabricated responses and finds no support for the view that these are disproportionately greater with the Cognitive Interview.

McSpadden, Schooler and Loftus provide a useful corrective to any euphoria induced by these findings by their description of a set of studies, all of which failed to find substantial evidence for a context effect.

McSpadden *et al.* employed the 'guided memory' procedure used success-fully by Malpass and Devine (1981), a design incorporating features from the seminal work of Smith and materials similar to Cutler and Penrod. Yet, context produced only a small and inconsistent effect upon performance.

One similarity in the result of both McSpadden *et al.* and Geiselman was a comparative failure to ameliorate the effects of misleading information encountered in the interim between observation and test, even when the information was furnished in a context different from that in which the events were staged or questioning took place. Some amelioration might have been predicted on the basis of the studies of Bekerian and Bowers (1983; see also Bowers and Bekerian, 1984) who have demonstrated context-sensitive processing in the misleading information paradigm developed by Loftus (1979).

One difference between the studies described in this volume and the work of Bekerian and Bowers lies in the nature of the context manipulated. For Bekerian and Bowers, context was defined as question ordering whereas for Geiselman and McSpadden, context is spatio-temporal in nature. There are, however, at least two studies which have reported such reductions when context has been defined in terms of physical environment. Mingay and Bekerian (1984) had subjects observe a slide sequence illustrating a cycling accident. Subsequently some subjects were exposed to misleading information embodied in leading questions before attempting a three-alternative, forced-choice recognition task. Subjects who chose a foil incorporating the erroneous information were more likely to choose the correct response on their second choice if context was reinstated by showing parts of the original slide sequence. Likewise, Gibling and Davies (1988) reported that subjects recalling the appearance of an individual observed in a shop-lifting incident were less likely to be influenced by the misleading features of a Photofit picture if, at the time of recall, they saw pictures of the shop interior and were reminded of the circumstances surrounding their original observation of the person involved. These positive findings suggest that Bekerian and Bowers' effect is not confined solely to the original paradigm and form of context manipulation. Nevertheless, as with the more direct stimulation of context-dependent memory, the circumstances under which the effects will manifest themselves remain to be defined.

McSpadden *et al.* suggest that a combination of particular subsets of individuals and varieties of incident may be necessary to spark context-sensitive recall. As we have noted, attempts in laboratory studies to iden-tify individual difference variables are at an early stage, while the range of situations and settings which have yielded positive findings form no very clear pattern. McSpadden *et al.* may well be correct in asserting that failures to obtain context reinstatement effects in conditions approaching a field setting have failed to reach the public record, but such null results do not in themselves negate the positive findings, as Geiselman emphasises. What is required is careful experimentation, based on hypotheses which make firm predictions as to when and when not a context effect will be observed (see Tiberghien, 1986, for an isolated example). Until such times as the conditions under which positive effects can be specified, Geiselman's admonition that it should be introduced as part of routine police questioning seems sound: it can do little harm and may yield valuable new information.

What of the use of contextual revival procedures in other settings? The idea that it might be used to assist the memory problems of amnesic patients receives little encouragement from Mayes' review. In a memorable phrase, Mayes describes the amnesics' immediate memories fading 'as do dreams on awakening'. It seems that contextual prompts, either semantic or physical, have little impact on the performance of those unfortunate individuals, though perhaps the full range of contextual revival techniques have yet to be explored. There needs to be more work which adapts existing laboratory paradigms for use with amnesic subjects. Tiberghien's (1986) recent studies on contextual influences on face recognition with prosopagnosic patients provides one useful starting point.

The use of contextual maintenance in the very young and the very old appears to be a fertile area for research. Howe's chapter provides a number of illustrations of how mental contexts stimulated in the child can trigger precocious cognitive skills. In the memory domain, Wilkinson (1988) has demonstrated that young witnesses can benefit greatly in their recall of events by the reinstatement of physical cues. Children taken on a walk in which a series of planned incidents occurred, were much better able to recall these when escorted to the spot by the experimenter, than if questioned in the conventional way. The great perceived danger of such techniques is the production of inventive fantasy rather than veridical recall, an accusation frequently levelled against that other familiar physical prompt of the child witness, the anatomically correct doll (White, Strom, Santilla and Halpin, 1986). However, Wilkinson was able to find no evidence that her subjects were abnormally prone to confabulation under reinstatement conditions, a finding parallelled by Geiselman and Padilla (in press) when the Cognitive Interview was employed with young children.

In comparison, the significance of contextual cueing in aiding the memory of the elderly is a neglected area, whether in the long-term recall of autobiographic material or the retrieval of newly imparted skills or essential information. One feature of the treatment of the elderly and infirm tends to be the uprooting of the individual on health and safety grounds from their own home and their placement in a new and often alien hospital or residential environment. It may well be that the comparative absence of a web of supportive context accelerates retrieval deficits and accentuates the symptoms of memory loss associated with dementia.

In episodic memory, argue Mayes, Bekerian and Conway, and others, the linking of particular traces to particular contextual information provides a ready means of discrimination and effective access. There is, however, a negative side of this differentiation which is seen when a task demands retrieval of information learned in one context which must be applied in another: the theme of Lockhart's contribution and one touched on by Howe. They offer many examples, in both juvenile and adult problem-solving, where such transfer of knowledge does not take place. It is tempting to see such functional fixity or domain-specific behaviour as an adverse effect of contextual coding. Indeed the process of learning for positive transfer can be construed as a process of decontextualising learning. A piece of information, such as the name or appearance of an acquaintance, may initially be retrieved via the circumstances of the original encounter. Subsequently, however, as the person becomes better known and the information is retrieved and deployed at different times and in different settings, so the information floats free of its original contextual boundaries and takes on a very different character. Information, in effect, moves from the episodic to the semantic domain (Amy and Tiberghien, 1988). This process, it might be predicted, would be associated with a gradual freeing of the constraints of contextually-determined usage. Symptomatic of this progression, perhaps, is the observation of Young, Hay and Ellis (1985) that real-life problems of identification failure of faces in different contexts are much more serious for distant acquaintances than for familiar friends (though recognition failures for the latter are not unknown, see Thomson, 1988).

A second source of contextual error can arise when a known context leads to a novel stimulus being classified as familiar: Thomson in his contribution instances examples of not only verbal material but also persons being prone to this form of error in laboratory studies of context. To pursue an argument developed earlier, it seems plausible that stimulus familiarity may influence probability of erroneous recognition. Where the stimulus represents a highly familiar person, such context-based errors seem unlikely to occur in real life, unless there is a high degree of similarity between target and novel distractor: the wartime exploits of a look-alike actor successfully impersonating Field Marshal Montgomery or the film stunt person doubling for the expensive star come to mind as isolated examples of an effective exploitation of such context-based errors. However, in the main, as Thomson and most of his fellow authors are at pains to emphasise, reinstatement of context, either through mental manipulation or physical placement, provides the single most effective method for recovering old memories.

Clearly there is much still to be learned about context, both as a construct in theory and its practical utility in remembering. This book has given some indication of the range of application as well as the diversity of research subsumed under this title. As with all live contemporary issues, this collection of papers raises as many issues as it clarifies or resolves. However, in the wake of this work, it seems unlikely that future theories of memory will ignore its pervasive and sometimes perverse influence on mental processes.

## REFERENCES

Amy, B. and Tiberghien, G. (in press). More about context and cognition. *Journal for the Integrated Study of AI, Cognitive Science and Applied Epistemology.*

Baddeley, A.D. (1982). Domains of recollection. *Psychological Review, 79*, 97–123.

Bekerian, D. and Bowers, J. (1983). Eyewitness testimony: were we misled? *Journal of Experimental Psychology; Learning Memory and Cognition, 9*, 139–145.

Blaney, P. (1986). Affect and memory: a review. *Psychological Bulletin, 99*, 229–246.

Bower, G.H. and Mayer, J.D. (1985). Failure to replicate mood-dependent retrieval. *Bulletin of the Psychonomic Society, 23*, 39–42.

Bowers, J. and Bekerian, D. (1984). When will post-event information distort eyewitness testimony? *Journal of Applied Psychology, 69*, 466–472.

Davies, G. and Milne, A. (1985). Eyewitness composite production: a function of mental or physical reinstatement of context. *Criminal Justice and Behaviour, 12*, 209–220.

Fernandez, A. and Glenberg, A.M. (1985). Changing environmental context does not reliably affect memory. *Memory and Cognition, 13*, 333-345.

Fiedler, K. and Stroehm, W. (1986). What kind of mood influences what kind of memory: the role of arousal and information structure. *Memory and Cognition, 14*, 181–188.

Fisher, R. and Geiselman, R. (1988). Enhancing eyewitness memory with the Cognitive Interview. In M. Gruneburg, P. Morris and R. Sykes (Eds), *Practical Aspects of Memory: Current Research and Issues*, Vol. 1, Chichester: Wiley, pp. 34–39.

Geiselman, R. and Padilla, J. (in press). Cognitive interviewing with child's witnesses. *Applied Cognitive Psychology.*

Gibling, F. and Davies, G. (1988). Reinstatement of context following exposure to post-event information. *British Journal of Psychology, 79*, 129–141.

Harris, J.E. (1980). Memory aids people use: two interview studies. *Memory and Cognition, 8*, 31–38.

Horowitz, L. and Prytulak, L. (1969). Redintegrative memory. *Psychological Review, 76*, 519–531.

Loftus, E. (1979). *Eyewitness Testimony*, Cambridge, Mass.: Harvard University Press.

Malpass, R. and Devine, P. (1981). Guided memory in eyewitness identification. *Journal of Applied Psychology, 66*, 343–350.

Mingay, D. and Bekerian, D. (1984). Does once misled mean always misled? Paper presented at the Conference of the British Psychological Society, London, December.

Mueller, J.H., Lenhart, K. and Gustavson, K. (1987). Study habits and contextual dependency as a function of test anxiety level. Paper presented at the Fifth International Conference on Affect, Motivation and Cognition, Nags Head, NC, May.

Saufley, W.H., Osaka, S. and Bavaresco, J. (1985). Context effects: classroom tests and context independence. *Memory and Cognition*, **13**, 522–528.

Smith, S.M. (1986). Environmental context-dependent recognition memory using a short-term memory task for input. *Memory and Cognition*, **14**, 347–354.

Thomson, D.M. (1988). Eyewitness identification: can jurors assess its accuracy? In M. Gruneburg, P. Morris and R. Sykes (Eds), *Practical Aspects of Memory: Current Research and Issues*, Vol. 1, Chichester: Wiley, pp. 175–181.

Tiberghien, G. (1986). Context effects in recognition memory of faces: some theoretical problems. In H.D. Ellis, M. Jeeves, F. Newcombe and A. Young (Eds), *Aspects of Face Processing*, The Netherlands: Nijhoff, pp. 88–104.

Tulving, E. and Thomson, D.M. (1973). Encoding specificity and retrieval processes in episodic memory. *Psychological Review*, **80**, 353–370.

White, S., Strom, G.A., Santilla, G. and Halpin, B.M. (1986). Interviewing young sexual abuse victims with anatomically correct dolls. *Child Abuse and Neglect*, **10**, 519–529.

Wilkinson, J. (1988). Context effects in children's event memory. In M. Gruneburg, P. Morris and R. Sykes (Eds), *Practical Aspects of Memory: Current Research and Issues*, Vol. 1, Chichester: Wiley, pp. 107–111.

Young, A.W., Hay, D. and Ellis, A. (1985). The faces that launched a thousand slips: everyday difficulties and errors in recognising people. *British Journal of Psychology*, **76**, 495–524.

# Author Index

347

# Subject Index